Inside
Administrative Law

Inside
Administrative Law
What Matters and Why

Jack M. Beermann

Professor of Law and Harry Elwood Warren Scholar
Boston University School of Law

Law & Business

AUSTIN   BOSTON   CHICAGO   NEW YORK   THE NETHERLANDS

Printed in the United States of America.

5 6 7 8 9 0

ISBN 978-0-7355-7961-3

Library of Congress Cataloging-in-Publication Data

Beermann, Jack M.
    Inside administrative law : what matters and why / Jack M. Beermann.
       p. cm.
    ISBN 978-0-7355-7961-3
    1. Administrative law — United States. I. Title.

    KF5402.B444 2011
    342.73'06 — dc22

                        2010043844

About Wolters Kluwer Law & Business

Wolters Kluwer Law & Business is a leading provider of research information and workflow solutions in key specialty areas. The strengths of the individual brands of Aspen Publishers, CCH, Kluwer Law International and Loislaw are aligned within Wolters Kluwer Law & Business to provide comprehensive, in-depth solutions and expert-authored content for the legal, professional and education markets.

CCH was founded in 1913 and has served more than four generations of business professionals and their clients. The CCH products in the Wolters Kluwer Law & Business group are highly regarded electronic and print resources for legal, securities, antitrust and trade regulation, government contracting, banking, pension, payroll, employment and labor, and healthcare reimbursement and compliance professionals.

Aspen Publishers is a leading information provider for attorneys, business professionals and law students. Written by preeminent authorities, Aspen products offer analytical and practical information in a range of specialty practice areas from securities law and intellectual property to mergers and acquisitions and pension/benefits. Aspen's trusted legal education resources provide professors and students with high-quality, up-to-date and effective resources for successful instruction and study in all areas of the law.

Kluwer Law International supplies the global business community with comprehensive English-language international legal information. Legal practitioners, corporate counsel and business executives around the world rely on the Kluwer Law International journals, loose-leafs, books and electronic products for authoritative information in many areas of international legal practice.

Loislaw is a premier provider of digitized legal content to small law firm practitioners of various specializations. Loislaw provides attorneys with the ability to quickly and efficiently find the necessary legal information they need, when and where they need it, by facilitating access to primary law as well as state-specific law, records, forms and treatises.

Wolters Kluwer Law & Business, a unit of Wolters Kluwer, is headquartered in New York and Riverwoods, Illinois. Wolters Kluwer is a leading multinational publisher and information services company.

This book is dedicated to the memory of Iris Beermann.

Summary of Contents

Contents

Chapter 4. Scope of Judicial Review of Administrative Decisions 109

Chapter 5. Advanced Issues in Agency Decisionmaking: Reasoned Decisionmaking, Cost-Benefit Analysis and Impact Statements

Preface and Acknowledgments

Administrative law is everywhere in the American legal system, from the smallest local dispute about whether a town should cut down a potentially dangerous tree to the great national controversy over whether the U.S. Environmental Protection Agency should regulate the gases that cause global warming. Administrative law cuts across multiple areas of the law, and is also relevant to the study of political science, public policy, and numerous other subjects.

This book was written primarily for use by law students taking a law school course in Administrative Law. As an experienced teacher of Administrative Law, my aim is to explain the subject clearly and succinctly, but without compromising the depth that the subject demands. The course in Administrative Law is rewarding, but it can also be challenging and demanding. Any effort to dumb down the presentation in this book would render it useless. What I have tried to do in this book is to communicate the material at the level I would use if the reader were one of my students asking for an explanation of an area that was giving him or her trouble in class.

This book should prove helpful to non-law students as well. It would serve as a useful overview of administrative law in the United States for undergraduate and graduate students studying political science. This book would also serve as a useful reference for lawyers and public servants who encounter administrative law in their day-to-day professional activities.

To enhance the utility of the book, each chapter contains the following features:

- An **Overview** that briefly introduces the topics discussed in the chapter.
- **FAQs** (Frequently Asked Questions) that give readers clear and cogent answers to issues that commonly pop up in an Administrative Law course.
- **Sidebars** that add some color to the coverage of administrative law, offering readers some parenthetical insights.
- **Key terms** in boldface that will help the reader learn the language of administrative law.
- A **Summary** near the end of each chapter that offers a quick and easy guide to the most basic points covered in that chapter.
- A **Connections** feature at the very end of each chapter that helps fit the points made in that chapter with the other chapters in the book and the complete subject of administrative law.

Finally, I would like to thank numerous people who helped make this book possible, including my casebook co-authors Ron Cass and Colin Diver, Dean Maureen O'Rourke of the Boston University School of Law for material and moral support, my colleague Gary Lawson for always being available to talk through the latest (or earliest) issue in administrative law, the ten anonymous reviewers who provided valuable suggestions for improving the manuscript, research assistants Ben Narodick, Crystal Callahan, Mark Cianci, Alex Freundlich, Aaron Shue, Phillipa Skow, and Daniel Suraci, and all of the students in my Administrative Law courses over the years at Boston University School of Law, DePaul College of Law, and Harvard Law School.

Jack M. Beermann
Boston, Massachusetts
December 2010

P.S. It is always helpful to have comments from readers. Please contact me at *beermann@bu.edu* with any comments or suggestions for improving future editions of this book.

Inside
Administrative Law

Introduction to Administrative Law

1

What exactly is administrative law? Part of the plan for this chapter is to answer that question,

and to explore a few important general issues surrounding administrative law, including where administrative law comes from, and what theoretical perspective or perspectives might expand the horizons of our insights into administrative law.

Administrative law regulates the exercise of authority by executive officials, including officials of agencies that are formally independent of the executive branch. It includes constitutional law, statutory law including the Administrative Procedure Act (APA), and common law principles predating the APA. Administrative law is everywhere in our legal and political system, ranging from monumental decisions by the President of the United States to determinations by local officials in their daily interactions with private citizens. It is thus vital for every lawyer to have a solid understanding of the principles of administrative law.

Administrative law encompasses a fantastically wide range of subjects. Topics covered in administrative law include constitutional law subjects such as separation of powers and procedural due process; statutes governing agencies in areas as varied as environmental law, labor law, occupational safety, and motor vehicle safety; the structure and workings of the various agencies; procedural requirements for adjudication and rulemaking; enforcement discretion; methods of enforcement; government tort liability; and freedom of information.

When studying administrative law, our focus is usually on the sources of agency power, the constitutional limits on that power, the procedural requirements for the exercise of agency power, and the availability and scope of judicial review of agency action. A fuller understanding of administrative law can be achieved by analyzing agency structure and agency action under the public interest and public choice theories of regulation. Public interest theory analyzes administrative law with reference to the public policy goals of the government. Public choice theory analyzes administrative law with reference to the political environment and realities of the administrative system.

A. WHAT IS ADMINISTRATIVE LAW?

1. The Sources of Administrative Law
2. Administrative Law's Recurring Issues

B. THE ORIGINS AND ROLES OF ADMINISTRATIVE AGENCIES

1. The Origins of the "Administrative State"
2. Agencies in the Governmental Structure
3. Explanations for the Growth of the Administrative State
4. The Functions of Administrative Agencies
5. Judicial Review of Agency Action

C. PUBLIC INTEREST AND PUBLIC CHOICE EXPLANATIONS OF REGULATION AND THE STRUCTURE OF ADMINISTRATIVE AGENCIES

1. Public Interest Theory of Regulation
2. Public Interest Theory of Agency Structure
3. Public Choice Theory of Regulation
4. Public Choice and Agency Structure
5. Judicial Power and Administrative Law

A. What Is Administrative Law?

Administrative law is the branch of law that regulates the exercise of authority by officials and agencies executing the law under authority granted by the legislature. The scope of administrative law is as great as the scope of the government itself. To name but a few administrative functions, federal agencies administer environmental laws, provide subsidies to farmers, regulate drugs and medical devices, distribute welfare and social security benefits, police the borders and airports, and administer transportation and worker safety programs. Administrative law comprises the substantive and procedural doctrines that enable and control the officials and agencies in the administrative system.

It is vital for every lawyer to have a solid understanding of the principles of administrative law. The breadth and depth of government regulation has grown exponentially in the last one hundred years. Administrative law is everywhere in our legal and political system, ranging from monumental decisions by the President of the United States, for example on whether to regulate pollutants believed to cause global warming to determinations by local officials in their daily interactions with private citizens, for example on whether a business can advertise with a sign on the sidewalk. Administrative law touches nearly every transaction or controversy in litigation. While it is impossible to master the intricacies of the numerous existing regulatory systems, grounding in the general principles of administrative law is important preparation for the issues that will arise.

Administrative law originated in common law actions directed at officials exercising government power, including mandamus, prohibition, and certiorari. Federal administrative law is largely a statutory and constitutional creation, although some pre-APA common law elements survive. In this book, the focus is on federal law, although the states have administrative law that resembles federal law.

One of the most important elements of understanding administrative law is to recognize the boundary between law and politics. Administrative agencies function in a highly political environment, and often there is great policy disagreement between Congress and the Administration. Each agency is likely to have its own culture and its own degree of connection to politics. Courts engaged in judicial review of administrative action mediate this boundary, sometimes requiring strict agency adherence to apparent statutory commands while other times providing substantial space for agency discretion by deferring on matters of substance and by recognizing limits to the justiciability of cases challenging agency action.

(1) The Sources of Administrative Law

Administrative law derives mainly from five sources. First, the Constitution of the United States affects administrative law by limiting innovation regarding the structure of government and the degree to which Congress may grant power to agencies and retain supervisory authority over those grants of power. Further, constitutional due process considerations deeply affect agency procedures, often requiring relatively formal procedures when government action is based on particularized attention to the situation or conduct of regulated parties such as benefits recipients, permit applicants, and government employees.

The second main source of administrative law is the Administrative Procedure Act (APA), a federal statute that was passed in 1946 after a lengthy effort to bring greater coherence to administrative law and ensure adequate mechanisms for supervising agencies. The influence of the APA is pervasive, and its current application embodies decades of judicial experience reviewing the output of the administrative state. The APA contains detailed provisions on agency procedure and judicial review of agency action. The APA includes procedures for rulemaking, adjudication, and informal action, and prescribes when agencies must publish their actions. The APA, as amended, also includes open records and open meetings requirements as well as a procedure for congressional review of agency rules.

```
F     A     Q
```

Q: What if an agency's enabling act is inconsistent with the APA?

A: The agency's enabling act, or any specific statute directed at an agency, governs. The APA provides a general rule when no other statute provides a different rule or procedure. Specific statutes such as an agency's enabling act normally take precedence over the APA.

The third main source of administrative law comprises statutes directed at a particular agency or group of related agencies. The main such statute is what we call an agency's "organic statute" or "enabling act," the statute that establishes an agency and prescribes its mission. Organic statutes and other statutes directed at a particular agency are important sources of law regarding the procedural and substantive constraints on that agency's actions, and should be closely consulted whenever issues arise concerning the legality of agency action. Particular agency statutes take precedence over the APA so that, for example, if the agency's organic statute provides a different procedural model or different standard of judicial review from the APA, the particular statute governs.

The fourth main source of administrative law comprises generally applicable federal statutes that govern agency action but are not directed at any particular agency or set of agencies. This category includes statutes such as the National Environmental Policy Act, which requires all agencies to consider the environmental impacts of their actions. There are numerous statutes like this that place both formal and substantive obligations on agencies.

The fifth and final main source of administrative law is the common law of administrative review that existed before the APA was enacted. Courts sometimes still refer to the common law doctrines, either as a way of understanding APA provisions or even as independent sources of limits on agency action. The APA preserves administrative common law in two somewhat distinct ways. First, some of the APA's provisions are impossible to understand and are actually cryptic references to a body of law outside the APA. A good example of this is APA §706(2)(f)'s provision on when agency action is subject to de novo review. The provision basically states that de novo review is available when de novo review is available, requiring resort to another body of law to break into the circle of reasoning. Second, and more fundamentally, the APA itself, in §559, preserves "additional requirements imposed by statute or otherwise recognized by law." The reference to "otherwise recognized by law" is understood by at least one prominent administrative law scholar to refer to the common law.[1] In addition, APA §703 states that if a particular statute does not provide for judicial review or if statutory remedies are inadequate, "any form of legal action, including actions for declaratory judgments or writs of prohibitory or mandatory injunction or habeas corpus" is available. This preserves pre-APA forms of legal action when the remedies under the APA are not adequate.

In addition to the five primary sources of administrative law discussed above, agency rules are also an important subject of study. Agencies promulgate procedural and substantive rules. In administrative law, we tend to focus on agency procedural rules, except when substantive agency rules provide a vehicle for studying the scope of judicial review of agency action.

---

[1]Kenneth Culp Davis, *Administrative Common Law and the Vermont Yankee Opinion*, 1980 Utah L. Rev. 3, 10.

(2) Administrative Law's Recurring Issues

Certain issues recur in almost all administrative law controversies. First, it is important to identify the source of agency power, which is usually the agency's enabling act. That statute will contain the terms of Congress's delegation of power to the agency along with explicit and implicit limits on that power. This includes the identification of agency procedural power, e.g., whether the agency has the power to engage in rulemaking, whether it has the power to adjudicate, or whether it has the power to collect information via subpoena or through inspections. Second, beyond the source of power, the agency's enabling act and other statutes will contain substantive guidelines that the agency must follow in the use of its delegated power. Courts on judicial review insist that agencies act in accordance with the substantive standards established in governing statutes. Third, the APA, other statutes, and the Constitution specify the procedures that agencies must follow when using their delegated power. Fourth, the APA and other statutes including enabling acts contain provisions that govern judicial review including setting the standard of review, the circumstances under which review is available, and specifying who can seek review and at what stage of the administrative proceedings. Finally, the separation of powers principles of the Constitution may limit Congress's ability to structure the agency in novel ways. These constitutional limits arise from specific provisions of the Constitution and through doctrines derived from the general principle of separation of powers.

The heart of administrative law is procedure. Procedural requirements arise from the Constitution, the APA, administrative common law, the agency's particular statute, and other statutes that place obligations on administrative agencies, such as the National Environmental Policy Act, which requires agencies to prepare environmental impact statements under certain circumstances. The availability of judicial review is determined by application of the APA and the agency's particular statute, and it is important to be aware of when review is available and what actions are reviewable. Constitutional doctrines such as standing and ripeness, as well as administrative common law, can also influence the availability of judicial review.

The APA and the agency's particular statute determine the scope of judicial review — what standard the reviewing court applies. The scope of judicial review determines how deferential the reviewing court will be to the agency's decision. Agency enforcement power may be limited by a particular statute, the APA, and the Constitution. Private parties may attempt to force agencies to bring enforcement actions or they may attempt to enforce regulatory norms themselves, without agency involvement.

F   A   Q

Q: What if an agency's enabling act says nothing about judicial review or does not specify the appropriate standard or scope of review?

A: The APA provides for judicial review of most final agency actions for which there is no other adequate remedy in court, and it specifies the appropriate scope of review for each category of agency action. Therefore, if an agency's enabling act says nothing about judicial review, the APA normally provides for review and specifies the standard of review.

B. The Origins and Roles of Administrative Agencies

(1) The Origins of the "Administrative State"

There has been administrative law throughout the history of the United States, at least since the first Congress under the present Constitution met in 1789 and established the Departments of Foreign Affairs, War, and Treasury, and placed a Postmaster General within the Department of the Treasury. The Constitution identifies the President as the repository of the executive power but also anticipates the existence of Departments of government that will carry out executive functions.

The label "administrative state" signifies something different, namely that the regulatory reach of the government has expanded greatly through the proliferation of numerous agencies created to address various perceived problems that need attention from the federal government. The administrative state as we know it began in 1887 with the establishment of the first modern regulatory agency, the Interstate Commerce Commission (which has since been eliminated but not until 1996). Antecedents to the administrative state have existed as long as the republic. For example, the first Congress authorized the President to appoint an official to estimate import duties. Import duties were a very important source of income for the federal government and continue to be an important area of federal policy.

Sidebar

CREATION OF DEPARTMENTS

Although the Constitution refers to the Departments of Government, Departments are created by legislation, not by the Constitution itself. In 1789, Congress established three Departments of Government: Foreign Affairs, War, and Treasury. Today, there are fifteen Departments, including the recently created Departments of Homeland Security and Veterans Affairs. The Departments are headed by Secretaries, except for the Department of Justice, which is headed by the Attorney General. Department Heads are appointed by the President with the advice and consent of the Senate.

(2) Agencies in the Governmental Structure

Congress establishes agencies and executive branch offices and specifies their placement within the government structure. Most federal administrative agencies are within a Department of the executive branch, in a chain of command with the President at the apex. For example, the National Highway Transportation Safety Administration (NHTSA) is located within the Department of Transportation. The Department of Transportation is headed by the Secretary of Transportation, and NHTSA is headed by an Administrator, a subordinate of the Secretary. The Environmental Protection Agency is an agency within the executive branch that has not been placed within any Department, and thus the EPA Administrator's immediate supervisor is the President. Agencies that Congress has placed within the traditional executive branch structure are often referred to as "executive agencies."

Congress has designated some agencies, such as the Federal Communications Commission (FCC), as "independent agencies." Typical of independent agencies, the FCC is headed by five commissioners appointed by the President for five-year terms. Independent agencies are not within any department of the federal government and are not under the supervision of the President or a cabinet officer. Independent agencies normally have four characteristics: (1) they are headed by multi-member commissions or boards; (2) the agency heads serve for a term of years usually longer than the term of the President; (3) the agency heads may not be removed without good cause; and (4) the agency must be bipartisan with the usual requirement being that no more than half plus one of members (e.g., three of five) may be of the same political party. There is an ongoing constitutional controversy over the status of independent agencies, with a strong belief in some quarters that any effort by Congress to insulate an agency from complete presidential control is unconstitutional under the Constitution's vesting of all executive power in the President.

(3) Explanations for the Growth of the Administrative State

The administrative state has grown in response to the increased size and complexity of the economy and increased demand from interest groups and voters for more regulation. The economic depression of the 1920s and 1930s created great demand for regulation to prevent recurrence of economic problems and for benefits programs to safeguard against poverty. The environmental movement of the 1960s and 1970s created great demand for federal environmental regulation. As government programs have grown, so has the administrative state. New agencies have been established, and existing agencies have increased in size. Even with the wave of deregulatory thinking since the late 1970s, the overall size and scope of the federal government has not decreased.

(4) The Functions of Administrative Agencies

As the name implies, administrative agencies administer government programs by exercising power delegated by Congress. Therefore, the functions of administrative agencies are as varied as the programs established by Congress. Administrative agencies perform a wide variety of functions in the United States at the local, state, and federal levels. While this book focuses on federal agencies, almost everything said here applies to state agencies as well.

Distribution of Benefits. Administrative agencies distribute government benefits such as welfare, disability benefits, old-age benefits, medical care for poor people and seniors, loan guarantees

---

Sidebar

AGENCY HEADS

Agencies within a Department of the executive branch are usually headed by a single Administrator who is appointed by the President with the advice and consent of the Senate and who is under the supervision of the Head of the Department within which the agency is located. The EPA is headed by an Administrator, appointed by the President and confirmed by the Senate, but is not in a Department and thus is under the direct supervision of the President and no other official. Independent agencies are headed by multiple Commissioners or Board Members appointed by the President with the advice and consent of the Senate, but are not under the supervision of any Department Head or the President.

Sidebar

AGENCIES ARE EVERYWHERE

Administrative agencies are everywhere and affect all of our lives every day. Local agencies include zoning and planning boards, parks and recreation commissions, conservation boards, police review boards, motor vehicle authorities, water and sewer commissions, parking authorities, and many more. It is difficult to imagine spending a single day without being affected by one or more agencies.

for home buyers and students, and subsidies for industries such as agriculture. Agencies often adjudicate disputes that arise in these areas.

Granting of Licenses and Permits and Enforcement of Standards. Agencies rule on requests for licenses and permits in a wide variety of areas, including the construction and operation of nuclear power plants, logging on federally-owned forest land, operation of stockyards, ownership and operation of television and radio stations, the sale of insurance, the operation of commercial airlines, and the scores of occupations that require licensing, such as lawyers and doctors. In addition to granting licenses, agencies monitor and enforce compliance with regulatory standards in the areas in which licenses and permits are required.

Policymaking. Federal agencies make important policy decisions in most of the areas in which they administer government programs. Congress often delegates power to agencies in very broad terms that leave important matters to agency discretion, including such things as whether to require automobiles to be equipped with new safety and pollution control devices; how much of certain pollutants may be released into the air and water; the proper conditions for conducting elections to determine whether employees will be represented by a labor union; whether an interstate highway should be built through parkland; and the requirements for obtaining the various benefits, licenses, and permits administered or required by federal law in numerous areas.

Sidebar

AGENCY PROCEDURES

Agencies administering welfare benefits or licensing and permit programs usually employ adjudicatory procedures, in no small part because of due process requirements. Agencies making broad policy determinations usually employ legislative rulemaking procedures that normally satisfy due process in that context.

Management of Resources and Government Property. Agencies manage natural resources such as parks and wilderness areas and they oversee the use, maintenance, acquisition, and disposal of government property.

Policymaking Methods and Procedures. Agencies make policy in a variety of ways, each of which is studied in depth in this book. Policymaking methods include legislative rulemaking, adjudication, and informal procedures sometimes referred to as informal adjudication. Agencies engage in a variety of enforcement methods including internal agency proceedings, litigation in court against alleged violators, criminal enforcement of regulatory standards in cases of serious violations, and informal monitoring and compliance negotiation. The Administrative Procedure Act and other statutes determine the procedures agencies must follow in each regulatory situation.

(5) Judicial Review of Agency Action

When Congress delegates policymaking authority to agencies, the authority is circumscribed by the terms stated in the statute delegating the authority and also by the general judicial review provision of the APA. Judicial review is the tool Congress uses to ensure that agencies (and the President) follow the terms of the delegations. Almost all final agency action is subject to judicial review under various standards of review contained in APA §706 such as the arbitrary and capricious test and the substantial evidence test. On judicial review, courts determine whether the agency has followed all prescribed procedures, whether the agency has respected the terms of the delegation from Congress, and whether the agency action meets relatively deferential standards of good policy.

C. Public Interest and Public Choice Explanations of Regulation and the Structure of Administrative Agencies

Administrative law inevitably involves looking at the substance of agency action, especially when courts apply the substantive standards of review under the APA. The public interest and public choice theories are the two major approaches to understanding and evaluating the work of agencies. The public interest theory of regulation focuses on the policies involved in the regulation while the public choice theory focuses on the politics of regulation.

(1) Public Interest Theory of Regulation

Public interest theory explains administrative law based on traditional notions of the policy aims of regulation. Public interest theory holds that regulation is desirable in several, often related, situations such as preventing parties from externalizing costs, preventing monopolization that leads to higher prices than would exist with more competition, providing subsidies when desirable goods and services are underproduced, providing information that consumers need to make informed choices, and so on. Much public interest analysis of regulation focuses on whether the regulation is cost effective, i.e., whether the costs of the regulation to the regulated parties are less than the benefits produced for society as a whole.

Traditional regulation often involved creating monopolies to encourage the production of goods and services and then regulating the resulting enterprises to keep prices and service at an acceptable level. Regulation takes the place of the market in such areas. Examples of this type of regulation involve public utilities such as electric power and telephone service. When these industries began, government granted a monopoly over the provision of service so that the company had an adequate incentive to wire all homes and businesses. The price and terms of the contract between the utility and its customers were then heavily regulated to keep prices below the level that a monopolist would be able to charge and to ensure that all customers were provided with adequate service.

Government regulation or service provision is also viewed as desirable when the market will underproduce a valued good or service because it is non-excludable, i.e., it is impossible to force all users to pay or when the choice of some not to pay would reduce the provision of the service below the optimal social level. These issues are often referred to as "collective action problems." Payment for public goods, such as the national defense or scenic parkland, must be compelled through the tax system. Otherwise, no one would voluntarily pay, and the good would be underproduced. In some areas, it might be possible to exclude, but the lack of universal service would lead to inefficiency. For example, it might be possible to have private companies provide fire protection, but if a fire breaks out at a building that has not purchased fire protection, neighboring structures may be placed at risk, and it would be cheaper overall if everyone were forced to pay for service. Inequalities of information in the marketplace might also justify government regulation in the form of mandatory disclosure. Consumers may value the information but be unable to bargain for it because of lack of market power or lack of sufficient information to even know what information to look for. This view of the public interest justifies, inter alia, food product labeling; efficiency ratings on products like automobiles, air conditioners, and refrigerators; and securities market disclosures.

Collective action problems can also lead to overuse of a resource, which also provides a public interest reason for regulation. For example, a river might be able to handle a limited amount of pollution before it becomes dangerous or unfit as drinking water or for recreational uses. Each individual user will try to maximize his or her own gains without regard to the welfare of others or the overall good. Assuming the river's value as drinking water and for recreation is greater than its value as a place to dump pollutants, government regulation may be necessary to maintain the river's optimal condition by limiting pollution to the tolerable level. In many situations, transaction costs including enforcement difficulties would make it impossible to accomplish the regulatory goal through private contract or other nongovernmental means.

(2) Public Interest Theory of Agency Structure

Public interest theory evaluates the structure of agencies based on whether they are well suited to perform their functions. If the agency's function is to make policy in an area requiring scientific expertise, the structure should be designed to maximize the input of experts. If the agency's function is to award benefits or adjudicate disputes under a particular legal scheme, the agency should be designed with process values in mind. In general, agencies should be structured to optimize the achievement of public interest goals.

(3) Public Choice Theory of Regulation

Public choice theory explains regulation as a product of the political process in which parties with political power enlist government coercion to achieve goals that they could not achieve in a free market. One major reason for regulation, according to public choice theory, is the desire of government officials to increase their power and maximize their benefits from the regulatory scheme. Public choice observes that often the strongest impetus for regulation comes from government officials who see an opportunity to gain influence and create post-government employment opportunities for themselves in the industries they regulate.

Public choice also sees a collective action problem behind much government regulation. Private beneficiaries of regulation use their influence, often in the form of contributions to congressional campaigns, to procure regulatory benefits that they could not obtain in a free marketplace. Although there are plenty of interest groups that represent the general public on matters such as the environment or consumer issues, smaller industry-oriented interest groups often find it easier to organize and influence government policy than the less cohesive general public. Policies that sound good in theory often are twisted to favor small, organized interests at the expense of the general welfare. For example, when the federal government began regulating mileage and emissions from automobiles, powerful automobile manufacturers persuaded the government to regulate their largest, lowest mileage and highest polluting vehicles, SUVs, under the lenient standards applicable to trucks.

Public choice rebuts each of the public interest explanations for regulation with an explanation based on political power. For example, public choice explains regulation of externalities as a victory of the more powerful party who could not prevent the other party's activity, either through the market or through traditional tort law such as nuisance. The public choice theorist would explain that there is no objective reason for preferring the interests of a quiet residential property owner over the interests of a noisy manufacturing business that residents dislike.

Public choice theorists are skeptical of claims that monopolies are necessary and view monopolies as governmentally enforced subsidization of politically powerful businesses. In the public choice view, utilities with monopoly rights tend to earn excessive profits, and the existence of the monopoly lowers the incentive to create more efficient and more desirable products and services. The ability of the public to politically resist monopoly creation is low because each consumer may suffer only a small negative effect from the monopoly.

Public choice theorists see very few genuine public goods and view government compulsion in most public goods areas as tending toward overproduction of the good involved. For example, private schools and private parks exist, and they would be more efficiently provided if government did not use its power of taxation to create public competitors. Government intervention occurs because of the political power of the beneficiaries of the regulation.

Public choice theorists suspect that forced disclosure of information results in overproduction of information — which means that consumers and producers are forced to pay for information they do not want. The market would determine how much information people want, and government intervention occurs because powerful consumer advocates lobby for tougher regulation (which in turn increases their support from consumers). Sometimes businesses lobby for more information disclosure. This can occur, for example, when producers of higher-quality products use government regulation to force competitors to disclose unfavorable facts.

Sidebar

PUBLIC CHOICE OR PUBLIC INTEREST

Public choice understandings underlie the movement in recent decades toward deregulation and market solutions to regulatory problems. The more regulation seems biased toward political power, the more it seems contrary to the public interest. Recent problems in the banking and other industries, however, have reinvigorated public interest arguments in favor of regulation. At a minimum, public choice concerns teach the desirability of a healthy skepticism toward regulation while recent events counsel against blind adherence to a complete laissez-faire attitude.

(4) Public Choice and Agency Structure

Public choice theorists explain agency structure as created to maximize the influence of those parties, including members of Congress, most keenly interested in the output of the agency. When Congress wishes to maximize its own influence, it often creates an independent agency or otherwise structures the agency to insulate it from presidential control. Interest groups lobby for agency structure to increase their regulatory success. For example, when the Occupational Safety and Health Administration was created, labor unions lobbied to place it in the Department of

Labor where they had the most influence, while business interests wanted authority placed in an independent agency to reduce the influence of organized labor.

(5) Judicial Power and Administrative Law

Public interest theories of administrative law see judicial review of agency action as providing a neutral forum for ensuring that agencies obey Congress's instructions, act rationally, and are not captured by powerful interests. Public choice theories of administrative law see judicial review as a mechanism for enforcing the bargain arrived at in Congress or of satisfying constituencies that are concerned with unchecked agency power. For example, if powerful interests believe they will have greater success in an agency than in Congress, public choice predicts that such interests will lobby for (and may get) weak judicial review, or no judicial review at all.

The public choice and public interest theories are in some sense competitors but in other senses are complementary. The biggest way in which they compete is that public choice theorists often seek to look behind the public interest–oriented reasons offered for regulation and reveal both that the regulation is actually not in the public interest and that narrow private interests had the upper hand in the political process that led to the regulation. This is because narrow interests with a great deal of money at stake often have an advantage in the ability to organize and lobby for or against legislation over diffuse interests (like all citizens) who may, in the aggregate, have more at stake. However, they can be complementary, for example if public choice analysis reveals that a narrow interest was defeated by a surprisingly well-organized broader interest or if a public interest analysis raises questions about the wisdom of regulation that can be answered by revealing the underlying politics.

SUMMARY

■ Administrative law regulates the exercise of authority by executive officials, including officials of agencies that are formally independent of the executive branch. Administrative law is everywhere in our governmental system.

■ Administrative law is derived from constitutional law, statutes including agency enabling acts, the APA, other statutes imposing obligations on administrative agencies, and common law principles.

■ In administrative law, it is important to focus on the sources of agency power, the constitutional limits on that power, the procedural requirements (both statutory and constitutional) for exercise of agency power, and the availability and scope of judicial review of agency action.

■ The "administrative state" as we know it today originated with the creation of the Interstate Commerce Commission in 1887, although agencies and administrative law existed long before that.

■ Some agencies are located within a department of government. Others are within the executive branch but not located within any department. Still others, known as "independent agencies," are not located within any department and are not considered under the direct supervision of the President.

■ Administrative agencies perform a wide variety of functions including distributing benefits, licensing and regulating numerous businesses and industries, granting permits for a wide variety of activities, and making and enforcing health and safety rules.

■ The public interest analysis of administrative law analyzes regulation from the perspective of the public policy goals sought to be achieved such as cleaning the air and water, preventing abusive business practices, and producing an optimal level of public goods.

■ The public choice analysis of administrative law analyzes regulation from the perspective of the political forces that result in regulation and the structure of agencies, such as how narrow but organized interests seem to capture the attention of agencies while unorganized broad interests such as the public at large have difficulty advancing their interests in the administrative process.

■ The public interest and public choice views are in some sense complementary in that they help understand why in some situations regulation appears to be in the public interest while in other situations regulation appears to be contrary to the public interest but highly beneficial for a small organized interest group.

CONNECTIONS

Sources of Law

For many issues in administrative law, several sources of law may be relevant including the APA, the agency's enabling act, generally applicable statutes such as the National Environmental Policy Act (see Chapter 5), administrative common law, and the constitutional principles.

Public Interest or Public Choice?

Whenever you analyze an administrative law issue, ask yourself if your understanding is informed by public interest or public choice understandings or both. If it's only one or the other, try bringing the other category of understanding into view.

Separation of Powers and Administrative Law

2

Separation of powers is an important concern in Administrative Law. Although we no longer spend half or two-thirds of the Administrative

O V E R V I E W

Law course trying to figure out the proper place of agencies in government, separation of powers issues usually take up a substantial part of Administrative Law courses, and separation of powers concerns lurk beneath the surface of many of the most apparently mundane administrative law issues, such as rulemaking procedure and freedom of information. Therefore, it is important for the administrative law student to have a good working knowledge of separation of powers concepts and doctrines across a range of issues. The issues in this chapter include the nondelegation doctrine's limits on the delegation of discretion by Congress to agencies, the competition between the President and Congress over control of administrative agencies including the establishment of so-called independent agencies, the constitutionally required procedures for appointing Officers of the United States who execute the law, the constitutionality of legislative and line item vetoes, the constitutionality of agency adjudication in light of the Constitution's vesting of the judicial power in the federal courts, and other questions that arise concerning the balance of power among the branches, mainly between Congress and the President. We also explore the unitary executive theory, which supports complete presidential control over the execution of the laws.

A. **FRAMEWORK FOR UNDERSTANDING SEPARATION OF POWERS**

B. **THE NONDELEGATION DOCTRINE**

 1. Nondelegation Foundations
 2. The Strict Nondelegation Doctrine in the Early Twentieth Century
 3. The Current Lenient Nondelegation Doctrine

C. **SEPARATION OF POWERS AND THE STRUGGLE FOR CONTROL**

 1. The Struggle for Control
    a. Informal Congressional Influence
    b. Formal Congressional Influence
    c. The Legislative Veto and Review of Regulations
 2. Appointment of Administrative Officials
 3. Removal of Executive Branch Officials
    a. Congressional Involvement in the Removal Process
    b. Restrictions on Presidential Removal of Administrative Officials
 4. Direct Presidential Control over Administrative Agencies
    a. Centralized Review
    b. The Line Item Veto
    c. Signing Statements

D. **ADJUDICATION BY NON–ARTICLE III ADJUDICATORS**

 1. *Crowell v. Benson* and the Public Rights Versus Private Rights Doctrine
 2. The Bankruptcy Courts
 3. The Current Test for Adjudication in Non–Article III Tribunals

A. Framework for Understanding Separation of Powers

The Constitution creates three branches of government and assigns to each the exercise of one of the three main powers of government. The Constitution does not mention **separation of powers** in so many words, yet the notion that powers were divided among the three branches of government was understood by the Framers of the Constitution to be one of the pillars of the new structure they were creating, along with federalism and the doctrine of limited, enumerated powers. Separation of powers makes numerous appearances in the Constitution in the form of particular provisions and procedures that together form the structure of the government of the United States. These include the procedures that govern the creation and execution of the law and the fundamental constitutional prohibition on concurrent service in the legislative and executive branches of government. Even when no particular constitutional provision is relevant, separation of powers concerns may be implicated by action that appears to shift the balance of power among the three branches. What we shall see is that by and large the courts are strict in their enforcement of particular constitutional provisions that relate to separation of powers but they are relatively deferential to other government actors when called on to enforce a more amorphous separation of powers principle. Therefore, each time you confront a separation of powers problem, it is useful to begin by asking whether the issue implicates a specific constitutional clause or whether the legal issues involved concern more general questions of the proper distribution of power within the government.

Separation of powers is embodied in numerous constitutional provisions that establish the structure of the government. As a practical matter, the operation of individual provisions like these is more important to separation of powers than the application the overarching principle of separation. For example, the **Incompatibility Clause**, Art. I, §6, prohibits executive branch officials from also serving in Congress, creating a strict separation between the executive and legislative branches of government. Note that many provisions of the Constitution subject the branches of government to a measure of control by another branch. For example, the **Presentment Clause**, Art. I, §7, requires presentation of legislation to the President for signature or veto, providing the presidency with protection from overreaching by Congress. And the **Appointments Clause**, Art. II, §2, requires the advice and consent of the Senate before the President may appoint "Officers of the United States." These provisions raise an important point, that separation of powers must be understood as a system of separated powers with checks and balances rather than a system of isolated separated powers. It is virtually impossible for the federal government to take any important action without the concurrence of at least two of the three branches, providing checks and balances in many forms across the spectrum of government action.

While it is impossible to capture the constitutional principle of separation of powers in any simple formula, the following framework may help us to analyze the range of separation of powers problems we will encounter. The first element of the framework has to do with the attitude the Supreme Court generally takes when confronted with separation of powers questions. In general, the Supreme Court has insisted that all specific procedures spelled out in the Constitution be followed. Examples include the procedures that Congress must follow to make law and the procedures that govern the appointment of officials who engage in the execution of the laws. Regardless of the strength of normative arguments in favor of departing from the constitutionally prescribed procedures, the Court has by and large required strict adherence to them.

The Court has not been very strict, however, when the allegation is that some action, usually legislative innovation, transgresses general separation of powers limits. Without a specific procedural requirement to enforce, the Court applies a totality of the circumstances test and asks whether a branch's ability to perform its constitutionally assigned function has been impermissibly burdened, or unduly trammeled upon or impeded. In recent decades, the Court has rejected the more categorical approaches taken in an earlier day and has allowed great flexibility so long as no specific provision of the Constitution has been transgressed.[1]

Sidebar

KEY SEPARATION OF POWERS PROVISIONS IN THE CONSTITUTION

Art I: §1. All legislative Powers herein granted shall be vested in a Congress of the United States, which shall consist of a Senate and House of Representatives.

§6. [N]o Person holding any Office under the United States, shall be a Member of either House during his Continuance in Office.

§7. Every Order, Resolution, or Vote to which the Concurrence of the Senate and House of Representatives may be necessary . . . shall be presented to the President of the United States; and before the Same shall take Effect, shall be approved by him, or being disapproved by him, shall be repassed by two thirds of the Senate and House of Representatives. . . .

Art. II: §1. The executive Power shall be vested in a President of the United States of America.

§2. [H]e shall nominate, and by and with the Advice and Consent of the Senate, shall appoint Ambassadors, other public Ministers and Consuls, Judges of the supreme Court, and all other Officers of the United States, whose Appointments are not herein otherwise provided for, and which shall be established by Law: but the Congress may by Law vest the Appointment of such inferior Officers, as they think proper, in the President alone, in the Courts of Law, or in the Heads of Departments.

§3. [H]e shall take Care that the Laws be faithfully executed[.]

Art III: §1. The judicial Power of the United States, shall be vested in one supreme Court, and in such inferior Courts as the Congress may from time to time ordain and establish. The Judges, both of the supreme and inferior Courts, shall hold their Offices during good Behavior, and shall, at stated Times, receive for their Services a Compensation which shall not be diminished during their Continuance in Office.

The second element of the framework is to understand that in most situations, the Court does not apply a conceptual understanding of the powers of the branches of government, but rather mainly ensures that each branch observes the procedures that apply to it when taking action with legal effects. This statement obviously needs elaboration. A "conceptual understanding" of separation of powers would sort each possible governmental action into a category of powers and then allow only the branch that has power over the particular category to take the action. For example, if under a conceptual understanding the specification of the gas mileage requirements for automobiles was found to be a legislative matter, only Congress could specify the requirements (by legislating) and it would be unconstitutional for an agency to make rules on the subject. Conversely, if this were considered an executive function, it would be unconstitutional for Congress to specify the requirements in a statute.

While the conceptual approach might be a plausible way to understand separation of powers, it is not how the law has evolved. As the Supreme Court noted as far back as 1825 in an opinion by Chief Justice Marshall, "Congress may certainly delegate to others, powers which the legislature may rightfully exercise itself." *Wayman v. Southard*, 23 U.S. (10 Wheat.) 1, 20 (1825). Rather, the primary understanding of separation of powers is that each branch must observe the limitations that apply to it, that the limitations are mainly procedural, and as long as all required procedures have been observed, the substantive content of governmental action does not usually implicate separation of powers. Returning to the example of gas mileage requirements, to determine whether legislation prescribing such requirements is consistent with separation of powers, rather than ask whether prescribing mileage requirements is a legislative

---

[1]It must be noted that this means that the Court does not view the "Vesting Clauses," i.e., the first sentences of each of the first three articles of the Constitution, as specific procedures that must be followed. More on this below.

function, the only real legal question would be whether Congress followed the constitutional requirements for making law, i.e., whether a bill was passed by a majority in each House of Congress and was presented to the President. With regard to agency rulemaking on the subject, the legal question would be whether the agency acted in accordance with a constitutionally valid delegation of authority from Congress or, in the much rarer case, in accordance with a power specifically granted to the President in the Constitution. If the judiciary got into the act, for example by prescribing mileage requirements as a remedy in a case before the courts, the question would still be largely procedural, asking whether the court had jurisdiction under a constitutionally valid statute and whether the constitutional requirements for a case or controversy were met.

A contrary conceptual approach to separation of powers would mean that each branch of government is confined to exercising those powers within its particular conceptual sphere. It is, however, often difficult to identify which branch "owns" a particular power and which power a branch is exercising in any particular action. While separation of powers analysis does contain some elements of this conceptual approach, the conceptual approach is not the dominant focus in most situations. Rather, separation of powers analysis is usually pragmatic rather than conceptual, asking whether the system is functioning properly rather than whether a power, by definition, belongs to a particular branch.

A third element to understanding separation of powers is to recognize that no branch may exercise a power that is constitutionally assigned to another branch unless the Constitution specifically allows it. At first glance, this element may seem inconsistent or at least in tension with the rejection of the conceptual approach to separation of powers, but a deeper understanding should reveal that it is not. Let's use the example of the President's veto power to illustrate this element. The Constitution assigns the legislative power to Congress and if that were all the Constitution said about the legislative power, it would be impermissible for the President to become involved in the actual legislative process. Similarly, the Constitution assigns the President the power to appoint Officers of the United States, and if that were all the Constitution said on that subject, it would be impermissible for the Congress to become involved in the appointments process. In both of these cases, however, the Constitution says more. The Presentment Clause allows the President to become involved in the legislative process by signing or vetoing legislation. The Appointments Clause allows Congress to become involved in the process of appointing Officers of the United States by requiring the advice and consent of the Senate before the President's nominees may be appointed. Without a specific authorization in the Constitution, it is impermissible for a branch to exercise or interfere with a power that is constitutionally assigned to another branch.

A more precise statement of this third element is that unless it is allowed by a specific constitutional provision, it is unconstitutional for a branch of government to interfere with the exercise of a power that is textually committed to another branch. The best illustration of this principle comes in the area of the appointment power. As noted, the Constitution assigns the power to appoint Officers of the United States to the President with the advice and consent of the Senate. The Supreme Court has made it clear that the President has the exclusive power to make the actual appointments, and that the House of Representatives may not play any role at all in the process, since it is not mentioned in the Appointments Clause.

The reason that this element appears somewhat inconsistent with the rejection of the conceptual approach to separation of powers is that it depends on conceiving of a function as belonging to a particular branch, such as the appointment of executive officials belonging to the executive branch or the enactment of legislation as belonging to Congress. There is some truth to this analysis, but the Supreme Court has not gone very far in the direction of the conceptual view. In fact, the analysis does not depend completely on an understanding of the nature of the particular power but rather on the fact that the particular power is textually committed by the Constitution to a particular branch. Textual commitment carries with it the negative pregnant that no other branch can be involved in the exercise of the power. So, for example, when the Constitution states that the legislative power is vested in Congress, that should be understood as a textual commitment of the power to enact laws to Congress. But it tells us very little substantively about when government must act through laws as opposed to agency rules or judicial decree.

The view that the conceptual approach has been rejected is tested most strongly when the power to remove Officers of the United States is considered. The Constitution does not mention removal of officers except through impeachment and removal by Congress, and the Supreme Court has rejected any other role for Congress in the process of removal, although it has allowed Congress legislatively to place restrictions on the President's power to remove officers. The removal jurisprudence, which is discussed in detail below, may appear conceptual along the following lines—the power to remove an Officer of the United States is conceptually executive, and therefore Congress may not participate in the removal process because it has only legislative, and not executive, power.

While this view makes sense, there is a simpler explanation that is consistent with the rejection of the conceptual approach. The Constitution's assignment of the impeachment and removal power to Congress implicitly denies Congress any other involvement in the removal of Officers. Otherwise, Congress could legislatively eliminate the procedural requirements for impeachment and removal by legislating some other process for congressional removal of Officers of the United States. By confining Congress to impeachment and removal as the congressional method for participating in the removal of Officers of the United States, the Constitution implicitly assigns the ordinary removal power to the President (because officers clearly do not have life tenure given that such tenure is textually provided in the Constitution to federal judges) and it prohibits Congress from participating in the removal of officers except via the impeachment process.

F   A   Q

Q: Why did the Constitution include the Senate in the process of appointing Officers of the United States? Why can't the Senate also participate in their removal?

A: The Senate's role in appointments, like its role in the adoption of treaties, provides a check and balance on the President's exercise of the executive power. The Senate cannot participate in the removal of Officers of the United States because the Constitution by implication grants that power to the President, under the following reasoning: The Constitution specifies that certain officials, namely federal judges, have life tenure (during "good behavior") implying that other officers do not have life tenure. This means that someone must have removal authority, and the logical someone is the President, the official with appointive authority. Why not with the advice and consent of the Senate? The Constitution specifies that the Senate tries impeachments, which can result in the removal of an official. By negative implication, any other congressional participation in the removal of Officers of the United States would be inconsistent with this plan.

The final element of our separation of powers framework is that separation of powers must be understood as a system of separated powers with checks and balances. Recall Madison's statement in Federalist No. 48 that "unless these departments be so far connected and blended as to give to each a constitutional control over the others, the degree of separation which the maxim requires, as essential to a free government, can never in practice be duly maintained." The constitutional structure normally does not immunize any single branch from supervision by the others. The closest that the Constitution comes to this involves the Supreme Court's power to determine the meaning of the Constitution, as famously recognized in *Marbury v. Madison*, 5 U.S. (1 Cranch) 137 (1803), where only the difficult and rarely employed power to amend the Constitution, shared by Congress and the States, provides an actual check on the Supreme Court's power. The powers contained in the Constitution are shared among the branches through various procedural and substantive devices — the President checks Congress through the veto power while Congress controls the President through substantive legislation and the power of the purse and so on. Separation of powers should always be thought of in conjunction with checks and balances.

Over time, numerous controversies involving separation of powers have erupted. Some have involved the application of particular constitutional provisions such as the Appointments Clause while others have involved the more general question of whether some innovation violates the principle of separation of powers. Often, it is not certain which type a case is until the Supreme Court decides it. The remainder of this chapter looks at separation of powers issues of both types, drawing on the framework set forth above to help deepen our understanding of the issues.

B. The Nondelegation Doctrine

The **nondelegation doctrine** holds that Congress may not delegate its legislative power to the President, an agency, or any other entity inside or outside of government. It is axiomatic that only Congress has the constitutional power to legislate. Congress cannot pass a law authorizing someone else, such as a federal agency, the President, a private organization or a congressional committee, to write statutes and place them in the United States Code. In that sense, it is a truism that the Constitution prohibits Congress from delegating its legislative powers, and the early cases said so in so many words. The nondelegation doctrine is about preventing Congress from avoiding that basic restriction by delegating away so much discretionary power that someone else in effect has been granted the power to legislate. However, as we shall see in the pages that follow, the nondelegation doctrine has never prevented Congress from granting a great deal of discretionary authority to executive officials, and today Congress satisfies the nondelegation doctrine by supplying only an "intelligible principle" to guide that discretion.

The reason that the nondelegation doctrine is not a serious impediment to delegation of discretionary authority by Congress is that discretion is inherent in the execution of the law. Especially today, as government confronts more complicated and important problems, it would be impossible for the executive branch to execute the law without exercising some discretion. The nondelegation doctrine prohibits excessive delegation of discretionary powers by the Congress to the President, federal agencies and private entities, although most cases involve delegations to federal agencies. In essence, the nondelegation doctrine describes the boundary between legislation and execution of the law. This doctrine derives from separation of powers concerns because if Congress has delegated its legislative power, someone else is exercising a power that has been constitutionally assigned to Congress.

<table>
<tr><td>

Sidebar

SOURCES OF THE NONDELEGATION DOCTRINE

The nondelegation doctrine is derived from the Constitution's grant of legislative power to Congress and from the structural aspects of the Constitution that make clear that only Congress has the power to enact federal laws. Art. I, §1 provides: "All legislative powers herein granted shall be vested in a Congress of the United States, which shall consist of a Senate and House of Representatives." Further, the Presentment Clauses of Art. I, §7, prescribe the legislative process under which bills must pass both Houses of Congress to become law.

</td><td>

There are some preliminary issues we should address before delving into the nondelegation doctrine. The first is why we care about nondelegation. Unlike other separation of powers problems, delegation does not involve one branch seizing power from another branch (which is often called **"aggrandizement"**) or interfering with another branch's exercise of its powers. It is not like, for example, Congress attempting to appoint Officers of the United States or to participate in the removal of such officers. In those cases, Congress is arguably interfering with the execution of the laws. In delegation controversies, Congress has voluntarily delegated discretion to another government entity, and Congress remains free to legislatively narrow or take back the delegation. Is there any reason beyond constitutional fundamentalism that leads us to worry about delegations by Congress to the executive branch?

</td></tr>
</table>

The primary reason we should be concerned about excessive delegation is related to the practical basis for separation of powers, namely that separation of powers was viewed by the Framers as necessary to preserve liberty. Allowing Congress to delegate might make it too easy for the federal government to make new law. This could increase the volume of law and lower its quality. One virtue of requiring the participation of so many actors, namely both Houses of Congress and the President, in the process of legislation is that it makes it difficult to legislate. Making it more difficult to legislate preserves freedom from regulation, which is a basic value underlying the U.S. legal system. Further, making it easier to legislate could prejudice quality control, allowing lower quality law to slip through.

Another concern, related to the first, is that if Congress can delegate its legislative power to agencies that can produce law more easily than Congress itself, the demand for law may increase because potential beneficiaries of new law will have a greater incentive to spend time, energy, and money on pressuring Congress and agencies for new law rather than on more productive ventures. In turn, opposing groups will be forced to devote resources to defending themselves from possible regulation targeted against them. This diverts resources from production toward political activity to procure or avoid government-enforced redistribution.[2]

Finally, and perhaps most fundamentally, excessive delegation contributes to what may be termed a "democracy deficit."[3] Agency lawmaking tends to be less democratic than law made by Congress. Agencies often function outside public view. Narrowly focused interest groups may have even relatively more influence on agency lawmaking than they do in Congress where media exposure tends to be much greater than the exposure of agencies. Some agencies appear to be captured by powerful interest groups, and agency officials often leave government to work at high paying jobs in the industry they formerly regulated. Related to this, delegation allows Members of Congress to avoid accountability for their actions. They may know full well what an agency is likely to do once it receives a delegation, but the Members of Congress can still credibly deny responsibility and point the finger at the President or agency officials.

(1) Nondelegation Foundations

As noted, some early cases stated that the Constitution absolutely prohibits the delegation of legislative authority from Congress to the executive branch. However, this did not mean that Congress may not assign discretionary authority to the executive branch, but only that any delegated authority had to be executive in nature and not legislative. This principle has not changed over time. What has changed is the analysis that the Court applies to determine whether the nature or scope of the delegated authority is permissible.

In the earliest cases, after reciting the rule that the Constitution prohibits delegations, the Court upheld delegations on the ground that Congress had made the legislative decisions and the executive branch was merely filling in details or acting under Congress's instructions when certain facts were found to exist. Under this analysis, the discretion exercised by executive officials was not legislative but rather was discretion inherent in the execution of the

Sidebar

APPLICATION OF SEPARATION OF POWERS

The nondelegation doctrine is one of the applications of the separation of powers principle that has not been built upon the requirements of a particular constitutional provision or procedure. It is related to the **Vesting Clauses**, the sentences at the beginning of the first three articles of the Constitution vesting power in each branch, mainly the Vesting Clause of Article I, which vests the Constitution's legislative power in Congress. Contrary to the views of some commentators, the Vesting Clauses lack sufficient substantive clarity to have much effect on the law. One can agree that only Congress has legislative power without having any idea what is actually exclusively legislative action. The generality of the Vesting Clause analysis may help explain why the nondelegation doctrine has not been applied very strictly.

laws. Congress does not delegate legislative authority merely by enabling executive officials to exercise discretion in the enforcement of the law. As long as the executive branch is filling in details in a program created by Congress, executive action has not crossed into the exclusive legislative territory of Congress.

There are several noteworthy examples of cases in which the Court upheld delegations to the executive branch on the basis that Congress had made the legislative

---

[2]See Jonathan Macey, *Promoting Public-Regarding Legislation Through Statutory Interpretation: An Interest Group Model*, 86 Colum. L. Rev. 223 (1986).
[3]See Theodore Lowi, *The End of Liberalism* (1979).

decision and delegated executive authority to the President or some other executive authority. In a very early case, *The Brig Aurora*, 11 U.S. (7 Cranch) 382 (1813), the Court upheld Congress's delegation to the President of the authority to lift an embargo of European trade when he found that the subjects of the embargo had "ceased to violate the neutral commerce of the United States." The statute was attacked on the ground that it was an unconstitutional delegation of legislative power because its effectiveness depended on a proclamation by the President. To this argument, the Court responded, rather vaguely, that "we can see no sufficient reason, why the legislature should not exercise its discretion in reviving the act of March 1st, 1809, either expressly or conditionally, as their judgment should direct."

Other early cases followed this pattern of drawing the line between legislation and execution of the law based on the idea that discretion in execution was permissible when Congress legislated the parameters of a program and some other government entity filled in the details. In *Wayman v. Southard*, 23 U.S. (10 Wheat.) 1 (1825), the Court approved a delegation of power to the federal courts to make their own rules of procedure. The Court recognized the difficulty and novelty of the questions posed in the case, stating that "[t]he line has not been exactly drawn which separates those important subjects, which must be entirely regulated by the legislature itself, from those of less interest, in which a general provision may be made, and power given to those who are to act under such general provisions to fill up the details." Id. at 20.

Through the early twentieth century, the basic doctrine remained the same. In *Field v. Clark*, 143 U.S. 649 (1892), the Court upheld a delegation of power to the President to impose tariffs when the President found a need for them due to unequal treatment by another country. Finally, in *United States v. Grimaud*, 220 U.S. 506 (1911), the Court rejected a rancher's challenge to a fine levied for violating a regulation restricting grazing that was promulgated by the Secretary of Agriculture under a broad delegated power to protect the national forests from "fire and depredations." In all these cases, the Court held that the delegation was permissible since only the power to "fill up the details" had been delegated.

What was missing from the Court's jurisprudence was a methodology for deciding what were "details" that could be "filled up" by others and what decisions had to be made by the legislature. In *Wayman*, the Court implied that the standard was importance, but that notion was not carried through in later cases. Finally, in *J. W. Hampton, Jr. & Co. v. United States*, 276 U.S. 394 (1928), the Court created a test for permissible delegation that has remained the law to the present day. In that decision, reviewing a law granting the President authority to alter tariff rates, the Court stated that a delegation is permissible when Congress "lay[s] down by legislative act an **intelligible principle** to which the person or body authorized to fix such rates is directed to conform." *Hampton*, 276 U.S. at 409. Congress had delegated authority to the President to alter tariffs when the President found that statutorily established tariffs did not equalize the costs of production between the United States and competing foreign countries. In the course of approving this delegation under familiar nondelegation doctrine concepts, the Court announced its new intelligible principle test. Although the Court did not provide a definition of "intelligible principle," it was clear that the Court intended to allow agencies to exercise a great deal of discretion.

(2) The Strict Nondelegation Doctrine in the Early Twentieth Century

The New Deal era of the 1930s witnessed an explosion in regulatory programs designed to achieve and maintain economic recovery from the Great Depression. The Supreme Court greeted New Deal legislation with a great deal of skepticism, and the nondelegation doctrine provided one of the weapons the Court found in its arsenal to use against what it viewed as excessive government intervention into private economic affairs. For the first, and so far only, time in U.S. history, the nondelegation doctrine was relied upon to invalidate federal statutes. A total of three federal statutory provisions were invalidated by the Supreme Court in the 1930s as violating the nondelegation doctrine.

The first statute declared to violate the nondelegation doctrine was a provision of the National Industrial Recovery Act (NIRA) which granted the President broad powers to regulate the economy during the Great Depression. One provision granted the President power to exclude petroleum products from interstate commerce if they were produced or marketed in violation of state restrictions. In *Panama Refining Co. v. Ryan*, 293 U.S. 388 (1935), this provision was declared unconstitutional on the ground that it contained no standard guiding the President's decision of whether to invoke his powers in a particular case. The Court stated "the Congress has declared no policy, has established no standard, has laid down no rule. There is no requirement, no definition of circumstances and conditions in which the transportation is to be allowed or prohibited." Id. at 430. The Court rejected a defense of the statute based on its necessity, concluding that necessity could not be allowed to alter the constitutional structure.

The Court was careful to distinguish, on two related bases, the NIRA from other statutes delegating authority to the executive branch. The first and most fundamental basis is that delegations are constitutional when Congress lays down substantive standards and agencies promulgate "subordinate rules . . . within the framework of the policy which the Legislature has sufficiently defined." Id. at 429. "Sufficiently defined" means that Congress has supplied an "intelligible principle." Id. at 430. The second basis for distinguishing prior cases was procedural. The Court noted that in prior cases it has insisted not only that agency decision making be substantively constrained but that Congress prescribe a "certain course of procedure" that the agency must follow in promulgating binding standards. The Court's reasoning implies that nondelegation doctrine problems are exacerbated when the lack of procedural constraints raises due process concerns.

The next decision invalidating a statute under the nondelegation doctrine added a pair of procedural concerns to its reasons for disapproval. In *Schechter Poultry Corp. v. United States*, 295 U.S. 495 (1935), the Court invalidated another NIRA provision that granted the President the power to approve, and thus make legally binding, codes of "fair competition" that would be drafted and submitted by private trade organizations. In *Schechter Poultry*, several individuals and a related business were convicted of violating a code that had been approved by the President regarding the conduct of the poultry business in the area around New York City. The code of fair competition was designed to improve business conditions apparently by controlling competition that resulted in reductions in wages and losses of jobs within the industry.

F   A   Q

Q: What were the factors that contributed to the invalidation of the NIRA provisions that were struck down as violating the nondelegation doctrine?

A: There were three main factors: (1) The Justices were apparently uncomfortable with the unprecedented extension of federal regulatory power over the economy. (2) The provisions granted the executive discretion without telling the President when or how to exercise it. (3) Some of the provisions appeared to delegate power to make law to private groups.

The substantive ground for invalidating the NIRA provision for codes of fair competition was the same as the Court relied upon for invalidating the provision at issue in *Panama Refining*, i.e., that it contained insufficient standards guiding the President's discretion over whether to approve a particular code of fair competition. The problem with both provisions, according to the Court, was that the President could legally decline to take action under any set of circumstances. Congress had specified a set of statutory purposes including: to remove obstructions to the flow of interstate commerce, to promote industry by allowing cooperation among trade groups, to promote cooperation between management and labor, to eliminate unfair competitive practices, to promote the full utilization of productive capacity, to increase consumption, to reduce unemployment, and to conserve natural resources. The Court found that this set of statutory purposes did not provide adequate constraints on the President's discretion over whether to approve a particular code primarily because the concept of "unfair competition," which was at the heart of the statute, was too vague to provide any real constraint on the President's action.

The Court was also not convinced that the conditions imposed by the Act on the President's approval were sufficient to save the Act from the nondelegation challenge. The Act conditioned the President's approval of a code on findings that the private groups promulgating the codes were representative and did not impose inequitable conditions on membership and that the code would not promote monopolies or discriminate against small businesses. The Court found that these restrictions did not constrain the President in making the basic decision of whether to approve or disapprove a particular code — even if the President found all the required conditions were met, he still had compete discretion over whether to approve the code. As the Court stated, "the proponents of a code, refraining from monopolistic designs, may roam at will, and the President may approve or disapprove their proposals as he may see fit." Further, the statute granted the President the power to prescribe conditions on his approval, again without, to the Court, sufficient legislative guidance.

Schechter Poultry added two procedural points to the analysis. First, the Court supported its decision to invalidate the provision with the fact that the codes were drafted by private groups. To the question whether Congress may delegate its law-making power to a private group, the Court replied resoundingly that "[s]uch a delegation of legislative power is unknown to our law, and is utterly inconsistent with the constitutional prerogatives and duties of Congress." 295 U.S. at 537. Of course, this analysis begs the question of whether Congress has delegated legislative power to the private group. Because the code could not become effective without presidential action, the Court recognized that the real question was whether the delegation of authority to the President to approve or disapprove proposed codes was sufficiently constrained to meet nondelegation doctrine concerns. Second, the Court reinforced the concern it expressed in *Panama Refining* over the lack of public process. The Court noted that in other cases in which broad delegations had been upheld (such as the delegation to the FCC of the power to act in the public convenience, interest, or necessity in regulating the broadcasting industry), the existence of statutorily mandated agency procedures was an important safeguard against the evils of delegation.

The concern over delegations to private groups was decisive in the final decision invalidating a federal statute under the nondelegation doctrine, *Carter v. Carter Coal Co.*, 298 U.S. 238 (1936). In that case, the Court struck down a statute that authorized coal producers to elect local boards with power to set minimum prices for coal in their districts. The Court rejected this delegation out of hand, characterizing it as "legislative delegation in its most obnoxious form for it is not even delegation to an official or an official body . . . but to private persons whose interests may be and often are adverse to the interests of others in the same business." *Carter Coal*, 298 U.S. at 311.

These decisions, taken together, constitute the high water mark in the history of the nondelegation doctrine. Never before and not since, despite many opportunities, has the Supreme Court declared a federal statute unconstitutional under the nondelegation doctrine. It is not even clear if nondelegation concerns were the real

Sidebar

PRACTICAL NECESSITY AND NONDELEGATION

Although the Court rejected "necessity" as a basis for approving the delegations of power in the NIRA that had been struck down, in *Yakus* the Court said that practical necessity was an important factor in judging the permissibility of a delegation, stating that "[t]he Constitution as a continuously operative charter of government does not demand the impossible or the impracticable. It does not require that Congress find for itself every fact upon which it desires to base legislative action or that it make for itself detailed determinations which it has declared to be prerequisite to the application of the legislative policy to particular facts and circumstances impossible for Congress itself properly to investigate."

motivating factor behind these decisions. The New Deal was a period of enormous expansion of federal regulation of the economy. The opinions in the cases exude hostility toward what the majority Justices viewed as interference with private property and contract rights and with the expansion of federal power into areas that had been previously regulated only by the states. Thus, it may be that the temporary expansion of the nondelegation doctrine may have been born more out of a general concern over excessive government regulation and the expansion of federal power than over the values underlying the nondelegation doctrine.

(3) The Current Lenient Nondelegation Doctrine

Shifting political winds and changes in the membership of the Supreme Court soon returned the law to the traditionally lenient nondelegation doctrine. In the first post–New Deal case, the Court upheld a relatively broad delegation of discretion to an administrative agency and employed reasoning reminiscent of the early "fill up the details" cases. See *Yakus v. United States*, 321 U.S. 414 (1944) (upholding delegation to an agency to fix "generally fair and equitable" rent and price ceilings).

In addition to signaling a return to a more lenient nondelegation doctrine and accepting necessity as a permissible basis for delegation, although the Court did not actually mention the intelligible principle standard, the *Yakus* opinion came closer than any opinion until that time to providing a definition of what constitutes an "intelligible principle." The Court stated:

> The essentials of the legislative function are the determination of the legislative policy and its formulation and promulgation as a defined and binding rule of conduct — here the rule, with penal sanctions, that prices shall not be greater than those fixed by maximum price regulations which conform to standards and will tend to further the policy which Congress has established. These essentials are preserved when Congress has specified the basic conditions of fact upon whose existence or occurrence, ascertained from relevant data by a designation administrative agency, it directs that its statutory command shall be effective.

321 U.S. at 424-25. Anticipating the objection that agencies often go beyond mere fact finding, the Court continued:

> It is no objection that the determination of facts and the inferences to be drawn from them in light of the statutory standards and declaration of policy call for the exercise of judgment, and for the formulation of subsidiary administrative policy within the prescribed statutory framework.

Id. Relatively general statutory purposes or broadly stated instructions to agencies will supply an intelligible principle and thus meet the requirements of the nondelegation doctrine, and it is consistent with nondelegation norms for agencies to exercise substantial policy judgment in carrying out programs established by Congress.

Soon after *Yakus*, the Court explicitly reverted to the "intelligible principle" standard for evaluating whether Congress has delegated legislative power. In *Lichter v. United States*, 334 U.S. 742 (1948), the Court cited *Hampton* and quoted the "intelligible principle" standard in rejecting a nondelegation challenge to a statute that allowed the United States to recover "excessive profits" from wartime government contractors. The Court has rejected each of the many nondelegation challenges to federal statutes that have been brought in the last sixty-plus years. There have been episodes, one in 1980 and another in 1999, that raised the specter of a more stringent nondelegation doctrine, but neither actually moved the law away from the leniency of the intelligible principle standard.

In *Industrial Union Department, AFL-CIO v. American Petroleum Institute (The Benzene Case)*, 448 U.S. 607 (1980), the Court relied upon the nondelegation doctrine to narrowly construe the Occupational Safety and Health Administration's (OSHA) authority to prescribe occupational health and safety standards. The American Petroleum Institute and others challenged an OSHA regulation that severely reduced permissible occupational exposure to benzene, a carcinogen. The challengers argued that the rule was not adequately supported by evidence in the rulemaking record that the reduction was necessary to protect the health of exposed workers. The agency argued that it had a statutory duty to regulate carcinogens to the lowest possible level of exposure that was technologically and economically feasible. The plurality rejected the agency's position and construed the statute, in part on nondelegation grounds, to require a threshold finding of a significant risk in the workplace before the agency was authorized to promulgate a workplace safety standard. The plurality stated that without the significant risk requirement, the statute might be unconstitutional under the nondelegation doctrine. The nondelegation violation here would apparently be the lack of guidance on when the agency was authorized or expected to pursue the goal of a virtually risk-free workplace. Unfortunately, from the plurality's opinion, it is actually difficult to see how the nondelegation doctrine is relevant to the case.

The use of the nondelegation doctrine as a reason to construe a statute narrowly in the *Benzene Case* was not without precedent. For example, in *Kent v. Dulles*, 357 U.S. 116 (1959), the Court relied upon nondelegation grounds to construe narrowly a statute granting the Secretary of State discretion over the issuance of passports. The Secretary had denied passports to Kent and others due to their alleged communist sympathies. The Court held that the statute granting discretion to the Secretary to deny passports did not include denials for these alleged beliefs and associations. The Court additionally relied upon the threat to liberty that such discretion would pose, leaving it unclear just how important nondelegation norms were to the decision in the case.

Since the *Benzene Case*, the Court has rejected several delegation challenges, some of which presented arguments for heightened nondelegation scrutiny based on the subject matter of the delegations involved, including delegations of revenue-raising power and delegation of powers related to criminal punishment. In both situations, the Supreme Court has rejected any special review under the nondelegation doctrine, falling back on the familiar intelligible principle standard. In *Touby v. United States*, 500 U.S. 160 (1991), the Court upheld a delegation of power to the Attorney General to place a drug on a list of controlled substances, thus creating criminal liability for the sale or manufacture of the drug. *Touby* argued that the intelligible principle test was too lenient in cases involving executive creation of criminal liability. In *Touby*, the Court upheld the delegation without deciding whether a more stringent test was required for delegations of the power to create crimes. Soon after, however, the Court definitively rejected heightened

Sidebar

POLICIES BEHIND NONDELEGATION DOCTRINE

The *Benzene* plurality may have based its construction of the statute on the nondelegation doctrine in reaction to Justice Rehnquist's *Benzene* concurrence, in which he argued that the statute violated the nondelegation doctrine because the agency's choice of when to pursue the goal of a virtually risk-free workplace is statutorily unconstrained. Justice Rehnquist argued that the Court should reinvigorate the nondelegation doctrine for three reasons:

(1) it forces Congress, the representative branch of government, to make important policy choices;

(2) it increases the guidance under which agencies act; and

(3) it facilitates judicial review by requiring more definite statutory standards against which courts can measure administrative decisions.

Justice Rehnquist's effort to revive the nondelegation doctrine failed, and he gained only the support of Chief Justice Burger in a later opinion attacking the same provision of the OSH Act. See *Textile Manufacturers Institute v. Donovan*, 452 U.S. 490 (1981).

REJECTION OF STRICTER RULE

In *Skinner*, 490 U.S. at 220-21, the Court explained its rejection of a stricter nondelegation rule for revenue related statutes as follows:

> Article I, §8, of the Constitution enumerates the powers of Congress. First in place among these enumerated powers is the "Power To lay and collect Taxes, Duties, Imposts and Excises. . . ." We discern nothing in this placement of the Taxing Clause that would distinguish Congress' power to tax from its other enumerated powers . . . in terms of the scope and degree of discretionary authority that Congress may delegate to the Executive[.] From its earliest days to the present, Congress, when enacting tax legislation, has varied the degree of specificity and the consequent degree of discretionary authority delegated to the Executive in such enactments.

nondelegation scrutiny in the area of criminal enforcement. See *Loving v. United States*, 517 U.S. 748 (1996). Similarly, after first entertaining the idea, the Court rejected heightened review of nondelegation challenges to the exercise of revenue raising power in *Skinner v. Mid-American Pipeline Co.*, 490 U.S. 212 (1989).

The Court rejected a novel structural argument for a stricter nondelegation doctrine in *Mistretta v. United States*, 488 U.S. 361 (1989). In that case, the Court applied the intelligible principle test to uphold the Sentencing Reform Act, which delegated the authority to promulgate mandatory federal sentencing guidelines to the United States Sentencing Commission. The Court held that the Act's declaration of purposes and goals, and its specification of the factors to be considered by the Commission, provided a sufficient intelligible principle. The Court rejected Justice Scalia's dissenting argument that the statute was unconstitutional because the Sentencing Commission was, in effect, a mini-legislature since it had no function other than promulgating the guidelines. For Justice Scalia, such a mini-legislature was unconstitutional because its discretion was not incident to the performance of an executive function.

Q: Has the Supreme Court ever accepted an argument that there should be heightened nondelegation scrutiny because of the subject matter of a particular delegation?

A: No. The Court has rejected every attempt to heighten nondelegation scrutiny, refusing to heighten scrutiny when Congress delegates authority in the areas of criminal enforcement and revenue raising. In fact, the argument for heightened scrutiny in the revenue area is weak given that some of the earliest cases upholding delegations, including *Field v. Clark*, involved tariffs, which were a very important source of federal revenue at the time.

Despite the Supreme Court's consistent rejection of nondelegation challenges over many decades, the breadth of agency discretion granted by many regulatory statutes inspires litigants to continue to press nondelegation challenges. Most recently, in the second recent episode in which it appeared at least possible that the nondelegation doctrine might be revived, the D.C. Circuit held that the more than thirty-year old Clean Air Act, at least as applied, violated the nondelegation doctrine. *American Trucking Associations, Inc. v. U.S. Environmental Protection Agency*, 175 F.3d 1027 (D.C. Cir. 1999). This court's attempted revival of the nondelegation doctrine came with a twist under which the agency could cure a violation of the nondelegation doctrine by adopting a construction of its statute limiting its own discretion. The American Trucking Associations (ATA) challenged the EPA's promulgation of National Ambient Air Quality Standards (NAAQS) for ozone and particulate matter. The Clean Air Act (CAA) requires EPA to establish standards "requisite to protect the public health" with an "adequate margin of safety." This language obviously grants the EPA a great deal of discretion to choose the level of pollution it would allow. ATA argued on judicial review of the NAAQS that the CAA violated the nondelegation doctrine.

The D.C. Circuit found a violation of the non-delegation doctrine not so much because the statute lacked an intelligible principle but rather because EPA had not adopted an intelligible principle to confine its own discretion. The problem, to the court, was that there was no pre-existing principle either in the statute or in any announced EPA rule that directed the choice among numerous possible levels for the various pollutants EPA regulates. While this lack of a pre-existing principle for choosing among numerous possible regulatory regimes might have been viewed as a violation of the nondelegation doc-trine, the Court of Appeals reasoned that under the *Benzene Case*, a limiting construction might provide an intelligible principle for a statute that would otherwise be unconstitutional under the nondelegation doctrine, and that under cases under which courts are required to defer to agency statutory interpretations, the agency ought to be given the first chance to adopt the limiting con-struction. The court thus remanded the case to the EPA to allow that agency to construe the statute to avoid the constitutional violation.

Sidebar

DELEGATION OF LEGISLATIVE POWER?

In addition to reaffirming the lenient "intelligible principle" test, the decision provoked an interesting theoretical argument between the majority and concurring Justices. Justice Scalia, writing for the majority, expressed the issue in the case as whether Congress had delegated legislative power. If it had, the stat-ute was, to him, unconstitutional. To Justice Scalia, any delegation of legislative power is per se unconstitutional. Justice Stevens, in a concurring opinion joined by Justice Souter, urged the Court to admit that under the non-delegation doctrine, Congress was allowed to delegate legislative power, with the "intelligible principle" doctrine providing a limit on such delegations. Is this merely a semantic argu-ment, or is there something real at stake in this debate?

The Supreme Court reversed the D.C. Circuit's decision and rejected its novel understanding of the nondelegation doctrine. See *Whitman v. American Trucking Associations, Inc.*, 531 U.S. 457 (2001). The Supreme Court reaffirmed the intelligible principle test for deciding whether a statute contains sufficient guidance to pass muster under the nondelegation doctrine and held that the CAA's language, requir-ing NAAQS that are "requisite to protect the public health" with an "adequate margin of safety," easily meets that test. To the Supreme Court, and to most observers of the decision, the D.C. Circuit's remand to the agency to create its own intelligible principle made no sense in light of the nondelegation doctrine's primary purpose of ensuring that Congress makes the important legislative decisions. The Supreme Court stated that "[t]he idea that an agency can cure an unconstitutionally standard-less delegation of power by declining to exercise some of that power seems to us internally contradictory. The very choice of what portion of the power to exercise would itself be an exercise of the forbidden legislative authority."

Justice Scalia's majority opinion points toward even greater leniency in the application of the nondelegation doctrine, presenting it as virtually nonjusticiable. The opinion does not actually define "intelligible principle." Rather, Justice Scalia simply compares the language of the Clean Air Act to the language of several other statutes that have survived nondelegation challenges, pointing out that the Clean Air Act is "well within the outer limits of our nondelegation precedents."[4] Justice Scalia then concludes "we have 'almost never felt qualified to second-guess Congress regarding the permissible degree of policy judgment that can be left to those executing or applying the law.'"[5] This borders on an argument that nondelegation challenges are nonjusticiable, which would make official what seems to be an unofficial rule that nondelegation challenges are never successful.

F   A   Q

Q: Might there be another attempt to revive the strict nondelegation doctrine in the near future?

A: Perhaps Justice Thomas would be willing to pick up where the late Chief Justice Rehnquist left off. In a concurring opinion in *Whitman*, Justice Thomas expressed "concern" that the intelligible principle doctrine may be inconsistent with the Constitution's grant of legislative power to Congress. Justice Thomas noted that the parties did not base their arguments in *Whitman* on the text of the Constitution, and he expressed a willingness, in a future case, "to address the question whether our delegation jurisprudence has strayed too far from our Founders' understanding of separation of powers."[6] Given the Court's unanimous agreement on the outcome in *Whitman*, even if Justice Thomas concludes that the intelligible principle doctrine is too loose, he is unlikely to change the result without a significant change in views, or membership, on the Court.

Sidebar

DORMANT NONDELEGATION DOCTRINE?

Even though the Court continues to evaluate challenges to delegations on the "intelligible principle" standard, the Court always manages to find sufficient legislative guidance to withstand attack. Whatever the reason or reasons, the Court's hospitable attitude toward delegations, and the fact that no statutes have been struck down on delegation grounds since the 1930s, may mean that the nondelegation doctrine is dormant and no longer poses a substantial bar to congressional delegation of discretion to agencies or to the President. The doctrine may, however, serve as a reminder to Congress that there is a limit to the amount of discretion that it may delegate.

Why has the Court been so lenient with regard to the nondelegation doctrine? There are several reasons why the Court may not find it necessary or wise to enforce a strict nondelegation doctrine. First, in line with Justice Scalia's sentiment, the Court may find it impossible to construct a doctrine precise enough to enforce, and thus has decided to leave the matter virtually to the discretion of Congress. Second, unlike many other separation of powers problems, the nondelegation doctrine does not present a problem of aggrandizement, of one branch seizing power at the expense of another branch. Congress voluntarily delegates discretion to the executive branch and is free to rein it in any time. Third, the complexity of the problems confronting contemporary government may have led the Court to view delegation as preferable to any realistic alternative. It would be impossible for

---

[4]*Whitman*, 531 U.S. at 474.
[5]*Whitman*, at 474-75, quoting *Mistretta v. United States*, 488 U.S. 361, 416 (2989) (Scalia, J. dissenting).
[6]*Whitman*, 531 U.S. at 487 (Thomas, J. concurring).

government to function under current conditions without granting a great deal of discretion to those who execute the laws. Finally, the Court may be convinced that the presences of alternative legal and political safeguards against agency overreaching may help validate an otherwise questionable delegation. For example, Justice Breyer has stated that nondelegation concerns are reduced when power is delegated to the President because the President is a visible, politically accountable official. *Clinton v. City of New York*, 524 U.S. at 469 (Breyer, J. dissenting). See also *Amalgamated Meat Cutters v. Connolly*, 337 F. Supp. 737 (D.D.C. 1971).

C. Separation of Powers and the Struggle for Control

(1) The Struggle for Control

Much of administrative law involves a struggle among Congress, the President, and even the federal courts to control the administrative process. Congress asserts its authority through various means of oversight and by structuring agencies to maximize congressional influence. The federal courts employ strict standards of judicial review (substantive and procedural) and broad doctrines of standing and ripeness to insert themselves into the administrative process. Most powerfully, however, the vesting of the executive power in the President of the United States in Article II, §1, provides a strong constitutional basis for a great deal of presidential control over the execution of the laws.

Article II, §1 of the Constitution provides that "The executive Power shall be vested in a President of the United States of America." The Constitution grants executive power to no other official. It thus vests all the federal executive power in the President of the United States. The power inherent in that grant, and in the office of the President, has historically not been very clear. One theory, known as the **unitary executive theory**, holds that because the Constitution vests all executive power in the President, any attempt by Congress to insulate officials and agencies from complete presidential control is suspect and probably unconstitutional. The unitary executive theory's primary doctrines include unrestricted power to appoint Officers of the United States, unrestricted power to remove officials at will, and complete power to direct the activities of all officials in the executive branch.

The unitary executive theory (whose advocates include Justice Scalia) is attractive for its simplicity and apparent adherence to constitutional text, but does not reflect governing law. Rather, the Supreme Court long ago rejected the proposition that "every officer in every branch of [the executive] department is under the exclusive control of the President." *Kendall v. United States*, 37 U.S. (12 Pet.) 524 (1838). Stated simply (and at risk of oversimplification), in *Kendall*, the Supreme Court held that Congress could legislatively require a postmaster to pay a judgment even over the objections of the President. In the course of this decision, the Court recognized that Congress has the power to impose duties on executive officials with which the President may not interfere. As the Court put it, "[t]o contend that the obligation imposed on the President to see the laws faithfully executed implies a power to forbid their execution is a novel construction of the Constitution, and entirely inadmissible." Id. at 613.

Presidents have resisted Congress's attempts to prohibit presidential interference in the exercise of powers delegated by Congress directly to other executive branch officials such as federal agencies, and it is by no means clear just how much control the President has as a matter of constitutional law. One proposition does seem clear: The President may not order his subordinates to violate the law. This would be inconsistent with the President's constitutional obligation, Art. II, §3, to "take Care that the Laws be faithfully executed[.]" For example, during the Korean War, after steel workers threatened to go on strike, President Truman issued an executive order directing the Secretary of Commerce to seize the nation's steel mills. The Supreme Court held that President Truman's order was invalid. The Court rejected the administration's arguments that the President's actions were within his power as commander-in-chief of the armed forces or within his power to enforce the laws. The Court noted that no statute authorized the seizure and that therefore the President was making, rather than simply enforcing, the law. See *Youngstown Sheet & Tube Co. v. Sawyer*, 343 U.S. 579 (1952).

In a famous concurring opinion, Justice Jackson argued that the question of presidential power was more complicated and that the Court should have looked beyond the question of whether the President was acting pursuant to statutory authorization. Justice Jackson stated that the President's power is at its greatest when acting pursuant to express or implied congressional authorization and at its weakest when acting contrary to Congress's will. Jackson argued that there is a category in the middle, which he dubbed the "zone of twilight," in which the President acts with neither support nor disapproval from Congress. In such cases the President's power to act may be concurrent with Congress's, and the lack of congressional authorization does not necessarily mean that the President, when exercising power, is engaged in lawmaking.

Justice Jackson did not actually provide a legal standard for evaluating the President's claim to power in cases falling within the zone of twilight. Rather, he stated that "[i]n this area, any actual test of power is likely to depend on the imperatives of events and contemporary imponderables rather than on abstract theories of law." 343 U.S. at 635-38 (Jackson, J., concurring). While this may be frustrating to one looking for guidance on the relative power of the President and Congress, it should not be surprising in light of the numerous important areas in separation of powers jurisprudence in which legal uncertainty dominates.

Sidebar

LEGALITY OF EXECUTIVE ORDERS

A pair of more recent decisions on the legality of Executive Orders has reinforced the notion that the President's authority to manage the executive branch does not include the authority to require agencies to act in a manner that is contrary to law. In *Chamber of Commerce v. Reich*, 74 F.3d 1322 (D.C. Cir. 1996), the Court of Appeals invalidated an Executive Order issued by President Clinton prohibiting federal agencies from contracting with companies that had hired permanent replacements for striking workers. The court found that this order was contrary to the National Labor Relations Act (NLRA), which allows employers to hire permanent replacements in some circumstances. However, in *Building & Construction Trades Dept., AFL-CIO v. Allbaugh*, 295 F.3d 28 (D.C. Cir. 2002), the Court of Appeals upheld an Executive Order issued by President George W. Bush prohibiting federal agencies from either requiring or forbidding their contractors to use a particular form of labor agreement known as a Project Labor Agreement. The court placed primary reliance on the President's inherent "supervisory authority over the Executive Branch." 295 F.3d at 33. The court also noted that President Bush's order purported to apply only "to the extent permitted by law," thus avoiding conflict with the NLRA.

Congress's interest in the activities of the executive branch does not end at the moment of delegation. Rather, Congress maintains a keen interest in monitoring and influencing the way agencies carry out the responsibilities they have been given through congressional delegation. Congress attempts to maintain control over agency action by both formal and informal means.

The independence of **independent agencies** is largely a product of the struggle for control between the President and Congress. Formally, Congress designates some agencies as "independent" in order to shield them from presidential influence. Congress states, in the enabling acts creating these agencies, that they are "independent" and not located in any department of the executive branch. These agencies are typically headed by commissioners appointed for a term of years by the President with the advice and consent of the Senate with removal by the President only for good cause. The term of years means that new presidents cannot immediately staff independent agencies with their own appointees, which substantially reduces the President's influence over these agencies. The original theory justifying independent agencies was the notion that agencies dealing with complex social problems should be able to apply their expertise free from political influence. However, it has become increasingly clear that Congress's motivation for making agencies independent may have had more to do with increasing congressional influence over them and less to do with shielding them from politics. This structure is designed by Congress to minimize presidential influence and maximize congressional influence over independent agencies.

Informally, Congress conducts extensive oversight of the executive branch, often acting through its committees, holding hearings, conducting investigations, and demanding information, especially when an agency takes controversial action. (Congress has also institutionalized its oversight rule by establishing the **Government Accountability Office** (GAO) (an arm of Congress) and granting it broad power to oversee agencies.) Individual Members of Congress contact agency heads to express their views on how agencies should act, and express displeasure when their constituents are harmed by agency action. Members of Congress also prevail on the President to appoint their staff members and allies to important agency positions, providing a conduit for influence over the agencies.

Congressional oversight of the executive branch raises separation of powers concerns, especially when Congress meddles in the actual execution of the law. The key distinction in this area is between informal methods of influence, which may raise concerns but are generally constitutional, and formal methods of influence, which may be unconstitutional unless Congress is careful to follow the procedures established by the Constitution for congressional action.

(a) Informal Congressional Influence

Informal congressional influence over the executive branch is ubiquitous. Members of Congress have numerous informal contacts with agency personnel to express their interests and the interests of their constituents in the outcome of agency action. Members of Congress also seek information from agency officials and summon them to committee hearings to explain their actions. Committees and the GAO investigate agencies and issue reports detailing alleged failings in the execution of the law. Members of Congress also informally pressure the President to appoint their preferred candidates to positions within the executive branch such as independent agency commissioners. These officials appointed to agency positions at the behest of a Member of Congress are often subject to great influence by the Member of Congress to whom they owe their appointments.

In general, while these informal methods of congressional oversight and influence may raise eyebrows, they do not violate separation of powers or any more specific constitutional provision. This is because informal oversight, by definition, does not involve any legally binding action by Congress, and thus the Constitution's lawmaking procedures do not apply. To take a simple example, if the Environmental Protection Agency decides to promulgate a rule suggested by members of a key congressional committee, so long as the EPA administrator promulgates the rule and not the congressional committee, the fact that the agency was informally influenced by Members of Congress does not violate separation of powers or any of the Constitution's procedural requirements.

F   A   Q

Q: What are the constitutional limits on Congress's oversight of the executive branch?

A: In general, Congress has the constitutional power to investigate, subject to presidential invocations of doctrines that protect secrecy within the executive branch, such as executive privilege. (See Chapter 13.) Congress can hold hearings and issue legislative reports, and it can informally try to convince executive branch officials to act in Congress's preferred way. However, to legally require any response from the executive branch, Congress must use Article I's legislative procedures. (See below.)

(b) Formal Congressional Influence

The legislative power provides Congress numerous opportunities to formally influence and even control the conduct of the executive branch. If Congress is dissatisfied with an agency's use of its delegated power, Congress can revise the terms of the delegation or specifically require or bar particular agency actions. Congress can also control agency action with funding provisions in appropriations bills, such as appropriations riders that prohibit the use of agency funds for specified purposes. Congress also increases its ability to informally influence agency action by creating independent agencies that are less subject to presidential control. Congress has also attempted to formally overrule agency regulations and other agency actions, and the Supreme Court has been careful to disapprove the procedures Congress has used when they do not conform to constitutional requirements.

One method of control Congress may wish to employ is to appoint its own members to executive branch positions. Unlike many foreign governmental systems, the United States Constitution prohibits service in both the executive and legislative branches. The Incompatibility Clause, Art. I, §6, cl. 2 of the Constitution, forbids Members of Congress from holding executive appointments during their terms in Congress. In addition to violating the Incompatibility Clause, it would violate separation of powers for Members of Congress to serve as administrators. For example, Congress designated certain Members of Congress (formally in their private capacities as airport users) to serve on the Metropolitan Washington Airports Authority, a board that administers the airports in the Washington, D.C., area. The Supreme Court held that the arrangement violated the Constitution, either because the authority's work would amount to legislation by a subgroup of Congress without bicameralism and presentment or because it involved congressional participation in the execution of the law. See *Metropolitan Washington Airports Authority v. Citizens for Abatement of Aircraft Noise, Inc.*, 501 U.S. 252 (1991).

(c) The Legislative Veto and Review of Regulations

One method Congress has used to supervise the executive branch is the **legislative veto.** Under the legislative veto, Congress reserved the power to reject agency action (usually regulations) with a vote, depending on the particular provision, of both houses of Congress, by one house of Congress, or in some cases even by a single congressional committee. Legislative vetoes were not presented to the President for signature or veto. For several decades, Congress employed the legislative veto to control agency action. The legislative veto's virtue is that it serves as a check on delegation, allowing Congress to delegate needed authority to the executive branch while retaining a relatively easy check on the executive branch. The legislative veto should thus be attractive to those concerned with excessive delegation.

> **Sidebar**
>
> **THE INCOMPATIBILITY CLAUSE**
>
> The Incompatibility Clause, Art. I, §6, cl. 2 of the Constitution, "no Person holding any Office under the United States, shall be a Member of either House during his Continuance in Office," is among the least known but most important structural provisions of the U.S. Constitution. This clause distinguishes the government of the United States from the governments of most other Western democracies in which ministers are drawn from the ranks of the legislature. By prohibiting administrative officials from also serving in Congress, the clause ensures that even when it is difficult to discern a line between executive and legislative powers, it will at least be clear that the same people will not be involved in the operations of both branches.

In *Immigration and Naturalization Service v. Chadha*, 462 U.S. 919 (1983), the Supreme Court held a one-house legislative veto unconstitutional because it violated the Constitutions requirements of bicameralism and presentment. In *Chadha*, the House of Representatives vetoed the decision of the Department of Justice to suspend Chadha's deportation. Suspension of deportation is a procedure under which an otherwise deportable alien is allowed to remain in the United States due to extreme hardship to the alien or the alien's family. At one time the only way a deportable alien could obtain relief from deportation was via a private bill in Congress authorizing permanent residency for the particular alien. This was too much of a burden on Congress, so after trying several different solutions, Congress passed a statute allowing the Attorney General to suspend deportation, subject to the possibility of a veto by either House of Congress acting alone.

The question whether the one-house veto violated the **bicameralism and presentment** requirements of the Constitution centered on whether the legislative veto was a legislative act. "Bicameralism" refers to the requirement that all legislation pass both the House and the Senate. "Presentment" refers to the requirement that all legislation be presented to the President for either signature or veto. If it was, bicameralism and presentment apply. If not, they don't, although then a separation of powers problem would arise, because with no applicable exception, the Constitution grants the House and Senate only legislative power. Congress may not both make and execute the laws. The Court defined legislative action as "action that had the purpose and effect of altering the legal rights, duties, and relations of persons . . . outside the Legislative Branch." *Chadha*, 462 U.S. at 952. Congress's action in *Chadha* was held to be legislative because the legislative veto required the Attorney General to deport Chadha when Chadha otherwise would have been allowed to remain in the United States.

Note that the definition of legislative action does not turn on the form of Congress's action but rather its effect. A test that turned on the form of Congress's action might ask whether the action created a new rule of law that would be applied in a multitude of situations or whether it was something that had traditionally been done through legislation, whether by a public law or a private bill. A formal test would be difficult to construct and easier to avoid. The effects test is simple to understand and easy to police. In order for Congress to take action with legal effect, it must legislate bicamerally with presentment to the President.

F A Q

Q: Are all legislative vetoes unconstitutional after *Chadha*?

A: The *Chadha* Court's definition of legislative action, i.e., action that affects the rights and duties of persons outside the legislative branch, combined with the Court's reliance on bicameralism and presentment means that whenever Congress (or a subset of Congress) takes action that affects the legal situation of someone outside of Congress, it must use the legislative process, namely bicameralism and presentment. Because the use of the legislative veto to counteract agency power was widespread, *Chadha* placed hundreds of federal statutes under a constitutional cloud. This means that any legislative veto short of full bicameralism and presentment cannot have any legal effect. Thus, Congress's only constitutional method of nullifying agency action is through legislation that passes both houses of Congress and is presented to the President for signature or veto.

If Congress cannot overrule the suspension of Chadha's deportation without bicameralism and presentment, why is it apparently permissible for Congress to allow the Department of Justice to adjust Chadha's status without bicameralism and presentment? In *Chadha*, the argument was made that if the bicameralism and presentment requirements apply whenever Congress affects someone's legal rights, these requirements should also apply to the Attorney General's actions regarding Chadha's deportability and, by extension, anytime an executive branch official or agency takes action that changes the law. This is essentially an argument for a hyper-strict nondelegation doctrine. The Court answered this argument in a key footnote in its opinion. The Court explained in *Chadha* footnote 16, 462 U.S. at 953, that when the executive branch takes action that affects a person's legal rights and duties, it is executing the law according to the terms of delegated authority. The only constitutional question regarding executive action is the nondelegation doctrine question of whether Congress has provided an intelligible principle. The non-constitutional legal question is whether the executive branch has been delegated the power to act. Bicameralism and presentment are not required for two reasons, first because these provisions apply to legislative and not executive action and second because adequate alternative safeguards, such as judicial review and congressional oversight, ensure that executive action does not go beyond the terms of delegated authority.

This analysis leads back to an argument that Justice Stevens made in his concurring opinion in the *Whitman* nondelegation decision. Justice Stevens supports his argument that the nondelegation doctrine allows Congress to delegate some legislative power with the observation that whether a power is legislative or not depends on the nature of the power, not on the identity of the entity exercising the power. This may be correct in some circumstances, but under *Chadha*, in the vast majority of situations in which delegation is at issue, the identity of the actor is key to determining whether a particular government action is constitutional.

When the Attorney General deports Chadha, or decides not to deport Chadha, the Attorney General is executing the law, namely the statute authorizing the Attorney General to act. When Congress does the exact same thing, under the Court's test, its action is legislative and must comply with the bicameralism and presentment requirements. This makes sense in light of the fact that Congress has no power to execute the law and, under Justice Scalia's understanding of the nondelegation doctrine, the executive branch has no power to legislate even if it does have the power to take discretionary action when power has been properly delegated.

After *Chadha*, there was a great deal of concern in Congress over the loss of the legislative veto as a device for controlling the exercise of delegated discretion. This issued simmered for years until, in a part of the Contract with America Advancement Act of 1996, Congress created a procedure, called the **Congressional Review Act**, in a new APA chapter (Chapter 8) under which agency rules may be rejected by a resolution that passes both Houses of Congress and is presented to the President. The resolution must be introduced in Congress within sixty session days of Congress receiving notice of the rule, and major rules cannot become effective until after the sixty days have expired. The law prescribes expedited procedures in Congress to ensure that resolutions are voted upon in a timely manner.

F   A   Q

Q: Can Congress still review administrative rules after *Chadha*?

A: Yes, but any process must comply with the Constitution's bicameralism and presentment requirements. In 1996, Congress enacted the Congressional Review Act, 5 U.S.C. §§801 et seq., which sets a process for expedited congressional review of regulations. In recognition of the unconstitutionality of legislative vetoes, the Act requires action by both Houses of Congress and Presentment to the President. The Act's primary innovation is the creation of an expedited process for consideration of legislation rejecting administrative rules.

What does the combination of a lenient nondelegation doctrine and a strict bicameralism and presentment requirement mean for separation of powers and the balance of power between Congress and the executive branch? If the legislative veto was viewed by Congress as a means of controlling the exercise of delegated authority, the balance would seem to have shifted toward more power in the executive branch. In response, Congress may be more reluctant to delegate and it may engage in more informal oversight, using arm-twisting tactics in place of legislative vetoes. Whatever the result, the Supreme Court appears to be more concerned with making sure that constitutional procedures are followed than with more abstract questions about the proper balance of power among the branches.

F   A   Q

Q: Is the Congressional Review Act likely to be an effective method of supervising administrative agencies?

A: Probably not. The President's power to veto any resolution disapproving a regulation means that this procedure is likely to provide Congress with a much less effective tool than the legislative veto. Most agencies are unlikely to promulgate major rules without at least tacit approval from the President, who would then be likely to veto a resolution of disapproval. It should therefore not be surprising that in the years that this procedure has existed, it has been used only once, and then in a period of transition between administrations. Congress disapproved a broad-ranging rule regulating ergonomic workplace injuries that was promulgated near the end of the administration of President Bill Clinton. By the time the resolution of disapproval was passed by Congress, the champion of the regulation had gone out of office and the new President, of a different party and with a different view on workplace safety regulation, was happy to sign the resolution.

(2) Appointment of Administrative Officials

The President has primary responsibility for appointing and removing agency officials, and Congress's role is limited by constitutional text and separation of powers principles. Regarding appointments, the text of the Constitution limits Congress's role to advice and consent by the Senate for appointments of officials executing the law. The Appointments Clause, Art. II, §2, cl. 2 of the Constitution, provides:

> [The President] shall nominate, and by and with the Advice and Consent of the Senate, shall appoint . . . all other Officers of the United States, whose appointments are not herein otherwise provided for, and which shall be established by Law: but the Congress may by Law vest the Appointment of such Inferior Officers, as they think proper, in the President alone, in the Courts of Law, or in the Heads of Departments.

There are two key elements to this clause. The first is that it covers the appointment of all "**Officers of the United States**" including both "**principal**" officers and "**inferior**" officers. Second, the clause identifies only three appointing entities, the President, the "**Courts of Law**" and the "**Heads of Departments.**"

The Appointments Clause specifies two procedures for appointing Officers of the United States. Absent action by Congress, every Officer of the United States is appointed by the President with the Advice and Consent (understood as majority approval) of the Senate. Congress may legislatively alter the process for the appointment of inferior officers by placing their appointment in the President alone or in the Courts of Law or Department Heads. Although the clause does not explicitly say so, it is understood that when Congress provides for the appointment of inferior officers by the Department Heads or Courts of Law, these appointments are also exempt from the advice and consent requirement. However, the default rule is appointment by the President with the advice and consent of the Senate — if Congress does not specify otherwise in a statute, this is the process for appointing all Officers of the United States.

F A Q

Q: Are inferior offices appointed by the President with the advice and consent of the Senate?

A: Yes, unless Congress legislatively provides otherwise. If Congress specifies, inferior officers may be appointed by the President alone, a Department Head or a Court of Law.

Four questions arise under the Appointments Clause:

1. Which officials are covered by the clause?
2. Which of the covered officials may be classified by Congress as "inferior"?
3. Who may appoint inferior officers? and
4. What consequences attach to a violation of the clause?

The first question requires identifying which officials are "Officers of the United States." In an 1878 decision, the Supreme Court stated that "all persons who can be said to hold an office under the government" were Officers of the United States who must be appointed in accordance with the Appointments Clause. *United States v. Germaine*, 99 U.S. 508, 510 (1878). This definition is very broad, and does not account for the possibility that some government employees are not Officers of the United States because of the nature of their duties or the degree of power they possess. Perhaps this is because the phrase "hold an officer under the government" is just as vague as "Officer of the United States."

In 1976, the Supreme Court refined the test enunciated in *Germaine* by providing that "any

Sidebar

TEST FOR OFFICER STATUS

Notice the similarities between the Court's test for who is an Officer of the United States ("an appointee exercising significant authority pursuant to the laws") and what action by Congress constitutes legislation ("action that ha[s] the purpose and effect of altering the legal rights, duties, and relations of persons"). The Court's separation of powers jurisprudence is occupied largely with ensuring that the federal government follows proper procedures when it acts to change or enforce the law.

appointee exercising significant authority pursuant to the laws of the United States is an 'Officer of the United States,' and must, therefore, be appointed in the manner prescribed by §2, cl. 2, of . . . Article [II]." *Buckley v. Valeo*, 424 U.S. 1, 126 (1976). The Court distinguished Officers of the United States from government officials who do not enforce the law but rather aid in the legislative function. Officials in the latter category may be appointed in a process different from that provided for in the Appointments Clause.

S i d e b a r

LANDRY AND FREYTAG

The D.C. Circuit, in *Landry v. FDIC*, 204 F.3d 1125 (D.C. Cir. 2000), held that administrative law judges who could only recommend agency action were employees and not officers simply because they could not make final decisions in any category of cases. The *Landry* court's distinction of *Freytag*, on the basis that *Freytag* was grounded upon the power of the special trial judges to make final decisions in some cases, does not appear to be faithful to the language of the *Freytag* opinion. The Supreme Court did not base its decision in *Freytag* on the fact that the special trial judges could make final decisions in minor cases, but rather that they exercised discretion and authority simply by presiding over trials.

S i d e b a r

OTHER OFFICIALS

There are officials whose appointment is specified elsewhere in the Constitution and thus who are not subject to the analysis described here. "Ambassadors, other public Ministers and Consuls [and] Judges of the supreme Court" are appointed by the President with the advice and consent of the Senate. The Constitution also prescribes the method of selecting Members of Congress and the President and Vice-President. The Constitution leaves to each House of Congress and the States the method of selecting officers of Congress and Electors for President, respectively. Interestingly, the Constitution does not prescribe a method for appointing judges of inferior federal courts, who historically have been appointed by the President with the advice and consent of the Senate.

There are two categories of federal government servants who are not "Officers of the United States" subject to the Appointments Clause. The first category comprises executive branch "**employees**" who work in the executive branch but are not "Officers of the United States" and therefore may be appointed (perhaps a better word would be "hired") in a process other than the ones specified in the Appointments Clause, such as a civil-service-type appointment process. Employees are officials without discretionary authority under the law. They assist and perhaps advise Officers of the United States, but they do not have any authority to enforce the law. Many "employees" are lower-level federal workers such as clerical workers, maintenance workers, mechanics, etc., who are employed by the federal government but exercise no discretion or authority to administer federal law. Officials who exercise discretion and authority are officers, not employees.

Congress's classification of federal government workers sometimes skirts the line of legality. For example, in *Freytag v. Commissioner of Internal Revenue*, 501 U.S. 868 (1991), a challenge was brought to the appointment of certain special trial judges by the Chief Judge of the Tax Court. One argument in favor of this appointment process was that the special trial judges were employees, not officers, and therefore their appointment was not governed by the Appointments Clause. The Court rejected this argument based on the discretion and authority involved in presiding over hearings even in cases in which the special trial judges could make only recommendations to tax court judges and not final decisions. Thus, the Supreme Court held that the special trial judges were "Officers of the United States" and therefore must be appointed pursuant to the Appointments Clause.

The second category of federal workers who are not covered by the Appointments Clause are people who work for Congress in aid of the legislative process and do not exercise any authority pursuant to the law. The Supreme

Court stated in *Buckley* that officials who perform functions such as collecting information for, and making reports to, Congress are not necessarily Officers of the United States and thus such officials may be appointed by Congress itself in a procedure not contemplated by the Appointments Clause. These activities are thought to be "merely in aid of legislation" and do not involve the exercise of authority pursuant to the laws of the United States. However, officials appointed by Congress may not exercise authority under the laws of the United States, such as prosecutorial or rule-making authority, because they have not been appointed in accordance with the Appointments Clause.

The second Appointments Clause question is which federal government officials must be appointed by the President with the advice and consent of the Senate, and which are inferior officers who may be appointed by the President alone, Department Heads, or the Courts of Law. To distinguish them from inferior officers, those officers who must be appointed by the President are often referred to as "principal" or "superior" officers.

The general understanding seems to be that principal officers are high-level officials in the executive branch and heads of independent agencies. Cabinet members and commissioners of independent agencies are principal officers because there is no one in the government hierarchy between them and the President. There is not a great deal of case law about whether a particular government official is a principal or inferior officer. This is probably because Congress has not been adventurous in altering the appointment process for relatively high-level officials in the executive branch. If anything, Congress errs in the other direction, prescribing presidential appointment with the advice and consent of the Senate for many officials Congress could classify as inferior. Nothing in the Constitution prevents Congress from reserving the appointment of all inferior officers to the President with the advice and consent of the Senate.

F   A   Q

Q: Why does Congress seem to keep the appointment of many possibly inferior officers under the standard appointment by the President with the advice and consent of the Senate procedure?

A: The best explanation of this is probably a desire to maintain a role for Congress in the appointment in the form of Senate confirmation. As a political matter, this helps Congress keep more control over the functioning of the executive branch.

Inferior officers are lower-level executive officials who are under the supervision of other executive officials beneath the President. Under the Ethics in Government Act, the independent counsel was appointed by a special panel of the United States Court of Appeals to investigate alleged wrongdoing by executive branch officials and could be removed by the Attorney General for cause, but was not under the direct supervision of the Attorney General or any other executive branch official. Each independent counsel was appointed to investigate and potentially prosecute a particular case involving particular officials. In *Morrison v. Olson*, 487 U.S. 654 (1988), the Court held that an independent counsel is an inferior officer. The Court relied on three factors to conclude that the independent counsel was an inferior officer: (1) the limited scope of the duties of the independent counsel; (2) the limited duration of the independent counsel's appointment; and (3) the fact that the Attorney General could remove the independent counsel for good cause. Justice Scalia argued in dissent that the independent counsel was not an inferior officer because she was not subject to the supervision of any higher official and because she was not bound to follow the policies of the Department of Justice.

Although Justice Scalia's view did not prevail in that case, the next time the issue came up Justice Scalia wrote an opinion for the Court basically applying the test he argued for in his *Morrison* dissent. In *Edmond v. United States*, 520 U.S. 651 (1997), the Court held that judges on a Coast Guard Court of Criminal Appeals, whose appointments were not limited in scope or duration as was the appointment of the independent counsel, were nevertheless inferior officers, primarily because their work "is directed and supervised at some level by others who were appointed by Presidential nomination with the advice and consent of the Senate." 520 U.S. at 663. The Court emphasized that the factors relied upon in *Morrison* were not intended to be exclusive. Because these judges were considered inferior officers, it was proper for Congress to vest their appointment in the Secretary of Transportation.

The third question is who may appoint inferior officers. As noted, the clause allows Congress to vest the appointment of inferior officers in "the President alone, the Courts of Law or in the Heads of Departments." In most cases, this inquiry will be straightforward—we know who the President is, and most of the time, we can easily identify courts of law such as the Supreme Court of the United States and heads of departments such as the Secretary of Transportation and the Attorney General. There are, however, some cases of uncertainty. For example, are the commissioners who head an independent agency "department heads" who can constitutionally be vested with the authority to appoint inferior officers within their agency? What about non–Article III courts? While we do not normally think of each independent agency as a separate department, because the independent agencies are not part of any traditional department, a negative answer to this question would mean that all officers within independent agencies would have to go through presidential appointment with the advice and consent of the Senate or be appointed by the head of a different department.

After decades of uncertainty, in the *PCAOB* decision, the Supreme Court finally decided that each independent agency is a "Department" capable of being vested with the power to appoint inferior officers. In *PCAOB*, the SEC was granted authority to appoint members of the Public Company Accounting Oversight Board, which was created as part of the Sarbanes-Oxley Act that had been passed in reaction to a rash of accounting scandals. The Court held that any "freestanding component of the Executive Branch, not subordinate to or contained within any other such component" should be considered a "Department" for purposes of the Appointments Clause. See *PCAOB*, 130 S. Ct. at 3163. This gives Congress a great deal of discretion over the vesting of power to appoint inferior officers.

PCAOB resolved an issue that had split the Court in the past. In *Freytag v. United States*, 501 U.S. 868 (1991), discussed above, the Court unanimously agreed that the Chief Judge of the Tax Court could appoint special trial judges, but it split 5-4, on the reason for this conclusion. A majority of five Justices held that the Tax Court was a "Court of Law" within the meaning of the Appointments Clause even though it was established under Article I and was not staffed with judges appointed pursuant to the provisions of Article III. These five Justices, in an opinion written by Justice Blackmun, rejected the notion that the Tax Court was a Department, arguing that the Framers were very concerned that Congress might attempt to weaken the executive branch by fragmenting the appointment power among many small entities within the executive branch. The other four Justices disagreed with this reasoning and concluded that the Tax Court is a Department and that therefore the Chief Justice was a Department Head within the meaning of the Appointments Clause. In an opinion by Justice Scalia, the dissenters reasoned that the ordinary meaning of "department" as used in the Constitution is each separate organization in government, no matter how small. (This is the standard adopted later by the majority in the *PCAOB* decision.) The dissenters vehemently disagreed with the notion that the Tax Court is a court of law, arguing that the Appointments Clause refers only to the Article III courts that can constitutionally exercise the judicial power of the United States.

Another question on which there is very little case law is whether there are limits on which inferior officers may be appointed by each appointing authority named in the Appointments Clause, i.e., the President alone, the Heads of Departments and the Courts of Law. The text of the Appointments Clause does not limit each appointing entity to appointments within their respective departments or branch. Usually, however, Congress allows Department Heads to appoint inferior officers only within their own departments, and it allows the Courts of Law to appoint officers within the judicial branch. There are exceptions to this, mainly involving the judiciary. Federal law provides that under certain circumstances, an interim United States Attorney is appointed by the local federal district court. And recall that the law creating the office of **Independent Counsel** provided that the independent counsel was appointed by a special panel of the United States Court of Appeals for the District of Columbia Circuit. An "independent counsel" was a special prosecutor appointed under the Ethics in Government Act to investigate executive branch officials free from oversight by the Department of Justice so as to avoid conflict of interest within the executive branch.

In *Morrison v. Olson*, 487 U.S. 654 (1988), the Supreme Court approved the appointment of the independent counsel, an executive branch official, by a court of law. The Court reasoned that this appointment made sense given the concern over conflicts of interest when the independent counsel was investigating executive branch officials, especially those within the Department of Justice where the power to appoint might otherwise be located. The Court, in dicta, stated that there were constitutional limits to Congress's ability to assign the appointment of inferior officers under the Appointments Clause. The Court suggested that some appointments might be incongruous. For example, appointments made across departmental lines or by a court appointing an official to a position unrelated to law or legal processes (such as an undersecretary of a department) may be incongruous. Although incongruous appointments may violate the separation of powers, the issue is not often raised because Congress normally does not provide for such appointments.

One thing we can say for certain about the appointment of both principal and inferior officers — Congress may not participate in their appointment except through the Senate's advice and consent power. In *Buckley v. Valeo*, 424 U.S. 1 (1976), the Court found the procedure for appointing Federal Election Commissioners was inconsistent with the Appointments Clause. Under the statute, two commissioners were appointed by the President, two were appointed by the president pro tempore of the Senate and two were appointed by the Speaker of the House. All were subject to confirmation by both Houses of Congress. The Court rejected any role for Congress in the process (other than the Senate's power of advice and consent) because Congress is not named as a possible appointing authority in the Appointments Clause. (The Court in *Buckley* did allow that Congress and its officials may participate in the appointment of officials who act merely in aid of legislation, such as officers who gather information or do research to help Congress decide whether and how to legislate.) Congress's powers, including power over the budget and other presidentially favored legislation, and the Senate's constitutional advice and consent power can effectively force the President to appoint persons who are favored by key members of Congress. Congress also formally influences appointments by requiring bipartisanship and by legislatively regulating the qualifications for agency membership and chairmanship. But Congress itself cannot play a formal role in the actual process of appointing Officers of the United States.

F   A   Q

Q: Can Congress constitutionally appoint anyone?

A: Yes, Congress can appoint its own officers and employees. For example, Congress can appoint people to draft legislation and do research on its behalf. Congress cannot, however, appoint anyone who exercises legal authority. Anyone who exercises legal authority is an Officer of the United States and must be appointed pursuant to the Appointments Clause.

The fourth and final question under the Appointments Clause is what consequences attach when Congress specifies an appointments process that is inconsistent with the Appointments Clause. The simple answer to this is that the Court does not declare the appointment void, but rather holds that the appointee may not perform functions reserved to officers of the United States, i.e., the appointee may not exercise authority pursuant to the law. In *Buckley v. Valeo*, for example, the Court ruled that the Federal Election Commission (FEC) could not engage in enforcement functions such as rulemaking and the bringing of civil lawsuits because four of its six members were appointed by members of Congress (two by the president pro tempore of the Senate and two by the Speaker of the House), but it could continue to perform other functions such as collecting information and making reports to Congress. These activities were held to be "merely in aid of legislation" and did not involve the exercise of authority pursuant to the laws of the United States. Therefore, they could be carried out by persons other than Officers of the United States.

Under this reasoning, Congress may appoint its own officials, but it may not assign executive functions to anyone not appointed in conformity with the Appointments Clause. However, officials appointed by Congress may not exercise authority under the laws of the United States, such as prosecutorial or rulemaking authority, because they have not been appointed in accordance with the Appointments Clause. Therefore, the FEC could not engage in rulemaking or other enforcement activities but could receive information and make reports to Congress.

APPOINTMENTS CLAUSE CHECKLIST

The following factors are important for determining whether an appointment complies with the Appointments Clause:

1. Does the official exercise authority pursuant to the laws of the United States? If so, the official is an Officer of the United States to whom the Appointments Clause applies. ☑

2. Is the official a high-level official with significant policymaking authority and little or no supervision other than the President? If so, the official is a Principal Officer who must be appointed by the President with the advice and consent of the Senate. ☑

3. Does the official exercise authority only under substantial supervision by higher-ranking officials within the executive branch? If so, the official is an inferior officer and Congress may specify appointment by the President alone, by a Department Head or by a Court of Law. ☑

4. Does the official exclusively carry out activities not involving discretion or policymaking activities, such as clerical or maintenance work? If so, the official may be a government employee (not an Officer) to whom the Appointments Clause does not apply. Civil service or similar appointment may be appropriate. ☑

5. Does the official act only in aid of the legislative process, such as performing research for Members of Congress? If so, the Appointments Clause does not apply and the official may be appointed in a process controlled by Congress. ☑

(3) Removal of Executive Branch Officials

It is often said that the person with the power to remove an official is the one with the power to control that official's conduct. In light of this common sense understanding, the balance of power among the branches of government is deeply affected by the allocation of the power to remove officials.

The Constitution does not mention the removal of officials except through impeachment, an extraordinary procedure under which the House charges and the Senate tries officials for "Treason, Bribery, or other high Crimes and misdemeanors." Impeachment by the House and conviction by the Senate result in removal from office. Constitutional silence on the process for removing officials under more routine circumstances is the foundation of a basic constitutional presumption that the President has the power to remove executive branch officials in the ordinary course. The idea underlying this presumption is that the removal of an executive branch official is itself an executive function reserved to the executive branch absent any contrary specification in the text of the Constitution. This understanding gives rise to the black letter law that in the absence of statutory restrictions, the President has the power to remove executive officials at will. This recognized power to remove executive officials is, however, sometimes subject to restrictions Congress may place on the President's removal power.

(a) Congressional Involvement in the Removal Process

Congress often attempts to restrict the President's power to remove executive officials, usually through statutory requirements that officials not be removed absent good cause such as incompetence or corruption or by specifying that agency officials (usually in independent agencies), once appointed, shall serve for a specified term of years absent cause for removal. Presidents tend to comply with these provisions grudgingly, contending that they unconstitutionally restrict the President's executive power. Congress has attempted to involve itself in the removal process, but the Supreme Court has rebuffed these attempts, holding both that Congress may not retain advice and consent power over removal of officials or assign the power to enforce the law to officials subject to removal by Congress.

The earliest case dealing with Congress's involvement in the removal process is *Myers v. United States*, 272 U.S. 52 (1926). In *Myers*, the Supreme Court ruled that Congress may not statutorily require the President to seek the Senate's permission before removing a local postmaster, an official considered to be performing purely executive functions. Although this case is sometimes thought of as establishing the President's unlimited constitutional power to remove purely executive officials, the holding is actually narrower, providing only that the Senate may not retain a role in the removal of such officials. The Court's opinion in *Myers*, written by Chief Justice and former President William Howard Taft, does contain language suggesting that the President has inherent constitutional authority to remove officials engaged in executive functions. However, the opinion also includes dicta suggesting that Congress may restrict the removal of inferior officers.

The only other significant decision on Congress's power to become involved in the removal of executive officials involved the assignment of power to establish binding budget targets to the **Comptroller General**, who heads an agency now known as the Government Accountability Office. That agency, which was formerly known as the General Accounting Office, has always been considered an agent of Congress both because of its duties and because of the appointment and removal process for the Comptroller General. The Comptroller General is appointed by the President from a list provided by Congress and is removable by a Joint Resolution of Congress, which is presented to the President. The agency's primary role has always been to advise Congress on the activities of the executive branch, mainly with regard to the expenditure of money appropriated by Congress. Because the Comptroller General's responsibilities were mainly in aid of Congress's legislative function and did not involve the execution of the laws, it was considered appropriate for Congress to retain power over the removal of the Comptroller, although a Joint Resolution is presented to the President for approval or veto.

Congress went beyond the Comptroller's purely legislative role when, in the Balanced Budget and Emergency Deficit Control Act of 1985, it granted the

Comptroller the power to establish potentially binding spending reductions to reduce the federal budget deficit. In *Bowsher v. Synar*, 478 U.S. 714 (1986), the Court held that it was unconstitutional to assign this responsibility to the Comptroller General because, as it had held in *Buckley v. Valeo*, only Officers of the United States may exercise significant authority under the laws of the United States. The Court further held that because of the congressional removal provision, the Comptroller is not an Officer of the United States.

The *Bowsher* Court expressed the problem with removal by Congress in terms very similar to those the Court employed when it rejected a role for Congress in the appointment of Officers of the United States. The Court noted that only Officers of the United States may exercise authority pursuant to law. It further held that the power to administratively establish binding spending reductions could be exercised only by Officers of the United States and that no Officer of the United States could be subject to removal by Congress except via the impeachment process. Also consistent with its approach in appointments cases, the Court did not strike down the removal provision but rather held that the removal provision placed the Comptroller General outside the category of Officers of the United States and thus the Comptroller could not exercise the authority purportedly granted by the statute.

(b) Restrictions on Presidential Removal of Administrative Officials

Although Congress has only occasionally attempted to involve itself in the removal process, is has more often attempted to reduce presidential control over administrative agencies by restricting the President's authority to remove officials. Most independent agency heads, for example, may be removed only for good cause such as corruption or malfeasance. In *Humphrey's Executor v. United States*, 295 U.S. 602 (1935), the Court held that Congress may require a finding of good cause before the President may remove a Federal Trade Commissioner. The Court distinguished *Myers* on the ground that Humphrey, as a Federal Trade Commissioner, exercised legislative rulemaking and adjudicatory powers that were appropriately shielded from excessive presidential influence, while the postmaster in *Myers* exercised purely executive functions. It should be noted, however that, Humphrey, as a commissioner of an independent agency, may not have been an inferior officer and thus the *Myers* dicta allowing restrictions on removal of inferior officers might not have applied to him.

> **Sidebar**
>
> **CONCEPTUAL APPROACH TO SEPARATION OF POWERS**
>
> The conceptual approach to separation of powers questions appears to be most relevant in understanding why Congress cannot participate in the removal of executive branch officials. Because the Constitution is silent on removal (except for impeachment) it could be argued that Senate confirmation means that the Senate should also be able to participate in removal. However, if as a conceptual matter removal is an executive function, without explicit constitutional permission, the Senate cannot participate in removal.

The Court's reasoning in *Humphrey's Executor* depends on principles that seem out of date today. The Court characterized the Federal Trade Commission as acting in a **quasi-legislative** capacity when it made legislative rules and in a **quasi-judicial** capacity when it adjudicated alleged violations. The Court stated that the President does not need complete control over the commissioners because they were agents of Congress and the federal courts when performing these functions. Current thinking would probably place all of these activities in the category of "execution of the law" that can be performed only by Officers of the United States. Justice Scalia's opinion in the *Whitman* case, for example, would deny that agencies exercise legislative power when they make rules. Rather, they are executing the law and happen to be acting in a form that resembles legislation. However, to the Court in 1935, the quasi-judicial and quasi-legislative nature of the functions performed provided an intellectual justification for restricting the President's control over independent agencies and thus over the removal of the heads of such agencies.

F   A   Q

Q: Is the current rule that Congress may restrict the President's power to remove inferior officers but may not restrict the President's power to remove principal officers?

A: No, that is not the current rule. *Humphrey's Executor* approved a restriction on the removal of a principal officer. Originally, the line between permissible and impermissible removal restrictions may have involved the nature of the officer's functions — no restrictions were allowed on the removal of purely executive officials *(Myers)* while restrictions were allowed on the removal of officials exercising judicial and legislative functions *(Humphrey's Executor)*. Later cases (see below) draw the line, if it can be called a line, at restrictions that cripple the President's ability to perform the constitutional functions of the presidency. This is a vague standard that is unlikely to be violated.

More recent decisions on the power to restrict the President's power to remove executive branch officials do not employ the categorical approach taken by *Humphrey's Executor*. This is because the current understanding does not view administrative rulemaking and administrative adjudication as legislative and judicial functions. Rather, both are viewed as a form of executing the law. This altered theoretical perspective has moved the Court away from the *Humphrey's Executor* approach toward an approach that asks the more direct question whether separation of powers requires that the President have unlimited discretion to discharge the particular official.

The legal standard the Court has constructed to evaluate removal restrictions is the rather lenient one of whether the removal restriction impermissibly burdens the President's ability to control the execution of the laws such that the President is unable to perform the constitutional duty to take care that the laws are faithfully executed. The Court applied this test, and explicitly disavowed the approach taken in *Humphrey's Executor*, in *Morrison v. Olson*, 487 U.S. 654, 691 (1988). In *Morrison*, the Court upheld a provision of the Ethics in Government Act that confined the removal of an independent counsel, an official exercising purely executive prosecutorial functions, to personal action by the Attorney General and only on a finding of "good cause." The Court rejected reading *Myers* as entitling the President to unlimited power to remove officials exercising executive functions. The Court also rejected reading *Humphrey's Executor* to confine Congress's power to restrict removal to officials exercising nonexecutive functions such as quasi-legislative and quasi-judicial power.

Justice Scalia, in dissent in *Morrison*, made two powerful arguments against the Court's decision upholding the removal restriction, first that the Court's legal standard is so loose and bereft of content that it provides little if any guidance on when removal restrictions are permissible and second, that eliminating the President's power to control prosecutions of executive branch officials is crippling to the President's ability to take care that the laws are faithfully executed.

In the *PCAOB* decision, the Court finally struck down a removal restriction on separation of powers grounds. The members of the PCAOB were subject to removal for cause by the Commissioners of the SEC who in turn are subject to removal, by the President, only for cause. Although the Court upheld the assignment of the power to remove PCAOB members to the SEC Commissioners, the Court held that the dual layer of for-cause insulation violates the general separation of powers standard because "[t]he result is a Board that is not accountable to the President, and a President who is not responsible for the Board."

(4) Direct Presidential Control over Administrative Agencies

(a) Centralized Review

Presidents have long struggled to control and coordinate the activities of administrative agencies, while Congress has attempted to insulate agencies from presidential influence. One important tool that recent presidents have used is requiring, by Executive Order, that agencies submit their proposed regulations to centralized review by the Office of Management and Budget, which is controlled by the White House. There are several routes that presidents have taken to gain greater control of agencies. President Reagan set a precedent that has been carried forward by all of his successors when he promulgated a comprehensive Executive Order, E.O. 12,291, establishing centralized review by the Office of Management and Budget (OMB) in the White House; that review has continued under subsequent administrations and is currently carried out by the Office of Information and Regulatory Affairs within OMB. As part of this regulatory review, agencies have been required to prepare a Regulatory Impact Analysis (RIA), which includes a cost-benefit analysis of their proposed regulations. OMB has attempted to influence agencies to produce more cost-effective regulation.

President Reagan's Executive Order 12,291 provoked outcries of political interference in agency rulemaking processes and even arguments that the President lacked the constitutional power to require agencies to submit their proposed rules to OMB for centralized review. The concern was that the Administration's focus on cost-benefit analysis would divert agencies from the congressionally prescribed goals of the statutes involved. As centralized review has become well established, the

Sidebar

ABOLITION OF INDEPENDENT COUNSEL

Although the opponents of the Independent Counsel law, including Justice Scalia, lost the legal battle over it, they ultimately won the war. After the lengthy, controversial, and apparently highly political investigation of President Bill Clinton, which resulted in his impeachment for lying under oath about a sexual relationship with a White House intern, Congress did not reenact the Independent Counsel provisions after they expired in 1999. Currently, if the Attorney General finds a conflict of interest, Department of Justice rules allow for the appointment of a special counsel to conduct the investigation and prosecution. Special counsels remain under the supervision and removal authority of the Attorney General. Whether this is adequate to combat illegality within the executive branch in light of the President's need for control is a matter of judgment.

constitutional concerns have faded, although concern over diversion of agencies from statutory policies is still raised occasionally. In recognition of the special position of the independent agencies, Presidents have not attempted to control them nearly as much as the agencies within the executive branch. For example, President Clinton required independent agencies to participate in a centralized regulatory planning process, but he did not require them to submit their proposed regulations to OMB for review. He revised President Reagan's order but maintained its basic structure in Executive Order 12,866.

Agencies' budget requests are channeled through OMB, giving the President another method of controlling agencies. Congress, of course, is free to set an agency's budget at the level it prefers. In the case of at least one agency, the International Trade Commission (ITC), Congress has statutorily provided that the agency must submit its budget directly to Congress without presidential review via OMB. This shields the ITC from presidential influence.

Through the **patronage system**, presidents historically maintained a great deal of control over the personnel within the executive branch. In a patronage system, party loyalists (or persons recommended by party loyalists) are chosen to fill positions at all levels in a new administration. In the **civil service system** that exists today, all but the highest government positions are filled through a merit selection process. Further, civil service employees have statutory job security that protects them from replacement when a new administration takes over.

The Supreme Court has held that the First Amendment also limits the President's right to replace government officials for political reasons. Most government employees have the right to engage in political activity, such as party membership and voting, and they may not be fired for exercising that right. Therefore, the President may replace, for political reasons, only officers where the need for loyalty to the President outweighs the officials' interest in engaging in the political activity — such as officials in confidential positions and officials who engage in relatively high-level policymaking.

(b) The Line Item Veto

In an attempt to control spending, Congress passed the **Line Item Veto Act of 1996**, under which the President was granted the power to cancel certain items of spending and tax benefits contained in legislation. This procedure is referred to as a "line item veto" because in effect it gives the President the power to veto particular lines in spending and tax benefit bills without vetoing the bill as a whole. The Act was aimed at spending and tax benefit items that Members of Congress insert into Appropriations Bills to benefit their constituents but that do not necessarily advance the overall public good. Such items are often referred to as "pork barrel" spending. Each Member of Congress has an incentive to obtain as many benefits for their own district as possible, and in order to keep the system going (which helps get them reelected) the Members of Congress tend to vote for each others' items. Because the items are contained in Appropriations Bills with hundreds or thousands of items, the President finds it impossible to veto the bill because that could cause a crisis such as a government or agency shutdown. Most state governors have some sort of item veto, which is thought to help discipline the legislature by allowing the governor to veto the items deemed wasteful without causing the government or a particular agency to close until a whole new bill can be drafted and passed. Similarly, it was hoped that the President could use the line-item veto power to cancel wasteful spending and tax benefits items.

The Act established the following procedure to allow the President to cancel items: First, the President was required to sign the bill in which the items were contained. Then, the President could cancel items by transmitting a message canceling specified items to Congress within five days of signing the bill. Substantively, the President was required to certify in the message that cancellation would reduce the federal budget deficit, and that cancellation would neither impair an essential government function nor harm the national interest. In a decision reminiscent of *Chadha*, the Supreme Court held this procedure unconstitutional since in effect it granted the President unilateral power to amend or repeal legislation. See *Clinton v. City of New York*, 524 U.S. 417 (1998).

The problem with the Line Item Veto Act was that once the President signed the bill passed by Congress, the entire bill became law, and only further legislation by both Houses of Congress could amend or repeal it. The Court rejected the argument that the President was merely exercising delegated discretionary authority to decline to spend appropriated funds on two related grounds. First, although the Court acknowledged that historically presidents have exercised discretion to decline to spend appropriated funds, the Court found that this provision went farther because it allowed the President to unilaterally alter the text and thus the legal effect of a duly enacted law. The second ground is that when the President cancels an item so soon after signing the bill, the President is rejecting Congress's judgment, not using discretion to further Congress's policy.

The Court's decision striking down the line item veto illustrates the important tendency discussed above that the Court tends to be intolerant of innovation regarding the procedures specified in the Constitution. This includes the Court's rejection of the legislative veto in *Chadha* based on derogation of the requirements of bicameralism and presentment, the Court's insistence in *Bowsher* on adherence to the Appointments Clause, and the Court's rejection of the line item veto as inconsistent with the established veto and lawmaking processes. In the Court's view, the Framers' concentrated attention to the procedural aspects of the Constitution leaves little or no room for innovation.

F A Q

Q: Is there a constitutional way to give the President line-item veto power?

A: Congress could include a line-item veto provision in the body of each appropriations bill or in each section of the bill, essentially giving the President the authority to decline to spend appropriated funds. Congress is, however, very unlikely to do this, if only because it would lead to protracted legislative wrangling over proposals to exempt some appropriations from the veto provision. Members of Congress may be in favor of the general concept of the line item veto, but they rarely, if ever, favor a veto of their own pet projects. Further, even if this solved the line-item veto problem, it might raise a nondelegation issue because no standard would govern the President's choice of which items not to spend.

(c) Signing Statements

Although the practice goes back many years, a controversy has arisen recently concerning presidential **signing statements.** Many presidents have issued statements when signing legislation. Some signing statements contain nothing of substance but can best be characterized as public relations, applauding or condemning Congress for some aspect of the legislation or mentioning some policy achieved or neglected by the bill being signed. Other signing statements state the President's view on the meaning of the bill being signed, perhaps as a counterweight to legislative history with which the President disagrees. While this last category of signing statements is sometimes controversial, the most controversial is a third category in which the President states that a provision of the bill being signed is actually or potentially unconstitutional and promising either to not execute that portion of the bill or to construe the bill to steer clear of unconstitutionality. The controversy is heightened when the claim of unconstitutionality is based on legislative infringement of inherent presidential constitutional power.

Generally speaking, signing statements themselves are never unconstitutional. The President has the right to say whatever he or she wants when signing a bill. The real controversy is over the effects of a signing statement, and this controversy raises deep and unresolved questions concerning presidential power and the separation of powers. One question is whether the President has a duty to veto any bill that in his or her opinion contains any unconstitutional provision or whether even if no such duty exists would a veto be better practice. What if the veto power is no help because the law was passed during a prior administration or the unconstitutionality was not apparent at the time the bill was presented for signature? In such cases, a second question is whether the President has the power to refuse to execute a law that, in his or her opinion, is unconstitutional. Does the President's duty to take care that the laws are faithfully executed take precedence over the President's promise, in the oath of office, to protect and defend the Constitution? On a more mundane level, should presidential statements on the meaning of a statute be considered by courts that may also look at congressional committee reports and floor debates for guidance on statutory meaning? While these questions may be unlikely to be answered definitively any time soon, they do help structure our thinking about many of the separation of powers issues raised above.

In thinking about whether the President should veto every bill containing an unconstitutional provision or whether the President should execute laws he or she believes are unconstitutional, consider the fact that Congress continues to place legislative vetoes, even committee vetoes, into bills that it passes and sends to the President. If Congress is free to pass patently unconstitutional provisions in important bills, perhaps the President should be forgiven for signing them and refusing to execute the unconstitutional portions.

D. Adjudication by Non–Article III Adjudicators

Article III of the Constitution vests the judicial power of the United States in the Supreme Court and in lower federal courts as established by Congress, which are staffed by judges with life tenure and protected compensation. These are referred to as "**Article III courts.**" On its face, the Constitution does not anticipate federal adjudication except in the federal courts. Nevertheless, since the flowering of the administrative state in the New Deal era, federal agencies and what have been denominated "**Article I courts**" have adjudicated disputes. Article I courts and administrative tribunals are not established as inferior courts pursuant to Article III of the Constitution, and administrative adjudicators do not have the protections of Article III judges, namely life tenure and protection against salary reduction.

Under current law, Article I adjudication is allowed when it does not threaten the policies and values underlying Article III's assignment of the judicial power to the federal courts. As we shall see in the pages that follow, when certain structural requirements are followed, the Supreme Court today liberally allows adjudication in non–Article III tribunals of claims between the federal government and private parties and of claims between private parties when such Article I adjudication occurs in a narrowly prescribed field that is important to the accomplishment of the goals of a federal regulatory program.

Some non–Article III tribunals resemble courts while others clearly present themselves as adjudicatory arms of regulatory agencies. Examples of Article I courts include the United States Tax Court, the United States Bankruptcy Courts, and the United States Court of Federal Claims. These entities function in a manner very similar to other courts but the judges do not have the life tenure and protected pay enjoyed by Article III judges. We also see adjudication in federal regulatory agencies such as the Federal Trade Commission, the Federal Communications Commission, and the National Labor Relations Board, to name a few. These agencies do not resemble Article III courts, are headed by political appointees, and adjudicate as an aspect of an overall regulatory mission that goes far beyond what courts traditionally do.

Although all non–Article III adjudication raises questions, in Administrative Law we focus mainly on adjudication within regulatory agencies. The course on Federal Courts looks more broadly at Article I adjudication. Agency adjudication raises a separation of powers problem because Article III vests the judicial power of the United States in the Article III courts. When Congress assigns adjudication to non–Article III tribunals, it arguably usurps the power of the Article III courts. It is not that some other branch is directly interfering with the judicial function but rather that Article III prohibits the assignment of the judicial power, including jurisdiction to adjudicate, to anyone other than Article III judges.

In a certain sense, the argument over agency adjudication can be conceptualized in a manner similar to the distinction between legislation and agency rulemaking. As the *Chadha* opinion makes clear, when Congress takes action that affects people's rights, it is legislation and Congress must employ the Constitution's procedures for legislating. When an executive agency promulgates a rule, under a delegation from Congress, the rule may contain exactly the same substantive provisions as a piece of legislation, the agency is executing the law, and bicameralism and presentment are not required. Similarly, when an agency adjudicates a matter within its jurisdiction it is not exercising the judicial power but rather is engaged in the execution of the law and is not required to employ Article III judges. However, just as there are limits to Congress's power to delegate authority to the executive branch, there are also limits to Congress's power to assign the adjudicatory function to a non–Article III tribunal.

In recognition of the fact that not all adjudication outside the Article III courts implicates the authority of those courts, the Supreme Court has approved of a great deal of agency adjudication. While originally such approval was limited to three categories — public rights, territorial courts, and military courts — recent cases have approved much broader adjudication in non–Article III tribunals.

Territorial and military courts are not relevant to the Article III issues that arise in administrative law.

The distinction between public rights and private rights was once vital to identifying the limits to federal adjudication outside of the Article III courts. Public rights disputes are controversies between a private party and the government over matters such as government benefits, taxation, and immigration. Many non–Article III tribunals, such as the Tax Court and the Court of Federal Claims, adjudicate claims between the government and private citizens. Private rights are disputes between two private parties in which the government's role is primarily adjudicatory. Over time, non–Article III jurisdiction over private rights has been expanded, raising serious constitutional concerns. In early cases raising the issue, the Supreme Court stated that while Congress has a great deal of discretion over the assignment of power to adjudicate public rights, Article III places severe restrictions on Congress's ability to assign adjudication of private rights disputes to non–Article III tribunals such as administrative agencies.

(1) *Crowell v. Benson* and the Public Rights Versus Private Rights Doctrine

The Longshoremen's and Harbor Workers' Compensation Act of 1927 assigned adjudication of workers' compensation claims for covered workers to the United States Employees' Compensation Commission, a non–Article III body. In *Crowell v. Benson*, 285 U.S. 22 (1932), after the Commission made an award to an employee, the employer sued, claiming, inter alia, that the assignment of adjudicatory power to the Commission was unconstitutional. The Supreme Court upheld the Commission's authority to adjudicate the claim, subject to certain restrictions.

The *Crowell* Court stated that **public rights** disputes may be assigned to non–Article III adjudicators, such as administrative agencies. "Public rights" are rights against the government, such as claims to government benefits. The roots of the public rights doctrine lay in the common law tradition of sovereign immunity. Because claims against the government were unknown at common law, such claims are not exclusively within the Article III judicial power. The *Crowell* Court characterized the assignment of adjudication of public rights disputes as "completely within congressional control." Although the analysis was framed in terms of factual issues, the *Crowell* Court may have intended to allow Congress to assign adjudication of both law and fact in public rights disputes to administrative agencies.

The adjudication of public rights may be assigned to administrative agencies for two reasons. First, because the historical understanding is that public rights disputes could have been decided within the government without any adjudication, the government's choice of an adjudicatory procedure within an administrative agency does not violate Article III. Even if due process property rights in government benefits now require adjudication, adjudication in an agency may satisfy due process. Second, since claims against the government were barred at common law by sovereign immunity, assigning their adjudication to administrative agencies does not deprive the Article III courts of any of their traditional jurisdiction. This does not prevent Congress from assigning public rights claims to Article III courts; it simply means that Article III jurisdiction is not mandatory.

In distinction from public rights disputes, adjudication of **private rights** disputes (legal disputes between private parties) in administrative agencies is suspect and may occur only under certain conditions, although in recent years the Court has been much more liberal in allowing private rights disputes arising out of federal regulatory schemes to be adjudicated in agencies. *Crowell* was the first case in which the Supreme Court approved the adjudication of a private rights dispute by an administrative agency. In *Crowell*, the Court approved agency fact finding on such issues as the "circumstances, nature, extent and consequences of the injuries sustained by the employee." The *Crowell* Court approved of deferential judicial review of an agency's non-jurisdictional factual determinations concerning the more mundane details of employees' claims for two reasons: First, because the Court viewed the agency's function as similar to that of masters and juries who often aid Article III judges in their fact finding; and second, because assigning the fact finding to an agency might actually preserve judicial power by not overwhelming the courts with numerous controversies.

F   A   Q

Q: What is the distinction between private rights disputes and public rights disputes?

A: A private rights dispute is a dispute between two private parties while a public rights dispute is a dispute between the government and a private party. Note that the distinction does not turn on the source of the rights involved — a statutory claim is still a private rights dispute if it is brought by one private party against another private party.

In order to preserve the domain of Article III courts, the *Crowell* Court placed important limitations on agency adjudication. The primary limits were that issues relating to the jurisdiction of the agency and issues of constitutional fact must be adjudicated de novo in the federal courts and that the courts must also decide issues of law de novo. In *Crowell*, jurisdictional fact issues included whether the claimant was actually an employee of the employer and whether the injury occurred on navigable waters (which was necessary for federal jurisdiction over the claim). With regard to constitutional issues, the Court held that the federal judicial power includes the power to make factual determinations necessary for federal regulatory power. The Court held that it was therefore appropriate for the district court to hold a trial de novo on these matters.

The *Crowell* Court relied heavily on the availability of judicial review to sustain the statute. The Court found that maintaining judicial control through judicial review, including de novo review of questions of law and jurisdictional facts, and deferential review of the non-jurisdictional facts was sufficient to satisfy the concerns of Article III. The Article III restrictions identified above regarding Congress's power to assign adjudication to non–Article III tribunals mean that in some situations, either exclusive jurisdiction in federal court, or at least de novo judicial review of agency determinations, is required. The Court stated that with regard to fundamental or jurisdictional facts, "the Federal Court should determine such an issue upon its own record and the facts elicited before it." Because the Court construed the statute in *Crowell* to allow such de novo review, the Court upheld the statute.

With regard to legal determinations in private right disputes, the Court implied that an Article III problem might exist if issues of law are reserved to determination by the agency. The Court noted that the statute in *Crowell* left the final determination of issues of law to the federal courts, albeit on review of initial determinations by the Commission. *Crowell* thus stands for the proposition that Article III requires, in private rights cases, judicial review (and perhaps de novo review) of legal issues.

Sidebar

STRICT SEPARATION OF POWERS

The decision in *Northern Pipeline*, together with the invalidation of the Federal Election Commission in *Buckley v. Valeo*, 424 U.S. 1 (1976) and the invalidation of the legislative veto in *INS v. Chadha*, 462 U.S. 919 (1983), led some to believe that the Supreme Court's new strict, apparently formalist, approach regarding separation of powers might ultimately lead to the invalidation of independent agencies and to severe restrictions on the activities of administrative agencies, including sharp limits on adjudication in agencies. As subsequent developments revealed, the Court chose a different path.

(2) The Bankruptcy Courts

For several decades after *Crowell*, the Court was largely silent regarding Congress's power to assign adjudicatory functions to non–Article III courts. Over time, the restrictions recognized in *Crowell* receded from legal consciousness until the Court decided that the bankruptcy courts that had been established by Congress in 1978 unconstitutionally exercised jurisdiction reserved to Article III courts. The Bankruptcy Code granted the non–Article III bankruptcy courts jurisdiction of all common law claims involving the bankrupt party. This was challenged as unconstitutional by a party to a contract dispute with a bankrupt entity. In *Northern Pipeline Constr. Co. v. Marathon Pipe Line Co.*, 458 U.S. 50 (1982), a divided Court struck down this provision of the Bankruptcy Act that gave bankruptcy courts (created under Article I and not Article III) jurisdiction over common law claims to which the debtor was a party. The Court was divided on the basis for the unconstitutionality of the bankruptcy courts' jurisdiction. The lead opinion (by Justice Brennan for himself and three others) applied a categorical approach, holding that Congress may delegate adjudicatory power to non–Article III tribunals in only three situations: (1) territorial courts in which complete federal control necessitates the creation of essentially local federal courts; (2) military courts or "courts martial"; and (3) public rights cases. Common law civil actions, held Justice Brennan, were not in any of the three exceptions to the vesting of the judicial power in the Article III courts. Thus, the Bankruptcy Act was unconstitutional.

Justice Rehnquist, joined by Justice O'Connor, concluded that the Bankruptcy Act was unconstitutional because it assigned adjudication to a non–Article III tribunal of a claim in the core of traditional Article III judicial power. Justice Rehnquist found it unnecessary to endorse Justice Brennan's categorical approach. Justice White (joined by three others) dissented, applying an analysis similar to his dissenting opinions in other separation of powers cases. He insisted that, on balance, the threat to Article III values posed by the bankruptcy court's jurisdiction over common law claims was outweighed by the policies advanced by the Bankruptcy Act's assignment of adjudicatory authority to those courts. Justice White argued that this balancing test was the proper approach to the problem, not the more categorical approaches adopted by the majority.

(3) The Current Test for Adjudication in Non–Article III Tribunals

In more recent cases, the Court has settled on a very accommodating approach to the powers of administrative agencies, including adjudication—an approach resembling Justice White's dissenting analysis in *Northern Pipeline*. The Court's current position recognizes broad congressional power to assign adjudication to administrative bodies. The Court applies a pragmatic test to determine whether the assignment of adjudicatory functions to an agency violates the separation of powers. Various factors determine whether the encroachment on the Article III courts' judicial power is so great as to threaten the separation of powers. Justice Brennan's categorical approach has been rejected by a majority of the Court, and thus there is no categorical bar to adjudication of private rights disputes in non–Article III tribunals, but certain limitations must be observed.

The current test for determining the constitutionality of a delegation of adjudicatory power to an agency is a balancing test that weighs the threat to Article III values against the concerns that led to the assignment of adjudicatory authority to the agency. The primary question is whether the assignment of jurisdiction to a non–Article III adjudicator threatens the institutional integrity of the federal courts. The Supreme Court has stated that its review will be most exacting when Congress assigns adjudication of a claim to an agency that is of the type traditionally within the jurisdiction of the Article III courts. Thus, in *Commodity Futures Trading Commission (CFTC) v. Schor*, 478 U.S. 833, 851 (1986), the Court stated that "where private, common law rights are at stake, our examination of the congressional attempt to control the manner in which those rights are adjudicated has been searching." The Court was also quick to point out, however, that the private, common law nature of the rights at stake was not determinative. In *Schor*, for example, the Court approved of the adjudication of private common law claims, raised as counterclaims to statutory actions, by the CFTC.

The broader the scope of the agency's jurisdiction, the more likely there will be a violation of Article III. Conversely, the more an agency's jurisdiction is confined narrowly to a particular area, the less the perceived threat to Article III values. Agency jurisdiction over congressionally created private rights disputes is seen as less threatening to Article III values than when the rights involved arise from another source, such as state law. Even though disputes involving congressionally created rights are technically private rights disputes and thus could be seen as within the core of Article III jurisdiction, the Court has treated congressionally created rights similar to public rights, perhaps because of the recognition that had Congress not acted, the statutorily created rights would not exist, and this would not seem like a threat to the Article III courts. Conversely, where common law or state statutory rights are involved, agency jurisdiction is less likely to be upheld against Article III challenge.

Things are a bit trickier when it comes to state-created rights that are closely related to rights created by federal statute. The Supreme Court has held that even when the agency's jurisdiction is over matters traditionally within the sphere of Article III adjudication such as state common law disputes, there is less of a perceived threat to Article III values when such jurisdiction is closely related to an area or dispute subject to extensive federal regulation. This is because of the reduced scope of the intrusion on Article III jurisdiction. Further, when the parties have a choice over whether to litigate their dispute in a non–Article III tribunal, there is even less of a perceived threat to Article III values than if the parties have no choice over the forum. However, because the structural interests of the Article III courts in preserving their authority cannot be waived by a litigant, the Article III issue remains even when the litigants have chosen the non–Article III forum.

When an agency must go to an Article III court to have its order enforced, it is less likely to present an Article III problem than if agency orders are self-enforcing. This is because the requirement of court enforcement ensures the involvement of Article III courts at some stage of the proceedings. If an entire dispute could be litigated without any involvement of the Article III courts, there would be a greater perceived threat on the jurisdiction of those courts and greater usurpation of the role of Article III courts.

The most recent comprehensive application of the pragmatic test is *CFTC v. Schor*, 478 U.S. 833 (1986). In *Schor*, the CFTC entertained state contract law counterclaims to a customer's federal statutory reparations action. Note that these are both private rights, one created by Congress (the reparations claim) and one created by state common law, the counterclaim for breach of contract. Schor brought a reparations proceeding in the CFTC against his broker Conti, alleging that Conti had violated federal law. Conti counterclaimed in the agency for breach of contract to recover the negative balance in Schor's trading account. After the broker Conti prevailed on both the reparations action and the counterclaim and Schor sought judicial review, the Court of Appeals for the D.C. Circuit raised, sua sponte, the issue of whether CFTC jurisdiction over the counterclaim was allowed under the CEA and whether such jurisdiction violated Article III under *Northern Pipeline.* The Court of Appeals read the CEA as not extending the CFTC's jurisdiction to common law counterclaims, largely to avoid the constitutional question that would arise if the statute were read differently.

The Supreme Court reversed, holding that the statute allowed the agency to take jurisdiction over common law counterclaims and that agency adjudication of common law counterclaims did not violate Article III. The Court stated that the result depends on several factors, including whether the "essential attributes of judicial power" remain in Article III courts versus "the extent to which the [agency] exercises the range of jurisdiction normally vested only in Article III courts, the origins and importance of the right to be adjudicated, and the concerns that drove Congress to depart from the requirements of Article III." *CFTC v. Schor*, 478 U.S. at 859.

The Court elaborated on the general understanding of the Article III limits on agency adjudicatory power as follows. First, agency adjudication of state law private rights is more likely to be constitutional if it involves a particularized area of law closely related to a federal regulatory scheme and does not cut across an entire class of traditionally judicially cognizable cases. Second, agencies may not exercise the inherent powers of courts of law such as the power to enforce judgments, issue writs of habeas corpus, issue contempt judgments, or preside over jury trials. Third, access to Article III courts should be preserved. Agency jurisdiction over state law private rights disputes should be concurrent with the jurisdiction of the Article III courts. Parties to a private rights dispute retain the freedom to choose an Article III court, ensuring that they are voluntarily presenting their dispute to an administrative tribunal. Fourth, judicial review of private rights disputes should be available in an Article III court under a standard of review that is stringent enough to ensure significant judicial involvement in resolution of the dispute. On questions of law, de novo review is preferable.

In *Schor*, the Court relied upon the following factors to conclude that in this case, there was no impermissible intrusion on the jurisdiction of the Article III courts: (1) the CFTC deals only with a particularized area of law; (2) the CFTC's orders are enforceable only by order of the District Court; (3) the factual decisions of the CFTC are judicially reviewable under a relatively nondeferential standard and its legal decisions are reviewed de novo; and (4) the CFTC does not exercise other powers normally reserved to district courts such as the power to preside over jury trials or issue writs of habeas corpus. Focusing more specifically on the fact that the CFTC was asserting jurisdiction over common law counterclaims, a factor weighing against the constitutionality of the statute, the Court stated that the limited nature of the common law jurisdiction, its close connection to the statutory reparations procedure, Congress's policy of providing an effective remedial scheme, and the fact that the federal courts retain concurrent jurisdiction over the claims all weigh in favor of the statute's constitutionality.

F   A   Q

Q: What led to the striking reorientation of Article III jurisprudence, from a categorical approach or at least an approach that was highly skeptical of adjudication of private rights by non–Article III federal tribunals, to a much more forgiving attitude?

A: There were probably several factors at work, but two are most prominent. First, Congress does not appear to have had overtly political motivations for establishing the non–Article III jurisdiction in areas such as commodities disputes and pesticide registration. Second, requiring Article III jurisdiction would create a high volume of relatively uninteresting and unimportant cases. On the first factor, the Court is likely to have a different reaction if it perceives that Congress has created non–Article III jurisdiction because it is unhappy with the outcome of cases in the Article III courts. Second, the Court might react differently if it found that Congress has redirected important matters to non–Article III tribunals. These, of course, are mere speculation and there may be matters of principle underlying the change that would still, for example, not allow Congress to assign jurisdiction over all claims involving a bankrupt debtor to a non–Article III bankruptcy court.

Thus, in *Schor*, the Court upheld agency adjudication of private common law counterclaims that were closely related to federal regulation of the business of marketing securities. Although the Court did not even seem cognizant of the fact that the reparations claims themselves are private rights that ordinarily would be adjudicated in an Article III court, implicitly the adjudication of these private claims was also approved since it is presumably an easier case than non–Article III jurisdiction over common law counterclaims.

Another example of a federal statute that allows adjudication of private rights disputes outside of an Article III court is the Federal Insecticide, Fungicide, and Rodenticide Act (FIFRA), which requires manufacturers of covered products to register their products with EPA. Under FIFRA, the EPA has authority to reject applications for registration if the manufacturer cannot establish that the product is safe and effective. The 1978 amendments to FIFRA allowed the EPA to use information submitted by one manufacturer to help evaluate an application for registration of a similar product by a second manufacturer. Because the information often consisted of valuable trade secrets, the second manufacturer was required to offer to compensate the first. If no agreement between the two manufacturers on the amount of compensation was reached, the parties were required to submit the compensation question to binding arbitration. The decision of the arbitrator was subject to judicial review but only for "fraud, misrepresentation or other misconduct." This procedure was challenged as violating Article III by placing jurisdiction over a private dispute in a non–Article III tribunal, here an arbitrator.

In *Thomas v. Union Carbide Agric. Prods. Co.*, 473 U.S. 568 (1985), the Court upheld the FIFRA amendments, relying largely on the ground that because the registration and use of pesticides is subject to heavy regulation, the compensation question was more like a public right than the typical dispute between two private parties. The Court stated that "Congress, acting for a valid legislative purpose pursuant to its constitutional powers under Article I, may create a seemingly 'private' right that is so closely integrated into a public regulatory scheme as to be a matter appropriate for agency resolution with limited involvement by the Article III judiciary." *Thomas*, 473 U.S. at 593. The Court also supported its holding by noting that the arbitrators' narrow jurisdiction did not threaten the judiciary's Article III powers and that limited judicial review was available to ensure that arbitrators did not exceed their authority.

These decisions substantially reorient the doctrines governing Congress's power to assign adjudicatory jurisdiction to non–Article III tribunals. The public rights doctrine has been essentially cast aside in favor of a new focus on whether agency jurisdiction is closely connected to a regulated field in which a narrow set of disputes is subject to non–Article III adjudication. The entire analysis is governed by a balancing approach that asks whether the independence and authority of Article III courts is threatened, rather than a potentially more restrictive, categorical approach. While scrutiny is somewhat heightened when matters within the core of traditional judicial powers are assigned to agencies, *CFTC v. Schor* and *Thomas v. Union Carbide* allow Congress great discretion to assign adjudication to non–Article III tribunals in areas related to federal regulation.

SUMMARY

- Separation of powers with checks and balances is one of the pillars of U.S. constitutional law yet it is not mentioned in the Constitution. Separation of powers should be understood as a collection of various procedural provisions in the Constitution and some general doctrines governing the distribution of power among the branches.

- Congress often delegates discretionary power to administrative agencies, and the nondelegation doctrine regulates how much discretionary authority Congress may delegate to an agency. The current understanding is that to satisfy the nondelegation doctrine, Congress must legislate an "intelligible principle" to guide the agency in its exercise of discretion. This is not very strict in application.

- The only way Congress may constitutionally take action that has legal effect outside the legislative branch is through the legislative process, which includes bicameralism and presentment. The legislative veto, which purported to allow a subset of Congress, such as one House or even a committee, and without presentment to the President, to reject agency action, is unconstitutional. Two House vetoes without presentment to the President are also unconstitutional.

- The Appointments Clause provides for the appointment of Officers of the United States by the President with Senate confirmation or, for inferior officers when specified by Congress, by the President alone, by a department head, or by the courts of law. Except for Senate confirmation and removal under the impeachment process, Congress may not participate directly in the appointment or removal of Officers of the United States.

- Congress may hire its own officials when their activities are in aid of legislation and not executive in nature. However, any official who exercises significant authority pursuant to the law must be appointed in accordance with the Appointments Clause.

- Congress may restrict presidential removal of officers and inferior officers, for example by requiring cause for discharge, as long as the restriction does not unduly interfere with the President's execution of the functions of the presidency. For very high-level officials and close presidential aides, the President is entitled to unrestricted power to remove them. After *Morrison v. Olson*, Congress's power to restrict presidential removal no longer depends on whether the officer is engaged in purely executive functions but turns rather on whether unrestricted removal is necessary for the President to carry out the constitutional functions of the presidency.

- Agency adjudication potentially conflicts with Article III of the Constitution, which vests the judicial power in the federal courts. Traditionally, Congress has had the power to assign adjudication in three categories to non–Article III tribunals: public rights (rights against the government that traditionally could have been resolved without any adjudication at all), military matters (which traditionally would have been heard in courts martial), and cases arising in territories (which were traditionally heard by non–Article III territorial courts).

- More recently, the Supreme Court has allowed Congress to assign even private rights disputes to non–Article III tribunals such as administrative agencies if the disputes arise in closely regulated fields and agency adjudication is necessary to make the regulatory scheme workable. For agency adjudication of private rights to be constitutional, there must be effective judicial review, and the essential attributes of judicial power, such as the power to preside over jury trials or issue final judgments, must remain in the courts.

CONNECTIONS

Ubiquity of Separation of Powers Issues

Separation of powers issues are lurking just below the surface of many areas of administrative law. For example, Justice Scalia has characterized liberal standing rules as an assault on the power of the President (Chapter 3). Other questions involving separation of powers concerns include: When should agency action be unreviewable as committed to agency discretion by law? (Chapter 3), should the President be able to engage in off-the-record contacts with administrative agencies? (Chapter 7), and how much information should the President be able to keep secret? (Chapter 14).

Agency Cannot Cure Nondelegation Violation

The notion that an agency can cure a nondelegation doctrine violation was inspired in part by the Court's *Chevron* doctrine, which allocates authority over statutory interpretation to agencies. See Chapter 4.

Cost-Benefit Analysis

For an extended discussion of cost-benefit analysis, which Presidents since Ronald Reagan have required agencies to do as part of their analyses of proposed rules, see Chapter 5.

The Availability of Judicial Review of Administrative Decisions

3

This chapter explores the who, what, when, and where of judicial review — who has standing to seek judicial review, what agency actions are reviewable, when is agency action subject to review, and where should review be sought, i.e., what court. Our focus is mainly on judicial review of administrative decisions under the Administrative Procedure Act (APA), but we will also look some at review of constitutional challenges to administrative action.

O V E R V I E W

On the where: A petition for review must be brought in a court with jurisdiction over the action. Jurisdiction involves which court can hear the petition for review and not whether the particular agency action is reviewable. Jurisdiction is thus distinct from reviewability.

On the what: APA §704 grants a right to obtain judicial review of "agency action made reviewable by statute and final agency action for which there is no adequate remedy in a court." There is a strong legal presumption in favor of judicial review of agency action meeting the above-stated criteria, but that presumption may be rebutted in two ways. First, judicial review is not available if a statute explicitly precludes judicial review. APA §701(a)(1). Second, judicial review is not available if agency action is committed to agency discretion by law. APA §701(a)(2).

On the who: Parties seeking judicial review must satisfy APA and constitutional tests for standing. The basic constitutional test for standing is that the party seeking judicial review must have suffered an "injury in fact" that was "fairly traceable" to the challenged conduct such that the injury is remediable by judicial action.

The APA, §702, limits standing to persons suffering legal wrong because of agency action and persons adversely affected or aggrieved by agency action within the meaning of a relevant statute. The Supreme Court has stated that "within the meaning of a relevant statute" means that the party seeking judicial review must be within the "zone of interests" addressed by the regulatory statute.

On the when: Unless a statute specifies otherwise, only final agency action is reviewable. The case must also be ripe and not moot, and when a statute or rule requires it, administrative remedies must be exhausted. An agency rule is not subject to pre-enforcement review unless it is fit for review and the petitioner would suffer serious hardship by waiting for the action to become ripe. Finally, if a petition for review is brought after the challenged agency action has ceased to have any adverse effects on the petitioner, the action may be moot.

A. Jurisdiction

The petition for judicial review must be brought in a court that has **jurisdiction** over the claim.

(1) Federal Court Jurisdiction over Petitions for Judicial Review

Federal court jurisdiction over any claim requires a statutory grant. The federal courts generally have jurisdiction over petitions for review of federal agency action under two statutory sources. First, some agency enabling acts often grant a right of judicial review and explicitly create federal court jurisdiction over petitions for review. Most such statutes grant jurisdiction over petitions for review to the U.S. Courts of Appeals. See, e.g., The Federal Trade Commission Act of 1914, 15 U.S.C. §45(c). A few grant jurisdiction to the district court. See, e.g., 42 U.S.C. §405(g), granting jurisdiction over review of social security determinations to the U.S. District Courts. Second, the general grant of federal question jurisdiction, 28 U.S.C. §1331, grants jurisdiction over petitions for review to the federal district courts. Claims for review of agency action arise under federal law, easily meeting the test for jurisdiction under §1331.

> ### Sidebar
>
> **JURISDICTION AND THE APA**
>
> The APA itself does not create federal jurisdiction over petitions for judicial review. At one time this was an important issue. In the past, there was an amount in controversy requirement for cases brought under federal question jurisdiction, which led some to argue for jurisdiction directly under the APA, to avoid the jurisdictional amount requirement in judicial review cases with small monetary value. After the jurisdictional amount requirement for federal question cases was repealed, the Supreme Court decided that the APA itself did not provide federal court jurisdiction over petitions for judicial review. See *Califano v. Sanders,* 430 U.S. 99 (1977). This has no effect today given the availability of federal question jurisdiction. Any petition for judicial review that meets other jurisdictional requirements may be brought in a federal court regardless of how little is at stake in monetary value.

F A Q

Q: What is the difference between jurisdiction and reviewability?

A: It is important to understand that jurisdiction and reviewability are separate issues, and the existence of one does not necessarily imply the existence of the other. Jurisdiction involves whether a particular court has the authority to hear a class of disputes. The fact that federal courts have jurisdiction over federal questions does not mean that all challenges to agency action based on federal law are reviewable in federal court or elsewhere. Reviewability is the equivalent of the existence of a cause of action, and involves whether a claim exists that may be brought in a court with jurisdiction. An action is reviewable only if, as elaborated below, a particular statute makes the agency action reviewable or if the action meets the requirements of APA §704. The fact that an agency action is reviewable does not answer the question of which federal court, if any, has jurisdiction over the claim.

(2) Deciding Which Court Is the Proper Forum for Judicial Review

In most cases the choice between the court of appeals and the district court is simple because either the agency's governing statute identifies the proper forum for judicial review or, in the absence of a statute stating otherwise, review is available in the district court. Most statutes that specify the forum provide for review of administrative action in the court of appeals. The most notable exception is the Social Security Act, 42 U.S.C. §405(g), which provides for district court review of orders denying or terminating benefits even though the agency has conducted a formal adjudication. In the absence of statutory authority for choosing the court of appeals, the federal question jurisdiction provision of 28 U.S.C. §1331 directs review to the district court.

Courts interpret specific statutes, whenever possible, to allow review in the court of appeals even in cases of informal agency action where there is no formal agency record to review. There are two reasons for this preference. The first is that judicial economy favors review in the court of appeals. If review is available in the district court, the losing party can appeal the district court's decision to the court of appeals. Two levels of judicial review signify greater delay and more resources devoted to review. See *Florida Power and Light Co. v. Lorion*, 470 U.S. 729 (1985). The second is that the Supreme Court has stated, as a fundamental principle of administrative law, that a reviewing court should judge the agency's action based on the record the agency had before it and not based on one created by the agency for the purposes of the litigation. See *Camp v. Pitts*, 411 U.S. 138 (1973); *Florida Power and Light Co. v. Lorion*, 470 U.S. 729 (1985). Thus, the Court has rejected the argument that a district court's trial procedures are necessary to assemble a record adequate for review because it conflicts with this fundamental principle.

F   A   Q

Q: Is there any simple way to distinguish between cases that belong in the district court and cases that belong in the court of appeals?

A: Basically, this is a statutory question that cannot be answered without looking at applicable statutes. It was sometimes said that there is a rule of thumb that the court of appeals has jurisdiction when an administrative record exists, and the district court has jurisdiction when a record does not exist. While it is true that as agency procedures become more formal, an adequate administrative record is more likely to exist, and thus district court procedures will be unnecessary to create a record for review, the presumption favoring court of appeals review of agency action is limited to when a statute exists that can be construed to grant jurisdiction over the cases to the court of appeals. Absent such a statute, regardless of the formality of agency proceedings or the adequacy of the record for judicial review, the only source of federal jurisdiction would be the general federal question statute, which provides for district court review.

Harrison v. PPG Industries, Inc., 446 U.S. 578 (1980), is an example of the Supreme Court's tendency to construe statutes in favor of jurisdiction at the court of appeals level. In *Harrison*, the EPA had determined that PPG's waste-heat boilers were subject to "new source" standards for "fossil fuel-fired steam generators." This determination was made informally, and PPG was notified of the decision by letter. PPG then sought judicial review directly in the Court of Appeals, which held that it lacked jurisdiction due to the informal nature of the proceeding and decision. The Supreme Court disagreed and construed the Clean Air Act's grant to the courts of appeals of jurisdiction over "final agency action" to include informal agency proceedings.

B. Reviewability

(1) Presumption in Favor of Judicial Review

The APA's judicial review provisions, together with a tradition based on the ideal of the rule of law, create a presumption in favor of reviewability of agency action. This presumption is consistent with the judiciary's role in protecting individuals from arbitrary exercises of government power and ensuring that government acts only when it has legal authority. Judicial review is thought to be necessary to keep agencies within the bounds established by Congress.

The presumption in favor of judicial review of agency action did not exist before the APA was enacted, and many agency decisions were not subject to judicial review. Common law writs, such as mandamus, were available to challenge only nondiscretionary (or ministerial) agency action. Any hint of executive discretion would sometimes lead federal courts to deny reviewability. For example, in *Decatur v. Paulding*, 39 U.S. (14 Pet.) 497 (1840), the Court refused to review a decision of the Secretary of the Navy to deny Mrs. Decatur a widow's pension. The Secretary denied the pension because on the same day that Congress passed the general pension law, it also passed a private bill granting Mrs. Decatur a pension. In the Secretary's judgment, Mrs. Decatur was entitled to one pension or the other, but not both. The Court denied review even though the determination seemed to be a matter of statutory interpretation, i.e., did Congress intend for Mrs. Decatur to have both pensions. The Court denied review, using very deferential language: "The Court could not entertain an appeal from the decision of one of the Secretaries, nor revise his judgment in any case where the law authorized him to exercise discretion, or judgment. Nor can it by mandamus, act directly upon the officer, and guide and control his judgment or discretion in the matters committed to his care, in the ordinary discharge of his official duties." 39 U.S. at 515. The Court also stated that "[t]he interference of the courts with the performance of the ordinary duties of the executive departments of the government would be productive of nothing but mischief, and we are quite satisfied that such a power was never intended to be given to them." Id. at 516.

Although some pre-APA courts favored judicial review of any allegation of official illegality, see *American School of Magnetic Healing v. McAnnulty*, 187 U.S. 94 (1902), the dominant pre-APA view held that review was available only when Congress explicitly provided for review. See, e.g., *Switchmen's Union v. National Mediation Board*, 320 U.S. 297 (1943).

(2) APA §704's Grant of Judicial Review: General Understanding

APA §704 provides for judicial review of "[a]gency action made reviewable by statute and **final agency action** for which there is no adequate remedy in a court." This statute creates a strong presumption of reviewability of final agency action. In essence it provides a cause of action for judicial review of final agency action when no other statute provides for review. The key provisions of §704 may be understood as follows:

The "agency action made reviewable by statute" provision is redundant. It merely states that if a statute other than the APA, such as an agency enabling act, provides for judicial review of a particular agency action, the action is reviewable under that provision. The only real substantive effect of this provision is to foreclose any argument that upon its passage the APA became the exclusive basis for judicial review. It also suggests that, absent contrary statutory provisions, the requirements of Chapter 7 of the APA, including the standards of judicial review, govern the remaining issues in judicial review even when another statute provides the basis for judicial review. APA standards of review are discussed in Chapter 4.

The "final agency action for which there is no adequate remedy in a court" provision creates a general entitlement to judicial review of final agency action. The standards for determining when an agency action is final are discussed below in the finality and ripeness section.

The requirement that there be "no other adequate remedy in a court" means that if Congress has provided a remedy other than APA judicial review for a particular agency action, APA review is not available unless the alternative remedy is not adequate. If a court finds the other remedy inadequate, review is presumptively available under APA standards of review. This provision may also mean that agency rules are not automatically subject to judicial review immediately upon promulgation. See Attorney General's Manual at 101. Rather, a rule would be immediately reviewable upon promulgation only if adequate review is not available when the rule is enforced. This is discussed further below in connection with ripeness and the *Abbott Laboratories* case.

(3) APA §704's Grant of Judicial Review: Agency Action

The APA's references to "**agency action**" mean that review under the APA is available only for "agency action." The judicial review chapter of the APA contains its own definition of "agency," see APA §701(b)(2), but that definition is almost identical to the one contained in the definitions section of the APA, §551(1). Agency means "each authority of the government of the United States," except, inter alia, Congress, civil and military courts, and the governments of territories and possessions of the United States. Despite the absence of an explicit exemption, the Supreme Court has decided that the President is not an agency within the meaning of the APA. *Franklin v. Massachusetts*, 505 U.S. 788 (1992). This means that personal action by the President is not subject to judicial review under the APA.

As defined in the APA, " 'agency action' includes the whole or a part of an agency rule, order, license, sanction, relief, or the equivalent or denial thereof, or failure to act." APA §551(13). This definition resulted in the recognition of an important condition on the availability of judicial review, that the petition must identify a particular agency action within the statutory definition that is being challenged.

The meaning of "agency action" is not obvious, as illustrated by the Court's decision in *Norton v. Southern Utah Wilderness Alliance*, 542 U.S. 55 (2004). The Southern Utah Wilderness Alliance sued the Department of Interior for allegedly not taking adequate steps as required by statute to safeguard certain federal lands in Utah for potential future designation as a wilderness area. The plaintiffs asked for injunctive and declaratory relief to compel the Department of Interior to protect the lands mainly from harm caused by recreational off road vehicles. The complaint relied on the APA provision that grants courts the authority to "compel agency action unlawfully withheld." APA §706(1). The Supreme Court rejected the plaintiffs' claims based on the APA's definition of "agency action," which refers to agency actions such as the issuance of (or decision not to issue) a rule, license, or order. The Court held that the complaint did not successfully allege that "agency action" had been unlawfully withheld because the complaint did not specify the particular discrete action the agency was legally required to take. The Court concluded that the APA's reference to "failure to act" refers to failure to take one of the actions specified in the definition of "agency action," not a general failure to take adequate steps to accomplish a statutory goal. This means that APA review is not available to challenge the general manner in which an agency regulates but rather must focus on one of the specific actions named in the APA.

(4) Nonstatutory Review

The APA explicitly preserves review under the pre-APA procedures such as petitions for mandamus, general federal question equity actions and actions for declaratory relief under the federal Declaratory Judgment Act. This non-APA category of review has been denominated "**nonstatutory review**," under which agency action that is covered by neither a specific review provision nor the APA is reviewed. The term "non-statutory review" is a misnomer, since these forms of non-statutory review depend at least to some extent on various statutes including APA §703, which provides that if the action for judicial review under the APA is inadequate or unavailable, the challenger may employ "any applicable form of legal action, including actions for declaratory judgments or writs of prohibitory or mandatory injunction or habeas corpus, in a court of competent jurisdiction." APA §559 also explicitly preserves "additional requirements imposed by statute or otherwise recognized by

law," which has been interpreted to mean that Congress did not intend for the APA to displace the federal courts' traditional common law powers in administrative law. See Kenneth Culp Davis, *Administrative Common Law and the Vermont Yankee Opinion*, 1980 Utah L. Rev. 3, 10.

The question then becomes what law determines the availability of these non-statutory remedies such as mandamus, certiorari, and injunction. The answer turns out to be **federal common law**. There are some statutory aspects—from the very beginning, in the All Writs Act provision, §14 of the Judiciary Act of 1789, Congress granted the federal courts the power to employ the traditional writs known to courts at that time. However, no federal statute specifies the conditions under which each writ should be granted. Rather, the federal courts fashion appropriate actions and remedies when the APA and other specific regulatory statutes do not cover the particular issues involved, applying the same common law methodology they employed before passage of the APA.

Thus, as we have seen, the entitlement to judicial review comprises both statutory and non-statutory elements. Because most judicial review arises under the APA, little attention has been paid to the non-statutory aspects of judicial review, but in light of the APA's explicit provision for non-statutory methods of review, it remains an important aspect of administrative law.

(5) Statutory Preclusion of Review: APA §701(a)(1)

APA §701 specifies two situations in which APA judicial review is not available: when "**statutes preclude judicial review**" and when "agency action is **committed to agency discretion by law**."

APA §701(a)(1) provides that judicial review is not available when "statutes preclude judicial review." Statutory preclusion often involves agencies with their own elaborate internal review mechanisms. Normally, for a statute to preclude judicial review, it should explicitly mention judicial review. The best example of such a statute was old §211(a) of the Veterans' Administration Act, which provided that the "decisions of the [Veterans' Administration] on any question of law or fact under any law administered by the Veterans' Administration [VA] . . . shall be final and conclusive and no other official or any court of the United States shall have power or jurisdiction to review any such decision[.]" A statute like this precludes review of the administrative action specified — decisions of law and fact by the agency under any law it administers.

F   A   Q

Q: Why would Congress preclude judicial review of agency action?

A: Usually, practical considerations lead Congress to preclude judicial review. These considerations include a high volume of relatively routine fact-bound determinations in a specialized regulatory or benefits scheme. Sometimes, internal review procedures are preferred to minimize delay. In some situations, however, Congress's motives may be less benign. Congress may preclude review because it fears the results of judicial review. Perhaps the fear is that courts will be too solicitous of benefits claimants' interests or insufficiently sensitive to government policies.

A statute that precludes review of agency action does not preclude a constitutional challenge to the substantive statute itself, because in such a case the court would be reviewing a decision by Congress, not the agency. For example, a conscientious objector to military service challenged the constitutionality of a statutory provision, administered by the Veterans' Administration (VA), that limited eligibility for certain veterans' benefits to people who had actually been on active duty in the armed forces. The VA argued that since §211(a) barred review of the denial of benefits, the conscientious objector could not challenge that denial in court even on the ground that the statutory provision excluding conscientious objectors was unconstitutional. The Supreme Court rejected the VA's argument and held that that §211(a) did not bar the claim because the challenge was not to agency action but rather was to Congress's decision to exclude non–active duty personnel from the benefits. See *Johnson v. Robison*, 415 U.S. 361 (1974).

There are powerful reasons against reading a statute precluding review of agency decisions to preclude judicial review of the constitutionality of the statute being administered. The contrary view would allow Congress to in effect amend the Constitution by passing an unconstitutional statute and insulating it from judicial review. This would be contrary to fundamental principles regarding the legal status of the Constitution.

When a statute **channels** review in particular ways or on behalf of particular parties, it may be argued that this implicitly means that Congress has precluded review of other, closely related, agency actions or in favor of parties other than those named in the statute. For example, suppose a statute grants an agency the power to suspend and revoke licenses to sell a product, let's say pesticides. Suppose further that if the license to sell a pesticide is suspended, the process continues and culminates either in revocation or a decision against revocation, at which time the suspension ends. The statute includes an explicit grant of review over decisions revoking a license but does not mention review of suspensions. The fact that the agency's enabling act explicitly provides for review of decisions regarding revocation implies that Congress has implicitly precluded review of suspension orders or orders denying suspension. While the Court has stated as a principle of administrative law that the fact that some administrative actions are made reviewable by statute does not, by itself, support an inference that other actions under the same program are not reviewable, *Bowen v. Michigan Academy of Family Physicians*, 476 U.S. 667 (1986), the Court has also held that the provision of a method of review for a particular action may implicitly preclude alternative methods of review of the same action. *United States v. Erika, Inc.*, 456 U.S. 201, 208 (1982). This preclusion should be narrow, according to the Court, based on Congress's general attitude favoring judicial review of all executive action and the overall importance of the right to review.

Sidebar

REVIEW FOR CONSTITUTIONALITY

One practical reason supporting the decision in *Johnson v. Robison* is that many agencies will not address the constitutionality of the statutes they administer. Agencies have viewed resolving constitutional challenges to their statutory authority as beyond their competence. Often, they leave resolution of such challenges to the courts.

F A Q

Q: What is the difference between statutes that preclude judicial review and statutes that channel judicial review?

A: Statutes that preclude review prohibit any review of particular agency actions whatsoever. Statutes that channel review allow review but require that review be sought under the procedure specified.

When Congress grants standing to seek review to a particular class of parties, this may implicitly mean that Congress meant to preclude other parties from seeking review. Implicit preclusion due to channeling of review to particular parties occurs only when an agency's enabling act is very explicit about who can obtain review. In *Block v. Community Nutrition Institute*, 467 U.S. 340 (1984), for example, consumers and a nonprofit nutrition advocacy group sought review of a decision by the Secretary of Agriculture that increased the price of certain milk products. A milk handler also sued. The statute specified that milk handlers could obtain judicial review but only after they exhausted remedies provided by the Secretary. The Court held that under these circumstances, review on behalf of parties other than milk handlers was implicitly precluded by the statute that granted review only to milk handlers and channeled that review through the administrative process. Similarly, in the above example concerning suspension and revocation of licenses, if the statute granted review only in favor of licensees, the argument arises that third parties, such as users of the licensed product, cannot seek review.

A related issue that often arises with regard to channeling of judicial review is whether a provision that channels and precludes other methods of review of an individual determination precludes review of challenges to general procedures that an agency is applying in administering the statute. In *Bowen, supra*, the Court rejected the argument that general challenges were implicitly precluded by statutory provisions channeling review of individual determinations. It appears therefore that a statute that channels review of individual determinations under a program might not normally bar review directed at the administration of the program as a whole.

Even channeling accompanied by an explicit statutory bar of judicial review of determinations on the merits of individual cases may not bar review of general challenges to the administration of the program. In *McNary v. Haitian Refugee Center, Inc.*, 498 U.S. 479 (1991), a statute creating a new category of legal immigrant workers provided that "[t]here shall be no . . . judicial review of a determination respecting an application for adjustment of status under this section except in accordance with this subsection" and that "there shall be judicial review of . . . a denial [of the new status] only in the judicial review of an order of exclusion or deportation[.]" Despite the explicit language of the statute, the Court held that as long as no individual status determination was challenged, the statute did not bar disappointed applicants and their advocates from pursuing, in a class action, constitutional and statutory challenges to the procedures used in the program as a whole. The challengers cited a number of procedural problems including inadequate interpreters for non–English speaking immigrants, and the inability of applicants to present their own witnesses and evidence in the hearings. The Court read "determination respecting an application" to refer to a decision on a single application, not to the agency's general policies regarding how the hearings are held, and thus review of the general challenges was not precluded.

Chief Justice Rehnquist raised an interesting challenge to the majority's reasoning in his dissent in *McNary*. In his view, the statutory channeling provision was irrelevant to whether review was available. Rather, Chief Justice Rehnquist argued that the APA's grant of review, which extends to "final agency actions," does not extend to general challenges to the way an agency administers its program. The APA would grant review of final denials of the special status, but review of denials is channeled to review after deportation or exclusion proceedings. This argument may be bolstered by the later decision in *Norton v. Southern Utah Wilderness Alliance*, 542 U.S. 55 (2004), that reviewable "agency action" includes only challenges to discrete actions by agencies, not general challenges to the way an agency is carrying out its responsibilities. The majority's response to Chief Justice Rehnquist's argument is that review of a single denial, and only after the applicant was found to be subject to deportation or exclusion, would not provide effective review of the allegedly widespread failure of the agency to comply with applicable statutes and constitutional provisions. For example, evidence of widespread violations would not be available to individual applicants and it would not even be relevant to whether a particular application should have been granted.

(6) Committed to Agency Discretion by Law: APA §701(a)(2)

APA §701(a)(2) bars judicial review of agency action "committed to agency discretion by law." That provision, a descendant of the now-abandoned notion that discretionary administrative action was never reviewable, can be understood in three different ways — all of which reinforce the idea that certain decisions have been left to agency discretion and are free from judicial review. These are the "no law to apply" approach, the "deeming clause" approach, and the "traditionally unreviewable" approach.

In the *Overton Park* decision, the Court explained that agency action is "committed to agency discretion by law" when the governing "statutes are drawn in such broad terms that in a given case there is **no law to apply**." See *Citizens to Preserve Overton Park v. Volpe*, 401 U.S. at 410, quoting S. Rep. No. 752, 79th Cong., 1st Sess., 26 (1945). Judicial review is not possible in such cases because there is no discernible statutory standard against which to judge the legality of agency action. Because Congress normally attempts to give agencies statutory guidance, this exception to reviewability of final agency action is rarely met and even in those cases in which the exception applies, there were special reasons in addition to the vagueness of the statutory standard to think that precluding review is appropriate. These circumstances are explained below.

Sidebar

"DISCRETION" AND "DISCRETION"

The unreviewability of decisions "committed to agency discretion by law" under APA §701(a)(2) may appear to be inconsistent with the APA's judicial review provision, §706(2)(A), allowing review of agency action for **"abuse of discretion."** While the two provisions use the word "discretion," its meaning in each provision is quite distinct. In §701, agency "discretion" denotes situations in which the agency has final say over the matter so that its decision should not be questioned in court. In §706, "discretion" connotes judgment, which is subject to review for serious errors.

In *Webster v. Doe*, 486 U.S. 592 (1988), the Supreme Court held that the decision to fire an employee of the Central Intelligence Agency (CIA) was committed to the discretion of the director of the CIA because the governing statute, which provided that the director had the power to terminate the employment of CIA employees "whenever he shall deem such termination necessary or advisable in the interests of the United States," was so vague that it did not supply courts with law to apply in order to determine whether the director's decision was within statutory bounds.

In addition to the vague nature of the standard ("necessary or advisable in the interests of the United States"), the Court suggested that agency action is also "committed to agency discretion by law" when the statute suggests that Congress intended for the agency to have final authority over a decision. Such statutory provisions may be referred to as "deeming clauses." In *Webster v. Doe*, the statutory language, by stating that the director may terminate employees when he "*deem*[s]" it in the interests of the United States, assigned final authority to dismiss CIA employees to the director. The statute does not state that it must actually be in the national interest to terminate the employee — only that the director must deem it to be so. The Court observed that "[t]his standard fairly exudes deference to the Director." *Webster v. Doe*, 486 U.S. at 600. Another example is *Lincoln v. Vigil*, 508 U.S. 182 (1993), in which an agency's allocation of funds from a lump sum appropriation was held committed to agency discretion by law partly on the "**deeming clause**" theory but without an explicit deeming clause. A lump sum appropriation leaves it to the agency to determine how to spend the money, subject to broad statutory guidelines such as promotion of the health of Indians as was the case in *Lincoln*. The Court found that a lump sum appropriation is essentially a congressional determination that the agency, within broad parameters, should determine how to spend the money — in effect an implicit "deeming clause" under which Congress grants unreviewable discretion to the agency to decide how to apportion the lump sum.

In his separate opinion in *Webster v. Doe*, Justice Scalia argued for a novel understanding of "committed to agency discretion by law." In explaining the words "by law" in the phrase "committed to agency discretion by law," Justice Scalia stated that "by law" refers to a body of common law of reviewability under which certain subject matter categories of agency action were traditionally unreviewable. In support of this position, Justice Scalia relied upon *Heckler v. Chaney*, 470 U.S. 821 (1985). As we shall see, that reliance was misplaced.

Heckler v. Chaney held that, in most cases, agencies' decisions on whether to bring an **enforcement action** against a particular violator were "committed to agency discretion by law." In *Heckler*, the Court held that §701 (a)(2) barred review of the Food and Drug Administration's (FDA) decision not to take enforcement action against states that administered capital punishment by the lethal injection of drugs that were not approved for that particular use. The Court held that it was up to the agency to balance the various factors that are relevant to the agency's decision whether to take action against a particular violation of law, and that therefore judicial review of a decision not to take enforcement action is ordinarily not available.

The Court's analogy in *Heckler* to the discretion of prosecutors in criminal law supports understanding *Heckler* as adopting a **categorical approach** to reviewability under which the exercise of enforcement discretion is a category in which review is precluded. However, it is clear that *Heckler* is actually an application of the "no law to apply" standard to an area in which "law to apply" is unlikely to exist. *Heckler* created a rebuttable presumption that decisions not to bring enforcement actions are unreviewable. The presumption against reviewability of prosecutorial decisions is rebutted when "the substantive statute has provided guidelines for the agency to follow in exercising its enforcement powers." See *Heckler v. Chaney*, 470 U.S. at 832. In other words, review is available when there is law to apply. For this understanding, the *Heckler* Court relied upon *Dunlop v. Bachowski*, 421 U.S. 560 (1975). In *Dunlop*, the Court held that the Secretary of Labor's refusal to bring a lawsuit challenging the results of a union election was reviewable because, under certain circumstances, the relevant statute required the Secretary to sue. The statute provided that if the Secretary finds probable cause to believe that the law governing union elections was violated, the Secretary "shall, within sixty days after the filing of such complaint, bring a civil action against the labor organization as an entity in the District Court of the United States." *Dunlop*, 421 U.S. at 563. The *Heckler* Court stated that in *Dunlop* "the statutory language supplied sufficient standards to rebut the presumption of unreviewability." See *Heckler*, 470 U.S. at 833. (It is, however, difficult to locate such a finding in the actual *Dunlop* opinion.)

Given that *Heckler* makes clear that when statutory standards constrain prosecutorial discretion, courts will review the exercise of that discretion, *Heckler* is not authority for the categorical approach argued for by Justice Scalia in his *Webster* dissent. However, when reviewable, enforcement decisions are reviewed very deferentially. The agency's decision is upheld unless the administrator fails to provide plausible or rational reasons for the failure to prosecute. In *Dunlop*, for example, the Court may have felt compelled by the statute's mandatory language ("shall . . . bring a civil action") to review the decision not to sue, but the Court clearly stated that the review is to be very deferential, insisting only that the Secretary articulate rational reasons for failing to bring the required civil action.

Although *Heckler* was virtually the only (very weak) prior suggestion in a majority opinion of the categorical approach to nonreviewability, the Court unanimously held, in *Lincoln v. Vigil*, that there are categories of administrative decisions that are unreviewable under the "committed to agency discretion by law" provision because these categories have traditionally been held to be committed to agency discretion. Justice Souter's opinion for the *Lincoln* Court stated that "[o]ver the years, we have read [APA] §701(a)(2) to preclude judicial review of certain categories of administrative decisions that courts traditionally have regarded as 'committed to agency discretion.'" *Lincoln v. Vigil*, 508 U.S. 182, 192 (1993). Justice Souter's assertion that the Court had previously applied the categorical approach was based on meager evidence — he cited primarily to a concurring opinion by Justice Stevens and a dissenting opinion by Justice Scalia. Regardless, a unanimous Court in *Lincoln* itself agreed to the categorical approach to "committed to agency discretion by law."

In *Lincoln*, the Court went on to hold that the allocation of funds from a lump sum appropriation is not reviewable, in part, because it is "another administrative decision traditionally regarded as committed to agency discretion." *Lincoln v. Vigil*, 508 U.S. at 191. The Court had even less evidence for this tradition than it had for the existence of the categorical approach to unreviewability discussed above. The Court cited to a Court of Appeals decision written by then-Judge Scalia that held that the allocation of funds from a lump sum appropriation was not reviewable because there was no law to apply, *International Union, United Auto., Aerospace & Agricultural Workers v. Donovan*, 746 F.2d 855, 663 (D.C. Cir. 1984), and to a 1975 opinion of the Comptroller General explaining that committee reports specifying the use of funds from lump sum appropriations have no legal effect. Judge Scalia's opinion for the Court of Appeals did not even hint at the categorical approach or that there was a tradition of unreviewability regarding allocations from lump sum appropriations.

Even if the Court's legal reasoning was flawed, there are good reasons to conclude that agency allocations from lump sum appropriations should not be subject to judicial review. The nature of a lump sum appropriation is that there is no law to apply to allocation decisions from among the usually numerous permissible statutory uses of the funds. However, although neither the text nor the legislative history of APA §701(a)(2) bear the meaning ascribed to it under the "traditionally unreviewable" approach, there is support, albeit not relied upon by the Court, for the "deeming clause" approach. There was a pre-APA understanding that judicial review was not available when a statute grants discretion in terms of the personal judgment of an official, using phrases such as "in his judgment" to describe the conditions for executive action. See *United States v. George S. Bush & Co.*, 310 U.S. 371 (1940). Section 701(a)(2)'s language was meant to incorporate this doctrine, but the Court did not come to this view until *Webster*, in which it noted that the inclusion of the word "deem" in the statute indicated that Congress meant for this to be a personal decision of the agency director, not reviewable by any other official or in court.

F A Q

Q: When an agency argues against reviewability based on no law to apply, isn't it admitting that there is a violation of the nondelegation doctrine?

A: There are two reasons why the lack of law to apply does not automatically violate the nondelegation principle. First, not all agency action involves delegated legislative power. For example, *Webster v. Doe* involved the power to terminate executive employees. The power to terminate an executive employee, and even the power to set the standards governing termination, may be viewed as an executive function. Many government officials are, and historically have been, subject to at-will employment, which means that the standards governing termination are set within the executive branch. Second, although there may be "no law to apply" for reviewability purposes, this does not necessarily mean that a statute does not contain an intelligible principle guiding the agency's exercise of discretion. Congress's general purposes may supply enough guidance to satisfy the intelligible principle standard without providing sufficient guidance to allow meaningful judicial review, especially given how lenient the intelligible principle doctrine has become over the years.

There are additional important examples of the nonreviewability of agency decisions involving enforcement discretion. In order for a charge of an unfair labor practice to go forward, the general counsel of the National Labor Relations Board (NLRB) must file a complaint with the NLRB. A decision by the general counsel not to file an unfair labor practice complaint with the NLRB is "final" under the statute creating the NLRB. The Court has long held that the decision not to file an unfair labor practice charge is an unreviewable exercise of agency prosecutorial discretion. See *NLRB v. Sears, Roebuck & Co.*, 421 U.S. 132, 136-38 (1975). The general counsel's unreviewable discretion to decide whether to file a complaint extends further to a decision to withdraw a complaint before a hearing. Therefore, if the general counsel reaches a settlement with the employer before a hearing is held, the terms of the settlement are not subject to judicial review. See *NLRB v. United Food and Commercial Workers*, 484 U.S. 112 (1987).

The Court reinforced its decision against review of pre-hearing settlement agreements in *Food and Commercial Workers* with the channeling argument that review of settlements was unavailable because the labor laws grant review of some post-hearing settlements but not the decision to withdraw a complaint before the hearing. If a settlement has been reached after a hearing or some other proceeding before the agency has been held, the decision to settle might be reviewable. This is because to settle the case once proceedings before an agency have begun, the agency must issue an order dismissing the case pursuant to the settlement. Such an order would be final agency action subject to judicial review under the statutes governing review of NLRB orders. However, courts are likely to be very deferential in reviewing orders dismissing enforcement actions as part of settlement agreements.

What about reviewability of agency decisions not to promulgate rules? After *Heckler*, the question arose whether decisions not to promulgate rules are similar to decisions not to bring enforcement actions and thus were not subject to judicial review, at least absent a statutory provision limiting the agency's discretion. The D.C. Circuit recognized that *Heckler v. Chaney* cast doubt on its prior cases finding that agency decisions not to promulgate rules are reviewable. However, that court found decisions not to promulgate rules reviewable and distinguished such decisions from non-enforcement decisions on three bases as follows:

> [R]efusals to institute rulemaking proceedings are distinguishable from other sorts of nonenforcement decisions insofar as they are less frequent, more apt to involve legal as opposed to factual analysis, and subject to special formalities, including a public explanation. *Chaney* therefore does not appear to overrule our prior decisions allowing review of agency refusals to institute rulemakings.

American Horse Protection Ass'n, Inc. v. Lyng, 812 F.2d 1, 3-4 (D.C. Cir. 1987). While the matter was thus settled in the D.C. Circuit, it remained unresolved at the Supreme Court level until the global warming case, *Massachusetts v. EPA*, 549 U.S. 497, 527-28 (2007), in which the Court adopted the D.C. Circuit's reasoning (quoting the language above), adding that parties have a procedural right to file petitions for the promulgation of rules, while they have no procedural right to participate in individual enforcement decisions. See id. (petitions for rulemaking "moreover arise out of denials of petitions for rulemaking which (at least in the circumstances here) the affected party had an undoubted procedural right to file in the first instance").[1] Thus, it is now settled law that agency decisions not to promulgate rules are subject to judicial review.

---

[1] APA §553(e) requires that agencies "give an interested person the right to petition for the issuance, amendment, or repeal of a rule." APA §555(e) requires agencies to answer petitions and give reasons for denials.

Although refusals to promulgate rules are susceptible to judicial review, the analogy to enforcement decisions gives rise to a sense that the standard of review should be more deferential than traditional hard look review under the arbitrary and capricious test. Here again, the Supreme Court adopted the D.C. Circuit's reasoning. The Court in *Massachusetts v. EPA* held that while review of non-promulgation decisions is available, "such review is 'extremely limited' and 'highly deferential.' " *Massachusetts v. EPA*, 549 U.S. at 527-28, quoting *National Customs Brokers & Forwarders Ass'n of America, Inc. v. United States*, 883 F.2d 93, 96 (D.C. Cir. 1989). It should be noted that the statutory standard of review is still the arbitrary, capricious, abuse of discretion standard of APA §706(2)(a), and nothing in the APA suggests that the standard has different meanings depending on the context.

The Court did not provide a satisfactory analysis of the most difficult question in *Massachusetts v. EPA*, having to do with the fact that the EPA had not made a formal judgment concerning the harmful effects of greenhouse gases. The Clean Air Act provides that the EPA Administrator "shall prescribe . . . [the] standard applicable to the emission of any air pollutant from . . . new motor vehicles which *in his judgment* cause, or contribute to, air pollution which may reasonably be anticipated to endanger public health or welfare. . . ." 42 U.S.C. §7521(a)(1) (emphasis supplied). The phrase "in his judgment" appears to make the inquiry subjective, and the statute contains no standard governing when the Administrator is actually required to make a judgment regarding any air pollutant, only that once the judgment is made, the Administrator must prescribe a rule that meets the statutory requirements.

The agency based its decision not to make a judgment concerning whether global warming gases should be regulated under the statute on various factors including the administration's preference for other, voluntary, programs, concern over impairing the President's ability to negotiate with other countries, and the administration's view that a comprehensive approach would be preferable to what it called "piecemeal" regulation involving automobile emissions. The majority opinion held that these policy judgments could not be relevant to the EPA Administrator's decision of whether to make a judgment concerning greenhouse cases because they were not derived from the Clean Air Act. The majority opinion thus held that the statutory criteria concerning whether greenhouse gases are a dangerous air pollutant also governs the Administrator's decision whether to make the judgment. As the dissent points out, this conclusion cannot be derived from the language of the statute, which contains no standard governing when the agency must make a judgment.

More generally, *Massachusetts v. EPA* indicates that the Court is split on the fundamental question of how to treat statutes that condition an agency's obligation to make a rule on the formulation of a judgment that a rule is necessary to achieve the goals of the statute. Many regulatory statutes condition agency action on a judgment that certain statutory criteria for regulation are met, and few prescribe when the agency must take the first step and make a judgment. The (slim) majority held that statutory standards governing agency action after a judgment is made also govern the agency's decision on whether to make the judgment in the first place. While the minority assumed that an agency may need a reasonable basis to refuse to exercise its judgment on a condition precedent to rulemaking, the minority would hold that absent explicit statutory standards governing the decision whether to make a judgment, any reasonable basis will do, including the reasons the EPA gave for its decision not to make a judgment regarding the harmful effects of greenhouse gases.

(7) Preclusion of Review of Constitutional Questions

The Court has not decided whether Congress may preclude judicial review of constitutional challenges to agency action. Because precluding judicial review of constitutional challenges itself raises a serious constitutional question, courts have interpreted statutes precluding judicial review to preclude review only of nonconstitutional questions, while preserving review of constitutional issues. For example, in *Johnson v. Robison*, 415 U.S. 361 (1974), the Court held that a statute barring review of decisions of the Veterans' Administration did not bar a constitutional challenge to the statute the VA was charged with administering. See also *Webster v. Doe*, in which the Court held that while a legal challenge to the firing of a CIA officer was not subject to judicial review, a constitutional challenge to the same action was subject to review. Justice Scalia, in his dissent in *Webster*, argued that Congress has the power to preclude review of constitutional issues. The issue will only be resolved authoritatively if Congress unmistakably bars the review of constitutional challenges and a challenge to that bar is brought to court.

It would be very surprising if the Court found that Congress has the power to preclude review of the constitutionality of a statute. Such a power would give Congress de facto power to amend the Constitution by passing an unconstitutional statute and precluding courts from ruling on the constitutionality of that statute. Imagine, for example, if in one of the numerous legislative veto provisions Congress has passed even after the *Chadha* decision, Congress provided that no court may review the constitutionality of the legislative veto. It would be completely inconsistent with basic assumptions about the U.S. legal system, and with the process for amending the Constitution, to allow Congress to preclude judicial review of the constitutionality of a statute.

A different set of concerns governs whether a statutory preclusion of review should be read to also preclude review of constitutional claims against executive branch actions. Here we are assuming that the statute itself is constitutional but the claim is that it has been administered unconstitutionality and Congress has precluded judicial review even of constitutionally based challenges to the executive action. The Supreme Court has expressed concern over the constitutionality of preclusion under these circumstances and has accordingly read statutes not to preclude such review. Precluding review in such cases is not as serious as precluding constitutional challenges to statutes themselves, because at least Congress would be able to step in (by repealing the preclusion) if the executive branch abused its authority. However, it still seems unlikely that the Court would approve of precluding judicial review of constitutional challenges to agency action.

Justice Scalia has rejected any special rule against preclusion of constitutional challenges to agency action. In *Webster v. Doe*, Justice Scalia dissented from the holding that Doe could challenge the constitutionality of his termination even though non-constitutional review was not available because the decision was committed to agency discretion by law. Justice Scalia disagreed with the notion that preclusion of constitutional challenges raises a serious constitutional question. He argued that there are many situations in which constitutional claims are not available because of particular constitutional provisions, such as the **Speech or Debate Clause** (which immunizes Members of Congress against any civil or criminal challenges to their legislative acts) and the long tradition of **sovereign immunity**, which is partially codified in the Eleventh Amendment. It might be argued in response that the serious constitutional question involves allowing Congress to determine legislatively the reviewability of constitutional claims, but Justice Scalia responds to this argument by pointing out that Congress already determines the extent to which the United States waives its sovereign immunity and allows damages suits against the government based on constitutional violations. In the end, there is no resolution to this disagreement, except to say that so far, the majority of the Supreme Court believes that preclusion of review of constitutional challenges to agency action raises a serious enough constitutional question that the Court has avoided resolving the issue thus far by construing statutes not to preclude such claims.

The issue of precluding review of constitutional questions should not be confused with the distinct question of whether there is a constitutional entitlement to judicial review of non-constitutional claims. This breaks down into two inquiries; first whether Article III requires judicial review and second whether due process requires judicial review of agency decisions. The Article III question is discussed above under the rubric of separation of powers — in some circumstances Article III allows adjudication in administrative agencies only if, inter alia, non-deferential judicial review is available. A due process entitlement to judicial review is less clear. Normally, due process concerns the fairness of the procedures applied, not the particular institution conducting the hearing. While due process does require a neutral decision maker, neutrality can be achieved without Article III life tenure. Otherwise, many state courts and federal administrative adjudicators would be constitutionally deficient. In the public rights area in which judicial review may not be required by Article III, a hearing within an agency before an administrative law judge acting independent of other agency officials may be sufficient to satisfy due process.

C. Standing to Seek Judicial Review

A party seeking judicial review must have **standing** to sue. In general, as government regulation became more pervasive during the twentieth century, the Supreme Court has expanded the category of parties with standing to seek review of government action. Standing problems arise most often in actions seeking injunctive (or similar) relief regarding an agency's treatment of a party other than the one seeking review. It may be unclear whether the agency's action has injured the party seeking judicial review and whether holding the agency action unlawful (and setting it aside) will alter the plaintiff's situation.

Sidebar

THIRD PARTIES HAVE STANDING PROBLEM

Standing involves identifying the proper party to challenge agency action. Normally, a regulated party has no problem establishing standing. With regard to third parties such as competitors or citizens interested in environmental protection, standing depends on various constitutional, prudential, and statutory factors.

A regulated party rarely if ever has a standing problem. For example, if the EPA orders automakers to increase the gas mileage of the cars they manufacture, there is no doubt that as regulated parties the automakers have standing to seek review of that order. Rather, standing problems arise when third parties such as competitors and environmentalists seek judicial review of the regulatory treatment of someone else. For example, even though it would cost them sales revenue, oil companies would have a more difficult standing argument than auto manufacturers if they seek review of the order directing automobile manufacturers to increase the gas mileage of their new cars. However, the expansion of standing in recent years makes it increasingly likely that an injured third party will have standing to seek review of the regulatory treatment of someone else.

Typical categories of **third parties** who are likely to complain about the treatment of someone else include business competitors, individuals (and interest groups) representing the public interest, and customers. Business competitors might complain that the regulated parties with whom they compete are being treated too leniently. Individuals (and interest groups representing them) might complain that the environmental laws are not being enforced strictly enough against polluting industries. Customers might complain that sellers are being treated too leniently (for example because products are unsafe or overpriced) or too strictly (resulting in unavailability or higher prices for goods or services).

There is great disagreement on the Supreme Court over basic standing principles. Many of the key decisions on standing are badly split, often 5-4. This makes it difficult to make generalizations about standing doctrine with much confidence that the rule announced today will be followed tomorrow. Therefore, standing rules must be approached with caution so that today's decision not to follow the reasoning of last Term's (5-4) decision will not come as a surprise.

F   A   Q

Q: How does standing differ from reviewability?

A: Standing and reviewability are distinct concepts. Standing concerns who, if anyone, is the proper party to challenge government action. Reviewability concerns whether the particular government action may be attacked by anyone, even someone with standing to do so. For example, if Congress were to provide that the denial of a particular immigrant status is unreviewable, an immigrant denied that status would almost certainly have standing to seek review, but the statute might preclude the court from actually reviewing the determination. Conversely, a statute might make decisions to allow drilling for oil reviewable, but no one may have standing to challenge drilling in an area that is so remote that no people are directly affected by the drilling.

(1) No Third-Party Standing: The Old Legal Right Test

Early standing doctrine generally denied standing to third parties, prohibiting anyone from challenging the regulatory treatment of someone else. Standing was recognized only for parties whose own **legal rights** had been allegedly violated by agency action. Parties injured by agency treatment of others lacked standing to seek judicial review. Cases involving regulation of competitors best illustrate the limits on standing implicit in the legal right test: A business entity's claim that regulation of a competitor (or lack of a legally required regulation) gives the competitor an unfair advantage would be rejected on the ground that the plaintiff's own legal rights were not at stake. For example, in *Alexander Sprunt & Son, Inc. v. United States*, 281 U.S. 249 (1930), the Court rejected a claim that the Interstate Commerce Commission (ICC) had set railroad shipping rates for Sprunt's competitors too low, thereby injuring Sprunt's business. The Court stated that even though Sprunt was injured, Sprunt did not have standing because Sprunt's only legal right was to be charged reasonable rates itself. That legal right was not implicated when the ICC lowered the rates charged to Sprunt's competitors.

In 1940, the Court ruled that Congress had the power to override the legal right test and, in effect, appoint competitors as **private attorneys general** to vindicate the public interest by keeping agencies within legal bounds. This means that the legal right test was not of constitutional pedigree because if it was, Congress could not override it. In *FCC v. Sanders Bros. Radio Station*, 309 U.S. 470 (1940), the Court held that Sanders Bros, had standing to challenge the award of a radio station license to a competitor because Congress had statutorily granted a right to judicial review of FCC orders to any person whose "interests are adversely affected" by an order of the FCC. The legal right test for standing was criticized because it required the plaintiff to establish a key element of the claim on the merits (whether his or her legal rights were implicated) at an early stage of the litigation, just to establish standing. This criticism led to the abandonment of the legal right test in favor of the "zone of interests" test as discussed below.

(2) Standing in Administrative Law under the APA: APA §702 and the Zone of Interests Test

APA §702 states, in part, that "[a] person suffering legal wrong because of agency action, or adversely affected or aggrieved by agency action within the meaning of a relevant statute, is entitled to judicial review thereof." The first clause of APA §702 is the legal right test. Thus, the APA grants standing to anyone whose legal rights are allegedly violated by agency action. The second clause of §702 appears to liberalize standing beyond the legal right test to all those injured by the agency action, but is limited by the phrase "within the meaning of a relevant statute." Because this language is somewhat obscure, it is unclear how much APA §702 expands upon the legal right test.

In *Association of Data Processing Service Organizations, Inc. v. Camp*, 397 U.S. 150 (1970), the Court held that to have standing the plaintiff must show two things: a constitutionally sufficient injury and that "the interest sought to be protected by the complainant is arguably within the **zone of interests** to be protected or regulated by the statute or constitutional guarantee in question." *Data Processing*, 397 U.S. at 153. The *Data Processing* Court discarded the legal right test on the ground that it went to the merits and should not be relevant for purposes of standing. In its place, the Court erected the zone of interests test, which limits APA standing to those parties whose interests were important to Congress in formulating the regulatory scheme.

The zone of interests test limits standing to a subset of those injured by the challenged action but is broader than the legal right test. *Data Processing* presented the classic competitor's challenge to administrative action. The Comptroller of the Currency allowed national banks to sell certain data processing services to their customers and to other banks. The data processors, competitors of the national banks in the data processing field, challenged the Comptroller's ruling as violating statutory restrictions on the activities of national banks. The Court held that because the statute restricting banks to banking and related activities was concerned not only with the financial health of the banks, but also with the interests of parties in competition with banks, the data processors were within the zone of interests of the statutory scheme and thus had standing to seek judicial review. The zone of interests test takes a political, rather than legal, view of standing because it asks not whether the plaintiff has a legal right at stake but rather whether the plaintiff's interests were considered by Congress or the regulatory body.

Although the zone of interests test appeared to fall into disuse after *Data Processing*, it has enjoyed something of a revival in recent years. In *Air Courier Conference of America v. American Postal Workers Union*, 498 U.S. 517 (1991), the Court denied standing to postal workers who challenged the Postal Service's decision to give up its monopoly over international remailing services—a method for saving money over airmail rates when sending a large volume of mail overseas. The Court held that postal workers were not within the zone of interests of the statute that created and regulated the United States Postal Service's monopoly over the mail. The only issue considered by Congress, according to the Court, was the public interest in an efficient mail service. However, in most cases in which it has come up, the Court has found that the party challenging agency action is within the zone of interests. See, e.g., *Federal Election Comm'n v. Akins*, 524 U.S. 11 (1998) (voters are in the zone of interests of election laws requiring political committees to disclose information); *National Credit Union Admin. v. First Nat'l Bank & Trust Co.*, 522 U.S. 479 (1998) (competing banks are within the zone of interests of statute regulating the scope of credit unions' business); *Bennett v. Spear*, 520 U.S. 154 (1997) (ranchers and others seeking to limit reach of the Endangered Species Act are within the zone of interests addressed by the Act because the Act's citizens' suit provision allows suits by "any person").

(3) General Standing Principles

Standing law is derived from three sources; constitutional law, prudential principles, and statutes. Article III's limitation of federal judicial power to "cases" or "controversies" entails standing requirements of **injury**, **causation**, and

---

Sidebar

STANDING AND PUBLIC INTEREST LITIGATION

The transformation of standing law from the legal right test to the zone of interests test reflects movement in administrative law away from the private law model of litigation toward the adoption of a more public law–oriented model of litigation. This transformation is, to a great extent, the result of the recognition that third parties, and often the entire public, are just as interested in the outcome of an administrative process as the immediate subject of regulation. The effects of economic regulation may be felt by competitors just as acutely as they are felt by the subject of the regulation, and environmental regulation may be as important to the public at large as it is to the polluter. Congress recognizes this when it includes a citizens' suit provision in a regulatory statute, which places all citizens or all persons within the zone of interests. And the courts have recognized this by liberalizing the situations under which third parties have standing to challenge administrative action.

However, this does not mean that third parties are on the exact same footing as the subjects of regulation. As the Court has stated explicitly, it is more difficult to establish standing when a third party challenges an agency's treatment of someone else. See *Lujan v. Defenders of Wildlife*, 504 U.S. 555 (1992). Third parties face problems establishing **causation** and **redressability** (standing requirements that are discussed below) that do not exist when the regulated party seeks judicial review. The actions of the regulated party (and not the government's actions) may independently cause the plaintiff's injuries and ordering the government to act differently may not change the regulated party's conduct in a way that is beneficial to the plaintiff.

redressability. Judge-made prudential rules reject standing when a party attempts to raise what is called a "**generalized grievance**" or assert someone else's rights. These requirements (called "**prudential**" limitations) are, according to the Supreme Court, necessary to confine the courts to their proper role in government. Prudential limitations prevent courts from deciding "abstract questions of wide public significance," especially when "judicial intervention may be unnecessary to protect individual rights." *Warth v. Seldin*, 422 U.S. 490, 499-500 (1975). Statutes may limit or expand the range of persons eligible for standing to challenge particular agency action, but expansion may not go beyond constitutional limits. Each of these sources of standing law is elaborated below.

(4) Constitutional Standing: The "Injury-in-Fact Fairly Traceable" Test

Injury

Article III of the Constitution grants the federal courts jurisdiction over various classes of "cases" and "controversies." This grant can also be understood as a limitation — the jurisdiction of the federal courts extends only to genuine cases or controversies. The federal courts may not render advisory opinions or adjudicate cases without a real dispute in which a party may benefit from a judicial remedy. This limitation of jurisdiction to cases and controversies has given rise to the basic constitutional requirements for standing — namely that the plaintiff has suffered an injury-in-fact that is fairly traceable to the challenged conduct and redressable by a favorable judgment. These requirements ensure that the plaintiff has a real legal controversy with the defendant, not just an abstract disagreement. While the constitutional requirements for standing are relatively simple and straightforward, they have been applied so inconsistently over the years that it is very difficult to generalize from the decisions. The most one can hope for is to understand the arguments in the cases and try to make sense of their reasoning.

Sidebar

BASIC REQUIREMENTS FOR STANDING

The basic requirements for standing are simple to state even if they are uncertain in application. To have standing, a plaintiff must have suffered an injury in fact that was caused (**fairly traceable**) by the challenged conduct such that a favorable judgment will remedy it.

The most basic requirement for standing is that the plaintiff must have suffered an injury. To satisfy this requirement, the plaintiff must be "significantly affected" by the challenged conduct. An abstract interest in a regulatory scheme is not sufficient to establish standing. Rather, the plaintiff must be among those actually injured by the challenged conduct or policy. For example, in *Sierra Club v. Morton*, 405 U.S. 727 (1972), the Court held that the Sierra Club's abstract interest in environmental protection was not sufficient to establish standing to oppose the granting of a development permit in previously undeveloped parkland. The Court stated that, for standing purposes, only a person who had used and planned to continue using the parkland in its undeveloped state would have a sufficient injury to bring suit to prevent the development. The Sierra Club may have been trying to establish a principle that interest groups have standing to sue to advance the purposes of the group — if so, they failed in this attempt as the Court held that actual injury is required for standing. Thus, in all cases, it is vital that the plaintiff actually be among the injured. (Standing for organizations based on injuries to their members is discussed below.)

The rule in *Sierra Club* was applied to block standing for people interested in seeing endangered species to sue over U.S. government activity in foreign countries that was alleged to be contributing to the extinction of species. See *Lujan v. Defenders of Wildlife*, 504 U.S. 555 (1992). In the *Lujan* case, the plaintiffs based their claim on a provision of the Endangered Species Act that requires agencies to consult with the Secretary of the Interior before they engage in activities that might harm endangered species. The Secretary of the Interior re-interpreted this provision not to apply to U.S. government activities carried out in foreign countries. The plaintiffs challenged this interpretation and claimed standing based on their interest in seeing endangered species in Sri Lanka and Egypt that were threatened by projects supported by U.S. government aid. The Supreme Court denied standing because, although they had viewed the species in the past, none of the individual plaintiffs had concrete plans to go see them in the future. As Justice Kennedy explained in his concurring opinion, without concrete plans, given the great distances involved, it was not possible to assume that visits in the past made future visits likely.

The Supreme Court has held that that a broad class of injuries is constitutionally sufficient to form the basis of standing to sue. In general, the category of injuries that can form the basis of standing to seek review of government action has been expanded greatly over the years to encompass matters far beyond those that would have been recognized before the advent of the administrative state. In addition to traditional common law interests such as bodily integrity and property rights, standing can be based on **aesthetic** and **economic** interests, the freedom to exercise **rights** such as the right to speak or vote, and even the interest in receiving information in the hands of the government. Under current law, injury to a person's ability to view open spaces or study endangered species is sufficient for standing, although the person must establish that he or she has actually been subjected to the alleged injury. In its most important recent standing decision, the Court held that the State of Massachusetts had standing to challenge the EPA's refusal to regulate greenhouse gas emissions. Standing was based upon the fact that Massachusetts owns a great deal of coastal land, which is threatened by rising sea levels resulting from global warming. The basic injury requirement for standing is met by a wide variety of injuries, so long as the plaintiff is among those suffering concrete injury as a result of the conduct being challenged. *Massachusetts v. EPA*, 549 U.S. 497 (2007).

F   A   Q

Q: Did the fact that the State of Massachusetts was a plaintiff make standing easier in *Massachusetts v. EPA*?

A: The Court's opinion is not clear on this. On the one hand, the Court supports its standing analysis with observations concerning Massachusetts's special status as a state, including the fact that states depend on the federal government for some areas of regulation over which they would otherwise have control. On the other hand, the findings of injury, causation, and redressability result from relatively straightforward applications of traditional standing analysis.

Standing can also be based on the deprivation of a right created by Congress where, without the statute creating the right, standing would not otherwise exist. For example, *Havens Realty Corp. v. Coleman*, 455 U.S. 363 (1982), involved a violation of a federal fair housing statute that requires landlords to provide truthful information on the availability of rental property without regard to race. Havens Realty officials told an African American "tester" who pretended to be a prospective tenant that no apartment was available when it was showing vacant apartments to white applicants. Havens Realty argued that the tester did not have standing because, since he never intended to rent an apartment, the lie did not injure him. The Court rejected this argument on the basis that the federal fair housing statute gave the tester the right to truthful information without regard to race, and therefore the tester was injured simply by being lied to, regardless of his lack of intent to actually rent an apartment.

Congress's ability to legislate standing is limited by Article III's injury requirement. In many regulatory statutes, mainly in the environmental area, Congress has included **citizens' suit** provisions, which allow basically anyone in the United States to sue government officials who fail to carry out their responsibilities under the law. One of the plaintiffs' standing claims in *Lujan*, which was accepted by the Court of Appeals, was that the citizens' suit provision gave all persons a procedural right to the consultation that was required by the law and that therefore all persons, including the plaintiffs, were injured when the Secretary of Interior did not obey the law's requirements. The Court rejected this application of the doctrine that statutes can create rights the deprivation of which constitute injury for standing purposes. The Court held that Article III requires that the plaintiff suffer a distinct, concrete injury. The generalized interest in having the executive branch follow the law is not sufficient, even with the presence of a citizens' suit provision. Without this limitation, Congress would essentially be requiring federal courts to decide matters that are not constitutional cases or controversies within the meaning of Article III.

There is another class of injury that has been recognized in some relatively recent decisions that is best characterized as the potential reduction in expected benefits. A potential reduction in expected benefits has been recognized as an injury even without allegation or proof of actual losses, and appears to substantially loosen standing rules. This doctrine is best illustrated by two decisions, *Northeastern Florida Chapter of Association of General Contractors v. Jacksonville*, 508 U.S. 656 (1993) and *Bennett v. Spear*, 520 U.S. 154 (1997). *General Contractors* involved an affirmative action set-aside program under which the City of Jacksonville, Florida, set aside 10 percent of its public works contracts for minority- and women-owned businesses. The Court approved standing for white contractors to challenge the program even though none of them had ever been denied a contract based on the program's criteria. The lack of a single contract denial raises the question whether there was even an injury alleged, but the Court reconceptualized the interests affected and ruled that the contractors had standing since they were injured in their ability to compete on an equal footing with minorities entitled to the preference. The decision appears to recognize a new sort of injury, namely damage to the ability to compete for a benefit.

The recognition of an injury to the ability to compete has not been confined to equal protection cases in which equality concerns may support the notion that a party is injured just by having to meet a higher standard than other applicants for a benefit or contract. In *Bennett v. Spear*, 520 U.S. 154 (1997), the Court allowed a group of ranchers to challenge a reduction in the overall quantity of available irrigation water in a regulated watershed even though none of them alleged that their own allocation of water had been reduced. The Court held that the allegation that less water was available in the aggregate was sufficient for standing because "it is easy to presume specific facts under which petitioners will be injured — for example . . . distribution of the reduction pro rata[.]" Id. at 168.

F A Q

Q: Do Members of Congress have standing to sue over interference with their lawmaking powers?

A: Members of Congress have sued over the legality of the pocket veto, under which the President vetoes legislation at the end of a Term of Congress without actually returning the bill, and over alleged violations of the Origination Clause, under which revenue-raising bills must originate in the House of Representatives. While the D.C. Circuit has upheld standing in such cases based on the injury to the ability of Members of Congress to exercise their constitutional powers, *Moore v. United States House of Representatives*, 733 F.2d 946 (D.C. Cir. 1984), it appears that the Supreme Court would disagree and reject standing in such cases. In *Raines v. Byrd*, 521 U.S. 811 (1997), the Court ruled against standing for particular Members of Congress to challenge the Line Item Veto Act on the basis that "the institutional injury they allege is wholly abstract and widely dispersed" among the Members of Congress. Note that in *Moore*, the D.C. Circuit ruled that it would exercise its equitable discretion and decline to order any remedy in the case even if the procedure used to pass the bill in question was unconstitutional.

Sometimes, it will be difficult to distinguish the question of whether a party has been injured from the question of whether the injury is caused by the challenged conduct. For example, in the *SCRAP* case, *United States v. Students Challenging Regulatory Agency Procedures (SCRAP)*, 412 U.S. 669 (1973), a group of law students sought judicial review of the Interstate Commerce Commission's approval of an increase in freight rates charged by railroads on the basis that the increase would cause a decrease in recycling, which would in turn cause an increase in air pollution and litter in the Washington, D.C., area where they lived. Potential physical harm from unclean air and aesthetic harm from litter are sufficient injuries for standing, but if the increase in freight rates did not have the alleged effects, the plaintiffs would not have been injured by the challenged conduct.

The more recent decision in *Massachusetts v. EPA*, that the State of Massachusetts has standing to challenge the EPA's refusal to regulate carbon dioxide and other greenhouse gases, presents a similar puzzle. Massachusetts's alleged injury was damage to its coastline due to rising sea levels caused by global warming. The injury may not exist if the causal connection is not real. For the purposes of understanding the injury requirement, it is necessary to understand that if causation is present, these injuries are sufficient to satisfy the injury requirement for standing.

"Fairly Traceable"

The second requirement for standing is that the injury must be "**fairly traceable**" to the challenged conduct of the government defendant, or in other words, the government conduct challenged must have actually caused the injury. While the concept of causation is not a difficult one to grasp, the cases do not analyze causation in a consistent fashion. Standing is granted in some cases and denied in others based on causation without clear reasons for the different outcomes. This is perhaps best illustrated by looking at pairs of cases in which different results have been reached.

The Supreme Court decision that is thought of as a high-water mark for permissive standing doctrine is *United States v. Students Challenging Regulatory Agency Procedures (SCRAP)*, 412 U.S. 669 (1973), discussed above, in which law students challenged the Interstate Commerce Commission's freight rates on the basis that an increase would cause a decrease in recycling, which would in turn cause an increase in air pollution and litter. By contrast, in *Simon v. Eastern Kentucky Welfare Rights Organization, Inc. (EKWRO)*, 426 U.S. 26 (1976), lack of causation was fatal to standing for a group of people who were denied free medical care at hospitals and wanted to challenge the Internal Revenue Service's (IRS) alleged leniency regarding the requirement that tax-exempt hospitals provide free care to indigent patients. The plaintiffs were denied free care after the IRS issued a Revenue Ruling loosening free care requirements for charitable institutions. The Court held that the lack of availability of free medical care was not traceable to the Internal Revenue Service's lax enforcement of requirements for charitable status in part because even if the IRS revised its policy, the hospitals might decide to forgo tax-exempt status rather than provide more free care.

F   A   Q

Q: Can the standing decisions be explained simply by viewing them as result-oriented?

A: This is a commonly held view. Some critics have given up on trying to explain standing doctrine in legal terms and view the Supreme Court as stretching to grant standing when it wants to reach the merits and deny standing when it would prefer to avoid deciding them. Even if this critique is accurate, it is important in litigation (and on law school exams!) to be conversant with the doctrinal terms in which standing decisions are expressed even if the true bases for standing decisions are not revealed in the Supreme Court's opinions.

Another pair of cases further illustrates the inconsistencies in Supreme Court standing doctrine: *Warth v. Seldin*, 422 U.S. 490 (1975) and *Northeastern Florida Chapter of Association of General Contractors v. Jacksonville*, 508 U.S. 656 (1993). In *Warth*, the Court rejected builders' and potential residents' claims that zoning laws prevented low-income housing from being built in the Town of Penfield, New York. The Court's primary basis for denying standing was causation — the builders could not identify a project that had been turned down, and thus potential residents could not establish that their inability to live in Penfield was caused by the zoning as opposed to general economic conditions that made low-income housing in Penfield economically unrealistic. This insistence that the plaintiffs in *Warth* point to an actual proposed project that had been turned down stands in contrast with the *General Contractors* decision (and with *Bennett v. Spear*) in which reduction in the ability to compete for a benefit was held sufficient for standing. Recall that in *General*

Contractors, the Court allowed a group of white contractors to challenge an affirmative action program even though they could not show that they had lost a single contract due to the affirmative action program. In terms of causation, it seems just as likely that restrictive zoning laws have an effect on the zoning process as set-aside programs have an effect on the contracting process. More fundamentally, the more recent decisions seem to dispense with the requirement that the party seeking standing actually be among those injured by the challenged conduct unless merely having to compete for a contract or benefit under more restrictive rules is sufficient injury in and of itself.

Another relatively liberal application of standing requirements is the decision in *Massachusetts v. EPA*, 549 U.S. 497 (2007), on whether the State of Massachusetts has standing to challenge the EPA's decision not to regulate motor vehicle emission of greenhouse gases thought to be causing global warming. The Court flirted with the notion that standing rules should be liberalized when the plaintiff is a state on the ground that states represent their sovereign interests in protecting the health and welfare of their people. However, the Court's actual standing analysis is traditional, holding that Massachusetts has standing because global warming injures it in its capacity as owner of coastal lands likely to be affected by rising sea levels resulting from global warming. The biggest problem for Massachusetts's standing claim is that greenhouse gases from motor vehicles in the United States contribute so little to global

> ### Sidebar
>
> **STANDING AND RACE DISCRIMINATION**
>
> The *General Contractors* rule would not seem out of step with standing doctrine had it been confined to cases involving racial discrimination. It is understandable that the Court would want to grant standing to victims of explicit racial discrimination even if they cannot prove that the results of any government process would have been different without the racial classification. However, when the Court extended this reasoning to the ranchers in *Bennett v. Spear*, it raised serious questions about its commitment to confining standing to those actually injured by the challenged governmental conduct.

warming that Massachusetts suffers no measurable injury from them and thus would not be measurably helped even if EPA were ordered to regulate them. To this the Court answered that it is sufficient for Massachusetts to have standing that greenhouse gases within the EPA's jurisdiction make even a small contribution to global warming that would be slowed by more stringent regulation.

Redressability

Finally, to have standing the plaintiff must also show that the remedy sought against the defendant will redress the injury. The issue of **redressability** looks at whether the plaintiff has a personal stake in the outcome of the litigation such that the plaintiff will benefit if the court grants relief. Redressability is thus in most cases the flip side of causation: If ending the challenged conduct would cure the injury, obviously the challenged conduct caused the injury. Conversely, if the challenged conduct did not cause the alleged injury, logically a remedy requiring a halt to the challenged conduct is not likely to redress the injury. For example, in *SCRAP*, the redressability question was whether reducing freight rates would lead to more recycling, and thus less litter in the parks and cleaner air. Because the Court accepted the argument that the rate increase caused litter and air pollution, it was committed to accepting the argument that reducing the rates would decrease litter and air pollution. In *EKWRO*, the redressability question was whether better IRS enforcement of the requirement that tax-exempt hospitals provide free care to indigents would actually lead to the hospitals treating more indigents. Here the Court ruled against redressability, holding that it was not clear that the hospitals would treat more indigents. Rather, they might simply forgo tax-exempt status if the loss in donations would be less costly than providing more free care.

In the global warming case, *Massachusetts v. EPA*, 549 U.S. 497 (2007), the redressability problem was a bit different. The dissent argued that the contribution of greenhouse gases from new automobiles was so small that their effect on global warming and thus harm to Massachusetts's coastal lands was immeasurable. The majority held that the injury was redressable because EPA regulation would reduce emissions and thus slow global warming at least to some extent. The dissent viewed it as "pure conjecture" that stricter regulation by the EPA would likely prevent the loss of any of Massachusetts's coastal land.

A different sort of **procedural injury** than the type rejected in *Lujan* was also relevant to the majority's view in *Massachusetts v. EPA*. The *Lujan* Court had explained, in a very interesting footnote, that procedural rights can contribute to standing, but only if the procedural rights are in support of efforts to combat a concrete injury. The *Lujan* Court stated in footnote 7, 504 U.S. at 573:

> There is this much truth to the assertion that "procedural rights" are special: The person who has been accorded a procedural right to protect his concrete interests can assert that right without meeting all the normal standards for redressability and immediacy. Thus, under our case law, one living adjacent to the site for proposed construction of a federally licensed dam has standing to challenge the licensing agency's failure to prepare an environmental impact statement, even though he cannot establish with any certainty that the statement will cause the license to be withheld or altered, and even though the dam will not be completed for many years. . . .

The Court in *Massachusetts v. EPA* relied on this footnote to hold that the procedural right (granted in the Clean Air Act) to seek judicial review of the EPA's rejection of the rulemaking petition was a procedural right that supported the claim for standing as long as "there is some possibility that the requested relief will prompt the injury-causing party to reconsider the decision that allegedly harmed the litigant." Justice Scalia, the author of the *Lujan* footnote, would disagree with its application in *Massachusetts v. EPA* because he would find that Massachusetts had not established that it was suffering concrete injury due to the EPA's failure to regulate greenhouse gases.

An injury may not be redressable if a court is without power to craft an enforceable order against the official engaged in the illegal conduct. In *Lujan v. Defenders of Wildlife*, 504 U.S. 555 (1992), a plurality held that since a remedy would require the cooperation of federal agencies who were not parties to the case, the injury was not redressable because a court cannot issue a judgment against a nonparty. However, in *Franklin v. Massachusetts*, 505 U.S. 788 (1992), a majority of the Court found redressability even though the President, who was not a party to the case, was the official responsible for the challenged conduct. *Franklin* involved a challenge to the 1990 census, which Massachusetts claimed had undercounted its citizens. Massachusetts sued the Secretary of Commerce, Head of the Department that conducted the census, but the final census numbers are by law transmitted to Congress by the President. The Court stated that it expected that the President would act in accordance with the Court's decision on the merits even though it doubted that a court could issue a binding order against the President.

There is also an element to standing that is analogous to **mootness**, namely that past harm may not provide the basis for prospective relief. Standing requires that the plaintiff's concrete stake in the outcome of the case must exist at the time the lawsuit is filed. While a plaintiff might be eligible for damages based on past harm, harm must continue for the plaintiff to have a claim for injunctive relief as well. For example, in *Steel Company v. Citizens for a Better Environment*, 523 U.S. 83 (1998), the Court rejected standing for an environmental group that challenged the Steel Company's failure, in past years, to submit required information to the EPA concerning the presence of hazardous and toxic chemicals. The Court ruled that remedies such as a declaration that the company had

> ### Sidebar
>
> **STANDING AND REMEDIES**
>
> Most cases that present standing issues are cases in which the plaintiff seeks prospective relief of some kind, such as an order setting aside agency action or an injunction or declaratory judgment. The redressability question is whether the plaintiff will be among those who benefit from the remedy. Plaintiffs who seek damages rarely have standing problems because it is pretty clear that if they are entitled to damages, the reviewing court can provide effective relief to them.

violated the law in the past and even the imposition of civil fines (which would go to the government, not the plaintiff) based on past violations were insufficient for standing because they did not redress any present harm suffered by the plaintiff. However, in another context, the deterrent effect of a civil penalty toward future violations was held sufficient to satisfy the redressability requirement for standing even though the defendant had halted the illegal conduct. See *Friends of the Earth, Inc. v. Laidlaw Environmental Services, Inc.*, 528 U.S. 167 (2000) (Friends of the Earth has standing to sue Laidlaw for civil penalties payable to the United States even though Laidlaw had ceased its illegal discharges of pollutants into the river). This conclusion seems to be in tension with the apparently contrary view of the Court in *Steel Company*.

CONSTITUTIONAL STANDING CHECKLIST

1. Is the plaintiff the regulated party? If so, there is rarely a standing issue. ☑

2. If the plaintiff is not the regulated party, has the plaintiff suffered a concrete and particularized injury? If so, the plaintiff meets the injury requirement for standing. ☑

3. If the plaintiff has suffered an adequate injury, was the injury caused by (fairly traceable to) the challenged conduct? If so, the plaintiff meets the causation element of standing. ☑

4. Will an available judicial remedy redress the injury? If so, the plaintiff meets the redressability element of standing. ☑

5. Is the plaintiff's interest in the manner merely abstract, with no personal effects or involvement? If so, the plaintiff lacks standing. ☑

(5) Prudential Limits on Standing

The prudential limits on standing are judge-made doctrines that limit access to the federal courts beyond the basic constitutional standing requirements. Two prudential requirements have been recognized. First, the courts should not hear a case involving a **generalized grievance** that the government is not following the law. Rather, the plaintiff must be distinct from the general populace in that he or she is particularly affected by the alleged illegality. As discussed above, the simple claim that government is not following the law is not only barred by the prudential generalized grievance doctrine, it also does not constitute injury sufficient to satisfy Article III. A generalized grievance is one that should be resolved by the political branches, not by the courts. The generalized grievance doctrine does not necessarily bar all cases involving widespread harms. In *SCRAP*, for example, the Court stated that the fact that many people are injured by government action should not prevent standing, lest the most widespread and injurious government illegalities become beyond judicial reach. However, the widespread injury must be more than simply an allegation that the government is violating the law.

The generalized grievance rule is applied most strongly in challenges to government action brought by people in their capacity as taxpayers claiming that the government is violating the law. For example, the generalized grievance doctrine bars suits by taxpayers challenging how government spends its revenues. Since the plaintiffs' only injury in these cases is an injury suffered by all citizens or taxpayers, the Court has held that the issue should be resolved in a political, rather than legal, forum. Despite the generalized grievance doctrine, taxpayers have been allowed to challenge government spending as violating the First Amendment's ban on establishment of religion. *Flast v. Cohen*, 392 U.S. 83 (1968). This is supported on the ground that the Establishment Clause is a constitutional restriction on the taxing and spending power and thus there is a sufficient nexus between the taxpayer status and the claim so that the generalized grievance bar should not apply. However, in *Valley Forge Christian College v. Americans United for Separation of Church and State*, 454 U.S. 464 (1982), the Court held that taxpayers could not, due to the generalized grievance doctrine, challenge a government department's decision to transfer surplus property to a religious school. More recently, in *Hein v. Freedom from Religion, Inc.*, 551 U.S. 587 (2007), a plurality held that the *Flast* exception to the taxpayer nexus requirement does not apply when executive branch action allegedly violates the Establishment Clause. Concurring Justices would have eliminated the *Flast* exception altogether. These and similar decisions make it unclear whether the Establishment Clause exception to the generalized grievance doctrine in tax cases is likely to survive much longer.

More recently, the Supreme Court held that citizens of Colorado lacked standing to challenge the application of a Colorado statute governing the way congressional elections are held in Colorado. After the Colorado legislature did not agree on a redistricting plan after the 2000 census, a state trial court adopted a plan. Later, the state legislature adopted its own plan, but the Colorado Supreme Court blocked the legislative plan from taking effect on the ground that under Colorado law, redistricting is allowed only once every ten years. The plaintiffs brought suit in federal court, alleging that the Colorado Supreme Court's application of the Colorado statute violated the Elections Clause of the United States Constitution, Art. I, §4, cl. 1, because it was too far removed from the actual statutory language to satisfy the Election Clause's requirement that the "Times, Places and Manner of holding

Elections for Senators and Representatives, shall be prescribed in each State by the Legislature thereof." The U.S. Supreme Court held that this was "precisely the kind of undifferentiated, generalized grievance about the conduct of government that we have refused to countenance in the past." *Lance v. Coffman*, 549 U.S. 437, 442 (2007) (per curiam).

Second, a party must assert his or her own rights and may not litigate the **rights of a third party** even if the plaintiff is injured by the violation of the other party's rights. For example, suppose a shopkeeper has many customers who use food stamps, and her sales decrease significantly after the government allegedly illegally cuts off the food stamps of many of the customers. The drop in sales indicates that she is injured by the cutoff of food stamps to her customers. She may sue alleging that she was injured when the government violated the legal rights of the food stamp recipients by illegally cutting off their food stamps. However, she may not have standing to challenge the food stamp cutoff because she would be asserting the rights of third parties — the food stamp recipients. She may also have a zone of interests problem because it is uncertain whether the food stamp program is concerned with the well-being of those who sell food to food stamp recipients. (She would have standing to challenge a government decision that she could no longer accept food stamps as that affects her own legal rights.) To overcome the prudential problems, she would have to establish an exception to the bar against asserting the rights of a third party, and she would have to show (through the statute or legislative history) that shopkeepers' interests were within the zone of interests of the food stamp program.

The ban on asserting third-party rights keeps the courts out of disputes in which the persons primarily affected — those whose rights are actually at stake — have decided not to assert their rights. Further, the actual right-holder may have a greater incentive and greater ability to assert the rights than another party, who although injured, may not be as seriously affected and may not have complete information. Finally, third-party litigation may duplicate litigation between the government and the right-holder, and right-holders should have the primary opportunity to assert their own rights.

There are exceptions to the ban on asserting third-party rights. Plaintiffs have been allowed to assert the rights of a third party when there is an impediment to the rights-holder asserting his or her own rights, the plaintiff has a close relationship with the third party whose rights are at stake, and the plaintiff has a strong incentive to litigate to protect those rights. For example, health care providers have been allowed to litigate the right of their patients to receive contraceptives or abortions because they are in a confidential relationship with their patients and

Sidebar

DEFINITION OF THIRD-PARTY RIGHTS

The ban on asserting the rights of a third party uses the term "third party" in a different sense than earlier in this chapter when we were discussing standing for third parties to challenge the treatment of someone else. There, the issue was whether government's lenient treatment of a regulated party was sufficient for standing for third parties who were injured thereby, for example when people who breathe are injured by lenient treatment of polluters. There, the plaintiff is not asserting a right that belongs to the polluter and may in fact be the intended beneficiary of the regulation. In the current discussion of third-party rights, the plaintiff is asserting that someone else's rights have been violated, such as the food stamp recipient whose benefits have been unlawfully terminated, and the question is whether the plaintiff has standing to assert those rights. The usual answer is "no."

the providers' own professional success depends upon their ability to provide the products or services. Further, persons seeking abortions and contraceptive products and services might have privacy interests that prevent or discourage them from litigating their own rights. Similarly, during the civil rights movement (and perhaps even today) African Americans seeking to vindicate their right to live in a previously segregated community might have feared reprisals from whites seeking to maintain segregation. Under such circumstances, courts have allowed third parties with close relationships to the rights-holders to litigate the claims. In the First Amendment context, the Court has allowed parties to argue that a statute that might constitutionally be applied to them is unconstitutional as applied to others; thus it should be struck down as overbroad on the theory that the existence of the overbroad statute chills the exercise of important First Amendment rights.

There is controversy over whether the generalized grievance doctrine is prudential or based in Article III. Justice Scalia has, on more than one occasion, characterized the generalized grievance doctrine as an element of Article III standing, stating once that a generalized grievance does not present an injury adequate to satisfy Article III's injury-in-fact requirement, *Friends of the Earth, Inc. v. Laidlaw Environmental Services (TOC), Inc.*, 528 U.S. 167, 204 (2000) (Scalia, J. dissenting), and stating on another occasion more generally that a generalized grievance does not establish an Article III case or controversy. *Federal Election Comm'n v. Akins*, 524 U.S. 11, 31 (1998) (Scalia, J. dissenting). He had a majority for this view in *Lujan*, which held that the procedural injury alleged in that case (government not following procedures required by statute) was a generalized grievance and that

> [w]e have consistently held that a plaintiff raising only a generally available grievance about government — claiming only harm to his and every citizen's interest in proper application of the Constitution and laws, and seeking relief that no more directly and tangibly benefits him than it does the public at large — does not state an Article III case or controversy[.]

Justice Scalia is correct that earlier cases posit a strong relationship between the generalized grievance doctrine and Article III, but the relationship among Article III, citizens' suit provisions, and the generalized grievance doctrine is not completely clear. The fact that many people, even all mankind, are injured does not mean that the injury is a generalized grievance. Rather, it is a generalized grievance when no particular individual is harmed in any way other than the general harm of government illegality. The majority in *Massachusetts v. EPA*, 549 U.S. 497 (2007), understood the doctrine this way, holding basically that if

Sidebar

BAN ON ASSERTING THIRD-PARTY RIGHTS AND ZONE OF INTERESTS TEST

The ban on asserting a third party's rights may seem to be in tension with the elimination of the legal right test for injury and the substitution of the zone of interests test. Under the zone of interests test, parties are allowed to challenge agency action without alleging that their own legal rights are at stake. The only legal rights at stake may be the rights of the third party whose lenient treatment by the government caused the injury to the plaintiff. However, the right-holder here will not seek judicial review because the problem is that the right-holder is being treated too leniently. Therefore, unless the plaintiff is allowed to seek judicial review, there will be none.

every person in the United States will be concretely harmed by global warming, every person in the United States has standing to challenge government action related to global warming.

F   A   Q

Q: May Congress overrule the prudential limitations on standing?

A: Yes. Because the prudential limitations on standing are judge made and not consti-tutionally compelled, Congress has the power to overrule them. However, Congress must respect constitutional minima for standing. As long as constitutional injury, causation, and redressability requirements are met, Congress may constitutionally grant standing for parties to litigate third-party rights and for citizens to litigate generalized grievances. Congress can easily bring a party within the zone of interests of a statute by mentioning that party's interests either in the statute itself or in the legislative history. Citizens' suit provisions effectively eliminate the zone of interests requirement since the statute grants the right to sue to all citizens.

---

(6) Associational Standing

Associations, such as interest groups and trade associations, have standing to litigate their own claims and also the claims of their members. When an association sues on its own behalf, it must meet normal standing requirements, i.e., it must have an injury that is traceable to the challenged conduct such that a remedy will cure the injury. We know from the *Sierra Club* and *Lujan v. Defenders of Wildlife* cases that an association does not have standing to sue based only on the abstract interests of its members in an issue such as environmental protection or wilderness and species preservation. For an association to sue on behalf of its members, it must establish three elements:

1. that the members themselves would have standing to sue;
2. that the interests the association is suing over are within the association's purpose; and
3. that the litigation will not be adversely affected by the absence of individual plaintiffs.

Hunt v. Washington State Apple Advertising Comm'n, 432 U.S. 333 (1977).

While the first two requirements are relatively simple to understand, the mean-ing of "not be adversely affected by the absence of individual plaintiffs" is not obvi-ous. The primary meaning of this requirement is that the remedy must not require the participation of individual plaintiffs, for example by requiring individualized proof of damages for a monetary remedy. Where prospective relief such as a declar-atory judgment or injunction is sought, this is normally not a problem. Associational standing may not be appropriate when damages are sought on behalf of association members because in such cases individualized proof of damages is normally required.

D. The Timing of Judicial Review: Finality, Ripeness, Exhaustion of Administrative Remedies, and Mootness

(1) The Constitutional Underpinnings of Ripeness and Mootness

The ripeness and mootness doctrines are related to the constitutional requirements for a case or controversy, namely that the plaintiff is injured by the challenged conduct and the injury will be remedied by a favorable judgment. When a case is brought too early or too late, either there is not yet an injury sufficient for standing or the injury has ended, and a favorable judgment will not remedy it. For example, if a person brings a petition for judicial review of a regulation before the agency has attempted to enforce the regulation against the petitioner, the action may not be ripe because the petitioner has not yet been injured by the regulation. If the agency repeals the challenged regulation before or during judicial review, or if the challenger is no longer subject to the regulation, the case may be moot because the petitioner is no longer injured. However, the ripeness and mootness doctrines are more flexible than basic standing requirements and thus may not, in all circumstances, be constitutionally based.

> **Sidebar**
>
> **TIMING OF REVIEW**
>
> Traditional justiciability doctrines of ripeness, exhaustion of administrative remedies, and mootness govern the timing of judicial review. Claims may not be brought too early (ripeness), too late (mootness), and (in some cases) without first exhausting administrative remedies.

(2) Finality and Ripeness in Administrative Law: The APA's Grant of Review of "Final Agency Action"

APA §704 grants a right to judicial review of "**final agency action** for which there is no adequate remedy in a court." The "final agency action" provision is essentially a ripeness requirement, which excludes from review any agency action that is not yet final. Courts also apply ripeness requirements in addition to the APA's finality requirement, although, as discussed below, there is a question whether this is proper, or whether courts should find an action ripe for review whenever the action meets statutory (including APA) standards of finality.

Finality of Adjudications

Agency adjudications are final when the adjudicatory process in the agency has completely ended (including whatever appellate review is legally required within the agency), and the agency has issued its order. During the adjudicatory process, the ALJ or agency normally makes numerous rulings on the scope of the issues, the evidence, the sufficiency and meaning of pleadings, etc. Although an individual ruling may be final in the practical sense because it will not be revisited in the course of the adjudication, the adjudicatory process is not final for the purposes of judicial review until the agency issues a final order. Subsidiary issues may be reviewed at the end of the case, but normally all review must await the issuance of a final order by the agency. See APA §704.

In review of adjudication, finality normally entails ripeness. Once an agency has issued an order in an adjudication involving a regulated party, the order is likely to be ripe for judicial review. It is possible to imagine non-ripe aspects of an order. For example, an agency might, in the course of adjudication, announce a rule of law that it intends to apply in future adjudications raising the same issues. If the agency did not apply the new rule to the parties involved in the adjudication in which the new rule was announced, a court might want to defer resolution of the legality of that new rule of law until it is actually applied. But in most cases, the issuance of an order is final and ripe for judicial review.

Finality of Rulemaking

The finality and ripeness issues are a bit more complicated when it comes to rulemaking. Technically speaking, a rule is final once the rulemaking process is completed and the agency issues the final rule by publishing it in the Federal Register. However, the Supreme Court has held that rules are not necessarily ripe for review when issued. Rather, some rules are ripe upon promulgation while others may not be reviewed until they are enforced, with judicial review essentially providing a defense to an enforcement action brought by the agency.

There is a textual basis in the APA for delaying review of agency rules until they are actually enforced. Recall that APA §704 grants judicial review of "final agency action for which there is no adequate remedy in a court." Not all final agency action is subject to review, only final agency action for which there is no adequate legal remedy in a court. APA §704. Many regulatory statutes provide that agency orders are enforceable only in court. For example, the National Labor Relations Board must petition a court of appeals to enforce its orders. In some cases, using the invalidity of a rule as a defense to a petition for enforcement may be an adequate remedy in a court, which would mean that immediate review of the rule would not be available.

Ripeness and Review of Agency Rules: Fitness and Hardship

The Supreme Court has not based its ripeness doctrine for agency rules on the APA. Rather, even though APA §704 appears to grant a right to review of "final agency action for which there is no adequate remedy in a court," and the Court acknowledged that rules are final upon promulgation, the Court has created an additional ripeness requirement wholly detached from any statutory mooring. The Court's doctrine holds that a rule is ripe for judicial review upon promulgation (before enforcement) only if the issues are **fit** for judicial review and the party seeking review would suffer substantial **hardship** if review was delayed until after enforcement. *Abbott Laboratories v. Gardner*, 387 U.S. 136 (1967). If the fitness and hardship tests are not met, a party subject to a rule must wait to challenge the rule as a defense to enforcement, typically in an agency-initiated enforcement proceeding.

F   A   Q

Q: Does the promulgation of a rule constitute "final agency action" under the APA?

A: The *Abbott Labs* Court concluded that the promulgation of a rule pursuant to §553's notice and comment rulemaking provision is final under APA §704 because it is clearly the end of the process of formulating the rule — there are no further administrative steps needed to give the rule the force of law. Further, requiring an enforcement order before judicial review may be sought would restrict judicial review to orders, and nothing in the APA confines the availability of judicial review to review of "orders." However, because of the independent problem of ripeness, the Court allows pre-enforcement review of regulations only when the fitness and hardship tests are met.

The source of the fitness and hardship test is unclear. It does not come from the definition of "final agency action" under the APA since the Court in *Abbott Labs* decided that a rule is final agency action when it is promulgated. It is not part of a constitutional ripeness requirement since the Court will allow review immediately upon promulgation if Congress so specifies. It must, therefore, derive from a prudential concern with ripeness under which the Court tries to avoid premature resolution of disputes when possible.

An issue is fit for pre-enforcement judicial review if no further factual development is necessary for the issue to be resolved. What this means is that the easiest cases for pre-enforcement review are cases that raise purely legal issues. The *Abbott Labs* case is an example in which judicial review of a rule raised purely legal issues. In *Abbott Labs*, a regulation was promulgated requiring drug manufacturers to use the generic name, along with the trade name, of medication every time the trade name appeared on the drug's packaging. The drug manufacturers immediately challenged the "every time" requirement, and the only issue in the case was whether the Food and Drug Administration (FDA) had statutory authority for the "every time" requirement. The Court held that this issue was fit for preenforcement review because it was purely legal. There were no issues regarding particular labels or particular situations that would need to be resolved in order to decide on the legality of the rule. An issue is not fit for immediate judicial review when it is unclear what the regulation means or when it is likely to be applied. In a companion case to *Abbott Labs, Gardner v. Toilet Goods Association, Inc.*, 387 U.S. 158 (1967), a cosmetics manufacturer sought immediate review of a regulation requiring cosmetics manufacturers to permit FDA inspectors to have "free access" to certain manufacturing facilities. The Court held that the issue was not fit for review because it was unclear when the FDA would actually order inspections.

There is sufficient hardship to warrant pre-enforcement judicial review if it would be very expensive to comply with the regulation immediately (which might ultimately be overturned) and if special problems would arise for a party who violated the regulation to provoke an enforcement action (in order to get judicial review of the rule). In *Abbott Labs*, the Court held that the hardship was sufficient because it would be very costly for the drug manufacturers to print new labels and destroy those already in stock. Further, violation of the regulation carried with it the risk of criminal penalties and seizures of improperly labeled medication. It would damage the drug manufacturers' reputations to willfully violate an agency regulation if they ultimately lost on judicial review, and the Court noted that public confidence is very important to the drug industry.

There is not sufficient hardship for immediate judicial review if the regulation promulgated would not be expensive to comply with and if there are no substantial impediments to challenging the legality of the regulation on judicial review of an enforcement action. In *Toilet Goods*, the regulation provided that the cosmetics manufacturers must allow inspections or lose the certifications that allowed them to market their cosmetics. The Court held that there was not sufficient hardship for immediate judicial review despite the fact that the agency had the power to immediately suspend certification, and thus ban the sale of the company's products, if access were denied. The Court based its holding on the fact that the regulation did not actually require the manufacturers to change their behavior, and they could promptly challenge any suspension of certification services on judicial review.

F A Q

Q: Should pre-enforcement review be the norm?

A: Justice Thomas, in a dissenting opinion in *Shalala v. Illinois Council on Long Term Care, Inc.*, 529 U.S. 1, 33 (2000), argued that the case law is best explained as embodying a "longstanding presumption in favor of pre-enforcement judicial review." Justice Thomas's basic argument in favor of such a presumption is that review delayed is often review denied because a party who must await enforcement before seeking review of a rule will often find it cheaper to knuckle under and obey the agency's rule even if there is a good argument that the rule is unlawful. Justice Thomas does not think that each individual party seeking review should have to prove hardship. Rather, he believes that because hardship exists in most cases, courts should presume that pre-enforcement review is available and deny it only in those rare cases in which there is good reason not to allow it.

Note that Justice Thomas's analysis proceeds from a presumption in favor of judicial review and that the value of judicial review is largely to ensure that the executive branch follows the law. This particular commitment to the rule of law is not shared by all members of the Court. For example, recall that Justice Scalia found in his *Morrison v. Olson* dissent that one of the primary protections provided to the executive branch by separation of powers was the power to control whether executive branch officials were investigated and prosecuted for their wrongdoing. And in his opinion for the Court in the *Lujan* case, Justice Scalia explained that "vindicating . . . the public interest in government observance of the Constitution and laws . . . is the function of Congress and the Chief Executive" not the function of the courts. To allow standing based merely on executive violation of the law, without concrete injury to any particular party, would, according to the opinion, "permit Congress to transfer from the President to the courts the Chief Executive's most important constitutional duty to 'take Care that the Laws be faithfully executed.' " *Lujan*, 504 U.S. at 577.

Finality and Informal Agency Action

Sometimes it is difficult to discern whether **informal agency action** is final and reviewable. If further proceedings are contemplated to determine whether a violation has actually occurred, the issuance of a citation alleging a regulatory violation is not final. If, however, the agency makes a determination that a regulated party must pay a fine or change its conduct, no matter how informally that determination is made, if no further agency proceedings are contemplated, the determination is final and likely to be ripe for judicial review.

Finality is more difficult to determine when regulated parties seek advice or permission to engage in a course of conduct from an agency. Regulated parties seek guidance from agencies all the time, often informally by writing a letter to an agency. In general, the more formal the agency action is, the more likely it is going to constitute final action. However, when an informal agency action has the effect of granting or denying permission to take a requested course of action, a court might consider it as final agency action even though the decision was made without any formal procedures. For example, the Secretary of Transportation's approval of the route and design of the interstate highway involved in the *Overton Park* case was final agency action, despite the fact that it was made without a rulemaking or adjudicatory procedure.

Agencies provide informal guidance by letter or other methods all the time, and normally such actions are not final and reviewable. For example, the Sixth Circuit held that an agency web site posting stating that plaintiff's antilock braking system for trucks did not meet NHTSA's safety standards was not reviewable because it was tentative and based on incomplete information and because it had no legal consequences. See *Air Brake Systems, Inc. v. Mineta*, 357 F.3d 632 (6th Cir. 2004). If, however, an agency responds informally to an inquiry from a regulated party that a certain course of conduct would violate the law or is subject to a specified regulatory burden, the agency's response may be final and subject to immediate judicial review. See *National Automatic Laundry and Cleaning Council v. Shultz*, 443 F.2d 689 (D.C. Cir. 1971). The determination of whether such agency action is final is similar to the "fitness and hardship" tests that govern whether review of a regulation may be sought immediately upon promulgation, without waiting for an enforcement action. For example, a national bank asked the Comptroller of the Currency, who is in charge of enforcing legal restrictions on national bank activity, whether it may offer a new banking product without violating restrictions imposed by federal law. The Comptroller answered by letter that the bank would be violating the law if it offered the product. Because the informal ruling has the effect of denying the bank permission to offer the product, the Seventh Circuit found that immediate judicial review is available in such a case. See *First National Bank of Chicago v. Comptroller of the Currency*, 956 F.2d 1360 (7th Cir. 1992).

If the agency answers a request for action with a firm statement that it has decided not to act, that decision can be a "final agency action" subject to judicial review. However, if an agency has not answered a request for action or has explained its inaction as a delay for further study of whether action is appropriate, inaction may not be final agency action subject to judicial review. Generally, whether agency inaction has ripened into a refusal to act is a factual question concerning the significance of inaction in the particular context. See *Oil, Chemical & Atomic Workers Union v. OSHA*, 145 F.3d 120 (3d Cir. 1998). Courts are reluctant to review agency action for excessive delay because such review infringes on the agency's prosecutorial discretion. Nonetheless, in extreme cases in which an agency has delayed excessively when it is statutorily required to act, a court may find the delay reviewable and order the agency to act. See *Public Citizen Health Research Group v. Chao*, 314 F.3d 143 (3d Cir. 2002).

If agency inaction occurs in the context of an exercise of an agency's prosecutorial discretion, even if the agency inaction amounts to a final decision not to act, the agency's inaction will not be reviewable unless the agency's statute meets the requirements for review of prosecutorial discretion, i.e., it must contain criteria under which the agency is required to act. Normally, this requirement is satisfied by a statute that requires agency action in an emergency, because Congress tends to define emergency circumstances and prescribe agency action when the definition is satisfied.

(3) Exhaustion of Administrative Remedies Prior to Seeking Judicial Review

One of the oldest, most established doctrines in administrative law is that challengers must **exhaust** remedies within the agency before seeking judicial review. Courts have applied this doctrine most strongly in cases of agency adjudication where there are normally one or two appeals available within the agency. However, in APA cases, there is no general exhaustion requirement beyond APA §704's finality requirement. Only when a statute or rule requires exhaustion does the requirement apply in a case subject to the APA. *Darby v. Cisneros*, 509 U.S. 137 (1993). More on this below.

Sidebar

TIMING OF REVIEW IN EMERGENCIES

Perhaps the strongest case for reviewability of an agency refusal to take enforcement action exists when the agency is required to act in an emergency and a member of the public petitions for agency action claiming that there is an emergency. Agency inaction in the face of a claimed emergency may amount to a final rejection of the claim that an emergency exists. For example, the Secretary of Agriculture had the power (since transferred to the EPA) on a finding of an imminent hazard to the public, to order an immediate suspension of the registration of a pesticide and to continue the suspension during a process for determining whether the registration should be cancelled. In addition to cancellation, environmental groups petitioned for immediate suspension of the registration of the pesticide. More than a year after the petition for suspension was filed, the Secretary had not acted on it. The Court of Appeals held that delay in granting a suspension is reviewable since the delay is tantamount to a denial of suspension because the delay indicates that the Secretary does not agree with the petitioner that there is an imminent hazard to the public. However, the court found it necessary on two occasions to remand the suspension issue to the Secretary for findings so that it could effectively review the Secretary's decision. See *Environmental Defense Fund v. Hardin*, 428 F.2d 1093 (D.C. Cir. 1970); *Environmental Defense Fund v. Ruckelshaus*, 439 F.2d 584 (D.C. Cir. 1971).

F A Q

Q: What is the difference between ripeness and exhaustion of remedies?

A: Sometimes the two are the same: In some circumstances, a claim against an agency may not be ripe until available remedies are exhausted especially if the initial decision is preliminary and only after the later remedy is exhausted does the agency decision appear to be actually final. However, in many situations the two issues are distinct. For example, suppose a prisoner claims the food he is being served is lacking in sufficient nutritional value. That claim would be ripe as soon as the prisoner was served one allegedly bad meal. However, if there is a procedure within the prison for complaining about the food, exhaustion principles might require the prisoner to use that complaint system before bringing the claim to court. Now suppose the prisoner hears that the prison is considering switching to a new food service company with a reputation for serving substandard food. Ripeness principles might require delaying any suit alleging that this vendor's food is substandard until after the vendor is actually chosen and begins to serve food.

The requirement that parties seeking judicial review of agency action exhaust their administrative remedies before going to court is one of the pillars of the common law of judicial review. It applies even if the claim is that the agency lacks jurisdiction. A party who claims that an agency lacks jurisdiction to subject the party to an enforcement hearing must await a final agency order and challenge the agency's jurisdiction on judicial review. The regulated party may not seek an injunction against the hearing. See *Myers v. Bethlehem Shipbuilding Corp.*, 303 U.S. 41 (1938). In *Myers*, the NLRB charged Bethlehem with unfair labor practices. Rather than seek a hearing on the complaint before the Board, Bethlehem went straight to federal court to enjoin further administrative proceedings on the ground that it was not engaged in interstate commerce and thus not within the Board's jurisdiction. The Supreme Court held that Bethlehem should have sought relief first in the agency, based on a well-established common law requirement of exhaustion.

Under traditional administrative law understandings, there are three exceptions to the requirement of exhaustion of available administrative remedies. Exhaustion is not required if

1. exhaustion would cause undue prejudice to the protection of the rights at issue;
2. the administrative agency lacks power to grant effective relief; or
3. the exhaustion would be futile because the administrative body is biased or has predetermined the issue.

See *McCarthy v. Madigan*, 503 U.S. 140 (1992).

For example, in *McCarthy*, a prisoner sued prison officials for damages because of alleged unconstitutional conditions in the prison. There is an administrative process within the prison under which an order to improve the conditions can be issued, but no damages can be awarded. The prisoner was not required to exhaust administrative remedies because the remedy sought in the lawsuit — damages — was not available in the administrative proceeding. *McCarthy v. Madigan*, 503 U.S. 140 (1992).

The policies behind the exhaustion requirement include avoiding needless judicial intervention into administrative affairs, allowing an agency to correct its own errors, and sharpening the issues and the record for judicial review. See *McCarthy v. Madigan.*

Despite the venerability and attractiveness of the exhaustion doctrine, the Supreme Court has taken a wholly statutory approach with regard to exhaustion of remedies in cases governed by the APA, holding that there is no exhaustion requirement in addition to the finality criteria of APA §704. APA §704 states that an agency action is final even if further appeal within the agency is available "unless the agency otherwise requires by rule and provides that the action meanwhile is inoperative, for an appeal to superior agency authority." Because of this provision of §704, the Court has held that exhaustion in cases governed by the APA is required only of those remedies expressly required to be exhausted by statute, or when an agency rule requires appeal within the agency before judicial review and when the administrative action is made inoperative pending that review. *Darby v. Cisneros*, 509 U.S. 137 (1993). If APA §704 is met, no further exhaustion is required.

> ### Sidebar
>
> **EXHAUSTION AND FINALITY**
>
> Note the difference between the Court's treatment of §704's exhaustion provision and its treatment of §704's finality provision. In *Abbott Labs*, the Court expressly found the issuance of a rule to be "final agency action" within the meaning of §704, but it still constructed a non-statutory test for ripeness of challenges to rules. With regard to exhaustion, however, the *Darby* Court insisted that under the terms of the statute, courts could not require exhaustion without a basis in a valid statute or rule.

(4) Mootness: When Is It Too Late to Seek Review?

A case is moot if there is no longer a live controversy between the parties. If a party is no longer subject to an agency rule, or if the agency repeals the rule, a claim for judicial review of the rule may be moot. For example, if a prisoner seeks injunctive relief to improve prison conditions and is released from prison, the prisoner's claim is highly likely to be moot. The released prisoner may still have a damages claim for past treatment, but no longer has a live controversy with the prison over treatment in the future. Mootness has sometimes been characterized as standing over time—a plaintiff in essence loses her standing when she is no longer subject to the challenged agency conduct.

Mootness is a flexible doctrine, and moot cases are allowed to continue under certain circumstances. The most prominent exception to the mootness doctrine is when the claim is "capable of repetition yet evading review." These cases often involve inevitable mootness when the time necessary for litigating a claim is longer than the time the plaintiff will have an actual controversy. For example, a pregnant woman who seeks an injunction against a law that restricts abortion may not be able to litigate the claim within the period of pregnancy. Such a case is not moot because otherwise all such claims will be moot by the time they are resolved.

A moot case may also be allowed to proceed where the mootness is caused by the defendant's decision to voluntarily cease the challenged conduct. In such cases, the courts have reasoned that as long as the defendant is free to resume the challenged conduct, the case should be allowed to go forward, lest all efforts at resolution are frustrated by voluntary cessation until after the case is dismissed for mootness. This exception is not satisfied if an agency is forced to change its rules—for example by a statutory amendment by Congress—because then the agency is not free to resume the challenged conduct.

SUMMARY

■ A petition for review must be brought in a court with jurisdiction over the action. Jurisdiction involves which court can hear the petition for review and not whether the particular agency action is reviewable. Jurisdiction is thus distinct from reviewability. The most common issue is whether the case belongs in the district court or court of appeals. If a statute provides for review in the court of appeals, that's where the case belongs. Otherwise, the petition should be filed in the district court.

■ The APA grants a right to obtain judicial review of "agency action made reviewable by statute and final agency action for which there is no adequate remedy in a court" to persons suffering "legal wrong" because of agency action, or "adversely affected or aggrieved by agency action within the meaning of a relevant statute."

■ There is a strong legal presumption in favor of judicial review of agency action.

■ Judicial review is not available if a statute explicitly precludes judicial review. APA §701(a)(1).

■ Judicial review is also not available if agency action is committed to agency discretion by law. APA §701(a)(2). This exception is satisfied where the governing statute supplies no law or clear standards for a court to apply to judge the correctness of agency action, where the governing statute appears to vest unreviewable discretion in the agency, and where the agency action falls into a category of agency action that has traditionally been unreviewable.

■ Parties seeking judicial review must satisfy APA and constitutional tests for standing. The basic constitutional test for standing is that the party seeking judicial review must have suffered an "injury in fact" that was "fairly traceable" to the challenged conduct such that the injury is remediable by judicial action. For standing under the APA, the party also must be within the zone of interests addressed by the regulatory statute.

■ Only final agency action is reviewable. Further, the case must be ripe and not moot, and administrative remedies must be exhausted.

■ Although agency rules are final when promulgated, judicial review of a rule must await enforcement unless the petitioner establishes fitness for immediate review and hardship if review is delayed until after enforcement.

■ In cases governed by the APA, there is no exhaustion requirement separate from the APA's finality criteria. However, ripeness concerns may delay judicial review. In non-APA cases, courts may require exhaustion of administrative remedies unless one of the traditional exceptions applies.

CONNECTIONS

Reviewability and Separation of Powers

Many of the issues that come up in reviewability and standing cases implicate separation of powers because they involve whether Congress has the power to subject executive action to scrutiny in court. Justice Scalia has made separation of powers an explicit element of his standing analysis. The availability of judicial review is also important to separation of powers analysis because judicial review may reduce concerns over excessive delegation to agencies. See Chapter 2.

Reviewability and Scope of Review

Once reviewability is established, the next big issue is the scope or standard of review. See Chapter 4.

Citizens' Suits as an Alternative to Review

In recent years, Congress has included citizens' suit provisions in many regulatory statutes. These grant a statutory right to almost anyone to challenge agency action. However, citizens' suit plaintiffs must meet constitutional standing requirement. For more detail on citizens' suits, see Chapter 9.

Procedural Injuries

Administrative law is largely procedural, and the Supreme Court has recognized parties injured by administrative action should have standing to challenge procedural violations even if they cannot prove that the agency would have ultimately acted differently had it followed proper procedures. For more on APA procedural requirements, see Chapters 7 and 8.

Scope of Judicial Review of Administrative Decisions

OVERVIEW

This chapter examines the scope of judicial review of agency action, including how to decide which standard of review applies, and what each standard means when applied to various types of agency action. The chapter includes examination of the special rules that govern judicial review of agency legal interpretations and judicial review of an agency's denial of a petition for rulemaking. As we shall see in this chapter, many issues concerning judicial review boil down to how much deference the reviewing court will afford to the agency.

Unless the agency's enabling act or some other statute states otherwise, the standard of review of agency action is determined by applying Administrative Procedure Act (APA) §706. APA §706 lists the various standards of judicial review that apply to agency action. While some of the standards apply to all agency action, others apply only when specified in the particular provisions of APA §706. The arbitrary, capricious standard of review, which is considered the APA's most deferential standard, applies to all agency action. The substantial evidence test applies only to formal adjudication and formal rulemaking, and de novo review applies rarely, only when new factual issues properly arise for the first time on judicial review or when agency adjudicatory procedures are inadequate.

APA §706 directs reviewing courts to examine the whole record when conducting judicial review, not merely those parts of the record that support the agency's action. The record consists of the information the agency had before it at the time it made its decision. Post hoc rationalizations for agency action are disfavored because the agency's action is judged on the record available at the time the decision was made.

For agency action to survive review under the arbitrary, capricious test, the agency must apply the correct legal standard, consider all relevant factors, evaluate alternatives, and explain its conclusions on issues raised in the decisionmaking process. An agency action is considered arbitrary or capricious when the agency fails to consider all relevant factors, considers irrelevant factors, or makes a clear error in judgment. The agency decision must not be so irrational that the court cannot help but conclude that the decision was not the product of the application of agency expertise to the problem. In recent decisions, the courts have insisted that agencies consider only those factors contained in governing statutes.

The arbitrary, capricious standard also applies to the review of agency decisions denying petitions to initiate rulemaking. However, the Supreme Court has said such review is extremely limited and highly deferential. Similarly, the D.C. Circuit has said that a decision not to initiate a rulemaking should be reversed only for compelling cause, such as plain error of law or a fundamental change in the factual premises previously considered by the agency. In the analogous situation of an agency refusal to take enforcement action (in the rare setting in which such a refusal is reviewable), the Supreme Court stated that the reviewing court should ordinarily look only at the agency's statement of reasons for not taking enforcement action and should reverse only if the statement is completely irrational.

Judicial review of agency statutory interpretation of a statute administered by the agency is conducted under the *Chevron* standard. Under *Chevron*, the first step is to decide whether Congress's intent on the matter is clear. If it is, the agency must follow Congress's clear intent and the Court will reverse any agency interpretation contrary to that intent. However, if Congress's intent is not clear, either because the statute is ambiguous or because Congress explicitly delegated interpretive power to the agency, the reviewing court should uphold any permissible interpretation made by the agency. *Chevron* applies only when Congress intended that agency interpretations have the force of law. The *Mead* case teaches that the best indication that Congress intended for agency interpretations to have the force of law is when Congress authorized the agency to use "relatively formal procedures" such as notice and comment rulemaking or formal adjudication. If *Chevron* does not apply, the *Skidmore* standard applies, which tells courts to look at all the circumstances to determine whether the agency's interpretation merits deference.

The less deferential substantial evidence test requires that agency decisions be supported, on the record as a whole, by enough relevant evidence as a reasonable mind might accept as adequate to support the agency's conclusion. This test is the same standard under which courts review jury verdicts. When agency action is reviewed de novo, the reviewing court decides the matter anew, without regard to the agency's decision.

The APA instructs reviewing courts to "hold unlawful and set aside" agency action that fails to meet the applicable standard of review. When courts reject agency action on judicial review, they tend to remand the matter to the agency, largely because courts do not have the authority to step into an agency's shoes and take positive action. Rather, the courts view their role as telling agencies what they may or may not do. In some circumstances, particularly on review of individual benefits or permit adjudications, the reviewing court may reverse the agency and order the award of the benefit or permit when it appears that the agency has no basis for denial.

A. CHOOSING STANDARDS OF JUDICIAL REVIEW UNDER THE APA

1. APA §706 Standards of Review; Definition and Mechanics
2. How to Decide Which Provision of §706 Applies

B. DEFINING AND APPLYING THE STANDARDS OF REVIEW

1. Arbitrary, Capricious
2. Special Cases: Review of Decisions Not to Regulate or Enforce, Deregulation, and Agency Policy Changes
3. Special Case: Agency Statutory Interpretation

C. REVIEW OF QUESTIONS OF FACT AFTER AGENCY ADJUDICATION: THE SUBSTANTIAL EVIDENCE TEST

1. The Substantial Evidence Test Defined
2. The Substantial Evidence Test Applied

D. DE NOVO REVIEW OF QUESTIONS OF FACT

E. REMEDIES ON JUDICIAL REVIEW

A. Choosing Standards of Judicial Review Under the APA

The **scope of judicial review** is established in virtually every case by a statute that specifies a standard against which agency action is measured by the reviewing court. The most common statutory source is the APA, which lists several standards of review. Most of the APA's standards apply to all agency action while some, namely the substantial evidence test and de novo review, apply only in specified circumstances. However, if an agency's enabling act contains a provision establishing a standard of review that differs from the applicable APA standard, which many do, the enabling act provision takes precedence over the APA standard. The following table contains a simplified model of the applicability of APA standards of judicial review.

Form of Agency Action	APA Standard of Review
Formal Adjudication	Substantial Evidence[*]
Formal Rulemaking	Substantial Evidence[*]
Informal (Notice and Comment) Rulemaking	Arbitrary, Capricious, Abuse of Discretion, Not in Accordance with Law
Informal Agency Action[**]	Arbitrary, Capricious, Abuse of Discretion, Not in Accordance with Law
Agency Adjudication with Inadequate Procedures	Trial De Novo
New Issues after Non-adjudicatory Agency Enforcement	Trial De Novo (of new issues)

---

[*] As discussed below, pp. 118–119, in some decisions, courts appear to review the facts in these cases under the substantial evidence standard and the policy decisions under the arbitrary, capricious test.

[**] "Informal agency action" refers to the great mass of agency action that is done informally, that is not within the confines of any specific procedural model. The term "informal adjudication" is also sometimes used to refer to this category.

The two standards of review that most commonly apply to agency action are the "**arbitrary, capricious, an abuse of discretion or otherwise contrary to law**" standard and the "**unsupported by substantial evidence**" standard. The arbitrary, capricious standard, which applies to informal rulemaking and informal agency action more generally, is supposed to be the most deferential among the commonly applied standards. The substantial evidence test, which applies to formal adjudication and formal rulemaking, is supposed to be somewhat less deferential. However, in actual practice it is often difficult to detect much of a difference, especially because there is great variation in how the standards are applied among courts and even across cases in the same court.

The remainder of this chapter proceeds in three steps as follows. First, the standards of judicial review contained in APA §706 are defined. Second, the chapter looks at how we decide which of the various standards of review applies in a particular case. Third, the various standards of review are analyzed in the context of the situations in which they each apply.

(1) APA §706 Standards of Review; Definition and Mechanics

Given the centrality of the APA to judicial review of agency action, it is worthwhile to begin our examination of the scope of judicial review by quoting APA §706 in its entirety:

> §706: To the extent necessary to decision and when presented, the reviewing court shall decide all relevant questions of law, interpret constitutional and statutory provisions, and determine the meaning or applicability of the terms of an agency action. The reviewing court shall:
>
> (1) compel agency action unlawfully withheld or unreasonably delayed; and
>
> (2) hold unlawful and set aside agency action, findings, and conclusions found to be —
>
> (A) arbitrary, capricious, an abuse of discretion, or otherwise not in accordance with law;
>
> (B) contrary to constitutional right, power, privilege, or immunity;
>
> (C) in excess of statutory jurisdiction, authority, or limitations, or short of statutory right;
>
> (D) without observance of procedure required by law;
>
> (E) unsupported by substantial evidence in a case subject to sections 556 and 557 of this title or otherwise reviewed on the record of an agency hearing provided by statute; or
>
> (F) unwarranted by the facts to the extent that the facts are subject to trial de novo by the reviewing court.
>
> In making the foregoing determinations, the court shall review the whole record or those parts of it cited by a party, and due account shall be taken of the rule of prejudicial error.

APA §706 thus directs courts to "hold unlawful and set aside" agency action that fails to meet the applicable standard of judicial review. Some of the standards of review listed in §706 incorporate legal standards found elsewhere such as the Constitution ("contrary to constitutional right, power, privilege, or immunity"), substantive statutes ("in excess of statutory jurisdiction, authority, or limitations, or short of statutory right"), and procedural statutes and rules ("without observance of procedure required by law"). Our focus here is largely on the three standards that relate directly to the substantive wisdom and legality of agency action, namely §706(2)(A), (E) and (F), the provisions that specify, respectively, the arbitrary, capricious standard, the substantial evidence test and de novo review.

Section 706 also instructs the reviewing court to "review the **whole record** or those parts of it cited by a party." This provision was meant to reject the practice that some pre-APA reviewing courts had adopted of looking only at those parts of the record that supported the agency's action. In some early cases of judicial review of agency action, if the record contained slight evidence to support the agency's decision, the reviewing court would affirm the agency even if the contrary evidence was overwhelming. Under the APA, the reviewing court must weigh the evidence in support of the agency against the evidence against the agency. Thus, agency action supported by some evidence might be overturned on review if there is overwhelming evidence in the record opposing the agency's action.

The record that was before the agency is supposed to be the exclusive basis for judicial review in two separate but related senses. First, reviewing courts should not look beyond the record that was before the agency at the time the agency made its decision. Second, the agency may not support its decision with information that it did not have at the time it made its decision or with post hoc rationalizations that were not offered at the time the decision was made. Further, courts prefer to look at the actual documents and other materials the agency had before it. Affidavits (or other evidence of the basis of the agency's decision created for the judicial review litigation) are disfavored and should only be used when it is not possible to create an adequate record out of the material that the agency had before it at the time it made its decision.

Sidebar

REVIEW ON THE RECORD

The Supreme Court has stated a strong preference for review based on the record before the agency at the time the decision was made. In *Citizens to Preserve Overton Park v. Volpe*, 401 U.S. 402 (1972), the District Court had based its review largely on testimony and affidavits of the officials involved in making the decision under review. The Supreme Court remanded the case to the District Court with instructions to examine the documents and other materials that were before the agency when it made its decision, and use affidavits and testimony about the decisionmaking process only when necessary to supplement the record.

(2) How to Decide Which Provision of §706 Applies

Those provisions of §706(2) with no textual guidance on when they apply are applicable to all reviewable administrative action. Specifically, subsections (2)(A) (arbitrary, capricious), (2)(B) (contrary to the Constitution), (2)(C) (without statutory authority), and (2)(D) (contrary to procedural requirements) apply to all agency action. Subsections (2)(B), (2)(C), and (2)(D) are rarely mentioned because it seems to go without saying that courts have the authority to ensure that all procedural requirements are followed and that agency action is taken only with statutory authority and within constitutional limits. Subsection (2)(A), however, which provides that agency action should be set aside if it is "arbitrary, capricious, an abuse of discretion, or otherwise not in accordance with law," is adverted to frequently. It is the substantive standard of review that is applied to the results of most agency rulemaking proceedings and also to most informal agency decisions. Because it has no limitations on its application, the arbitrary, capricious test is the standard that is applied when no other substantive standard of review applies.

F   A   Q

Q: What does it mean for a standard of review to be more or less deferential than an alternative standard?

A: Basically, the more deferential the review, the less carefully the reviewing court will scrutinize the agency decision. Under non-deferential review, the court will make sure that the agency decision is correct. Under deferential review, the court may ask only whether the agency's decision is rational within a range of possible reasonable outcomes.

The more deferential the standard of review, the more likely it is that a court will accept the agency's decision. Under deferential review, the reviewing court might affirm the agency decision unless it is patently obvious that the agency has made such a serious error that the decision is irrational. A court conducting deferential review may not scrutinize the record very carefully or demand much detail in the agency's reasoning. Conversely, less deferential review makes it more likely that the reviewing court will reject the agency decision. A court conducting non-deferential review is likely to look carefully at the record and demand a clear and comprehensive explanation from the agency. The least deferential standard is de novo review, under which the court re-determines the matter without regard to the agency's decision. The party challenging agency action will, if possible, argue for the application of a less deferential standard, while the party defending agency action, usually the agency, will argue for greater deference.

Unless a particular statute specifies a different standard, the arbitrary, capricious standard of judicial review applies to judicial review of **informal (notice and comment) rulemaking** and to review of **informal agency action.** "Informal agency action" is agency action for which no statute specifies a procedure or for which the statutory procedure is less formal than formal adjudication or informal rulemaking. For example, the decision of the Secretary of Transportation to approve the routing of an interstate highway through Overton Park in Memphis, Tennessee, reviewed in the *Overton Park* case, was an informal agency action because the statute requiring the Secretary's approval did not specify a procedure for making the decision. The Secretary and local authorities apparently held open hearings and received written input from interested parties, but they did not follow any statutorily prescribed procedural model. Informal agency decisionmaking is ubiquitous, and the standard of review in such cases is the arbitrary, capricious test.

The two other substantive standards of review in §706(2) (substantial evidence and de novo review) apply only to those agency actions specified in each provision. Subsection (2)(E) specifies that the substantial evidence test applies only to cases "subject to sections 556 and 557 of this title or otherwise reviewed on the record of an agency hearing provided by statute." Sections 556 and 557 are the formal adjudication and formal rulemaking provisions of the APA, and thus the substantial evidence test applies only when the results of formal procedures are reviewed.

As is discussed in more detail in Chapter 6 on choice of procedure, **formal rulemaking**, which denotes rulemaking conducted in an adjudicatory, trial-type procedure, is rare and courts tend not to require it unless the statute uses the precise language "on the record of an agency hearing." If a statute merely requires a "hearing" or "public hearings" before rules are issued,

Sidebar

INFORMAL RULEMAKING AND INFORMAL ACTION

The term "informal" as applied to agency procedures has different meanings in different contexts. "Informal rulemaking" is rulemaking conducted under APA §553's notice and comment procedures. "Informal agency action" denotes agency action taken informally, often with little or no notice or opportunity to comment. Some instances of informal adjudication resemble hearings, for example when a school administrator determines whether a student be dismissed for poor academic performance. Other instances are nothing like hearings, for example when the National Park Service rejects an application for a campsite at a National Forest.

courts normally interpret these terms as requiring only informal procedures. In fact, the word "hearing" has been interpreted to include paper notice and comment proceedings. When only a paper hearing is required, the substantial evidence test will not apply because the statute does not require either formal procedures under §§556 and 557 or rulemaking "on the record after hearing."

The APA is less clear on when **de novo review** applies. De novo review is the least deferential standard of review, basically allowing the reviewing court to re-determine the facts for itself without regard to any prior agency decision on the matter. Section 706(2)(F) provides that agency determination of facts should be overturned if "unwarranted by the facts to the extent that the facts are subject to trial de novo by the reviewing court." The statute does not tell us when "the facts are subject to trial de novo by the reviewing court." The Supreme Court, relying on a legislative committee report, has specified that de novo review is available only when the "[agency] action is adjudicatory in nature and the agency fact-finding procedures are inadequate [or when] issues that were not before the agency are raised in a proceeding to enforce non-adjudicatory agency action." *Citizens to Preserve Overton Park, Inc. v. Volpe*, 401 U.S. 402, 415 (1971). It should be noted that the Attorney General's Manual on the Administrative Procedure Act disagreed with this interpretation, stating that Congress meant to codify existing situations in which de novo review had been required by statute or judicial decision, not to establish a standard under which courts might prescribe de novo review in new situations.[1]

This entire discussion rests on the important assumption that the agency's enabling act or some other statute does not specify a standard of review other than the one that would apply ordinarily under the APA. Congress is free to specify a standard of review other than the one that would apply under the terms of APA §706. When Congress does so, the scope of review is governed by the particular statute, not the APA. For example, the Occupational Safety and Health Act specifies that OSHA rules made under informal rulemaking procedures are subject to review under the substantial evidence test.[2] (Absent this statutory provision, review would be had under the arbitrary, capricious test.)

Applying the substantial evidence test to informal rulemaking can be awkard, because it is unclear what it means for there to be substantial evidence in support of the sort of policy decision that is often the most important aspect of informal

Sidebar

STANDARD OF REVIEW FOR INFORMAL RULEMAKING

The Supreme Court has twice stated incorrectly in dicta that the standard of review for informal rulemaking conducted under APA §553 is the substantial evidence test. The Court first stated this in *Citizens to Preserve Overton Park v. Volpe*, 401 U.S. 402, 414 (1972) and then repeated it in *Lincoln v. Vigil*, 508 U.S. 182, 198 (1993). The standard of review for informal rulemaking conducted under APA §553 is the arbitrary, capricious test of §706(2)(A) because, as stated in §706(2)(E), substantial evidence applies only if proceedings are conducted pursuant to §§556 and 557, not to proceedings conducted under §553.

[1]Department of Justice, Attorney General's Manual on the Administrative Procedure Act 109, 111 (1947). The Attorney General's Manual was prepared shortly after the passage of the APA as a sort of guide to the new statute. It is often treated as authoritative on the meaning of the APA, but caution should be exercised in this regard because often the views expressed are more in favor of executive power than the language or history of the APA can bear.
[2]See 29 U.S.C. §655(f).

rulemaking. Perhaps the answer to this question may lie in the nature of rulemaking under the OSH Act. OSHA rules often involve assessment of the safe level or method of employees' exposure to a dangerous substance or process. Perhaps Congress expected that OSHA rules would be more fact based than the more policy-oriented rules issued by other agencies, making substantial evidence a workable standard of review. However, this is not a complete answer, since Congress has not subjected other agencies that make rules based on assessment of scientific facts, such as EPA pollution standards, to substantial evidence review. In the end, this puzzle may not be very important, since it remains unclear whether the choice between the two standards of review has a discernible effect on the outcome of cases.

The party challenging agency action will always argue for application of the least deferential standard of review, while the defender of the agency's action (usually the government) will argue for greater deference. To the party challenging agency action, the arbitrary, capricious test is a fall-back position in case the reviewing court rules against substantial evidence or de novo review. If the court decides that one of §706's less deferential standards of review applies, it will govern because it, in effect, subsumes the more deferential standard. Specifically, if substantial evidence or de novo review is applicable, because they are considered more demanding on the agency than the arbitrary, capricious test, and the agency's action survives substantial evidence or de novo review, it would of necessity also survive arbitrary, capricious review. Thus, even though technically the arbitrary, capricious test applies to all reviewable agency action, there is no reason to resort to it once the action has been reviewed under a less deferential standard.

B. Defining and Applying the Standards of Review

Once the choice of standard of review is made, the next step is to apply the chosen standard of review to the agency action being challenged. Because the application of each varies based on the context, the abstract statement of the particular standard is followed by discussion of how each works in various contexts.

(1) Arbitrary, Capricious

The most important standard of judicial review for our purposes is §706(2)(A)'s **"arbitrary, capricious, abuse of discretion or otherwise not in accordance with law"** standard, often referred to as the "arbitrary and capricious" test. This standard applies to most informal rulemakings and to other informal agency action. Although in pure volume of cases the substantial evidence test may apply more often (because it applies to thousands of formal agency benefits hearings), review of informal rule-making and other less formal agency action is generally more important and garners more attention than review of individual benefits hearings. As elaborated in the pages that follow, the arbitrary, capricious standard requires that agencies base their decisions on consideration of the factors relevant to the regulatory scheme, that they consider alternatives, that their policy conclusions make sense, that the logical path to their conclusions is discernible and that there be a rational connection between the facts found and the policy decisions made. Reviewing courts are not supposed to substitute their judgment for that of the agency but still must conduct a "thorough, probing, in-depth review."

The arbitrary, capricious test is the standard linguistically most suited to apply to agency policy decisions because when reviewing a policy decision, the question is not (or at least not only) whether there is sufficient evidence to justify the decision, but whether the agency decision makes sense in light of the principles and policies underlying the regulatory scheme at issue. Asking whether a policy decision is arbitrary, capricious, an abuse of discretion or not in accordance with law is a more sensible inquiry than simply asking whether it is supported by substantial evidence in the record. In fact, when a court reviews a pure policy decision made by an agency in the course of formal adjudication, it seems that the arbitrary, capricious standard applies to the policy aspect of the case, even though the substantial evidence standard clearly governs review of the agency factual determinations in formal adjudication. See *Allentown Mack Sales and Service, Inc. v. NLRB*, 522 U.S. 359, 364 (1998) (applying arbitrary, capricious standard to NLRB's rule, announced in formal adjudicatory proceedings, governing reasonable doubt concerning employees' continued support for union).

F A Q

Q: Does it really make any difference whether a court applies the arbitrary, capricious test or the substantial evidence test?

A: A great deal of doubt has been expressed over whether there is any detectable difference between substantial evidence review and arbitrary, capricious review of informal rulemaking. Substantial evidence review may allow for greater judicial scrutiny of the scientific or factual bases of agency rulemaking. This might help explain the result in *Industrial Union Dep't, AFC-CIO v. American Petroleum Institute (The Benzene Case)*, 448 U.S. 607 (1980), in which the Court performed relatively non-deferential review of an OSHA rule under the substantial evidence test, which by statute applies to rulemakings conducted under the OSH Act. The Court closely scrutinized the scientific basis for the OSHA rule under review and rejected the agency's more stringent limitation on workplace exposure to benzene as not supported by substantial evidence that the preexisting permissible level of exposure was dangerous.

What is a **policy** decision? A policy decision is a decision by an agency that determines whether regulation is necessary or desirable and what level or form of regulation is appropriate. In some contexts, policy decisions are embedded in more specific questions such as whether a permit or license should be granted or whether a particular project should be funded or approved. Policy decisions are heavily dependent on statutory authority and direction, and in fact as we shall see, reviewing courts have been pushing agencies making policy decisions to consider only the factors explicitly contained in governing statutes. Policy decisions are also heavily dependent on factual determinations, but usually of the legislative type rather than the adjudicatory type. Agencies making policy decisions must consider factual matters such as the current state of the world and how proposed regulation would affect that state, but these factual considerations are often predictive and implicate the agency's technical expertise and are not of the adjudicatory type, which involves determining particularities about a past event. For example, an agency considering whether to require a safety improvement to a product must consider, inter alia, whether the product is currently unsafe, and it must make predictions as to the cost of the improvement and the benefit it would produce in terms of increased safety.

Policy decisions are also intertwined with questions of statutory interpretation and authority. For instance, when the EPA decides what level of a pollutant should be allowed into the atmosphere, it is making a policy decision based on the statutory factors that govern the matter such as health and welfare of the public. By contrast, when the EPA decides whether it has statutory authority to address an issue it may be making a decision of pure statutory interpretation, which may involve a more statutory focus than the typical case of arbitrary, capricious review.

For example, suppose the Occupational Safety and Health Administration (OSHA) decided to regulate exposure to secondhand tobacco smoke in the workplace. When it decides whether regulation of secondhand smoke is necessary, it will look at facts concerning the effects of tobacco smoke on workers, whether regulation would improve the situation, what regulation might cost, and whether there are likely to be any additional unexpected costs or benefits from the regulatory scheme. These are all determinations of legislative fact. OSHA will consider these facts in light of the statutory standard that governs worker safety standards. There may be a question regarding whether OSHA has statutory authority to regulate tobacco smoke at all, and this would be considered a pure question of statutory interpretation rather than a policy decision. Issues may arise concerning the appropriate scope of the regulation. When OSHA decides, for example, which workplaces should be regulated or what level of ventilation should be required in an area where smoking is allowed, it is back to making a policy decision.

As discussed above, agency policy decisions are usually reviewed under the arbitrary, capricious test. This test was first defined by the Supreme Court in *Overton Park* as requiring that agencies make decisions "based on a consideration of the relevant factors," including alternatives to the agency's proposal suggested by the record, without "a clear error in judgment," and under the correct legal standard. *Overton Park*, 401 U.S. at 415-16. When conducting an arbitrary, capricious review, courts must keep in mind that, while the inquiry is "searching and careful," the standard of review is "a narrow one [and t]he court is not empowered to substitute its judgment for that of the agency." *Overton Park*, 401 U.S. at 416. An additional consideration was added by the Supreme Court in the *Airbags Case, Motor Vehicle Manufacturers Association v. State Farm Mutual Automobile Insurance Co.*, 463 U.S. 29 (1983). In its opinion in that case, the Court stated that the agency must "examine the relevant data and articulate a satisfactory explanation for its action including a 'rational connection between the facts found and the choice made.'" Id. at 43, quoting *Burlington Truck Lines, Inc. v. United States*, 371 U.S. 156, 168 (1962). *Burlington Truck Lines*, from which the "rational connection" language is quoted, is a decision applying the substantial evidence standard of review to an instance of formal agency adjudication, supporting the suggestion that there is not much difference between the arbitrary, capricious and substantial evidence standards as applied to policy decisions.

The arbitrary, capricious standard is sometimes referred to as "**hard look review.**" The phrase "hard look" originally referred to the requirement, enunciated in a series of decisions by the Court of Appeals for the District of Columbia Circuit, that the agency must take a "hard look" at the issues. A particularly clear example of the D.C. Circuit's attitude is the following passage:

> The function of the court is to assure that the agency has given reasoned consideration to all the material facts and issues. This calls for insistence that the agency articulate with

reasonable clarity its reasons for decision, and identify the significance of the crucial facts, a course that tends to assure that the agency's policies effectuate general standards, applied without unreasonable discrimination. . . .

Its supervisory function calls on the court to intervene not merely in case of procedural inadequacies, or bypassing of the mandate in the legislative charter, but more broadly if the court becomes aware, especially from a combination of danger signals, that the agency has not really taken a "hard look" at the salient problems, and has not genuinely engaged in reasoned decision-making.

Greater Boston Television Corp. v. FCC, 444 F.2d 841, 851-52 (D.C. Cir. 1970), *cert. denied*, 403 U.S. 923 (1971). This standard is not as stringent as it may appear at first glance. The opinion elaborated that if the agency has acted appropriately, the court's role is limited:

If satisfied that the agency has taken a hard look at the issues with the use of reasons and standards, the court will uphold its findings, though of less than ideal clarity, if the agency's path may reasonably be discerned, though of course the court must not be left to guess as to the agency's findings or reasons.

Id. Considered in this way, the hard look standard's primacy concern appears to be ensuring that the agency has genuinely considered the issues presented in light of the record and the relevant factors, as opposed to having made a purely political decision, without regard to the state of the record.

In some later cases and in some of the commentary, the phrase "hard look" has taken on a different connotation, that when conducting judicial review, the reviewing court should take a "hard look" at the agency decision to determine whether it is supported by the record. As the D.C. Circuit has explained, "As originally articulated the words 'hard look' described the agency's responsibility and not the court's. However, the phrase subsequently evolved to connote the rigorous standard of judicial review applied to increasingly utilized informal rule-making proceedings or to other decisions made upon less than a full trial-type record." *National Lime Ass'n v. Environmental Protection Agency*, 627 F.2d 416, 451 n. 126 (D.C. Cir. 1980) (footnote omitted). See also *Maryland-Nat'l Capital Park and Planning Comm'n v. United States Postal Serv.*, 487 F.2d 1029, 1037-38 (D.C. Cir. 1973) ("Having expressed our view that we should carefully scrutinize this decision, and engage in a 'hard look' at the decision . . . , we turn to the possible significant adverse impact present in this case."). While in the vast majority of cases in which the phrase "hard look" is used it refers to the agency's duty to base its decision on a careful and thorough look at the record, it is sometimes used to refer to the reviewing court's similar responsibility.

In recent years, a great deal of focus has been paid to identifying the **relevant factors** that agencies are supposed to consider and the trend has been to confine agencies to considering the factors statutorily deemed relevant by Congress, rather than more general considerations that might motivate agency decisionmaking across a range of issues. The focus on statutory factors is by no means new. In *Overton Park*, the Supreme Court stated that the first inquiry in applying the arbitrary and capricious test is "whether the Secretary acted within the scope of his authority" i.e., whether the agency properly understood the statutory standard that applied to the matter. The Court elaborated that the district court, on remand, must "consider whether the Secretary properly construed his authority to approve the use of park land as limited to situations where there are no feasible [or prudent] alternative routes." *Overton Park*, 401 U.S. at 416. The relevant factors appear to be those made relevant by governing statutes.

The most significant recent move toward confining agencies to consideration of factors spelled out by Congress in the governing statute is the Supreme Court's opinion in the global warming case, *Massachusetts v. EPA*, 549 U.S. 497 (2007). In that case, a narrow 5-4 majority of the Court very clearly limited the EPA to considering statutory factors as against other sensible, but not statutorily-based factors. The procedural posture of *Massachusetts v. EPA* makes the Court's insistence on statutory factors even more striking. The statute required the EPA regulate air pollutants that, in the Administrator's "judgment cause, or contribute to, air pollution which may reasonably be anticipated to endanger public health or welfare." 42 U.S.C. §7521(a)(1). The Administrator had not made a judgment regarding the pollutants at issue (greenhouse gases) and gave several reasons for declining to regulate greenhouse gas emissions from automobiles, including scientific uncertainty, the existence of voluntary executive branch programs, potential impairment of negotiations with developing countries over global warming, and the "piecemeal" nature of regulating greenhouse gases from automobiles separate from other elements of an anti-global warming strategy. The Court rejected all of these justifications and more, on the basis that "its reasons for action or inaction must conform to the authorizing statute." Even when deciding whether to engage in rulemaking, agencies apparently may consider only those factors made relevant by statute and may not consider irrelevant factors, i.e., factors not made relevant by statute. It is apparently of no moment that an agency has good reasons for acting if those reasons are not within the universe of factors Congress has identified as relevant to the agency's decision.

As the dissent pointed out, the Court's reasoning is problematic because the statute does not explicitly address what factors are relevant to the Administrator's consideration of whether to make a judgment. The statutory factors relied upon by the Court are addressed to the considerations relevant to the Administrator's judgment on whether to act against an air pollutant that the Administrator finds is likely to endanger public health or welfare, not whether to make a judgment concerning a particular pollutant in the first place. See *Massachusetts v. EPA*, 549 U.S. at 549-50 (Scalia J., dissenting). Justice Scalia would defer to the Administrator's decision not to make a judgment if it had any "reasonable basis."

In addition to ensuring that agencies consider the statutory factors, courts have identified additional requirements when reviewing the substantive reasonableness of agency policymaking under the arbitrary, capricious test. One important element of reasoned decisionmaking is the requirement that agencies consider **alternatives** to their proposals that the record suggests. In *Overton Park*, this meant that the agency was required to consider the amount of disruption the highway would cause to the park and whether other proposals would be better in this regard. In the *Airbags Case*, the Court found that the agency erred by not considering mandatory airbags or mandatory non-detachable seat belts as alternatives to the detachable belts that the agency thought would not increase automobile safety.

See *Motor Vehicle Manufacturers Association v. State Farm Mutual Automobile Insurance Co. (The Airbags Case)*, 463 U.S. 29 (1983). In *Scenic Hudson*, the Second Circuit faulted the Federal Power Commission (FPC) for not adequately considering a gas turbine power plant as an alternative to a hydroelectric plant planned for the Hudson River. *Scenic Hudson Preservation Conf. v. FPC (I & II)*, 354 F.2d 608 (2d Cir. 1968) and 453 F.2d 463 (2d Cir. 1971), *cert. denied*, 407 U.S. 926 (1972).

As proof that they considered all relevant factors and alternatives, courts require agencies to **explain** their decisions on major issues that are raised during the decisionmaking process. This includes an explanation adequate to establish that the agency considered relevant factors, that it considered alternatives, and that it considered the comments made during the rulemaking process. For example, in the *Airbags Case*, the fact that the agency did not utter a word about an all-airbags alternative or about simply eliminating the option of detachable seat belts led the Court to conclude that the agency had not considered the relevant alternatives.

The arbitrary, capricious test also requires the reviewing court to confront head-on the **reasonableness** of the agency's decision. The Supreme Court has stated that the reviewing court must ensure that the agency has not "entirely failed to consider an important aspect of the problem, offered an explanation for its decision that runs counter to the evidence before the agency, or is so implausible that it could not be ascribed to a difference in view or the product of agency expertise." *Motor Vehicles*, 463 U.S. at 43. The reviewing court walks a fine line when reviewing the substantive plausibility of agency action. On the one hand, the court must take care not to substitute its policy judgment for that of an agency with superior expertise on the matter. On the other hand, the court must ensure that the agency took a "hard look" at the issues involved and actually applied its expertise in a plausible manner.

The importance of substantive review of agency decisionmaking turns largely on how **deferential** the reviewing court is toward agency action. The Supreme Court's decisions applying the arbitrary, capricious test do not appear to be consistent on this score. In some cases, such as the *Airbags Case* and *Massachusetts v. EPA*, the Court appears to apply a demanding standard when examining the agency's reasoning on matters of policy presumably within the agency's expertise. For a more recent very non-deferential review of agency decisionmaking (herein reviewing the National Highway Transportation Safety Administration's automobile mileage rules), see *Center for Biological Diversity v. National Highway Traffic Safety Administration*, 508 F.3d 508 (9th Cir. 2007).

Sidebar

NOVA SCOTIA FOOD PRODS.

In *United States v. Nova Scotia Food Prods. Corp.*, 568 F.2d 240 (2d Cir. 1977), the Second Circuit faulted the FDA for not providing an adequate response to comments that challenged the necessity of the proposed rules and alleged that the proposed rules would have serious economic consequences for the regulated party making the comments. The FDA promulgated new standards for the preparation of smoked fish because of reports of illnesses caused by the failure of the smoking process to eliminate harmful bacteria. The producers of a particular species of fish submitted comments containing scientific data indicating that their particular fish is safe without the FDA's preferred process and that the economic viability of their product would be destroyed if they were required to use the preferred process for their fish. The FDA promulgated a uniform process applicable to all species of fish without explaining why it rejected the data offered by the producers of that particular kind of fish. This, according to the court of appeals, made the rule invalid. This decision can also be characterized as faulting the agency for not considering the option of different requirements for particular species and for not considering the relevant factor of the potential destruction of the commercial viability of the particular species of fish.

In other cases, the Court applies what seems to be a fairly deferential standard of review, especially when the agency's action implicates agency expertise in technical areas. For example, in *Baltimore Gas & Elec. Co. v. NRDC*, 462 U.S. 87, 103 (1983), decided the same year as the *Airbags Case*, the Court approved a Nuclear Regulatory Commission rule that was based on an assumption that there would be "zero release" of radiation from spent nuclear fuel. The Court stated that the reviewing court "must remember that the Commission is making predictions within its area of special expertise, at the frontiers of science. When examining this kind of scientific determination . . . a reviewing court must generally be at its most deferential." This attitude of extreme deference to scientific judgments is not maintained consistently either in the lower federal courts or at the Supreme Court itself, which makes it somewhat difficult to make generalizations concerning the degree to which the courts defer to agency expertise.

Sidebar

ADEQUACY OF THE RECORD

Even when they conclude that an agency has made a substantive error, courts do not necessarily feel comfortable expressing direct substantive disagreement with agencies. Because of this, what we see in judicial decisions rejecting agency action is that they rarely take issue directly with the correctness or reasonableness of agency action. Rather, the court is more likely to say something like "the record before the agency does not support the rule." Although this looks like a rather moderate statement in that a better record might justify the rule, the court is actually saying that the agency's decision is unreasonable or implausible in light of the information it had before it.

F   A   Q

Q: How deferential is the arbitrary, capricious test?

A: It is not possible to provide a general answer to this question. In some decisions, reviewing courts apply the test in a highly deferential manner, recognizing superior agency expertise and political accountability as reasons to defer to agency decisions, especially on matters of policy entrusted by Congress to an agency. On other decisions, the courts apply the test in a non-deferential manner, treating the agency as excessively political and combing the agency's explanation for gaps in reasoning and inconsistencies. It is sometimes difficult to predict which version of the arbitrary, capricious test will be applied in a particular case.

(2) Special Cases: Review of Decisions Not to Regulate or Enforce, Deregulation, and Agency Policy Changes

Agencies are required to entertain and answer petitions for rulemaking. APA §553 states that "[e]ach agency shall give an interested person the right to petition for the issuance, amendment, or repeal of a rule." Further, APA §555(e) requires agencies to answer petitions and provide reasons for any denial. For a long while, it was an open question whether decisions not to regulate, such as the denial of a petition for rulemaking, were reviewable at all, and if they were reviewable there remained the question of the proper standard of review for such decisions. *Massachusetts v. EPA* provided answers to both of these questions.

As is discussed in more detail in Chapter 3, the Court held in *Massachusetts v. EPA* that the denial of a petition for rulemaking is reviewable. However, review of a denial of a petition asking an agency to conduct a rulemaking is conducted on an extremely deferential version of the arbitrary, capricious test: "Refusals to promulgate rules are . . . susceptible to judicial review, though such review is 'extremely limited' and 'highly deferential.'" *Massachusetts v. EPA*, 549 U.S. at 527-28, (quoting *National Customs Brokers & Forwarders Ass'n of America, Inc. v. United States*, 883 F.2d 93, 96 (D.C. Cir. 1989)). While the Supreme Court has not elaborated on what this deferential, limited judicial review involves, the D.C. Circuit, in the *National Customs* opinion, elaborated a bit, stating that "[w]e will overturn an agency's decision not to initiate a rulemaking only for compelling cause, such as plain error of law or a fundamental change in the factual premises previously considered by the agency." Id. at 96-97.

In the somewhat analogous situation of an agency refusal to take enforcement action (when such a refusal is reviewable because the applicable statute required agency enforcement in some circumstances), the Supreme Court stated that the reviewing court should ordinarily look only at the agency's statement of reasons for not taking enforcement action and should reverse only if the statement "evinces that the Secretary's decision is so irrational as to constitute the decision arbitrary and capricious." *Dunlop v. Bachowski*, 421 U.S. 560 (1975). Clearly, the Court does not want judicial review to interfere very much with agency discretion in deciding whether to regulate or take enforcement action.

F A Q

Q: Why are decisions not to regulate, such as denials of rulemaking petitions, reviewed on a more deferential version of the arbitrary, capricious standard?

A: Courts view the decision whether to regulate as highly discretionary and involving both the application of agency expertise and the resolution of competing claims on agency resources. These factors make courts very reluctant to overturn agency decisions not to engage in rulemaking or other regulatory activity.

Another setting in which it has been argued that the usual rigors of the arbitrary, capricious test should be relaxed is **deregulation**, when an agency revokes, rescinds, or relaxes an existing rule. The argument in favor of a more lenient standard of review is that deregulation is more like a refusal to regulate than a decision to impose regulation because it moves toward a state of less regulation rather than more regulation. Judicial review is most important, the argument goes, when regulatory burdens are imposed and is less important when regulatory burdens are reduced.

There are two problems with this argument for relaxed judicial review of deregulation. The first problem is that it is inconsistent with the realities of the regulatory process in which third parties are often intensely interested in the government's treatment of regulated parties. For example, deregulation in the environmental area may have serious consequences for people who live in an affected area. The realization that deregulation can have serious effects on third parties is the reason that the legal right test for standing was abandoned in favor of the zone of interests test. Second, there is no legal basis for distinguishing between the promulgation and rescission or revocation of a rule. If an agency goes through the §553 process, under the APA the agency action is reviewed under the arbitrary, capricious standard of §706(2).

In the most important case involving the proper standard of review for deregulation, the *Airbags Case*, it was argued that deregulation was analogous to a decision not to regulate and therefore should be unreviewable or reviewed on a very deferential standard. The Court rejected the argument for a more lenient standard of review of deregulation and held that the rescission of a rule is subject to the same standard of review as the initial promulgation of a rule. One reason for the outcome of this case was a particular provision of the Motor Vehicle Safety Act that subjects orders "establishing, amending, or revoking" an automobile safety standard to judicial review under APA §706. Because the Act equates orders revoking regulations with orders establishing regulations, the Court found that it should treat deregulation under the Act the same as regulation for purposes of judicial review. However, this reasoning should apply across the board. Section 706 subjects all reviewable agency action to the arbitrary, capricious test and makes no distinction between regulatory and deregulatory action. The APA itself (§551(5)) provides that revocation of a rule is done through rulemaking. Since the APA subjects all rulemaking to judicial review under §706, the structure of the APA also suggests that the revocation of a rule should be subject to the same standard of judicial review as the initial promulgation of a rule.

The final special case asks whether review under the arbitrary, capricious standard should be enhanced when an agency changes its view. There is a long tradition of courts scrutinizing agency decisions more carefully when they represent a change from past practice. Perhaps this is due to suspicion that politics rather than expertise are behind agency changes to longstanding policies. By demanding reasons beyond mere policy disagreement for abandoning the prior administration's decision to require passive restraints, the *Airbags* opinion made it more difficult for agencies to change their policies. More recently, however, the Court made it clear that the arbitrary, capricious standard is not heightened merely because the agency has altered its policy. In *FCC v. Fox Television Stations, Inc.*, 129 S. Ct. 1800, 1810 (2009), the Court reviewed the FCC's decision to tighten up on regulation of indecency on television by abandoning its prior policy that it would not bring enforcement action based on "fleeting" use of indecent language during live broadcasts. Fox argued that review should be more searching because the FCC had changed its longstanding policy. The Court's response was that "[w]e find no basis in the Administrative Procedure Act or in our opinions for a requirement that all agency change be subjected to more searching review." Id. The Court acknowledged that agencies must provide reasons for changes in policy, but held that review of those reasons would be no more stringent than review of the reasons given when an agency adopts a policy initially.

Sidebar

JUDICIAL AUTHORITY TO ADJUST THE STANDARD OF REVIEW

This analysis raises a further question about judicial authority to adjust the standard of review based on the context. We have seen at least two instances of the Supreme Court authorizing the application of a relaxed version of the arbitrary, capricious standard. Perhaps this is a compromise position meant to head off the argument against any review at all. However, it is not altogether clear that courts have the authority to vary the meaning of statutory language when they think that the applicable statute does not capture the particulars of the situation. Despite this concern for legitimacy, it has become accepted practice for courts to vary the strength of the arbitrary, capricious test when, in the courts' view, the context calls for a more deferential standard.

(3) Special Case: Agency Statutory Interpretation

Agencies must often interpret the statutes from which they derive their authority to act. There has long been disagreement and confusion over whether courts or agencies are primarily responsible for interpreting regulatory statutes. One of the most vexing and controversial questions in judicial review of agency action has been the degree to which courts should defer to agency statutory interpretation. The issue muddled along for decades until 1984 when the Supreme Court, in *Chevron U.S.A., Inc. v. Natural Resources Defense Council, Inc.*, 467 U.S. 837 (1984), appeared to announce a new and apparently very deferential standard for reviewing agency interpretation. However, deeper analysis reveals that *Chevron* has not resolved any of the preexisting difficulties in this area and has added its own layer of difficulty and confusion.

Competing Traditional Standards of Review of Agency Conclusions of Law. Before *Chevron*, there were competing traditions regarding judicial review of agency conclusions of law. Under one tradition, questions of law were reviewed de novo by courts on the theory that it is the judicial role to declare the law. The competing tradition held that courts defer to reasonable agency interpretations of law because agency expertise assists in understanding Congress's statutory commands and other legal issues within the agency's jurisdiction. A middle position held that deference to agency statutory interpretation decisions varied depending on numerous factors. See *Skidmore v. Swift & Co.*, 323 U.S. 134 (1944). Today, these questions are analyzed under the *Chevron* framework, which is detailed below.

Application of Law to Particular Facts. Courts have traditionally shown the greatest deference to agency decisions involving the application of law to particular facts. Such decisions are affirmed if they enjoy "warrant in the record" and a "reasonable basis in law." *NLRB v. Hearst Publications, Inc.*, 322 U.S. 111 (1944). In *Hearst*, the Court reviewed the NLRB's determination that people selling newspapers on the street were employees of the newspaper company entitled to the protections of federal labor laws, rather than independent contractors who would not be protected. In the first part of its *Hearst* opinion, applying traditional methods of statutory interpretation, the Court upheld the Board's decision not to apply the tort law definition of "employee" in determinations of employee status under the labor laws. The Court did not appear to defer to the Board at all. Rather, it appeared to decide de novo that Congress did not intend for the tort law definition to apply. In the second part of its *Hearst* opinion, the Court reviewed the Board's decision that the particular newspaper vendors were employees. In that part of the opinion, the Court was highly deferential to the Board's decision and stated that "where the question is one of specific application of a broad statutory term . . . the reviewing court's function is limited." *Hearst*, 322 U.S. at 131.

Issues of Statutory Authority. Under a competing tradition, which may be difficult to square with the deferential language in *Hearst*, courts have decided issues of agency statutory authority without deferring to an agency's interpretation of its enabling act. *Addison v. Holly Hill Fruit Products, Inc.*, 322 U.S. 607 (1944), illustrates this doctrine. In *Holly Hill*, agricultural workers and employees engaged in canning agricultural products "within the area" of agricultural production were exempted by Congress from the requirements of the Fair Labor Standards Act. The Act left it to the Administrator to determine the size of the area of agricultural production. The Administrator ruled that canning operations with more than seven employees would not be exempt even if they were in the "area" of agricultural production as previously defined by the Administrator. The Supreme Court, using traditional statutory interpretation methods, held that once the Administrator determined the "area" of agricultural production, there was no statutory authority to exclude canning operations from the exemption based on the size of the operation. The Court held that there was no occasion for deference to the agency since this was an issue of statutory authority.

The Court no longer distinguishes between issues of statutory authority and other statutory issues. Issues of statutory authority are analyzed, like other issues of statutory interpretation, under the *Chevron* doctrine outlined below.

Questions of Statutory Interpretation: The Chevron Test. In *Chevron, U.S.A., Inc. v. Natural Resources Defense Council, Inc.*, 467 U.S. 837 (1984), the Court announced what appeared to be a new standard for reviewing agency decisions involving interpretation of statutes administered by the agency. The Court stated that unless Congress has "directly spoken to the precise question at issue," reviewing courts should defer to agencies on questions of statutory interpretation as long as the agency's interpretation constitutes a permissible construction of the statute. It should be noted, however, that there are competing versions of the **Chevron test**, and the Supreme Court often fails to refer to *Chevron* in situations in which it appears that it ought to apply.

The first difficulty is that it is unclear whether *Chevron* applies to **pure questions of statutory interpretation** or only when the case involves application of a statutory standard to a particular situation or policy questions bound up with statutory meaning. Pure questions of statutory interpretation are those issues that involve only the meaning of the words of the statute. They do not involve applying those words to a particular situation. In a footnote in the *Chevron* opinion that has been quoted in subsequent cases, the Court stated that "[t]he judiciary is the final authority on issues of statutory construction and must reject administrative constructions which are contrary to clear congressional intent." 467 U.S. at 843 n. 9. In later cases, the Court added the word "pure" to this phrase, rendering it as "The question . . . is a *pure* question of statutory construction for the courts to decide." *INS v. Cardoza-Fonseca*, 480 U.S. 421, 446 (1987). This issue is elaborated upon below.

The Clean Air Act provision involved in *Chevron* regulated permits for the discharge of air pollution from a "stationary source." In *Chevron*, the Court reviewed the Environmental Protection Agency's (EPA) definition, contained in a regulation, of the statutory term "stationary source." The EPA adopted a new definition of "stationary source," which provided that all of the pollution-emitting devises in an entire plant could be treated as a single stationary source, as if the plant was encased in a giant bubble. This definition allowed greater flexibility for polluters who could, for example, increase pollution from one smokestack at a plant while decreasing pollution from another smokestack without needing a new permit for the increase at the former smokestack. The challengers argued that the statutory language required that each smokestack must be regulated as a separate stationary source. Whether the statutory term — "stationary source" — could bear the meaning ascribed to it by the EPA was deemed, by the Court, to be a question of statutory construction. Agency resolution of such questions is reviewed as follows:

> When a court reviews an agency's construction of the statute which it administers, it is confronted with two questions. First, always, is the question whether Congress has directly spoken to the precise question at issue. If the intent of Congress is clear, that is the end of the matter; for the court, as well as the agency, must give effect to the unambiguously expressed intent of Congress. If, however, the court determines Congress has not directly addressed the precise question at issue, the court does not simply impose its own construction on the statute, as would be necessary in the absence of an administrative interpretation. Rather, if the statute is silent or ambiguous with respect to the specific issue, the question for the court is whether the agency's answer is based on a permissible construction of the statute.

467 U.S. at 833-34.

This passage from the *Chevron* opinion has been understood as establishing a two-step process for judicial review of agency interpretations of statutes. **Step one of Chevron** asks whether Congress has directly spoken to the precise question at issue. If so, Congress's intent prevails. If the agency's interpretation conflicts with Congress's intent, the court should overrule the agency and replace the agency's interpretation with the interpretation required by Congress's intent. If Congress's intent is unclear, or if Congress explicitly left a gap for the agency to fill, the analysis moves to **step two of Chevron**, which is very deferential to the agency's view, upholding reasonable or permissible agency statutory construction.

In *Chevron* itself, the Court held that Congress had not directly spoken to the precise issue of whether each smokestack must be regulated as a stationary source, that the term "stationary source" was ambiguous, and that the agency's construction, employing the bubble concept, was permissible because it fell within the range of meanings that "stationary source" could bear.

The theory underlying deference to agency interpretations is that when Congress delegates authority to administer a statute to an agency, it also delegates power to the agency to fill gaps and clarify ambiguities in the statute. In other words, *Chevron* understands statutory silence or ambiguity to entail congressional intent to delegate interpretive authority to the agency, not to the reviewing court. *Chevron* distinguished between two different types of interpretive delegations (implicit and explicit) and established different standards for reviewing agency interpretations under step two, depending on whether the interpretive delegation to the agency is implicit or explicit.

The delegation of interpretive authority to the agency is implicit if it is due to inadvertent ambiguity in the language of the statute. In such cases, *Chevron* instructs the reviewing court to ask whether the agency's interpretation is "reasonable" or "permissible." An interpretation is permissible if it is "a sufficiently rational one to preclude a court from substituting its judgment for that of the [agency]." See *Chemical Manufacturers Association v. NRDC*, 470 U.S. 116 (1985); *Young v. Community Nutrition Institute*, 476 U.S. 974 (1986). This is a very deferential standard of review. Justice Stevens, the author of *Chevron*, attacked this approach (in dissent in *Young*) as too deferential and inconsistent with the judicial role in statutory interpretation.

The delegation of interpretive authority to the agency is explicit when the statute explicitly instructs the agency to fill a statutory gap or define a statutory term. In the case of an explicit delegation, *Chevron* stated that under step two, the agency interpretation should be upheld unless it is "arbitrary, capricious, or manifestly contrary to the statute." This is a paraphrase of APA §706's arbitrary, capricious standard, with "manifestly contrary to the statute" substituted for "otherwise not in accordance with law" raising once again the question discussed above concerning whether the Court should revise standards of review established by statute. In *Household Credit Services, Inc. v. Pfennig*, 541 U.S. 232 (2004), the Court explained that under this standard, agency interpretations should be upheld if they are "rational" and "reasonable." Given that this is very similar to the standard that governs review of agency interpretations in cases of implicit delegation, it is unclear whether the distinction between explicit and implicit delegations of interpretive authority will ever make a difference to the outcome of a case.

F   A   Q

Q: When does *Chevron* apply and when does the arbitrary, capricious standard apply?

A: This is the $64,000 question. If the Court had confined *Chevron* to pure questions of statutory meaning, the answer would be simple — *Chevron* would apply to statutory meaning and arbitrary, capricious review would apply to agency policy decisions even when the policy issue is bound up with statutory meaning. However, in *Chevron* itself, the Court stressed that agency expertise in matters of policy was an important reason for *Chevron* deference, and it has also stated, as noted above, that "pure" questions of statutory interpretation are for the courts. Unfortunately, there is no clear line between the domains of *Chevron* and arbitrary, capricious review.

There is also some confusion over whether step two is about the reasonableness of the agency's interpretation as a matter of the meaning of the words of the statute or is more about the reasonableness of the agency's policy decision to adopt the particular meaning. As part of the step two analysis in the *Chevron* opinion, in reviewing the agency's plant-wide definition of "stationary source," the Court concluded that "the EPA's use of that concept here is a reasonable *policy* choice for the agency to make." *Chevron* at 845 (emphasis supplied). See also *National Cable & Telecommunications Ass'n v. Brand X Internet Services*, 545 U.S. 967 (2005). This analysis appears to call for review of factors that would be relevant under ordinary arbitrary, capricious review of the substance of an agency policy. The Ninth Circuit recently rejected an EPA rule on the ground that the agency's construction of the statute was "arbitrary and capricious," and the analysis focused more on the wisdom of the agency's interpretation of the Clean Water Act than on the linguistic plausibility of the agency's construction. See *Natural Resources Defense Council v. United States Environmental Protection Agency*, 526 F.3d 591, 605-08 (9th Cir. 2008).

When *Chevron* was decided, it was very controversial, mainly because it was viewed by many as inconsistent with traditional administrative law views on statutory interpretation. Perhaps because of this, the application of *Chevron* has been inconsistent and confusing. To many observers, the *Chevron* decision seemed to be a radical break with the traditional understanding, exemplified by the well-known dictum in *Marbury v. Madison*, 5 U.S. (1 Cranch) 137, 177 (1803), that "[i]t is emphatically the province and duty of the Judicial Department to say what the law is." Further, insofar as courts were going to defer to agency decisions on questions of law, it appeared to conflict with §706 of the APA, which provides that "the reviewing court shall decide all relevant questions of law." This probably helps explain why, as we see below, some post-*Chevron* decisions do not look much different from review of statutory interpretation pre-*Chevron*.

The *Chevron* decision left several questions in its wake:

1. What factors will courts look at to determine whether Congress's intent is clear?
2. When will *Chevron* deference apply?
3. If *Chevron* deference does not apply, what standard of review applies instead?
4. What is the effect of the *Chevron* framework on agency efforts to change the interpretation of a statute, especially when the prior interpretation has already been judicially reviewed? and
5. Does *Chevron* apply to an agency's interpretations of its own regulations?

On the first question, *Chevron* itself stated that Congress's intent governs under step one when Congress has "directly spoken to the precise question at issue." Understood literally, this version of step one is very narrow, making it more likely that the reviewing court will go on to the very deferential step two. However, in subsequent cases, the Court sometimes applies a less deferential version of step one under which the reviewing court should attempt to ascertain Congress's intent using **traditional tools of statutory construction** including the language, structure, purpose, and legislative history of the statute being construed and other interpretive devices such as the canons of statutory interpretation. See *INS v. Cardoza-Fonseca*, 480 U.S. 421 (1987); *Dole v. United Steelworkers of America*, 494 U.S. 26 (1990). Under the less deferential version of step one, courts are more likely to find congressional intent on a matter and thus are more likely to reverse the agency.

The application of *Chevron* step one is one of the many areas under *Chevron* that has been inconsistent and confusing. In some cases, the Court looks for the "**plain meaning**" of the statute under review, and appears less concerned with whether the statutory meaning would appear different if other traditional tools of statutory interpretation were applied. See *MCI Telecommunications Corp. v. A.T.&T.*, 512 U.S. 218 (1994). In other cases, the Court uses all of the traditional tools of interpretation, and in such cases it is difficult to distinguish between pre- and post-*Chevron* practice. For example, in *Dole*, the Court found clear congressional intent after consulting statutory text, statutory object, and the statutory structure. The *Dole* Court even applied "[t]he traditional canon of construction, noscitur a sociis" to determine the unambiguous meaning of the Paperwork Reduction Act. See *Dole v. United Steelworkers*, 494 U.S. 26, 36 (1990). And in *Barnhart v. Thomas*, 540 U.S. 20, 26 (2003), the Court applied the canon known as the "rule of the last antecedent" to determine the clear meaning of the Social Security Act. The Court has also consulted legislative history and the provision's relationship to other statutes. The word "precise" does not appear in "traditional tools" decisions, freeing the reviewing court to apply relatively general indications of congressional intent.

In still another version of step one, the Court has sometimes found that a case is "extraordinary" and must be decided outside of the *Chevron* two-step framework. The best example of "**extraordinary cases *Chevron***" is the Court's decision that the Food and Drug Administration (FDA) does not have jurisdiction under the Food, Drug and Cosmetic Act to regulate the marketing of tobacco products. The Court found that the FDA lacked jurisdiction because of the unique legal history surrounding tobacco, which indicated that Congress did not intend the general language of the Act to grant the FDA jurisdiction over tobacco. *FDA v. Brown & Williamson Tobacco Corp.*, 529 U.S. 120, 142-43 (2000). The Court based its holding that the FDA lacked jurisdiction to regulate tobacco on Congress's general intent without regard to the statutory language. Congress had clearly not spoken to the precise question at issue of whether the FDA had authority to regulate tobacco and the statutory language giving the FDA the authority to regulate drugs and drug delivery devices appeared to apply literally to tobacco products.

On the second question, of when *Chevron* applies, there are two issues. The first is whether the particular statute being interpreted is one over which Congress delegated interpretive authority to the agency. *Chevron* applies only to statutes **administered by the agency** whose interpretation is at issue because it is only with regard to such statutes that Congress has delegated interpretive authority to the agency. Agency interpretations of the APA, for example, should not receive *Chevron* deference because no agency is charged with administering the APA. Likewise, if a statute's primary method of enforcement is through civil actions brought in court, agency views on the meaning of the statute will not receive *Chevron* deference. See *Adams Fruit Co. v. Barrett*, 494 U.S. 638 (1990). In such cases, the statute is "administered" by the courts, not the agency.

The second question concerning whether *Chevron* applies assumes that the agency has interpretive authority over the statute and asks whether *Chevron* applies to the particular interpretation. This issue breaks down into two questions, first whether Congress delegated lawmaking authority to the agency and second whether the case presents a "pure question of statutory construction," which is for the courts to decide. This second issue raises a serious difficulty with *Chevron*, namely whether *Chevron* is about deference to agency statutory interpretation or about deference to agency policy decisions.

Sidebar

FOUR VERSIONS OF *CHEVRON* STEP ONE

There are four different versions of *Chevron* step one. Under "original" *Chevron*, the case would be decided in step one only if Congress had explicitly answered the exact question at issue in the case. Under "traditional tools" *Chevron*, in some cases the reviewing court uses all the traditional tools of statutory interpretation from pre-*Chevron* practice to find clear congressional intent under step one. Under "plain meaning" *Chevron*, in some cases, the Court finds clear congressional intent using the plain meaning rule. Finally, in "extraordinary cases" *Chevron*, the reviewing court finds clear congressional intent based on an examination of the history and political context of the particular issue, which it finds leads to only one possible congressional intent.

Generally, an agency interpretation made in a relatively formal proceeding is more likely to merit deference than an agency interpretation made informally, or for the first time in litigation. The Supreme Court first held that informally rendered agency interpretations are not entitled to *Chevron* deference in *Christensen v. Harris County*, 529 U.S. 576 (2000). In that case, the Court held that *Chevron* deference did not apply to an interpretation contained in an "Opinion Letter" that an agency wrote in response to a letter from a regulated party asking whether the statute administered by the agency permitted a particular course of conduct. There were no public proceedings prior to the issuance of the opinion letter, and the opinion letter did not have the appearance of an authoritative, thoroughly considered decision. The Court stated that "[i]nterpretations such as those in opinion letters—like interpretations contained in policy statements, agency manuals, and enforcement guidelines, all of which lack the force of law—do not warrant *Chevron*-style deference."

The Court elaborated on the applicability of *Chevron* to informal agency decisionmaking in *United States v. Mead Corp.*, 533 U.S. 218 (2001). The *Mead* opinion contains the most thorough analysis of the framework for determining when *Chevron* applies. In *Mead*, the Court refused to accord *Chevron* deference to a statutory interpretation contained in a Customs Service "ruling letter" which, although it represented the agency's official position, was not based on "a process of rulemaking or adjudication." Mead Corp. imported loose leaf date book pages that are inserted into binders. The Customs Service classified these as "bound diaries," which meant they were subject to an import tariff. While the original decision was made by a regional field office, after Mead protested, a ruling letter was issued by the agency's central office in Washington, D.C., affirming that determination based, in part, on the agency's understanding of the statute governing tariff classifications. On judicial review, the Customs Service urged the Court to defer to the decision embodied in the ruling letter under *Chevron*.

The analysis of whether *Chevron* applies begins with a question of congressional intent—did Congress delegate to the agency the power to make authoritative decisions on the meaning of the statute? Or as the *Mead* Court put it, does it appear that Congress intended for agency interpretations to have the "force of law"? The *Mead* Court concluded that the most important indication that Congress intended for agency interpretations to have the force of law is when Congress authorized the agency to employ relatively formal procedures such as notice and comment rulemaking and formal adjudication. When Congress authorizes an agency to act informally, for example through opinion letters or informal guidance documents, that indicates that Congress did not intend for agency interpretations to have the force of law, and thus they would not receive *Chevron* deference.

Sidebar

CHEVRON STEP ZERO

In language that has been widely adopted, Cass Sunstein denominated the doctrine that governs whether *Chevron* applies as "**Chevron step zero**" because it is an issue that must be addressed before getting to the two-step *Chevron* framework. See Cass Sunstein, *Chevron Step Zero*, 92 Va. L. Rev. 187 (2006).

F   A   Q

Q: Why is Congress's intent to delegate to the agency the power to render authoritative interpretations so important to whether *Chevron* applies?

A: The *Chevron* framework is based on the notion that when Congress does not address an issue or when its statutory expression is ambiguous, it intends to delegate interpretive authority to the agency rather than to the courts. "We accord deference to agencies under *Chevron* . . . because of a presumption that Congress, when it left ambiguity in a statute meant for implementation by an agency, understood that the ambiguity would be resolved, first and foremost, by the agency, and desired the agency (rather than the courts) to possess whatever degree of discretion the ambiguity allows," *Smiley v. Citibank (South Dakota), N. A.*, 517 U.S. 735, 740-41 (1996). In *Chevron*, the Court also mentioned agency expertise and accountability as reasons to prefer agency interpretations over judicial construction, but the primary basis for *Chevron* deference is congressional intent. It should be noted that many commentators, and even Justice Scalia, have characterized this characterization of Congress's intent as "fictional."

Although authorization to employ rulemaking or formal adjudicatory procedures are good indications of congressional intent to delegate the power to make rulings with the force of law, the *Mead* Court was careful not to make any single factor decisive. With regard to the lack of rulemaking procedures, the Court stated that "the want of that procedure here does not decide the case, for we have sometimes found reasons for *Chevron* deference even when no such administrative formality was required and none was afforded." The Court relied upon additional factors to support its decision not to grant *Chevron* deference to the Customs Ruling in *Mead*, such as the fact that thousands of Customs Rulings are issued every year by numerous offices and on their terms cannot be relied upon by anyone other than the importer whose goods were the subject of the ruling.

Perhaps this means that an agency making fewer decisions in a more centralized manner at a high level within the agency hierarchy might receive *Chevron* deference even without rulemaking or formal adjudication. The Supreme Court, in an opinion by Justice Breyer, has suggested the following factors that might lead toward *Chevron* deference in a less formal setting: "the interstitial nature of the legal question, the related expertise of the agency, the importance of the question to the administration of the statute, the complexity of that administration, and the careful consideration the Agency has given the question over a long period of time[.]" *Barnhart v. Walton*, 535 U.S. 212, 222 (2002). In *Walton*, the Court approved an interpretation that was embodied in regulations but that had initially been arrived at less formally.

Justice Scalia dissented vehemently in *Mead*. Four of his many points criticizing the decision in *Mead* are worth noting here. First, Justice Scalia attacked the *Mead* opinion for its vagueness in refusing to construct clear rules on when *Chevron* applies. This aspect of *Mead* leaves the courts with flexibility, which may be desirable, but at the cost of uncertainty over when agency interpretations will receive *Chevron* deference. Second, related to this point, the vagueness of the Court's standard is guaranteed to generate extensive litigation over whether *Chevron* applies in any particular case. Third, Justice Scalia argued that when an interpretation represents the official position of an agency and is rendered by a high-level official, as was the case in *Mead*, *Chevron* ought to apply. Finally, Justice Scalia lamented that agencies will now engage in rulemaking in order to receive *Chevron* deference even if less formal procedures would have been otherwise adequate.

F   A   Q

Q: When might an agency interpretation receive *Chevron* deference even if the interpretation was not rendered in the course of a "relatively formal procedure"?

A: While the Court has not had the occasion to elaborate on this very much, a few possibilities should readily come to mind. One factor in favor of *Chevron* deference might be that an interpretation was rendered at or near the top of the agency hierarchy, for example by a cabinet Secretary or the heads of an independent agency. In *Mead*, the Court rejected *Chevron* deference in part because ruling letters could be issued by multiple regional agency offices. If this factor militates against *Chevron* deference, perhaps the more centralized the interpretive process, the more likely that *Chevron* will apply. Since *Mead* also relied upon the fact that the agency issued thousands of letter rulings each year, it would seem that if an agency makes only a very few interpretive decisions each year, it is more likely that *Chevron* deference will apply. *Chevron* deference might also be more likely to apply to a long-term consistent interpretation of a statute that has been widely known and relied upon. *Chevron* might also apply when agency expertise is important to understanding the meaning of technical statutory terms. While these are reasonable possibilities, *Mead* provides very little guidance on when *Chevron* deference will apply to an interpretation that was not the result of a relatively formal procedure such as rulemaking or formal adjudication.

The second sub-issue on the applicability of *Chevron* involves applying the language in *Chevron* and subsequent cases that assigns resolution of "issues of statutory construction" (*Chevron*, 467 U.S. at 843 n. 9) or "pure questions of statutory construction" (*Cardozo-Fonseca*, 480 U.S. at 446) to the courts. The Court has not elaborated upon the distinction between issues of statutory construction that are subject to *Chevron* and *pure* questions of statutory construction that are not. There are two possible understandings, although neither understanding is satisfying because they both leave serious questions about *Chevron*'s domain in their wake. First, perhaps *Chevron* does not apply to cases in which the only issue is the meaning of the words of the statute without application to any particular situation. Second, perhaps *Chevron* does not apply to cases in which statutory construction is not bound up with agency policy determinations.

The first possibility, that *Chevron* applies whenever the agency's interpretation is unconnected to any particular situation, is not very helpful. Ultimately, all instances of agency statutory construction are designed to apply to particular situations. Otherwise, why would the agency bother to announce its construction? In *Chevron* itself, the EPA's construction of the term "stationary source" was announced in a rulemaking, outside the context of any application to a particular pollution-emitting facility, and the Court applied its new two-step formulation in that case. In a recent dissent, Justice Stevens, the author of *Chevron*, argued that when reviewing the results of formal adjudication, the Court "has sometimes described the court's role as deciding pure questions of statutory construction and the agency's role as applying law to fact." *Negusie v. Holder*, 129 S. Ct. 1159, 1172 (2009) (Stevens, J. dissenting). Stress should be on the word "sometimes" for even if Justice Stevens's characterization of the scope of the "pure questions of statutory interpretation" doctrine is accurate, it does not represent a consistently applied limitation on the scope of *Chevron*.

The second possibility, that *Chevron* applies only when agency interpretation is bound up with policy issues, is intriguing but ultimately raises serious questions of its own. The Court, in *Chevron* itself, justified deference in part based on agency expertise in matters of policy entrusted to the agency. Undoubtedly, many issues of statutory construction involve policy questions. For example, in *Chevron* itself, the most important issue was whether the agency's construction of "stationary source" as consistent with the bubble concept made sense in light of competing policy questions left to the agency. The problem with this understanding is that it ignores the applicability of the arbitrary, capricious test to review of agency policy decisions. Under *Overton Park*, which also involved an issue of statutory interpretation (proper understanding of the statute limiting the use of parkland for highway construction), the *Chevron* Court should have asked whether the EPA, in adopting the bubble concept, had considered all relevant factors or committed an error in judgment so serious that the decision could not be attributed to the application of agency expertise.

In sum, the distinction between cases of statutory construction to which *Chevron* applies and "pure questions of statutory construction" for the courts is unclear and confusing and may not represent an actual limitation on the applicability of *Chevron*.

CHECKLIST ON WHEN *CHEVRON* APPLIES

1. Is the statute being construed administered by the agency claiming deference? If so, the *Chevron* framework may apply. ☑

2. Is the statute ambiguous concerning the matter in dispute? If so, the *Chevron* framework may apply. ☑

3. Was the statutory construction arrived at in a relatively formal proceeding such as rulemaking or formal adjudication? If so, the *Chevron* framework may apply. ☑

4. Even if the procedure employed was not relatively formal, was the interpretation carefully considered and was the interpretive process centralized, issued at a relatively high level within the agency, and the result of a relatively infrequently performed process? If so, the *Chevron* framework may apply. ☑

The next question that arises under *Chevron* is what standard applies when *Chevron* doesn't. In both *Christensen* and *Mead*, the Court held that a lesser form of deference, known as ***Skidmore* deference**, applies, under which agency interpretations are "entitled to respect . . . but only to the extent that those interpretations have the 'power to persuade.'" See *Christensen*, 529 U.S. at 588 (quoting *Skidmore v. Swift & Co.*, 323 U.S. 134, 140 (1944)). Under *Skidmore*, courts decide how much to defer to agency interpretive decisions based on "the thoroughness evident in its consideration, the validity of its reasoning, its consistency with earlier and later pronouncements, and all those factors which give it power to persuade, if lacking power to control." This is a pre-*Chevron* sliding scale of deference based on the totality of the circumstances, which, as Justice Scalia argued in his *Mead* dissent, can be very uncertain and unpredictable.

Another set of questions arises over the effect of prior judicial interpretations on the applicability of *Chevron* deference. The nature of deferential review is that there may be a universe of permissible interpretations, any of which would be upheld by the reviewing court. What happens if an agency changes its mind after the prior interpretation has been upheld on judicial review? In the *Brand X* decision, the Supreme Court made it clear that "[a] court's prior judicial construction of a statute trumps an agency construction otherwise entitled to *Chevron* deference only if the prior court decision holds that its constructions follows from the unambiguous terms of the statute and thus leaves no room for agency discretion." *Brand X*, 545 U.S. at 982. In other words, if an agency interpretation was upheld under *Chevron* step one, the agency may not adopt an inconsistent interpretation. However, if an agency interpretation was approved under step two as a permissible or reasonable construction, the agency remains free to change its mind and adopt another permissible construction, although the agency will probably be required to offer reasons for the change. And if an agency interpretation was rejected as inconsistent with the statute, *Chevron* deference would not allow the agency to try once again to adopt that interpretation. See *Lechmere Inc. v. NLRB*, 502 U.S. 527 (1992).

The applicability of *Chevron* may be affected by the lack of consistency of the agency's current interpretation with prior agency interpretations. Although the Court has stated that agency interpretations are not "carved in stone" and thus may be changed when appropriate, the existence of a longstanding contrary interpretation may lead courts to question the validity of any reinterpretation, especially if the prior interpretation received prior court approval, see *Maislin Industries, U.S. Inc. v. Primary Steel, Inc.*, 497 U.S. 116 (1990), or appears to be more consistent with other action taken by Congress and the agency. See *Food and Drug Administration v. Brown & Williamson Tobacco Corp.*, 529 U.S. 120 (2000) (characterizing longstanding FDA view that statute does not give the FDA authority to regulate tobacco as evidence that Congress did not intend to grant the FDA general regulatory power over tobacco). See also *Barnhart v. Thomas*, 540 U.S. 20 (2003) (longstanding agency interpretation entitled to greater deference). The Court has, on more than one occasion, stated that deference is reduced when an agency interpretation goes against the agency's prior interpretation. See, e.g., *INS v. Cardoza-Fonseca*, 480 U.S. 421, 447 n. 30 (1987). See also *Natural Resources Defense Council v. United States Environmental Protection Agency*, 526 F.3d 591, 605 (9th Cir. 2008). On the other hand, the Court has applied full *Chevron* deference to an interpretation of a statute that was rendered 130 years after the statute being interpreted was enacted. The Court stated that the delay was not relevant as long as ambiguity in the statute left a gap for the agency to fill. See *Smiley v. Citibank*, 517 U.S. 735 (1996).

Sidebar

AGENCY FLEXIBILITY AND *CHEVRON*

Agency flexibility is very important, and the Supreme Court has applied judicial review doctrines to allow agencies to change their positions based on changed circumstance and evolution of policy at the agency. In *Brand X*, the Court recognized that agencies are free to change their views on statutory meaning as long as they remain within the range of "permissible constructions" under *Chevron* step two. And in *Fox Broadcasting*, the Court rejected calls for heightened arbitrary, capricious review when an agency changes its policy.

What about agency interpretations of their own regulations? Should such interpretations receive *Chevron* deference? Long before *Chevron*, the Court held in *Bowles v. Seminole Rock & Sand Co.*, 325 U.S. 410 (1945), that reviewing courts should defer to an agency's interpretation of its own regulations "unless it is plainly erroneous or inconsistent with the regulation." 325 U.S. at 414. After *Chevron*, the Court rejected an argument that agency interpretations of their own regulations should receive *Chevron* deference, but rather should continue to be analyzed under *Seminole Rock*. See *Martin v. Occupational Safety and Health Review Commission*, 499 U.S. 144 (1991). However, *Seminole Rock*'s "plainly erroneous or inconsistent with the regulation" standard seems very deferential, perhaps as deferential as the more deferential versions of the *Chevron* standard.

A final complication under *Chevron* must be examined. In many cases in which *Chevron* would seem to apply, the Court does not cite it or apply its two-step framework. In cases reviewing decisions of the National Labor Relations Board, for example, the Court appears to have constructed a different standard of review, citing *Fall River Dyeing & Finishing Corp. v. NLRB*, 482 U.S. 27 (1987), rather than *Chevron* on the standard of review of legal determinations. The *Fall River* standard is whether the Board's decision is "rational and consistent with the Act," which on its face seems to be less deferential than *Chevron*. See *NLRB v. Health Care & Ret. Corp. of Am.*, 511 U.S. 571, 576 (1994). In many other cases reviewing agency statutory construction, the Court does not cite any deference doctrine, apparently reviewing interpretive decisions de novo. This adds even more uncertainty to the step zero question addressed in *Mead*.

CHEVRON DECISION TREE

1. Does the agency's decision involve statutory construction of a statute administered by the agency?

    If yes, go on to number 2 below.[3] If the case does not involve statutory construction, go to APA §706 to determine what standard of review applies. If the case involves statutory construction but of a statute not administered by the agency (for example construction of the APA), the court will review the construction de novo.
2. If the agency's decision involves construction of a statute administered by the agency, apply *Mead* to determine whether *Chevron* applies.

    a. Did the agency employ "relatively formal procedures" such as rulemaking or formal adjudication?
    b. Does the agency decision represent the official position of the agency rendered at a relatively high level within the agency?

---

[3]If the matter under review is a "pure question of statutory construction," the Court has stated that it is for the reviewing court, not the agency, to decide. Just when this is actually true is unclear.

    c.   Are there other factors that indicate that Congress intended to give the agency the authority to make decisions with the force of law?

       If in your judgment *Chevron* does not apply, go to number 3 below. If in your judgment *Chevron* does apply, go to number 4 below.

3. When *Chevron* does not apply, the reviewing court should determine whether the agency's construction is correct, applying the multi-factor *Skidmore* test to determine how much the court should defer to the agency's view.

4. When *Chevron* applies, ask under step one whether Congress's intent is clear. If it is, that is the end of the matter, because the agency and reviewing courts must apply the clear intent of Congress. Note that the step-one determination is made under various tests including original, directly spoken *Chevron*, traditional tools *Chevron*, plain meaning *Chevron* and extraordinary cases *Chevron*. If Congress's intent is not clear, go on to number 5 below.

5. If Congress's intent is not clear, ask whether the agency's construction is reasonable or permissible. If it is, the agency's construction governs. If the agency's construction is unreasonable or impermissible, the court may either remand the case to the agency to adopt a different construction or impose what it finds to be the reasonable or permissible construction of the statute. (As discussed above, although the Court sometimes uses "reasonable" and sometimes uses "permissible" it is unclear whether there is any difference between the two.)

C. Review of Questions of Fact After Agency Adjudication: The Substantial Evidence Test

The substantial evidence test is the standard of review for formal agency adjudication and formal rulemaking conducted under APA §§556 and 557 (or conducted on the record after a hearing pursuant to the agency's enabling act). In addition, some enabling acts specify that the substantial evidence test applies to that particular agency's informal rulemaking. In this section, we look at the meaning and application of the substantial evidence test. By contrast with other areas of administrative law, the meaning and application of the substantial evidence test have both been relatively stable over time, with little in the way of controversy.

(1) The Substantial Evidence Test Defined

The substantial evidence test pre-dates the passage of the APA and is the traditional standard for reviewing the results of formal agency procedures. Drawing on pre-APA precedents, "**substantial evidence**" is understood to mean "such relevant evidence as a reasonable mind might accept as adequate to support a conclusion." *Consolidated Edison Co. v. NLRB*, 305 U.S. 197, 229 (1938). This standard is the same one that is employed to determine whether there is sufficient evidence to submit an issue to a jury. In other words, substantial evidence is lacking when a judge in a jury trial would direct a verdict on the ground that a reasonable jury could have only one view of the facts. *NLRB v. Columbian Enameling and Stamping Co.*, 306 U.S. 292 (1939).

The most important innovation in the meaning and application of the substantial evidence test involves the provision of APA §706 that requires the reviewing court to look at the whole record of the agency action under review, not merely those parts of the record that support the agency's decision. This provision of §706, which was also included in contemporaneous amendments to labor laws, was meant to overrule a practice that some courts followed of looking only for substantial evidence in support of the agency's decision and not weighing that evidence against evidence in the record that points in another direction. Under the APA, a court performing substantial evidence review must look at the whole record, not only the evidence supporting the agency's decision, and must weigh the evidence supporting the agency's action against the evidence on the other side. Thus, a decision might fail the substantial evidence test, even though it is supported by some evidence, when that evidence is overwhelmed by other evidence in the record to the contrary.

(2) The Substantial Evidence Test Applied

A court performing substantial evidence review examines the evidence that was before the agency and determines, in a rather uncomplicated way, whether the agency's decision was reasonable in light of the evidence on the record. Two situations merit special attention. First, when an agency's decision is based (in whole or in part) on the credibility of witnesses, the agency's decision is entitled to great deference because the reviewing court reviews only the paper record without the opportunity to observe the demeanor of the witnesses. If the agency's decision relies on witness credibility, it takes a great deal of contrary evidence to convince a court that the agency's decision lacks substantial evidence.

Second, an agency's decision is subject to special scrutiny when the decision at the agency's highest level is inconsistent with an initial agency decision made by an official who actually heard the evidence. In most agencies, initial adjudicatory decisions are made by an ALJ, with appeal to the highest level of the agency before judicial review may be sought. The black letter rule in such situations is that the initial decision of the ALJ is part of the agency record that is reviewed in court. Therefore, when an agency reverses the decision of the trier of fact on appeal within the agency, the reviewing court must take that reversal into account in deciding whether the agency's decision is supported by substantial evidence. The ALJ's decision weighs against the agency's decision.

Because witnesses appear only before the ALJ, the reversal of an ALJ's decision poses special problems when witness credibility was important to the initial decision. In *NLRB v. Universal Camera Corp.*, 179 F.2d 749 (2d Cir. 1950), in an opinion by Judge Learned Hand, the Court of Appeals held that it could not take into account the fact that the agency had reversed the ALJ (then called a "Trial Examiner"), even when the initial decision was based in part on a credibility determination. The court found itself unable to formulate an appropriate standard of review that would take the ALJ's decision into account and remain consistent with the requirements of the substantial evidence test. The Supreme Court disagreed with the Court of Appeals and held that because the initial decision is part of the record under the APA, the reviewing court must take the initial decision maker's opinion into account when deciding whether the agency's conclusions are supported by substantial evidence. See *Universal Camera Corp. v. NLRB*, 340 U.S. 474 (1951). The Court, in remanding the case to the Court of Appeals, observed that "evidence supporting a conclusion may be less substantial when an impartial, experienced examiner who had observed the witnesses and lived with the case has drawn conclusions different from the Board's than when he has reached the same conclusion." *Universal Camera*, 340 U.S. at 496. The Court noted that Congress intended the APA's "substantial evidence on the record as a whole" provision to make judicial review somewhat less deferential than it had been before.

On remand, Judge Hand, again writing for the Court of Appeals, interpreted the Supreme Court's decision to mean that a reviewing court should not allow an agency to overrule an initial decision based on credibility determinations unless there is overwhelming evidence against the initial decision. In the particular case, the court held that since the initial decision was based in part on a credibility determination, the agency's reversal of that decision was not proper because the evidence supporting the agency's decision was not enough to overwhelm the credibility findings of the ALJ. See *NLRB v. Universal Camera Corp.*, 190 F.2d 429 (2d Cir. 1951). The concurring opinion on remand argued that the court's decision went too far in protecting ALJ credibility decisions from reversal by agencies. The strongest argument against the majority on remand is that APA §557(b) states that "[o]n appeal from or review of the initial decision, the agency has all the powers which it would have in making the initial decision except as it may limit the issues on notice or by rule." This appears to support the concurring opinion's contention that the majority went too far in protecting ALJ credibility determinations from reversal by the agency.

The *Allentown Mack Sales* decision mentioned above is an interesting case concerning the application of the substantial evidence standard. In the course of resolving controversies regarding whether a union continues to have the support of employees within the bargaining unit, the NLRB has constructed a set of rules under which the employer can challenge the union's continuation as representative of the bargaining unit. The NLRB's rules exist as precedent derived from opinions of the Board, not as rules promulgated in any rulemaking proceeding. In *Allentown Mack Sales*, the employer challenged the substance of the rules, and the Supreme Court evaluated that challenge under the APA's arbitrary, capricious test, even though the proceeding reviewed was a formal adjudication subject to the substantial evidence test. See *Allentown Mack Sales and Service, Inc. v. NLRB*, 522 U.S. 359, 364 (1998). When the Court then turned to evaluating whether the NLRB had good reason to reject the employer's evidence that it had a good faith doubt as to the continued support for the union, the Court applied the substantial evidence test. See id. at 366. This reinforces the notion that the substantial evidence test is much more suited to review of agency factual conclusions than policy decisions.

F	A	Q

Q: How does the substantial evidence test apply to review of policy decisions that are made in the course of formal adjudication?

A: In *Industrial Union Dep't, AFC-CIO v. American Petroleum Institute (The Benzene Case)*, 448 U.S. 607 (1980), the application of the substantial evidence test to OSHA informal rulemaking appeared to result in relatively non-deferential judicial review of the rule challenged in that case. This might lead to the conclusion that policy decisions made in the course of formal adjudication may be subjected to less deferential review than policy decisions reviewed under the arbitrary, capricious test. However, as noted above, in actual decisions, the reviewing court appears to apply a standard very similar to the arbitrary, capricious test to the policy aspects of formal adjudication, which means that ultimately the standard of review is unlikely to make much of a difference when policy conclusions, as opposed to factual decisions, are involved. See *Allentown Mack Sales and Service, Inc. v. NLRB*, 522 U.S. 359, 364 (1998).

D. De Novo Review of Questions of Fact

De novo review means review without regard to the agency decision—no deference at all. Trial de novo means that the facts are retried in the reviewing court. The possibility of de novo review arises from APA §706(2)(F), which states that the court should reverse agency action on review to the extent that the agency decision is "unwarranted by the facts to the extent that the facts are subject to trial de novo by the reviewing court." As discussed above, the statute does not tell us when de novo review applies, but the Supreme Court has adopted the language of a legislative committee report that explains that de novo review applies only in two rare circumstances: first when agency adjudicatory fact-finding procedures are inadequate, and second when new factual issues arise in an action to enforce nonadjudicatory agency action. See *Overton Park*, 402 U.S. at 415. De novo review means that the reviewing court considers the facts and reaches its own decision without deferring to the conclusions of the agency. Usually, in de novo review of facts, the facts are retried in the trial court.

> **Sidebar**
>
> **DE NOVO REVIEW OF FACTS AND LAW**
>
> APA §706(2)(F) adverts to de novo review of facts, not law. This does not mean, however, that courts should defer to agency legal decisions when conducting the trial de novo specified under the APA. Rather, it seems logical that legal issues would also be decided de novo, except of course that courts should apply any valid regulations including deciding under the *Chevron* framework whether to defer to agency statutory interpretation embodied in those regulations.

E. Remedies on Judicial Review

Reviewing courts have the power under APA §706 to "hold unlawful and set aside" agency action found not to meet the applicable standard of review. In many situations, courts do just that: They hold regulations null and void or order agencies to pay benefits or award permits unlawfully withheld. However, especially in rulemaking that involves policy questions, courts often choose to **remand** matters to the agency for further consideration without ordering the agency to change its decision. One of the reasons that reviewing courts may prefer remand to outright reversal is that courts seem to prefer to rest the rejection of agency policy decisions on procedural grounds such as inadequate notice or inadequate opportunity to comment. Courts shy away from direct substantive rejection of an agency's policy decision because agency decisions on matters of policy implicate agency expertise. Courts do not wish to appear to be substituting their judgment for that of the experts. Another reason for remand rather than outright reversal is that reviewing courts may not have the authority to step into the agency's shoes and make the discretionary decisions necessary to choose the course the agency will take after its initial decision has been rejected on judicial review.

Sidebar

"INADEQUATE RECORD TO SUPPORT THE RULE"

Even when the problem is the lack of support in the record for the agency's action (which means that on the record before the agency the decision was arbitrary or capricious), courts often characterize this substantive failing as the procedural-sounding problem of an inadequate record to support the agency action. An inadequate record, however, means that based on the record before the agency, the decision fails the applicable standard of review. Courts normally remand the matter to the agency for it to decide whether to change course or attempt to gather a sufficient record to support the rule.

After a court rejects an agency policy decision as arbitrary or capricious or lacking in substantial evidence (unless the court bases the rejection on a lack of agency power to act in the area or a statutory bar to the agency's policy choice), the agency may have the power to issue a new notice of proposed rulemaking and promulgate the same or a similar rule based on a new record or hold a new hearing to determine whether the evidence supports the agency's initial decision. See *Briscoe ex rel. Taylor v. Barnhart*, 425 F.3d 345 (7th Cir. 2005) (remanding denial of social security benefits for new hearing and rejecting district court's order calling for the immediate award of benefits). In *Briscoe*, the court rejected the argument that an immediate award of benefits was appropriate simply because the agency appears to have obstinately refused to apply governing law in its hearings on the application for social security benefits. Rather, the court concluded that benefits may only be awarded if the evidence before the agency establishes the entitlement. If the reviewing court's rejection of a rule was for legal reasons unrelated to the record (such as lack of legal authority or improper statutory interpretation), action by Congress may be necessary before the agency can promulgate a new rule to achieve the same policy result.

Remand of a matter to an agency may effectively amount to rejection because the agency may not actually reconsider the matter. Remand entails delay. Over time, agency enthusiasm for the initial decision may have faded with the emergence of new problems and new priorities — especially if a new administration has taken office.

From the perspective of the party challenging agency action, remand is sometimes not an adequate remedy. For example, a person applying for government benefits or a permit of some kind may suffer greatly because of the delay inherent in a remand, especially if the agency's decision and judicial review have already taken a great deal of time. Under some circumstances, a reviewing court will order the immediate payment of benefits or award of the permit rather than remand the matter to the agency for further consideration. Or the court will remand to the agency simply to give the agency the opportunity to calculate the amount of benefits owed, with the understanding that the agency does not have the discretion to deny benefits again on remand. See *Lingenfelter v. Astrue*, 504 F.3d 1028 (9th Cir. 2007) (remand for calculation of benefits only). This can be controversial — a dissenting judge in *Lingenfelter* would have remanded to the agency for specific findings on the evidence rather than ordering the agency to award benefits.

SUMMARY

- Unless the agency's particular statute states otherwise, the standard (or scope) of review of agency action is determined by applying APA §706.

- The substantial evidence test applies to formal adjudication and formal rulemaking. Arbitrary, capricious review is available in most other circumstances such as review of informal rulemaking and informal agency action generally.

- De novo review, which means review without any deference to the agency's decision, applies rarely, when new factual issues properly arise for the first time on judicial review or when agency adjudicatory procedures are inadequate.

- APA §706 directs reviewing courts to examine the whole record when conducting judicial review, not merely those parts of the record that support the agency's action. This is meant to alter pre-APA practice under which some courts only discerned whether some evidence in the record supported the agency. The record consists of the information the agency had before it at the time it made its decision.

- Post hoc rationalizations for agency action are disfavored because the agency's action is judged on the record available at the time the decision was made and based on the reasons given by the agency at the time it made the decision.

- The substantial evidence test, under which agency factual determinations in adjudicatory hearings are reviewed, requires that agency decisions be supported, on the record as a whole, by enough relevant evidence as a reasonable mind might accept as adequate to support the agency's conclusion. This is the same standard under which courts review jury verdicts.

- Questions of law were traditionally for courts to decide. However, contrary to this traditional view, the *Chevron* doctrine appears to instruct courts to defer to agency decisions of statutory interpretation unless Congress's intent on the matter is unmistakably clear. Application of the *Chevron* standard has been inconsistent over whether courts should look beyond Congress's clearly expressed intent and attempt to ascertain Congress's intent using traditional tools of statutory interpretation, the plain meaning rule, or other indications of congressional intent.

- *Chevron* applies only to decisions made employing "relatively formal procedures." When decisions of law are made informally, a lower level of deference, known as *Skidmore* deference, may apply.

- For agency action to survive review under the arbitrary, capricious test, the agency must apply the correct legal standard, consider all relevant factors, evaluate alternatives, and explain their conclusions on issues raised in the decisionmaking process. In addition, the decision reached must not be so irrational that the court cannot help but conclude that the decision was not the product of the application of agency expertise to the problem.

■ Substantial evidence review, which applies to formal adjudication, applies the "reasonable mind" standard familiar from judicial review of jury decisions in civil cases.

■ De novo review, under which courts re-decide the issues without regard to the agency's decision, applies only in rare circumstances when agency fact-finding procedures are insufficient or when new issues properly arise in court.

CONNECTIONS

Standards of Review

In deciding on the appropriate standard of review for agency inaction, including decisions not to bring enforcement action and decisions declining to engage in rulemaking, reviewability may also be a consideration. See Chapter 3.

Chevron and Separation of Powers

Separation of powers objections to the *Chevron* framework should be considered in light of the material in Chapter 2. Similarly, the degree of deference to agency adjudicatory decisions might be influenced by Article III considerations that militate in favor of effective judicial review and preservation of the essential attributes of the judicial power in the Article III courts. See Chapter 2.

Influences on the Degree of Deference

The degree of deference courts should show agency decisions is influenced by the degree to which agency expertise is important to the decision. The more technical the decision, the more deference. The discussion of cost-benefit analysis may be relevant here. See Chapter 5.

Deference to Procedural Decisions

There does not seem to be much if any deference to agency application of procedural requirements including the APA. For rulemaking procedures, see Chapter 7. For adjudicatory procedures, including due process requirements, see Chapter 8. For procedural requirements related to impact statements and the like, see Chapter 5.

Relevant Factors

With regard to relevant factors, agencies should be permitted to consider issues relevant to other applicable statutes such as the factors addressed in the EIS required by NEPA. See Chapter 5.

Advanced Issues in Agency Decisionmaking: Reasoned Decisionmaking, Cost-Benefit Analysis and Impact Statements

5

This chapter looks at some advanced and specialized issues in agency decisionmaking and how they are enforced on judicial review.

OVERVIEW

The chapter focuses on how administrative law advances reasoned decisionmaking and employs impact statements and cost-benefit analysis as part of that decisionmaking process. This chapter also looks at estoppel of agencies and the issue of agency nonacquiescence, i.e., instances in which an agency refuses to follow a lower court decision until the issue is determined authoritatively by the Supreme Court.

The ideal in administrative law is for agencies to engage in reasoned decisionmaking informed by their expertise and without excessive political influence. Agencies should consider only those matters that are made relevant by governing statutes. Cost-benefit analysis has been identified as a useful tool to improve agency policymaking and reduce the potential for arbitrary agency action, but courts will not require agencies to use it unless governing statutes clearly require it. Further, Executive Orders have required agencies to conduct cost-benefit analyses of their rules when such analysis is permitted by law.

Impact statements are another popular device for improving agency policymaking mainly by requiring agencies to consider important effects of their rules that they might not have otherwise considered. The most well-known type of impact statement is the environmental impact statement (EIS), which is required by the National Environmental Policy Act (NEPA), but agencies have been required to prepare impact statements on a wide variety of economic, social, and governmental effects of their rules. Impact statement requirements such as NEPA do not ordinarily require agencies to change their actions based on the impacts. Rather, impact statements ensure that both agencies and the public are aware of the effects of agency action, which can provide ammunition in the political process to those opposing agency action on relevant grounds.

In the realm of reasoned decisionmaking, courts conducting judicial review have imposed requirements of consistency and clarity on administrative agencies. The clarity requirement holds that agencies may act in some circumstances only under relatively clear rules. Related to this requirement is the principle that on judicial review, agency action is evaluated based only on those factors actually relied upon by the agency. The consistency requirement holds that agencies must treat like cases alike unless the agency states a new rule and explains the change. In some circumstances, this may mean that an agency must state a governing principle against which its individual actions can be evaluated for consistency. A related doctrine holds that agencies must follow their own rules, except that courts may not enforce internal agency rules that are not intended to benefit the public.

Agencies are not estopped by the conduct or erroneous statements of agency officials, especially when the expenditure of funds is involved. If an official gives erroneous advice, the agency may still insist on adherence to the correct rule. The government is normally not subjected to non-mutual collateral estoppel, which means that the government may relitigate an issue it has lost against another party. Relatedly, agencies may sometimes refuse to acquiesce in unfavorable court decisions especially when an issue is open in the particular federal circuit in which the agency action is taking place. Intra-circuit nonacquiescence, in which an agency adheres to its rule even in the circuit that rejected the agency's view, is probably unjustifiable and contrary to the rule of law.

A. REASONED DECISIONMAKING

1. Permissible Considerations in Agency Policymaking
2. Clarity and Consistency
   a. Clarity
   b. The *Chenery* Rule
   c. Consistency
   d. Agencies Must Follow Their Own Rules
   e. Estoppel of Administrative Agencies

B. COST-BENEFIT ANALYSIS

1. Presidential Directives to Apply Cost-Benefit Analysis
2. Statutory Cost-Benefit Requirements
3. Should Agencies Use Cost-Benefit Analysis?

C. IMPACT STATEMENTS

1. Regulatory Impact Statements
2. Environmental Impact Statements under NEPA

A. Reasoned Decisionmaking

As we have seen in Chapter 4's examination of the arbitrary, capricious standard, the ideal in administrative law is for agency policymaking to be the result of **reasoned decisionmaking**, understood as application of agency expertise to the factors made relevant by governing law, including statutes and regulations. The normal push and pull of the political process, changing circumstances, and the differing perspectives of various actors including Congress and the President often divert agency policymaking from the ideal. What follows elaborates and expands on that ideal and the issues that have arisen surrounding it.

(1) Permissible Considerations in Agency Policymaking

Agency policymaking should be the product of agency expertise as applied to governing statutes. The primary matters that agencies are permitted to take into account are derived from applicable statutes including the agency's organic statute, and other generally applicable statutes such as NEPA. Agencies are also generally permitted to take into account the views of the President and the administration, but only insofar as those views are consistent with governing statutes. Under normal principles of judicial review, agencies are required to consider the factors made relevant by statute and should not consider extraneous matters not statutorily relevant.

Recent developments have reinforced the prohibition against agencies taking into account factors that, while they may be reasonable, are not contemplated by governing statutes. The Supreme Court's decision in *Massachusetts v. EPA*, 549 U.S. 497 (2007), supports the notion that agencies should make policy by applying their expertise to the factors made statutorily relevant. The Court rejected agency consideration of factors that had long been thought appropriate for agencies to take into account, such as scientific uncertainty and the President's views on the best way to proceed in an area with international implications. That decision reviewed the EPA's decision not to engage in rulemaking, not the substance of a final rule, but it still appears to have implications for judicial review of agency policymaking generally. The Court stated that "its reasons for action or inaction must conform to the authorizing statute. . . . To the extent that this constrains agency discretion to pursue other priorities of the Administrator or the President, this is the congressional design."

This is not to say that the law does not allow administration policy to be taken into account by administrative agencies. The Supreme Court has repeatedly stated that it is permissible for agencies to consider the President's views. However, the final decision must be within the discretion granted by governing statutes and rules. Further, agencies should not present their decisions as the product of the give and take among interest groups. Formally, agencies are required to engage in reasoned decisionmaking by justifying their decisions based upon consideration of the legally relevant factors and agency expertise. While the realities of the political process make it unrealistic to assume that agencies avoid influence from affected interests, the decision must at least appear to be based upon a rational understanding of the legally relevant factors.

An obvious corollary to the obligation to consider only statutorily relevant factors is that agencies may not take into account irrelevant factors, i.e., political factors that are not within the considerations made relevant by statute or valid regulation. For example, the D.C. Circuit reversed the Secretary of Transportation's decision to build a bridge, in part, because the Secretary apparently was influenced by a congressman's threat to withhold funding for another project if the Secretary did not approve the bridge. See *D.C. Federation of Civic Associations v. Volpe*, 459 F.2d 1231 (D.C. Cir. 1971), *cert. denied*, 405 U.S. 1030 (1972).

(2) **Clarity and Consistency**

Courts have, in some circumstances, imposed obligations of **clarity and consistency** upon agencies. Briefly stated, agencies are sometimes required to operate under clearly stated substantive criteria, and they are sometimes held to a relatively strong obligation to treat like cases alike unless they explicitly disavow the substantive rule governing prior decisions. These requirements are closely related to Administrative Procedure Act (APA) standards of judicial review and should be understood in conjunction with them. In short, in some cases agency action that appears to be inconsistent with prior decisions or that does not proceed from a discernible standard has been held to violate APA §706's arbitrary, capricious standard of review.

(a) **Clarity**

Courts have held that certain agency action may be taken only pursuant to clear criteria. This is termed the "**clarity**" requirement. The clarity cases are in tension with decisions allowing agencies a great deal of discretion under the APA over whether to promulgate rules or decide issues on a case-by-case basis. Three reasons support the clarity requirements: notice to the party of the standards for government action, prevention of arbitrary agency action, and facilitation of review of agency action (both at higher agency levels and in the courts).

The instinct in favor of the clarity requirement is similar to the D.C. Circuit's reasoning under the nondelegation doctrine in the *American Trucking* case, discussed in Chapter 2. Recall that the Court of Appeals was concerned that the .08 ppm limit on ozone in the ambient air was not the product of a clear rule or set of decisionmaking criteria. Rather, the decision appeared somewhat ad hoc, derived from a general "all things considered" process of weighing the pros and cons of various possible limits. The Supreme Court rejected the D.C. Circuit's conclusion that this lack of a preexisting regulatory standard violated the nondelegation doctrine, but this decision does not foreclose application of the clarity requirement as a matter of non-constitutional judicial review doctrine.

It has been argued that even if the D.C. Circuit was incorrect in *American Trucking* as a matter of the nondelegation doctrine, the law recognizes that agency action can be arbitrary and capricious if it cannot be traced back to a preexisting standard.[1] This argument was based on *Pearson v. Shalala*, 164 F.3d 650, 660 (D.C. Cir. 1999), a case

---

[1]See Lisa Schultz Bressman, *Beyond Accountability: Arbitrariness and Legitimacy in the Administrative State*, 78 N.Y.U. L. Rev. 461 (2008).

in which agency action was held to be arbitrary and capricious because it was not derived from a preexisting standard. In *Pearson*, the manufacturers of dietary supplements challenged an FDA regulation that governed the health claims they could make regarding their products. The regulation required manufacturers to seek FDA permission to make health claims and stated that it would grant permission only if the health claims were supported by "significant scientific agreement" among experts in the field. After the FDA denied requests for permission to make health claims, the manufacturers sued and claimed, inter alia, that the failure of the FDA to define "significant scientific agreement" rendered the denials arbitrary and capricious. In essence, the manufacturers were challenging the agency action for lack of clarity.

The D.C. Circuit agreed with the manufacturers, holding that "the APA requires the agency to explain why it rejects their proposed health claims — to do so adequately necessarily implies giving some definitional content to the phrase 'significant scientific agreement.' We think this proposition is squarely rooted in the prohibition under the APA that an agency not engage in arbitrary and capricious action." *Pearson*, 164 F.3d at 661. This seems to be a relatively stringent clarity requirement, and it is not clear that this approach would be followed by courts with a more deferential attitude toward agency action than that often displayed by the D.C. Circuit.[2] "Significant scientific agreement" on its own is not so hopelessly vague that a court cannot intelligently evaluate the agency's reasons for granting or denying permission. It is not a precise standard, but it has sufficient content to ensure that the agency has applied its expertise, considered the relevant factors, and taken a "hard look" at the issues involved. Most courts, including the Supreme Court, do not require more.

The clarity requirement has arisen mainly in cases challenging state agency action as inconsistent with federal due process requirements. In light of more recent developments in due process norms, including the *Roth* line of cases defining property interests and the development of the *Mathews v. Eldridge* balancing test (see Chapter 8), it is unclear whether courts would adhere to these decisions today. It is also unclear whether the APA imposes a similar, non-constitutional requirement on federal agencies. The following cases are examples of situations in which clarity requirements have been invoked.

In *Soglin v. Kauffman*, 418 F.2d 163 (7th Cir. 1969), a case dealing with university discipline, the court held that the use of "misconduct" as the standard for imposing expulsion or prolonged suspension on university students violated the Fourteenth Amendment as too vague. (*Soglin* involved punishment of Vietman War era protestors by the University of Wisconsin-Madison, and the named plaintiff, Paul Soglin, was later elected mayor of Madison.) In *Hornsby v. Allen*, 326 F.2d 605 (5th Cir. 1964), the court held that the denial of a liquor license to a qualified applicant by the board of aldermen and mayor violated the Fourteenth Amendment if the aldermen and mayor had not established ascertainable standards governing their decisions. This decision seems inconsistent with the *Roth* standard for determining whether due process applies at all. The lack of ascertainable standards would imply that the licensee had no property interest in the license. However, there may be other reasons for not allowing local officials to have complete discretion over a business license such as the liquor license at issue in *Hornsby*.

In a case similar to *Hornsby*, *Holmes v. New York City Housing Authority*, 398 F.2d 262 (2d Cir. 1968), the Second Circuit held that the agency selecting families for

---

[2]Professor Bressman also cited *Checkosky v. SEC*, 139 F.3d 221 (D.C. Cir. 1998), as a case imposing a clarity requirement under APA judicial review.

public housing must operate under ascertainable standards, and where many more applicants are equally qualified for the housing available, the agency must adopt a procedure for choosing which applications to grant. Again, while there may be good reasons related to fairness and the potential for corruption and discrimination for requiring agencies dispensing benefits to operate under clear rules, the due process reasoning does not seem consistent with the *Roth* line of cases.

In the immigration area, there has been some inconsistency concerning the clarity requirement. In *Fook Hong Mak v. INS*, 435 F.2d 728 (2d Cir. 1970), the Second Circuit held that the Immigration and Naturalization Service (INS) was entitled to deny an application for discretionary review of an alien's immigration status on the basis of a Department of Justice regulation against status adjustment for aliens in the petitioner's category who applied for discretionary adjustment. The alien argued that the agency was required to examine, on a case-by-case basis, whether a particular alien met the statutory standards for adjustment of statute. The Court, in an opinion by Judge Friendly, held that the agency was entitled to promulgate a clear rule making a particular class of aliens ineligible for adjustment. In a similar controversy, however, the Ninth Circuit took a different view. In *Asimokopoulos v. INS*, 445 F.2d 1362 (9th Cir. 1971), the Ninth Circuit held that because the governing statute granted the INS "discretion" in deciding whether to adjust an alien's status, the agency could not deny an application based on its own rule limiting discretion. While this may seem to create the potential for less clarity, because the agency decision will now be based on discretion and not the rule, given that the discretion was built into the rule itself, in order to be clear, the court held that the agency must explain why it was declining to exercise its discretion in the particular case. In general, in the interest of clarity, most cases lean toward allowing discretion-limiting rules as the Second Circuit did in *Fook Hong Mak*.

Entitlement theory, which limits property and certain liberty interests to situations in which positive law contains criteria governing the decision, may undercut the reasoning of these cases. However, the Supreme Court has come down in favor of rules in the welfare area, stating in *Morton v. Ruiz*, 415 U.S. 199 (1974), that "[n]o matter how rational or consistent with congressional intent a particular decision might be, the determination of eligibility cannot be made on an *ad hoc* basis by the dispenser of the funds." Although a general doctrine requiring clear rules has not developed, and *Ruiz* is not a highly cited decision, there are strong reasons, constitutional and non-constitutional, for favoring rules over complete agency discretion in benefits decisions and any subject area in which individual liberty is at stake.

Sidebar

ARGUMENT FOR CLEAR RULES

There is great normative attractiveness to the doctrine that says that under certain circumstances, especially when important private interests are at stake, such as immigration status or the ability to live in public housing, government ought to proceed via relatively clear rules. Rules reduce the possibility of corruption and error, and provide a baseline for review whether in the agency or in court. However, rigid rules limit agencies' ability to adjust their actions to the exigencies or equities of a particular case.

The recent decision in *United States v. AMC Entertainment, Inc.*, 549 F.3d 760 (9th Cir. 2008), illustrates the fairness instincts underlying concerns over clarity in the law. That case involved applying the Americans with Disabilities Act to movie theaters with stadium seating. Soon after the Act was passed, the Department of Justice promulgated a regulation concerning sight lines for wheelchair users in entertainment venues. The regulation did not specifically address movie theaters with stadium seating because they did not exist until later. After AMC constructed numerous theaters in reliance on its understanding of the law as it stood at the time, which was confirmed by the issuance of building permits by numerous local authorities under standards that had been approved at the federal level, the Department of Justice began advocating a new understanding that would require expensive modifications of AMC's existing theaters. After a federal district issued an injunction requiring AMC to comply with this new understanding, the Court of Appeals for the Ninth Circuit reversed on the basis that the law was not clear at the time AMC built its theaters. The court linked this to constitutional due process concerns: "Because the injunction requires modifications to multiplexes that were designed or built before the government gave fair notice of its interpretation of §4.33.3, the injunction violates due process — and to that extent, its issuance was an abuse of discretion. . . . Due process requires that the government provide citizens and other actors with sufficient notice as to what behavior complies with the law." *AMC Entertainment, Inc.*, 549 F.3d at 762, 768.

(b) The *Chenery* Rule

Related to the clarity requirement is the well-established *Chenery* **rule** that agency decisions are evaluated, on judicial review, based on the reasons given by the agency at the time the decision was made. This is different from the rule that normally prevails on appeal of a judgment by a court where a judgment may be affirmed on any basis, not merely the lower court's reasoning in support of its decision. Under the *Chenery* rule, an agency may not, on judicial review, defend its decision on a basis that was not relied upon by the agency at the time it made the decision. However, if the court remands a matter to the agency because its explanation is inadequate, the agency may adhere to its original decision if it constructs an acceptable alternative explanation.

The *Chenery* case is the most famous example of the operation of this rule. The Chenery family managed and owned shares in the Federal Water Service Corporation. The corporation was in a reorganization under which holders of preferred stock would ultimately control the corporation. During the reorganization process, the Chenerys purchased a large block of preferred stock on the open market. The Securities and Exchange Commission (SEC) conditioned its approval of the reorganization on the Chenerys selling their stock back to the corporation. In support of this decision, the SEC relied solely upon traditional equity rules governing fiduciary relationships for its finding that the Chenerys' purchase of the preferred stock while the reorganization was pending was improper. On judicial review, the SEC defended its action as based not only on traditional equity principles but also with arguments based on the policies underlying the securities laws and its expertise in applying those laws.

In *SEC v. Chenery Corp. (I)*, 318 U.S. 80 (1943), the Supreme Court held that traditional equity rules did not provide an adequate basis for the SEC's order, and that the SEC could not rely upon its additional securities law justifications because they were not part of the SEC's contemporaneous explanation for its action. On remand to the agency, the SEC reaffirmed its decision but explained itself based upon its expertise in applying the policies underlying the securities law. This time, the Supreme Court upheld the SEC indicating that the SEC "has made what we indicated in our prior opinion would be an informed, expert judgment on the problem." *SEC v. Chenery Corp. (II)*, 332 U.S. 194 (1947).

One aspect of the decision in *Chenery II* may be inconsistent with the argument that administrative law principles require agencies to proceed from preexisting rules. There was no preexisting SEC rule that would have barred the Chenerys from purchasing the stock during the reorganization. The Supreme Court held that this was not fatal to the agency proceeding on a case-by-case basis, even if the agency's action had some retroactive effect. This decision is consistent with other decisions, discussed in Chapter 6, granting agencies a great deal of discretion over whether to act by rule or through case-by-case adjudication.

F   A   Q

Q: What is the basis for the *Chenery* rule? Why shouldn't an agency be able to raise a new argument on judicial review if that argument would have been sufficient to support the agency's decision?

A: The Supreme Court's justification for the doctrine is notion that Congress expects the agency's decision to be the product of its expertise, and a court cannot affirm based on an agency argument that does not embody the actual application of expertise in the particular case. This would be inconsistent with the agency's obligation to engage in reasoned decisionmaking. The *Chenery* Court stated, "If an order is valid only as a determination of policy or judgment which the agency alone is authorized to make and which it has not made, a judicial judgment cannot be made to do service for an administrative judgment. For purposes of affirming, no less than reversing, its orders, an appellate court cannot intrude upon the domain which Congress has exclusively entrusted to an administrative agency." *Chenery I*, 318 U.S. at 88.

Relatedly, the Court also explained that allowing an agency to defend its actions in court with reasons not relied upon at the agency level is inconsistent with the nature of judicial review, which evaluates agency action based on the reasons given by the agency. The Court stated that "[t]he Commission's action cannot be upheld merely because findings might have been made and considerations disclosed which would justify its order as an appropriate safeguard for the interests protected by the Act. There must be such a responsible finding." Id. at 94. The Court also supported the doctrine with the notion that allowing an agency to defend its decision based on a ground not relied upon at the agency level would upset "the orderly functioning of the process of review." Id. The implication here is that agencies might not feel obligated to disclose the true reasons for their actions, but would rather construct a fictional justification that it found most likely to survive judicial review.

Professor Kevin Stack has argued for an alternative normative basis for the *Chenery* rule. In his view, the *Chenery* rule is a forgotten corollary to the nondelegation doctrine under which agencies must explicitly ground the exercise of delegated discretion in reasons sufficient to withstand judicial review:

> By requiring the agency to expressly state the grounds for its action, *Chenery* erects a barrier to Congress's giving away its own prerogative to act without articulating grounds for its actions. Put another way, *Chenery* operates to impede Congress from delegating its own prerogative of obscurantism. On this view, part of the tradeoff for Congress's choice to delegate authority is that the recipient of that power must be more articulate about the grounds for its action than Congress would be.[3]

---

[3]See Kevin M. Stack, *The Constitutional Foundations of* Chenery, 116 Yale L.J. 952, 1000 (2007).

Whether it has a constitutional basis or not, the *Chenery* rule is a principle of administrative law. Reviewing courts may uphold agency action based only on the reasoning of the agency, even if it is apparent that on remand the agency will reaffirm its original decision with legally sufficient reasons.

(c) Consistency

It is often stated that agencies are required to be **consistent**, which means that they must treat like cases alike. As a corollary to this, agencies must offer an explanation when they treat apparently like cases differently. However, agencies are free to change their policies so that later cases are treated differently from earlier ones, but they must explain any changed policy, and the new policy must, of course, be consistent with governing statutes and acceptable under the applicable standard of judicial review.

This purported obligation to treat like cases alike is in tension with the general rejection of **discriminatory enforcement** claims. In discriminatory enforcement claims, which are discussed in more detail in Chapter 9, the subject of an agency enforcement action claims that others, usually competitors, are violating the same provision and that the agency should not be able to enforce an order against it unless and until it also issues an order against the other violators. These claims often involve competitors because the subject of the enforcement action claims that without enforcement against competitors, they will be disadvantaged in competition if they have to obey an order while their competitors do not. The Supreme Court has not been sympathetic to claims of discriminatory enforcement, holding that agencies have great

> ## Sidebar
>
> **CONSISTENCY IS A DIFFICULT STANDARD TO MEET**
>
> Although it seems that consistency would be a basic expectation of government in general and administrative agencies in particular, it is actually very difficult to enforce a consistency requirement. In areas with clear rules, such as benefits or license administration, requiring agencies to adhere to the rules ensures a measure of consistency. However, when agencies have discretion, and their expertise is involved, courts tend to be very deferential to agency action and consistency may be sacrificed in favor of flexibility.

discretion to choose their subjects of enforcement unless there is a "patent abuse of discretion." This reasoning undercuts the argument that there is an enforceable general obligation to treat like cases alike.

Agencies most often risk acting inconsistently in adjudication when each case is evaluated separately without a preexisting legislative rule governing the situation. Paradoxically, because there is no preexisting rule, but only agency opinions in the style of judicial opinions supporting prior orders, it is more difficult to detect inconsistency than when the agency is acting under a preexisting legislative rule. There are examples, however, in which courts have held that agency adjudicatory decisionmaking is void for inconsistency with prior adjudicatory action. For example, see *Shaw's Supermarkets, Inc. v. NLRB*, 884 F.2d 34, 41 (1st Cir. 1989) (Breyer, J.). That case involved a charge of an unfair labor practice by an employer for threatening reprisals if employees voted to unionize. In a series of opinions resulting in a well-established rule, the NLRB held that, in the absence of additional factors, such a threat did not inhere in a statement that the employer would "bargain from scratch" with a union (i.e., that the employer would not take into account the current level of wages and benefits but would take the position that all issues were open to negotiation). A management employee of Shaw's Supermarkets told employees, during a representation campaign, that if the employees decided to unionize, Shaw's would start the bargaining with minimum wage and workers' compensation and build from there. At the time, the employees were earning substantially more than the minimum wage. After the employees voted against unionization, the NLRB decided that the statements constituted unfair labor practices as threats of reprisals. This seemed inconsistent with the NLRB's prior decisions, and the NLRB made no effort to explain the apparent inconsistency. When the NLRB petitioned for enforcement of its order, the Court of Appeals refused to enforce it, holding that the NLRB's decision was inconsistent with the NLRB's own precedent. The court noted that if the NLRB wishes to change its rule, it must "[focus] upon the issue and [explain] why change is reasonable." *Shaw's Supermarkets, Inc. v. NLRB*, 884 F.2d 34, 41 (1st Cir. 1989) (Breyer, J.). See also *Brennan v. Gilles & Cotting, Inc.*, 504 F.2d 1255 (4th Cir. 1974) (agencies "must explain departures from agency policies or rules apparently dispositive of a case").

In a similar vein moving an adjudicatory agency toward consistency, the Supreme Court has not allowed adjudicatory agencies like the NLRB to exercise the same degree of freedom in their legal reasoning as is enjoyed by courts applying the common law methodology. *Allentown Mack Sales and Service, Inc. v. NLRB*, 522 U.S. 359 (1998), is a very interesting decision regarding consistency in adjudicatory agency decisionmaking. The case involved the NLRB's rules, developed in a series of adjudicatory proceedings as agency precedent, governing when an employer can cease to recognize a union or poll its employees on their support for the union, when it doubts that the union maintains the support of the represented employees. The NLRB's doctrine allows an employer to poll its employees or simply refuse to bargain when it has a "good faith reasonable doubt" about the union's continued majority support among employees. On its face, this seems like a relatively lenient standard, but in actual practice the NLRB had been applying a standard that, according to one law review article, required that the employer actually prove that a majority of the represented employees had repudiated the union.[4] One of the arguments made in support of the NRLB's finding that Allentown Mack had improperly polled its employees regarding their continued support for the union was that its decisions had required a higher standard of proof than might be apparent from the bare words of the governing precedential standard.

Justice Scalia's opinion for the Court in *Allentown Mack Sales* rejects the idea that an adjudicatory agency can re-shape a rule in application in a manner that appears inconsistent with language of the rule as announced. The opinion characterizes such action by an administrative

Sidebar

REASONED DECISIONMAKING IN ADJUDICATION

The Court's conclusion that the NLRB's opinion in *Allentown Mack* was not reasoned decisionmaking is ironic, given that the NLRB's creativity in construing its precedent does not appear to be different in kind from the creativity that the Court itself uses in elaborating legal doctrine in many areas including judicial review of administrative action. For example, consider the permutations of step one of the *Chevron* doctrine's standard that agencies and courts are bound when Congress has "directly spoken to the precise question at issue." The Supreme Court probably does not meet the standard of rationality it imposed on the NLRB in *Allentown Mack*.

[4]See Joan Flynn, *The Costs and Benefits of "Hiding the Ball": NLRB Policymaking and the Failure of Judicial Review*, 75 B.U. L. Rev. 387, 394-95 (1995) cited in *Allentown Mack Sales*, 522 U.S. at 372-72.

agency as inconsistent with the requirement that agency decisions be "logical and rational." The opinion characterizes the NLRB's actions as follows:

> The National Labor Relations Board, uniquely among major federal administrative agencies, has chosen to promulgate virtually all the legal rules in its field through adjudication rather than rulemaking. . . . But adjudication is subject to the requirement of reasoned decisionmaking as well. It is hard to imagine a more violent breach of that requirement than applying a rule of primary conduct or a standard of proof which is in fact different from the rule or standard formally announced. And the consistent repetition of that breach can hardly mend it. . . . The evil of a decision that applies a standard other than the one it enunciates spreads in both directions, preventing both consistent application of the law by subordinate agency personnel (notably ALJ's), and effective review of the law by the courts.

522 U.S. at 374-75. Thus, as exemplified by *Allentown Mack Sales*, when an agency announces a rule in an adjudicatory process, it must apply the rule as written. An agency may not modify a rule sub silentio, in the style of a common law court, by deciding cases in a manner that is inconsistent with the rule as announced and then defending its decisions on the basis of a practice inconsistent with the words of the rule. This decision is in line with what we have seen as an instinct within some courts to increase agency consistency by requiring agencies to proceed via and adhere to clearly stated general rules.

(d) Agencies Must Follow Their Own Rules

Agencies are normally required to follow their own rules, whether those rules have been adopted in a rulemaking proceeding or announced in the course of agency adjudication. If an agency wishes to change a rule, it must do so in a procedurally valid fashion and must explain the basis for the change. It cannot simply ignore the rule when the rule does not suit the agency's purposes, even if it would be reasonable for the agency to change the rule.

If an agency adopts a rule in a rulemaking or a formal adjudication, the agency may change that rule in a subsequent proceeding—a rule adopted in rulemaking may only be revised in a rulemaking proceeding, while a rule adopted in adjudication may be altered either in a subsequent adjudication or in a rulemaking proceeding. The new rule will be reviewed to determine whether it is within the agency's statutory authority and whether the record provides adequate support for it. In a change situation, judicial review is somewhat heightened because in addition to the usual factors, the court will ask whether the agency has adequately justified the change from the prior rule.

The general principle in favor of consistency, and the notion that agencies should follow their own rules, also casts doubt on agency attempts to change

Sidebar

PROCEDURAL REQUIREMENTS FOR CHANGING RULES

These procedural requirements for changing rules mean that an agency may not informally adopt a policy that contradicts the terms of a formally adopted rule. For example, in *National Family Planning and Reproductive Health Association, Inc. v. Sullivan*, 979 F.2d 227 (D.C. Cir. 1992), the court overturned an interpretive rule that was inconsistent with a rule that had been promulgated in a notice and comment rulemaking. Interestingly, the court did not simply state that the second rule was an invalid interpretation because it was inconsistent with the prior rule. It proceduralized the issue and stated that the interpretive rule was invalid because the agency cannot alter a rule promulgated pursuant to notice and comment without engaging in a new round of notice and comment rulemaking.

rules retroactively. Retroactive rule changes can appear unfair when a regulated party has relied upon existing rules and they can be viewed as an attempt to avoid the obligation to remain consistent. Retroactive lawmaking by Congress has been upheld on a relatively lenient standard of judicial review for constitutionality. However, retroactive rulemaking by agencies is another matter altogether. Concerns over fairness and consistency have led to a negative judicial reaction to retroactive changes to agency rules. Retroactive changes in agency rules are disfavored, especially when the changes have material retroactive effects on the regulated party. For example, in *Arizona Grocery Co. v. Atchison, Topeka & Santa Fe Rwy.*, 284 U.S. 370 (1932), the Supreme Court held that the Interstate Commerce Commission (ICC) could not order a railroad to make refunds to shippers on the ground that the railroad's shipping rates were unreasonable after the ICC had itself established that the very rates at issue were reasonable in a previous proceeding. The Court held that the rates could be changed prospectively but that retroactive reductions were impermissible. The railroad had a strong claim of reliance on the rates as established by the ICC.

More recently, the Supreme Court has reiterated that retroactive rule changes are disfavored and agencies may not issue them without specific legislative authorization. In *Bowen v. Georgetown University Hospital*, 488 U.S. 204 (1988), the Court held that the Department of Health and Human Services (HHS) could not retroactively recalculate Medicare reimbursements due to hospitals for 1981 and 1982 based on a regulation promulgated in 1984. The Court held that the Medicare Act did not allow retroactive rulemaking and that such rulemaking would be presumed unlawful absent a specific provision allowing retroactive rules. This singles out retroactivity for more restrictive treatment than other agency policy decisions that would be reviewed under the (usually) deferential arbitrary and capricious standard of judicial review. These cases illustrate that the Court looks upon retroactive agency action that has substantial monetary effects with suspicion because it upsets settled expectations and entails a great potential for arbitrariness.

As a further matter related to consistency, it is a general principle of administrative law that agencies should follow their own procedural rules, even when these rules go beyond the rights afforded by any statute or due process. This does not present a *Vermont Yankee* problem (see Chapter 7) because the court is enforcing the agencies' own rules and not imposing a rule on an unwilling agency. However, there is some uncertainty about whether there is actually a strictly enforced requirement that agencies follow their own procedural rules under all circumstances.

The decision that stands most strongly in favor of a requirement that agencies follow their own rules is *United States ex rel. Accardi v. Shaughnessy*, 347 U.S. 260 (1954). In that case, the Court required the Board of Immigration Appeals to follow its own procedural rule requiring the agency "to exercise its own judgment when considering appeals." Accardi had filed for habeas corpus after the Board of Immigration Appeals rejected his appeal from the denial of his application for discretionary relief from deportation. He alleged that the Attorney General had, in effect, ordered the Board to deny his appeal before the Board heard his case in violation of the regulations requiring that the agency exercise its own judgment. See also *Ballard v. Commissioner of Internal Revenue*, 544 U.S. 40 (2005) (tax court required to disclose recommendation of special trial judges because tax court's own rules require disclosure). The D.C. Circuit has referred to "[t]he Accardi doctrine" as requiring agencies to "follow their own rules." *Steinholdt v. FAA*, 314 F.3d 633, 639

(D.C. Cir. 2003). See also *Morton v. Ruiz*, 415 U.S. 199 (1974) (criticizing agency for not publishing eligibility criterion as required by agency's informally promulgated claims manual).

There are decisions, however, that cast doubt on the existence of any such doctrine, especially with regard to informally promulgated internal rules intended only to guide agency employees rather than benefit the public. In *Schweiker v. Hansen*, 450 U.S. 785 (1981), the Court approved the denial of retroactive Social Security benefits to an applicant even though an agency employee violated a provision of an agency manual that required the employee to advise the applicant to file a written application. The governing statute expressly required a written application before benefits could be granted retroactively. The Court relied on two factors in affirming the denial, first that courts must respect Congress's conditions on the expenditure of funds and second that the manual had no legal status but rather was intended only to provide guidance to agency employees. The Court has since, in a case involving whether an agency provided sufficient public notice of a program, reaffirmed the notion that "not all agency publications are of binding force." See *Lyng v. Payne*, 476 U.S. 926, 937 (1986).

F A Q

Q: Given the apparent inconsistency among cases involving the requirement that agencies follow their own procedural rules, what do the lower courts do?

A: Lower courts attempting to navigate between these two lines of cases have seized on reliance as a factor tilting in favor of requiring an agency to follow its own rules. If an agency promulgates a rule, even informally, and members of the public rely on that rule or are prejudiced by the agency's failure to follow the rule, courts have required agencies to follow the rule even if the informal process of promulgation would normally deprive the rule of the force of law. See *American Farm Lines v. Black Ball Freight Service*, 397 U.S. 532, 538-39 (1970); *Port of Jacksonville Maritime Ad Hoc Committee, Inc. v. United States Coast Guard*, 788 F.2d 705, 709 (11th Cir. 1986). In some cases, courts have characterized agency failure to follow an informally promulgated rule as violating due process. See *United States v. Hefner*, 420 F.2d 809, 812 (4th Cir. 1976). However, if an agency fails to follow a rule intended for internal use only, and if the complaining party cannot establish prejudice resulting from the failure, it appears that the failure to follow the rule will not provide a basis for relief to the private party. See *First Family Mortgage Corp. of Florida v. Earnest*, 851 F.2d 843, 844-45 (6th Cir. 1988).

Where does this leave us in terms of agency consistency? Strict enforcement of agency rules, whether formally or informally promulgated, would advance the cause of consistency, but not without costs. These costs would include the loss of agency flexibility to adapt to circumstances, the possibility that blunders by low-level officials could bind an agency, and the likelihood that federal funds would be spent contrary to the instructions of Congress. For these and perhaps additional reasons, the courts have not been willing to adopt a strict view, and in many circumstances have allowed agencies to escape the consequences of the failure to follow each and every feature of all of their rules.

(e) Estoppel of Administrative Agencies

Related to the question whether agencies are always bound to follow their own procedural rules is the issue of **estoppel** of agencies by the conduct or statements of agency employees. "Estoppel" is a situation in which a party cannot assert a legal argument, usually a defense, because of conduct that would make assertion of the defense inequitable. Estoppel against the government arises when an agency official provides erroneous advice to a member of the public that leads the member of the public to follow an incorrect procedure or take actions that lead to substantively bad consequences. For example, a claimant is instructed to use Form A to apply for a benefit when the correct form is Form B. When the error is discovered, the claimant may argue that because the agency told the claimant to file Form A, the government must provide benefits dating back to when that application was filed even though the law states that benefits are paid only beginning from the date that Form B is filed.

Sidebar

TWO FORMS OF "ESTOPPEL"

It is important to separate two uses of the concept of "estoppel," equitable estoppel by conduct or representations and collateral estoppel in litigation. Estoppel in the first sense involves a claim that it would be unfair to allow an agency to deny something, for example if an agency provides erroneous procedural advice and then tries to use the procedural failing against the private party. Estoppel in the second sense involves a claim that prior litigation estops the government from relitigating an issue on which it lost in the prior litigation.

The usual rule is that agencies are normally not estopped by the conduct or statements of agency officials. Erroneous advice given by an agency official (for example, by misstating the eligibility requirements for a government program) does not estop an agency from relying upon the program's actual requirements and denying claims even if the claimant relied upon erroneous advice.

The reasons relied upon for the lack of estoppel against the government are the constitutional prohibition against spending government funds except as appropriated by Congress, Art. I, §9, cl. 7, and that errors of low-level officials should not be allowed to establish government policy. While the Supreme Court has not adopted an absolute rule precluding estoppel of the government based on erroneous advice, it has come close, recognizing that the arguments in favor of such a rule are "substantial." See *Office of Personnel Management v. Richmond*, 496 U.S. 414, 423 (1990). However, Justice Stevens argued in *Richmond* against relying on the Appropriations Clause to resist estoppel against the government. In his view, "[t]he Constitution contemplates appropriations that cover programs—not individual appropriations for individual payments. . . . The dispute in this case is not

Sidebar

CONSTITUTIONAL RESTRICTION ON ESTOPPEL

Art. I, §9, cl. 7 of the Constitution states that "No Money shall be drawn from the Treasury, but in Consequence of Appropriations made by Law." This provides an argument against judicial allowance of benefits claims against the government due to estoppel when the claimant's application does not meet statutory requirements.

about whether an appropriation has been made; it is instead about what rules govern administration of an appropriation that has been made." 496 U.S. at 435 (Stevens, J., concurring in the judgment).

The operation of the rule against estopping the government may seem unfair when private parties rely on bad advice from government officials. For example, in *Federal Crop Insurance Corp. v. Merrill*, 332 U.S. 380 (1947), a local government official, acting on behalf of the Federal Crop Insurance Corporation, told farmers that their reseeded wheat was insurable against crop failure. The farmers paid the premium. After the crop failed, their claim was denied because it turned out that reseeded wheat was not insurable. The Court held that the erroneous statement of the local government official did not estop the government from denying that the crop was insurable. In the *Richmond* case, a retired government-employed welder received outdated oral and written information from a government employee on how much he could earn and still qualify for his disability annuity. Once he exceeded the statutory earnings limit, he was ruled ineligible for disability payments for the six-month period in which he earned too much income. The Supreme Court rejected his argument that the government should be estopped from cutting off his annuity because of his reliance on the outdated advice. The Court relied primarily on the constitutional prohibition on spending money except as appropriated by Congress, declining, as noted, to create a complete ban on applying estoppel against the government. See *Office of Personnel Management v. Richmond*, 496 U.S. 414, 424 (1990).

F	A	Q

Q: Is the rule against estopping the government absolute?

A: The rule against government estoppel is strongest when an expenditure of funds is involved because of the constitutional principle that funds should be spent only as specified by Congress acting under the Appropriations Clause. The Court has stated categorically that principles of estoppel cannot override the limitations placed by Congress on the expenditure of government funds. See *Office of Personnel Management v. Richmond*, 496 U.S. 414 (1990) (court cannot order government to pay pension to claimant who was given outdated information by his former government employer on how much outside income he could earn without losing pension benefits). See also *Schweiker v. Hansen*, 450 U.S. 785 (1981) (government not estopped by failure of official to advise eligible benefits applicant to file written application). In non-monetary cases, there have been instances in which estoppel has been applied against the government, but it is not clear that such cases would be followed today.

The most important case in which estoppel was applied against the U.S. government is *Moser v. United States*, 341 U.S. 41 (1951), notably involving a non-monetary claim. Moser, a Swiss citizen who resided in the United States with his American wife, was told in writing by the Swiss Legation, a representative of the Swiss government, that he could file for exemption from the draft in the United States and still apply for U.S. citizenship. This advice was contrary to a U.S. statute that prohibited persons who had sought an exemption from the draft from becoming citizens. Further, the form Moser filed for exemption from service clearly stated that filing the form disqualified him from citizenship. However, the Legation had relied on assurances from the U.S. Department of State that the U.S. statute would not affect rights under a treaty that existed between the two countries governing military service of each country's nationals in the other country. The relationship between the treaty and the statute is somewhat opaque, and this led the Court to hold that given his reliance on the erroneous information, Moser had not waived his right to citizenship. While this decision set off a storm of pro-estoppel decisions in lower courts, the Supreme Court has more recently been skeptical of estoppel claims. The Court stated in *Richmond* that if estoppel exists against the government in a non-monetary claim, it would be only in "extreme circumstances."

Estoppel by erroneous information should be distinguished from principles of **collateral estoppel** that apply in litigation, including litigation against the government. Collateral estoppel precludes a party from relitigating an issue that has already been litigated in a prior case between the same parties. For example, in *United States v. Stauffer Chemical Co.*, 464 U.S. 165 (1984), the Court held that once a lower federal court held that the EPA could not require Stauffer to open its premises to private inspectors, and the EPA chose not to appeal that decision, collateral estoppel barred the EPA from relitigating the issue against Stauffer in a different federal court.

In recent years, courts have recognized **non-mutual collateral estoppel**, under which a party is precluded from relitigating an issue that it lost on in litigation against another party. For example, depending on state law, if a product is found to be defective in a products liability suit, if the issue was fully litigated, the manufacturer may be estopped from relitigating that issue against a different plaintiff. However, the Supreme Court has stated that non-mutual collateral estoppel does not apply against the U.S. government. See *United States v. Mendoza*, 464 U.S. 154 (1984).

The *Mendoza* case involved the rights of Filipino members of the U.S. Armed Forces to apply for U.S. citizenship. A federal district court ruled in 1975 that the U.S. government had violated the due process rights of Filipinos in its administration of the program, basically by withdrawing the citizenship examiner from the Philippines, which prevented Filipinos from applying for citizenship. The District Court thus allowed the plaintiffs to apply for citizenship long after the program allowing them to apply based on their service for the United States in World War II had expired. The United States did not appeal that decision but when Mendoza, who was not a plaintiff in the 1975 case, petitioned for naturalization, the government sought to relitigate the issue so that it could deny Mendoza's petition as too late. The lower court held that the government could not relitigate the constitutionality of its administration of the program due to collateral estoppel, but in *United States v. Mendoza*, 464 U.S. 154 (1984), the Supreme Court held that non-mutual collateral estoppel did not apply against the United States, and thus the government was free to relitigate the issue of whether the administration of the program had violated Mendoza's due process rights.

The Court provided several reasons for rejecting the application of non-mutual collateral estoppel against the government. For one, the Court observed that non-mutual collateral estoppel would thwart the development of the law on issues that arise largely or exclusively in litigation with the government, because the first decision would bind the government in all future litigation. The Court feared that this would deprive the Court itself of the benefit of differing lower court approaches which it likes to have before it resolves an issue of federal law. This might lead it to grant certiorari earlier that it would otherwise prefer. It would also dampen the ability of the Solicitor General to take numerous factors into account in deciding whether to appeal a particular ruling—if non-mutual collateral estoppel applies, the Solicitor General would feel compelled to appeal the first adverse ruling. Finally, the Court observed that applying non-mutual collateral estoppel would either prevent or significantly hinder a new administration from revising legal positions taken by a prior administration.

Related to the inapplicability of non-mutual collateral estoppel to the federal government is the practice of **nonacquiescence**. When a lower federal court rejects an agency's position on a legal issue, such as the interpretation of a statute or the procedures the agency must apply in its decisionmaking process, the inapplicability of non-mutual collateral estoppel leaves the agency free to choose whether to acquiesce in the court's decision with regard to other regulated parties. The agency may decide to change its practice or it may not, in which case it may press its losing argument in another court, even if it already lost on the issue in a court of appeals. In such a case, it would press its argument in a different circuit. This sort of inter-circuit nonacquiescence, in which an agency refuses to follow a court of appeals decision from another circuit, is justifiable on the ground that the courts of appeals often disagree with each other, and only the Supreme Court can authoritatively resolve a split among the circuits. In fact, circuit splits provide the ideal setting for Supreme Court review.

Intra-circuit nonacquiescence may be viewed differently. In such cases, an agency elects not to follow a decision of the court of appeals even within the circuit that rendered the decision. This seems to be contrary to the rule of law and the purposes of judicial review, and thus is difficult to defend despite the inapplicability of non-mutual collateral estoppel. In cases of intra-circuit nonacquiescence, the agency knows that if a party seeks judicial review of the agency's decision that is contrary to the circuit's prior decision, the party will prevail. The agency may be hoping that the regulated party chooses not to seek judicial review, perhaps because of cost considerations or ignorance of the chances of prevailing on review. The dominant view seems to be that an agency should follow the decisions of the courts of appeals in the circuit within which the decision was rendered out of fidelity to the rule of law and fairness to affected parties.

A flagrant example of intra-circuit nonacquiescence occurred in the 1980s, when administrative decisions involving evidentiary standards in social security hearings provoked a strong reaction from the Second Circuit. The Second Circuit had a well-established rule regarding evidentiary standards in social security disability cases, which it developed in the course of judicial review of agency benefits denials. The Social Security Administration (SSA) took a different view that made it more difficult for claimants to prevail. Even after the Second Circuit rejected the SSA's standard, agency adjudicators continued to apply the SSA's standard until the particular claimant sought judicial review and prevailed, at which time the agency would hold a new hearing and apply the Second Circuit's standard at the second hearing. Remarkably, the agency insisted that it had acquiesced in the Second Circuit's rule, but it could not explain why so many Administrative Law Judges were applying the agency's prior standard. In *Schisler v. Heckler*, 787 F.2d 76 (2d Cir. 1986), the Second Circuit made a strong statement against intra-circuit nonacquiescence, and ordered the SSA to inform its ALJs of the proper standard to apply to future cases. The court clearly did not want to continue the seemingly never-ending parade of agency denials followed by judicial review, remand, and a new hearing at which the agency would apply the proper standard of proof and the claimant would be awarded benefits. See also *Stieberger v. Heckler*, 615 F. Supp. 1315 (S.D.N.Y. 1985), *vacated and remanded*, 801 F.2d 29 (2d Cir. 1980), in which the SSA's practice was condemned as illegitimate and a threat to the rule of law (under which agencies should follow the decisions of courts on legal matters within judicial cognizance).

B. Cost-Benefit Analysis

One method for improving and evaluating the rationality of agency decisionmaking is **cost-benefit analysis**. Under cost-benefit analysis, a policy is evaluated by comparing the policy's costs with its benefits. It has been argued that agencies should be required to conduct cost-benefit analyses regarding their major policy decisions and should not adopt a policy unless the benefits outweigh the costs. However, while it is useful in some contexts, cost-benefit analysis has serious limitations that prevent it from providing an overarching standard against which to judge every exercise of agency discretion.

(1) Presidential Directives to Apply Cost-Benefit Analysis

The most prominent appearance of cost-benefit analysis in administrative law is in the process of centralized review of agency regulations that has existed since President Reagan put it in place in 1981. As discussed above in Chapter 2, in Executive Order 12,291, President Reagan ordered all executive branch agencies to submit their proposed rules to the Office of Management and Budget (OMB) for review. He also ordered agencies, "to the extent permitted by law" not to take any regulatory action "unless the potential benefits to society for the regulation outweigh the potential costs to society." The order also required agencies to prepare a Regulatory Impact Analysis including cost-benefit analysis on all major rules, and, if permitted by law, to include cost-benefit analysis in its decisionmaking process. The Executive Orders have given the OMB the authority to review the cost-benefit analysis and require further analysis before the agency is permitted to finalize its rulemaking proposal. To some, this gave OMB an inordinate amount of power over the regulatory process, in contravention of statutory delegations of power to particular agencies.[5]

President Bill Clinton replaced Executive Order 12,291 with Executive Order 12,866, which maintained the basic structure of its predecessor. President George W. Bush operated under E.O. 12,866, with some revisions and additions. At this writing, President Barack Obama has begun a process designed to replace E.O. 12,866, but even if he issues a new Executive Order, he is also likely to maintain its basic structure.

Like its predecessor, E.O. 12,866 requires agencies to conduct cost-benefit analysis of proposed regulations. The order requires agencies to analyze alternatives including the possibility of not regulating. Agencies are also directed to follow certain guiding principles including using economic incentives and performance-based solutions instead of command and control regulation, basing decisions on the best available

---

[5] OMB's regulatory review functions under these Executive Orders are carried out by the Office of Information and Regulatory Affairs (OIRA) within OMB.

science, consulting with local and tribal governments, and writing regulations in plain language. The order also established a comprehensive executive branch regulatory planning process, which includes meetings of agency heads and regulatory advisors, the production by agencies of a unified regulatory agenda identifying rules under consideration, and the development by agencies of a forward-looking regulatory plan that describes future regulatory initiatives. The Executive Order also establishes a regulatory working group headed by the OIRA Administrator for the identification and analysis of rulemaking issues, such as "the development of innovative regulatory techniques" or "the methods, efficacy, and utility of comparative risk assessment in regulatory decision-making." The OIRA Administrator is also given authority to consult with outside groups on regulatory initiatives or existent regulations of concern to them.

Neither agency action nor OMB action under the regulatory review of Executive Orders is subject to judicial review. The orders explicitly confine themselves to the internal management of the executive branch and are not meant to create any legally enforceable procedural or substantive rights. Thus, while there has been political wrangling over the extent to which OMB should dictate agency policy, and legal academics have written extensively on the subject, centralized review has not been the subject of judicial analysis because the terms of the relevant Executive Orders are not legally enforceable. See *Meyer v. Bush*, 981 F.2d 1288, 1296-97 (D.C. Cir. 1993); *Michigan v. Thomas*, 805 F.2d 176, 187 (6th Cir. 1986). See also *Center for Science in the Public Interest v. Department of the Treasury*, 797 F.2d 995 (D.C. Cir. 1986) (agency may consider cost-benefit analysis under E.O. 12,291 when permitted by regulatory statute). But see *International Union, United Auto., Aerospace & Agr. Implement Workers v. OSHA*, 938 F.2d 1310 (D.C. Cir. 1991) (suggesting that OSHA has an obligation, under E.O. 12,291, to consider cost-benefit analysis when promulgating safety standards).

> ## Sidebar
>
> ### REVIEW OF "SIGNIFICANT REGULATORY ACTION"
>
> OIRA's regulatory review jurisdiction under E.O. 12,866 applies to "**significant regulatory action.**" "Significant regulatory action" is defined as any rule that will likely have an annual effect on the economy of $100 million or more or adversely and materially affect the economy, productivity, competition, jobs, the environment, public health or safety of any state, local, or tribal government or community. Also considered significant are regulatory actions that are inconsistent with action of another agency, action that would materially alter the budgetary impact of entitlement programs, or raise novel legal or policy issues.

(2) Statutory Cost-Benefit Requirements

Agencies often include cost-benefit analysis in their decisionmaking process, but they may do so only if the statutes governing agency action permit it. Under the arbitrary and capricious standard of judicial review, agencies must consider those factors, and only those factors, made relevant by statute. If an agency's organic statute requires an agency to perform cost-benefit analysis, it must do so. If the governing statute prohibits the agency from considering the costs of its actions, it may not do so. For example, the Supreme Court in the *American Trucking* case approved of the D.C. Circuit's longstanding view that the EPA may not consider costs when establishing National Ambient Air Quality Standards (NAAQS). *Whitman v. American Trucking Associations*, 521 U.S. 457 (2001). This makes sense because NAAQS are like a definition of clean air. Costs are more likely to be relevant at the implementation stage. If the agency's statute is consistent with the application of cost-benefit analysis but does not explicitly require it, courts are likely to allow, but not require, the agency to employ cost-benefit analysis as part of its decisionmaking process.

Many statutes require agencies to take action that is "reasonable" or "appropriate" in light of the circumstances. Advocates of cost-benefit analysis have argued that a general requirement of reasonableness should be understood as requiring that an agency make sure that the costs of regulation are not greater than its benefits. No regulatory action could be reasonable, the argument goes, if its compliance costs are greater than the benefits achieved by compliance. This argument has great intuitive appeal, and some legal theorists have insisted that no reasonable person would ever intentionally take action in which the costs exceed the benefits of acting, for example by placing fairness concerns ahead of economic efficiency.[6] However, courts have not read general standards, such as "reasonably necessary or appropriate," as requiring cost-benefit analysis. Rather, cost-benefit analysis is required only when the statute clearly requires it. However, formulations like "reasonably necessary" are likely to permit an agency to employ cost-benefit analysis if it so chooses.

For example, in *American Textile Manufacturers Institute v. Donovan*, 452 U.S. 490 (1981), the Court refused to read the OSH Act as requiring cost-benefit analysis. The Act, in §3(8), 29 U.S.C. §652(8), defines an "occupational safety and health standard" as a standard that is "reasonably necessary or appropriate" for the health and safety of workers. The Act also provides (in §6(b)(5), 29 U.S.C. §655(b)(5)) that with regard to toxic substances and harmful physical agents, OSHA should regulate at the level that assures, "to the extent feasible," that "no employee will suffer material impairment of health or functional capacity even if such employee has regular exposure to the hazard dealt with by such standard for the period of his working life." After OSHA promulgated standards regulating exposure to cotton dust, the textile industry argued that the agency should have conducted a cost-benefit analysis, under which it would have concluded that the costs of the new standard outweighed its benefits. The Court disagreed, holding that the statute's use of the word "feasible" precluded a cost-benefit analysis requirement and that reading the "reasonably necessary and appropriate" language to require cost-benefit analysis would eviscerate the statute's requirement of regulation to the extent "feasible." The Court also pointed out that other statutes explicitly require cost-benefit analysis—for example, by providing that an agency should act "if the benefits to whomsoever they may accrue are in excess of the estimated costs" or that an agency should not act when "the incremental benefits are clearly insufficient to justify the incremental costs." See *American Textile Manufacturers Institute v. Donovan*, 452 U.S. at 510. This means that general standards like "reasonably necessary" are not likely to be read to require cost-benefit analysis. See id. at 512.

(3) Should Agencies Use Cost-Benefit Analysis?

It is impossible in this book to analyze comprehensively the pros and cons of the use of cost-benefit analysis in agency decisionmaking. In most situations, it makes perfect sense to consider costs and to not promulgate regulations when the costs outweigh the benefits. There are, however, reasons to be cautious about cost-benefit analysis when, for example, the costs or benefits of regulation are difficult to quantify

---

[6]Louis Kaplow & Steven Shavell, *Fairness versus Welfare* (2002).

or if there is concern that the analysis is likely to be biased for political or other reasons. What follows is a brief discussion of the promise and the pitfalls of cost-benefit analysis.

One strong point in favor of agency use of cost-benefit analysis is that it would be a vast improvement over the vague and standardless decisionmaking that seems to prevail at some agencies. Cost-benefit analysis would force agencies to consider the consequences of their policies in a concrete, rigorous, and material way. Agencies would have to **quantify** the costs and benefits as much as possible, and **compare** those costs and benefits to the costs and benefits of potential **alternatives**. Cost-benefit analysis would at least appear to be more systematic than current practice at some agencies and it would provide a clear basis for comparison with other potential policies. Further, a cost-benefit analysis requirement would limit the potential for arbitrary agency action by specifying, in advance, a set of relevant considerations. Finally, cost-benefit analysis may reveal (in some cases) that when all the costs and benefits are taken into account, the proposed regulatory action will actually cause a decrease in social welfare.

Greater **comprehensiveness** is one of the benefits of cost-benefit analysis. Rather than focusing only the policies advanced by the proposed action, an agency properly applying cost-benefit analysis would have to look generally at all of the costs and benefits associated with the proposal. This may even include unintended side effects both positive and negative, assuming they can be foreseen. For example, the installation of catalytic converters in automobiles to reduce pollution required the removal of lead from gasoline. This, together with reductions in industrial lead emissions, caused a sharp decrease in the amount of lead in the bloodstream of children, which in turn lowered the incidence of health problems related to lead in children. This effect should be included in the calculus of the costs and benefits of the regulation, which was aimed primarily at other pollutants. However, another gasoline additive, while improving air quality, turned out to be highly soluble in water and may cause negative health effects when it seeps into ground water. This chemical, MBTE, has been added to gasoline to make it burn more cleanly. In addition to the cost of the additive MBTE itself, the health costs and costs of ground water pollution must be included in any cost-benefit analysis of the desirability of MBTE as a gasoline additive, measured against the benefits of reduced pollution as compared, of course, with alternatives.

> ### Sidebar
>
> **IMPROVEMENTS TO AGENCY DECISIONMAKING**
>
> Cost-benefit analysis is not the only way that decisionmaking could be improved. Even without cost-benefit analysis, agencies should engage in a comprehensive analysis of all proposals. Agencies should establish and clearly state policy goals, whether measured in dollars, fairness, equity, or some other measure. Agencies should identify all of the consequences of proposed rules, both direct and indirect, examine alternatives, identify non-quantifiable costs and benefits, and be willing to experiment with untried alternatives that may work better with lower negative effects.

Critics charge that cost-benefit analysis, while perhaps attractive in theory, does not, for a variety of reasons, fulfill its promise. The critics find that rather than provide increased rigor and certainty, cost-benefit analysis may actually increase the potential for arbitrary agency action by providing a false veneer of scientific analysis that hides contestable value choices and political bias. One great difficulty is that some costs and benefits are difficult to quantify. For example, it is difficult to place a monetary value on the cost of an illness or injury or the benefit of avoiding an illness or injury. More dramatically, it is even more difficult to place a monetary value on a

13645

Rules and Regulations

Federal Register
Vol. 66, No. 45
Wednesday, March 7, 2001

CONSUMER PRODUCT SAFETY COMMISSION

16 CFR Part 1500

Dive Sticks; Final Rule

AGENCY: Consumer Product Safety Commission.

ACTION: Final rule.

SUMMARY: The Commission is issuing a rule to ban certain dive sticks under the authority of the Federal Hazardous Substances Act.[1] Dive sticks are used for underwater activities, such as retrieval games and swimming instruction. They are typically made of rigid plastic and stand upright at the bottom of a swimming pool. Due to these characteristics, if a child jumps onto a dive stick in shallow water he or she may suffer severe injuries.

G. Final Regulatory Analysis

2. Potential Benefits of a Rule Banning Certain Dive Sticks

The reduction in the societal costs of injuries represents the societal benefits of a ban on certain dive sticks. Based on estimates from the CPSC's Injury Cost Model, the costs of impalement injuries, such as those from dive sticks, may range from about $9,000 for injuries that do not require hospitalization to about $100,000 for injuries that require hospitalization. These estimates are based on the costs of injuries involving punctures or lacerations to the victims' lower trunk or pubic region for children 5 to 9 years-of-age (the age range of the known victims). These cost estimates include the cost of medical treatment, pain and suffering, lost work time (including that lost by parents and caregivers), and legal and liability costs.

If we assume that the only cases that required hospitalization were the 5 incidents that required surgery, the total societal costs of the known incidents are about $527,000 (5 cases × $100,000 and 3 cases × $9,000) or an average of $52,700 a year since 1990. This is a low estimate of the total societal cost because it is based only on the cases known to CPSC. There may have been other injuries of which CPSC is not aware.

A useful measure for analytical purposes is the annual average injury cost per dive stick. This estimate is derived by dividing the average annual societal costs of injuries by the average number of dive sticks in use each year. As discussed earlier, the average number of dive sticks in use each year from 1990 to 1999 ranged from about 3 million units (assuming a 1 year product life) to about 5.5 million units (assuming a 4 year product life).

Therefore, the annual societal costs of dive stick injuries may range from about one cent per dive stick in use ($52,700 ÷ 5.5 million) to 2 cents per dive stick in use ($52,700 ÷ 3 million).

Since dive sticks may last from one to four years, the societal costs of injuries per dive stick over the entire life of the dive stick range from about 2 cents ($0.02 × 1 year) to about 4 cents ($.01 × 4 years). Since the benefit of a ban on certain dive sticks is the reduction in the societal cost of the injuries, the benefits of a ban that eliminates these injuries is about 2 to 4 cents per banned dive stick removed from or prevented from entering the market.

The average total annual cost of dive stick injuries of $52,700 is based on known injury cases from 1990 to 1999. However, as noted earlier, dive stick sales increased from less than 1 million per year to about 5 million. If rigid dive sticks that stand upright in water had not been recalled and their annual sales had leveled off at about 5 million units annually (the sales volume in the late 1990s), the product population model indicates that the number of dive sticks in use would have reached 8 to 20 million units within the next few years. Since we estimated that the societal cost of injuries per dive stick in use was about 1 to 2 cents, this indicates that the annual cost of dive stick impalement injuries would have reached approximately $160,000 ($0.02 × 8 million) to $200,000 ($0.01 × 20 million) per year had these dive sticks not been recalled.

The benefits of eliminating dive stick injuries most directly affect households with children, since all victims have been 9 years old or younger. However, since medical costs are generally pooled through insurance, and some of the benefits include a reduction in lost worktime of caregivers, the monetary benefits of the proposed rule would be diffused through society as a whole.

3. Potential Costs of the Rule

Rigid dive sticks that stand upright were removed from the U.S. market in 1999 when the Commission recalled dive sticks. Since then, when the CPSC has become aware of a rigid dive stick that stands upright being available in this country, the staff has taken action under the authority of section 15 of the FHSA to remove the dive stick from the market. The rule being issued now promulgates a ban on these dive sticks and establishes a performance standard for dive sticks. The performance standard establishes criteria for distinguishing dive sticks that are unlikely to pose impalement risks (and so are not banned) from dive sticks that may impose impalement risks (and therefore, are banned).

Manufacturers that produced the

banned dive sticks (or that continue to produce these dive sticks for sale in other countries) will incur some costs to modify their products to conform to the requirements of the rule. The CPSC staff believes that the modifications can be made with minimal impact on tooling and other production processes. For example, some manufacturers may be able to continue to use the same molds that they used for rigid dive sticks, but with a softer or more flexible plastic. Other manufacturers may be able to use the same material as before but adjust the center of gravity of the dive sticks so that they do not stand upright in water. Consequently, it seems reasonably likely that when the incremental cost of the changes are spread over large production runs, the cost will be no more than the benefits— 2 to 4 cents per dive stick manufactured.

The ban on rigid dive sticks that stand upright may reduce consumer utility if consumers prefer the banned dive sticks to the substitute products (i.e., dive sticks that do not stand upright, flexible dive sticks, dive rings, dive disks, and so on). However, because these substitute products serve essentially the same purposes and would cost about the same, the negative impact on consumer utility, if any, is unlikely to be significant.

4. Alternatives Considered

The Commission considered several alternatives to issuing this rule to ban certain dive sticks. These included (1) taking no action and relying on a voluntary standard or section 15 actions, (2) a labeling only requirement, and (3) changing the scope of the products subject to the ban.

(a) *Taking No Action and Relying on a Voluntary Standard or Section 15 Activities.*
There is no voluntary standard for dive sticks that addresses the impalement hazard, nor was a proposed standard submitted in response to the NPR. Even if one were developed, it would be difficult to enforce since dive sticks are relatively easy to manufacture and new firms could easily begin distributing the product. Therefore, compliance with a voluntary standard may be low.

(b) *Labeling Only Requirement.* The staff explored the possibility of a warning label instead of a ban. However, according to the Commission's Human Factors staff, a warning label is the least effective approach to reducing the number of injuries. A label that is highly visible and clearly communicates the hazard could have a significant impact at the point of purchase. However, a label on the package would not remain with the product after the sale, and because the product is intended for use in the water, it is likely that any label attached to the product itself would not last the life of the product.

Federal Register excerpts from the Consumer Product Safety Commission's cost-benefit analysis concerning whether to ban dive sticks that had caused injuries in users.

life lost or saved. In fact, different federal agencies place significantly different valuations on the lives saved or lost under their regulatory programs.

The difficulty in placing a monetary value on some costs and benefits may lead to leaving them out of a cost-benefit analysis, or it may lead to valuing only those effects that are easily quantifiable. This difficulty also led some analysts to fall back on the market as the only defensible method of valuation, since market pricing arguably reveals values better than any government estimate. If, for instance, the value of a human life is measured only by the wages the person would have earned, other factors such as the emotional, social, and educational effects on the family are not taken into account. For example, after the Supreme Court in the *Airbags* case rejected the Reagan Administration's decision to rescind the passive restraint requirement for new cars, the Department of Transportation reinstituted it and prepared a Regulatory Impact Analysis (RIA) of the costs and benefits of the requirement. This RIA concluded that the requirement was probably not cost effective, but on the benefits side of the ledger, it included only reductions in life, health, and automobile insurance premiums. It did not include any dollar amounts for the thousands of deaths and serious injuries that would be avoided when automobiles are equipped with passive restraints.

More abstract values such as fairness and equality may be short-changed in cost-benefit analysis even though most people would agree that they are fundamental values in society. Given the difficulty in valuing some effects, there may be regulatory programs that are desirable even if the quantifiable costs outweigh the benefits. Social considerations may favor regulation that does not make economic sense. Thus, it is understandable that courts require cost-benefit analysis only when Congress clearly indicates such a requirement.

C. Impact Statements

A common method for controlling or channeling the exercise of administrative discretion is to require the agency to prepare an **impact statement** that contains a detailed discussion of the likely effects of the proposed regulation, either comprehensively or focused on a particular type of impact. Impact statements tend to be used to force agencies to consider issues that are outside the scope of their mission. For example, the most commonly known impact statement is the **Environmental Impact Statement** (EIS), which is required for federal actions by the National Environmental Policy Act (NEPA). The EIS forces agencies in diverse areas such as commerce, finance, and land management to consider environmental effects that their own organic statutes might not include. Impact statements improve decisionmaking by forcing agencies to focus on the effects of their actions and by providing an opportunity for public scrutiny of the agency's plans. The use of impact statements has increased in recent decades in line with greater appreciation and awareness of the effects of agency action on issues outside the agencies' core missions.

Courts on judicial review have enforced impact statement requirements procedurally, by requiring that the impact statement include the required information and that it is included in the record of agency action. As we shall see, reviewing courts have also required agencies to consider the issues addressed in the impact statement but they have generally not required agencies to take any particular substantive action based on the contents of an impact statement. In other words, if an agency prepares a proper EIS, it can go ahead with its proposed action even at great environmental costs, as long as the record shows that the agency was aware of and considered those costs.

F   A   Q

Q: Assuming that agencies are generally not required to do more than "consider" the information contained in impact statements, is this purely procedural view of impact statements of any real value?

A: Purely procedural impact statement requirements can be of significant value both in policy terms and in the political process. Preparing impact statements may lead the agency to consider issues that would have otherwise not been relevant and might even lead the agency to make changes to reduce the impacts. Politically, advocates of the interests addressed in the impact statements may be able to rally political support based on the information contained in them.

(1) Regulatory Impact Statements

As noted above and in Chapter 2, President Reagan instituted, in E.O. 12,291, a requirement that agencies prepare a **Regulatory Impact Analysis** of their proposed rules, which would include a cost-benefit analysis of the proposal. This Executive Order and its successor, E.O. 12,866, have required agencies, as part of all major regulatory initiatives, to prepare detailed regulatory impact statements that comprehensively address the impacts of the proposed regulatory initiative. This and other required or proposed impact statements address economic effects, social effects, effects on other government programs or institutions, and/or environmental effects. While impact statement requirements and proposals have merit, they also have their problems. Requiring agencies to prepare detailed, comprehensive regulatory impact statements on every major initiative adds significantly to the substantial legal, political, and technical burdens agencies already face in formulating and implementing policy. A glance at the Federal Register reveals that the process of proposing a regulation or taking many other important actions has become very complicated and expensive, adding to the burden under which agencies operate and contributing to regulatory delay.

Sidebar

CONTENT OF IMPACT STATEMENTS

Impact statements are required widely under federal, state, and local law. There are numerous substantive impacts that are addressed by impact statement requirements including the environment, endangered species, small businesses, traffic and parking, government budgets, coastal erosion, and views of coastlines. At the state and local level, impact statements may be a key to deciding whether to go forward with a proposal. For example, with regard to zoning applications, the traffic and parking issues may be decisive. In some areas, however, impact statements add to the information in the regulatory record but cannot legally be used to prevent the agency's proposed action.

In addition to the time and expense of preparing impact statements, challenges to the adequacy of the statements place yet another weapon in the hands of parties resisting regulation. This can seriously frustrate and delay agencies' ability to regulate effectively. It may be easy for Members of Congress to satisfy their constituents' concerns by simply adding another impact requirement to the agency's responsibilities so that no significant concern goes unaddressed. But this entails potentially hidden costs that may reduce the social value of regulation. Based on these concerns, it may be better for Congress to be careful about adding to agencies' burden, and only require agencies to address impacts when it is worth the time and effort required to do so competently and usefully.

(2) Environmental Impact Statements under NEPA

As noted, the most common and widely known impact statement is the requirement under NEPA that federal agencies prepare an EIS regarding "major Federal actions significantly affecting the quality of the human environment." NEPA states that the EIS "and the comments and views of the appropriate Federal, State and Local [environmental agencies] shall . . . accompany the proposal through the existing agency review processes." 42 U.S.C. §4332(C). "Major federal action" includes all significant federal activity, including federal funding of actions carried out by other entities.

Although NEPA signifies Congress's adoption of environmental protection as a national goal, see 42 U.S.C. §4331, it contains very little in the way of operative substantive provisions.

While NEPA does provide that agencies should, to the fullest extent possible, act in accordance with the environmental conservation policies espoused in NEPA, this provision is too general to have any significant substantive effect. The primary explicit operative requirements of NEPA are the preparation of the EIS and the requirement that the EIS "shall accompany the proposal through the existing agency review processes." 42 U.S.C. §4332(C). This means that the EIS must be part of the record during agency consideration of its action.

NEPA does not explicitly state that the agency must actually consider the EIS once it is prepared and placed in the record, although the Supreme Court has found in the statute an implicit obligation to consider the environmental effects detailed in the statement. See *Strycker's Bay Neighborhood Council v. Karlen*, 444 U.S. 223, 227 (1980). NEPA certainly does not state that an agency must abandon a proposal if the EIS reveals that the environmental costs are very high. The Court has stated with regard to NEPA that "the only role for a court is to insure that the agency has considered the environmental consequences." *Strycker's Bay Neighborhood Council v. Karlen*, 444 U.S. 223, 227 (1980).

While environmentalists might prefer a statute with greater substantive bite, a purely procedural NEPA under which the agency must create and consider the EIS has value:

- First, it requires agencies with non-environmental missions to focus on the environmental impacts of their actions when otherwise they might not have considered them at all.
- Second, NEPA results in the expenditure of federal funds on investigating environmental effects that environmental interest groups might not be able to afford to examine.
- Third, and most important, NEPA creates a vehicle for political activity regarding environmental issues and provides information to fuel the debate. The existence of the EIS and the requirement that it be considered in the agency decisionmaking process make it much more likely that environmental costs will be considered by the agency or by Congress in response to agitation from the public.

F   A   Q

Q: What effects must agencies include in the EIS?

A: NEPA requires that the EIS consider **actual and potential effects on the physical environment**, such as pollution of air and water. The phrase "environmental effects" is capacious, encompassing a broad range of impacts. NEPA has been construed to cover more than what we traditionally think of as pollution. For example, agencies under NEPA must include a broad range of effects on the human environment — such as the displacement of social institutions — that a proposed major federal action may have on a community. In *Strycker's Bay Neighborhood Council v. Karlen*, 444 U.S. 223 (1980), the Court approved agency consideration of the effects a large concentration of federally funded low-income housing may have on the "social fabric and community structures."

The EIS must include analysis of the effects of the proposed federal action on the physical environment, broadly construed. There are, however, limits on the range of impacts that NEPA requires agencies to address and consider. Only actual effects on the physical environment must be considered in the EIS. Fear, even psychological harm, generated by a potential effect of a federal action need not be considered. See *Metropolitan Edison Co. v. PANE*, 460 U.S. 766 (1983) (Nuclear Regulatory Commission need not consider psychological damage caused by the fear of a nuclear accident; NRC did consider the risk of physical harm resulting from a nuclear accident). Further, agencies are not required to address matters over which they have no control. If an environmental effect would occur due to the action of someone else that the agency has no power to control, the agency need not address that effect in an EIS. For example, in *Department of Transportation v. Public Citizen*, 541 U.S. 752 (2004), the Supreme Court held that the Department of Transportation was not required to prepare an EIS on the effects of Mexican trucks on the U.S. environment because the President, not the agency, had the power to determine whether Mexican trucks should be allowed to enter the United States.

As part of the consideration of environmental effects, NEPA requires agencies, in the EIS, to consider "alternatives to the proposed action." 42 U.S.C. §4332(C)(iii). The question arises as to which alternatives the agency must consider. The potential alternatives to any action are, in theory, limited only by the power of the human imagination. In recognition of the potential for opponents of agency action raising limitless alternatives, the Supreme Court has limited the range of alternatives that the EIS must consider to those that are known and feasible at the time that the EIS is prepared. An agency is not required to consider an alternative that is not "reasonably available" at the time the EIS is prepared, and a party raising a novel alternative must provide the agency with sufficient information to allow the agency to evaluate their submissions intelligently. See *Vermont Yankee Nuclear Power Corp. v. NRDC, Inc.*, 435 U.S. 519 (1978). In *Vermont Yankee*, the Court held that the Nuclear Regulatory Commission was not required to consider "energy conservation" in an EIS as an alternative to the construction and licensing of a nuclear power plant because at the time the EIS was prepared, energy conservation was not a known, feasible alternative. That may seem strange to us today, but when energy was cheap, no one had considered conservation as an alternative to simply increasing supply to meet demand.

SUMMARY

- Agencies should engage in reasoned decisionmaking, applying their expertise and taking into account only those considerations made statutorily relevant.

- The clarity requirement holds that agencies may act in some circumstances only under relatively clear rules. It may violate due process for an agency to impose punitive measures when the rules under which the agency is acting are not clear.

- The consistency requirement holds that agencies must treat like cases alike unless the agency states a new rule and explains the change. A related doctrine holds that agencies must follow their own rules, except that courts may not enforce internal agency rules that are not intended to benefit the public.

- Related to clarity and consistency requirements, under the *Chenery* rule, on judicial review, agency action is evaluated based only on those factors actually relied upon by the agency.

- Agencies must normally follow their own procedural rules, except for rules that are unpublished and not intended to benefit the public but rather intended only to provide guidance to agency employees.

- Agencies are not estopped by the conduct or statements of agency officials. If an official gives erroneous advice, the agency may still insist on adherence to the correct rule. This rule is strongest when expenditure of federal funds is involved because the Supreme Court has stated that courts have no constitutional power to order the federal government to spend money except as specified by Congress in appropriations legislation.

- Non-mutual collateral estoppel does not apply against the federal government. Thus, the federal government remains free to relitigate issues on which it has lost against a different party.

■ Agencies sometimes refuse to acquiesce in court decisions that are contrary to the agency's position on a matter. Inter-circuit nonacquiescence, in which an agency applies its own rule except in the circuit in which its rule has been rejected, is justified by the system of regional courts of appeals under which splits in the circuits are resolved by the Supreme Court. Intra-circuit nonacquiescence, in which an agency adheres to its rule even in the circuit that rejected the agency's view, is probably unjustifiable and contrary to the rule of law.

■ Cost-benefit analysis has been identified as a useful tool to improve agency policy-making and reduce the potential for arbitrary agency action. Cost-benefit analysis also has its weaknesses, and courts have not required agencies to apply cost-benefit analysis unless clearly required by statute.

■ Impact statements are another popular device for improving agency policymaking. The most common type of impact statement is the environmental impact statement, under NEPA, but agencies have been required to prepare statements on a wide variety of economic, social, and governmental impacts of their actions.

■ Impact statements require agencies to focus on the effects of their actions and provide information that can be used in the political process to influence agency action.

■ NEPA does not explicitly impose upon agencies any duty beyond preparation of the EIS, and the Supreme Court has held that an agency meets its obligation under NEPA by preparing an adequate EIS and considering it during the decisionmaking process.

CONNECTIONS

Clarity and Consistency and Judicial Review
The clarity and consistency requirements must be considered in conjunction with the general standards of judicial review discussed in Chapter 4.

Clarity and Due Process
Clarity raises due process concerns (Chapter 8) because some courts have found a due process violation when unclear law has retroactive or punitive effects.

Clarity and Nondelegation
Clarity concerns were also behind the D.C. Circuit's attack on the Clean Air Act as violating the nondelegation doctrine. See Chapter 2.

Consistency and Agency Discretion
The consistency requirement is related to agency discretion over enforcement targets (Chapter 9) and agency choice between rulemaking and case-by-case adjudication (Chapter 6).

Executive Orders and Cost-Benefit Analysis

Presidential orders requiring cost-benefit analysis (Chapter 2) are relevant to the discussion in this chapter of cost-benefit analysis.

Public Choice and Procedural Impact Statements

Public choice analysis (Chapter 1) may help understand the value of purely procedural impact statement requirements.

Agency Choice of Decisionmaking Procedure

6

This chapter examines the rules and doctrines that govern an agency's choice of decisionmaking procedure. The major administrative law procedural models are rulemaking and adjudication, but agencies also make decisions informally, i.e., without going through either an adjudicatory or legislative process. Although agencies have a great deal of discretion when choosing the decisionmaking procedure for a particular action, statutes and constitutional norms may constrain that discretion.

The primary constitutional constraint on the choice of a decisionmaking procedure is due process. Due process requires notice and an adjudicatory hearing when agency action affects a particular party and is based on facts specific to the situation of that party. These facts are referred to as "adjudicative facts." When agency action is based on conditions common to many parties, the general facts involved are referred to as "legislative facts" and a legislative process is usually constitutionally sufficient.

The main Administrative Procedure Act (APA) procedural models are rulemaking and adjudication. Agencies have a great deal of discretion over which mode to use, although adjudication is required before an agency may issue an order directed at a particular party. Where no particular procedural model is statutorily or constitutionally required, agencies may make decisions informally, i.e., without using either rulemaking or a formal adjudicatory process. Because the APA divides all agency decisionmaking into two categories, rulemaking and adjudication, informal decisionmaking is often referred to as "informal adjudication." When making an informal decision, the agency must notify the party of its decision and provide a brief explanation of the decision.

An agency may not rely on an unpublished rule against any member of the public who lacks actual notice of the rule.

Although rulemaking is thought to be the proper procedure for announcing general rules, agencies, like common law courts, often announce new general rules in the course of deciding particular matters in adjudication. The Supreme Court has allowed agencies to make rule-like decisions in the course of adjudication on two theories, first, that the practice is within the traditional adjudicatory process and second, that subsequent applications of the rule to particular parties take place in a proper adjudication. There are policy reasons, including fairness to all regulated parties and superior fact-finding devices, favoring rulemaking as the procedure for formulating general policy-oriented rules.

The APA exempts several types of rules, such as policy statements and interpretative rules (commonly shortened to "interpretive rules"), from notice and comment procedures. For a rule to fall within an exemption, it must not be legislative, i.e., it must not add to or change existing legal obligations.

If an agency is required to make rules "on the record after opportunity for an agency hearing," the agency must employ formal rulemaking procedures under which rulemaking is conducted in an "on the record" adjudicatory proceeding. This procedure is disfavored, and courts construe statutes, whenever possible, not to require it. Agencies must follow their own formally promulgated procedural rules; and they may be required to follow informally promulgated procedural rules when a member of the public has relied on the rule and has been prejudiced by the agency's failure to follow it.

A. CHOICE OF DECISIONMAKING PROCEDURE UNDER THE APA

1. The APA and the Choice of Decisionmaking Procedure
2. Agency Discretion to Make Policy by Rule
3. Decisionmaking via Formal Rulemaking: When Are Formal Rulemaking Procedures Required?
4. Agency Power to Make Policy by Adjudication

B. INFORMAL DECISIONMAKING

1. Exceptions to the Applicability of §553
2. Policymaking by Manual or Other Internal Document: *Morton v. Ruiz*
3. Informal Decisionmaking More Generally: When May an Agency Act without Adjudication or Rulemaking?

C. CONSTITUTIONAL CONSTRAINTS ON CHOICE OF DECISIONMAKING PROCEDURE

1. The *Londoner* and *Bi-Metallic* Dichotomy
2. *Bi-Metallic Investment Co. v. State Board of Equalization*
3. Legislative Facts, Adjudicative Facts, and Due Process

A. Choice of Decisionmaking Procedure under the APA

The Administrative Procedure Act (APA) divides all administrative action into two procedural categories, **rulemaking** and **adjudication**. See APA §551(4), (5), (6) and (7). Rulemaking is the procedure for issuing a rule and adjudication is the procedure for issuing an order. "**Rule**" is defined as "the whole or a part of an agency statement of general or particular applicability and future effect designed to implement, interpret, or prescribe law or policy. . . ." "**Order**" is defined as "the whole or a part of a final disposition, whether affirmative, negative, injunctive, or declaratory in form, of an agency in a matter other than rule making but including licensing." The most natural understanding of this dichotomy may be that when an agency wants to announce a general policy to be applied more broadly than to particular parties before the agency, it must use rulemaking. However, agencies make general policies in both rulemaking and adjudication, and these definitions have not been construed to place serious constraints on this practice.

The consequences of policymaking by rule and by order are similar, although procedurally they operate somewhat differently. When an agency embodies a policy decision in a rule promulgated in a rulemaking proceeding, that rule immediately becomes binding law and everyone is expected to follow it immediately. In a subsequent enforcement action, the only issue will normally be whether the regulated party violated the rule. When an agency embodies a policy decision in an opinion produced as a result of an agency adjudication, the agency acts much like a common law court by announcing a new rule of law in the course of deciding the particular case before the agency and then applying it as precedent in subsequent enforcement actions, usually agency adjudications. While this latter practice has been attacked as illegitimate avoidance of rulemaking procedures, as we shall see below, the Supreme Court has recognized a great deal of agency discretion in choosing between rulemaking and adjudication.

Sidebar

ADJUDICATION REQUIRED FOR ISSUING ORDERS

Although the APA gives agencies a great deal of discretion over the choice between rulemaking and adjudication, it is clear that adjudication is the required process for issuing an order against a regulated party. With regard to rulemaking, things are not so clear because agencies, like courts, may formulate general legal rules in an adjudicatory process.

(1) The APA and the Choice of Decisionmaking Procedure

The APA does not explicitly regulate the choice of decisionmaking mode, but its definitions of "adjudication" and "rulemaking" provide some guidance on the choice of decisionmaking mode. In addition to the APA and the Constitution, an agency's enabling act may prescribe a particular policymaking mode. The APA explicitly provides for two decisionmaking models: rulemaking and adjudication. The first, "rulemaking," is defined as the "agency process for making, amending or repealing a rule." APA §551(5). "Rule" is defined as "the whole or a part of an agency statement of general or particular applicability and future effect designed to implement, interpret, or prescribe law or policy. . . ." APA §551(4). The second, "adjudication," is defined as the "agency process for the formulation of an order." APA §551(7).

"Order" is defined as "the whole or a part of a final disposition, whether affirmative, negative, injunctive, or declaratory in form, of an agency in a matter other than rulemaking but including licensing." APA §551(6). In short, the APA provides that everything that is not a rule is an order, and the process for formulating an order is adjudication.

It should be noted at this point that there are two varieties of rulemaking and two varieties of adjudication. The most frequently employed rulemaking procedure is commonly referred to as "**informal rulemaking**" or "**notice and comment rulemaking**." This type of rulemaking is governed by the procedures specified in APA §553, mainly **notice**, opportunity for public **comment**, and decision accompanied by a **concise general statement of the basis and purpose** of any rule adopted. The less commonly employed form of rulemaking is referred to as "**formal rulemaking**" because it involves rulemaking via formal adjudicatory procedures. The conditions under which formal rulemaking is required are discussed below.

On the adjudication side, there are also two varieties. The first, which is what most of us think of when we conceive of adjudication, is best referred to as "**formal adjudication**." Formal adjudication is conducted pursuant to APA §§554, 556, and 557, and includes the features of formal trials. The second variety of adjudication is known as "**informal adjudication**," and consists of everything else in administrative law, i.e., everything that is not a rulemaking or formal adjudication. The informal adjudication label results from the APA's division of all agency action into the rulemaking and adjudication categories. It might have made more sense to create a third category of agency action, perhaps called "informal agency action," which would include most of what is now referred to as informal adjudication.

The APA does not explicitly state when agencies must engage in rulemaking or adjudication to make policies. However, agencies must employ an adjudicatory process to issue orders against regulated parties and they must employ rulemaking to promulgate a rule that will be published in the **Federal Register** and codified in the **Code of Federal Regulations**. As far as the general question of the proper procedure to make policy determinations is concerned, agencies make rule-like determinations in both rulemaking and adjudication, and either is proper as long as the agency has the power to use the particular procedure and all applicable procedural requirements are observed.

An agency must employ some valid procedure, normally rulemaking or adjudication, for any significant policy decision. If an agency does not employ either rulemaking or adjudication, it risks having its policy overturned even if it followed a reasonable procedural model. For example, in *Sugar Cane Growers Cooperative of Florida v. Veneman*, 289 F.3d 89 (D.C. Cir. 2002), the agency promulgated a plan for

---

S i d e b a r

INFORMAL ADJUDICATION

When an agency makes a decision under a procedure not accounted for by the rulemaking or formal adjudicatory models, the agency has engaged in informal adjudication. For example, if someone applies for a passport and the Department of State rejects the application for insufficient documentation of citizenship, the denial is an order and the procedure that the agency followed falls into the category of informal adjudication, even though there was never a hearing in the usual sense of the word.

S i d e b a r

THE FEDERAL REGISTER

The Federal Register is a daily compilation of official government documents released to the public. The APA requires that certain agency documents be published in the Federal Register. The Code of Federal Regulations is a compilation of agency rules. Its organization follows that of the United States Code.

submitting and accepting bids for a program involving subsidies for plowing-under surplus crops, which included the "procedures all applicants must follow, the payment limitations of the program, and the sanctions that will be imposed on participants if they plant more in future years." The agency did not employ §553 rulemaking, but rather formulated the plan after informally consulting with some affected parties. The D.C. Circuit held that the plan was a rule that should have been promulgated pursuant to §553. The court rejected the agency's harmless error argument—that the agency would have arrived at the same result had it engaged in notice and comment rulemaking. That argument, concluded the court, would amount to a virtual repeal of §553 because it would be extremely difficult to prove that the agency would have made a different decision had it followed the APA. See also *Utility Solid Waste Activities Group v. EPA*, 236 F.3d 749 (D.C. Cir. 2000) (correction of "technical errors" in rule without notice and comment cannot be excused as harmless error).

(2) Agency Discretion to Make Policy by Rule

The most basic prerequisite to agency rulemaking is statutory authority to make rules. Absent statutory authority to make rules, an agency cannot do so. With such authority, rulemaking is obviously an appropriate procedure for making policy. Because rulemaking has several legal and policy advantages over adjudication and informal decisionmaking, courts prefer policymaking by rule and in doubtful cases, courts are likely to rule in favor of agency authority to make rules.

There are several recognized advantages to making policy by rule.

1. Policy decisions promulgated in a rule are likely to be clearer and more definite than informal policy or policy made through adjudication.
2. Rules better inform regulated parties of their legal duties and provide administrative law judges and courts with more guidance in enforcement actions and on judicial review.
3. Rulemaking simplifies the enforcement process by allowing an agency to establish a regulatory regime in a single rulemaking proceeding, which it then applies to regulated parties in individual adjudications. In these adjudications, often the only issue will be whether the regulated party violated the rule.
4. Policy decisions promulgated through rulemaking may be better than other decisions for three reasons. First, the legislative notice and comment process allows for greater public input into the decision and thus the agency may be better informed. Second, the legislative form of rules may allow for a better-crafted decision, with exceptions when appropriate. Third, rules allow agencies to impose comprehensive decisions at once

on all similarly situated regulated parties. This is fairer than singling out a violator for an adjudicatory test case. Comprehensive decisionmaking can save agency resources because the agency does not have to repeatedly establish the same point in numerous adjudications.

However, even when an agency has statutory authority to make rules, rulemaking can be controversial when a rule limits the issues that would otherwise be decided in a formal adjudicatory hearing. In those cases in which agency statutory rulemaking power is in doubt, regulated parties make several arguments against agency authority to make policy by rules. First, if the agency's organic statute appears to contemplate an adjudicatory process, regulated parties argue that Congress did not intend for the agency to have rulemaking power. The argument is that Congress intended that the agency hold a hearing on all issues, including whether the party's conduct violated the statute. Second, related to congressional intent, regulated parties have argued that when Congress establishes a statutory hearing process to determine regulatory violations or entitlements, the statute grants regulated parties a right to a hearing on all issues — including whether the alleged conduct violated the statute. By making a binding rule that defines certain conduct as a violation, the agency is arguably depriving the regulated party of the hearing granted by Congress on that issue.

This controversy has arisen in numerous cases, most notably *United States v. Storer Broadcasting Co.*, 351 U.S. 192 (1956), which rejected a challenge to a rule promulgated by the Federal Communications Commission (FCC) that set a limit on the number of broadcast stations any licensee could own. Storer, a licensee that desired to own more than the maximum allowable broadcast licenses, challenged the rule on both substantive and closely related procedural grounds. Storer's substantive claim was that the rule could not displace the governing statute, which specified that the FCC was supposed to grant or deny licenses based on the "public interest, convenience and necessity." Storer's procedural argument was that summary application of the rule to reject an application from Storer for an additional license would violate

that statutory requirement that an applicant receive a "full hearing" before a license application can be denied. Storer's argument was basically that it could not be denied an additional license unless it were determined after a full hearing that the additional license would be contrary to the "public interest, convenience and necessity" without regard to the FCC's rule limiting the number of licenses any one broadcaster could hold.

The Supreme Court rejected both of Storer's arguments. On the substantive issue, the Court construed the grant to the FCC of "general rulemaking power" as including power to make all rules "not inconsistent with the Act or law." The rule was thus substantively valid because the FCC could reasonably conclude that preventing concentration of media ownership was in the public interest. On the procedural issue, the Court held that once the FCC promulgated a valid substantive limitation on the "public interest" licensing standard, the full hearing requirement would be met if the FCC held a full hearing on all issues not determined by a valid rule and "provid[ed] a 'full hearing' for applicants who have reached the existing limit of stations, upon their presentation of applications . . . that set out adequate reasons why the Rules should be waived or amended." Thus, while the Court mostly rejected Storer's arguments, it required that agencies entertain colorable arguments that special circumstances militate against application of the otherwise valid rule in the particular circumstances. The basis of this requirement is apparently concern over the denial of what appears to be a statutorily required hearing on the issues determined in the rulemaking.

In certain cases, most notably regarding the Federal Trade Commission (FTC), some agencies long believed that they lacked power to make binding rules and instead were required to use an adjudicatory process to make binding policy. More recently, the FTC changed its view and concluded that it had power to issue substantive rules. When an agency changes its mind on a fundamental issue, the regulated parties may argue that the longstanding agency belief against rulemaking authority is evidence against agency power to make rules. It has also been argued that because agencies have only those powers granted to them by Congress, courts should (when in doubt) rule against agency power to prevent the executive branch from seizing power not delegated to it.

In general, courts have resolved doubts in favor of agency rulemaking power. Thus, so long as some statutory provision can be interpreted to grant rulemaking power and there is no compelling evidence to the contrary, courts are likely to recognize agency power to make policy through the issuance of binding rules subject to the requirement discussed above — that when an agency rule decides an issue that would otherwise be addressed at a hearing, the agency usually is required to allow the regulated party to argue that special circumstances mean the rule should not apply to the particular case. For example, the FTC has broad jurisdiction to order businesses to "cease and desist" from engaging in "unfair or deceptive acts or practices" in interstate commerce. For the first fifty years or so of its existence, the FTC formulated "cease and desist" orders through an adjudicatory process during which the FTC established both that the challenged practice violated the act and that the defendant had engaged in the unfair or deceptive practice. In the 1960s, the FTC decided to promulgate trade regulation rules that would establish that a particular practice was "unfair or deceptive," thus leaving for the hearing only the issue of whether the defendant had engaged in the practice. In 1971, the FTC adopted its first trade regulation rule, the so-called Octane Posting Rule, which specified that it was unfair and deceptive for sellers of gasoline to fail to post the octane rating of their products.

In *National Petroleum Refiners Association v. FTC*, 482 F.2d 672 (D.C. Cir. 1973), the Court of Appeals held that the FTC had the power to make binding trade regulation rules. The court focused primarily on a provision of the FTC Act that gave the FTC the power to make rules and regulations, although the petroleum refiners argued that Congress intended only to give the agency the power to make procedural rules and not substantive ones. The *National Petroleum* court found it persuasive that the FTC hearing process would be simplified, that regulated parties would have more certain knowledge of regulatory requirements, and that all members of an industry would be regulated at once if the FTC could make substantive rules — leaving for the hearing only the issue of whether the rules were violated. These advantages appeared so significant to the court that it resolved its doubts concerning the agency's rulemaking power in the agency's favor. In response to the argument that this procedure deprived the regulated parties of their right to a hearing to contest the issue of whether a particular practice is unfair or deceptive, the court stated that the party must be allowed an opportunity to argue that, due to special circumstances, the trade regulation rule should not be applied. Note also that because the FTC's jurisdiction is so broad, members of Congress became concerned, and Congress has legislated limits to the FTC's rulemaking power several times since the FTC began promulgating trade regulation rules.

F   A   Q

Q: Why is rulemaking viewed as a better procedure than adjudication for formulating general rules?

A: Rulemaking is a more open process that facilitates greater input from regulated parties. Rulemaking also allows for a comprehensive decision. It provides notice to all affected parties and it ensures equal treatment because all regulated parties are expected to obey the rule when issued whereas when adjudication is used, only the party against which an order is issued is expected to obey immediately.

In sum, rulemaking is viewed as a superior policymaking procedure, and courts tend to resolve doubts in favor of agency authority to make substantive rules. Once made, such rules are considered binding law and everyone is expected to follow them immediately. The existence of a valid legislative rule can serve to limit the issues that would otherwise be determined at an agency adjudicatory hearing, provided that the agency provides regulated parties the opportunity to argue that the rule should not apply in the particular case.

(3) Decisionmaking via Formal Rulemaking: When Are Formal Rulemaking Procedures Required?

Formal rulemaking is a rulemaking proceeding conducted pursuant to the formal adjudicatory procedures of APA §§556 and 557. Formal rulemaking is required when the agency's enabling act requires that rules are to be made "**on the record after opportunity for an agency hearing**." APA §553(c) states that "when rules are required by statute to be made on the record after opportunity for an agency hearing, sections 556 and 557 of this title apply instead of this subsection." Sections 556 and 557 prescribe formal, adjudicatory-type procedures. Rulemaking conducted under these provisions is referred to as "formal" or "on the record" rulemaking.

Because it is such an expensive and cumbersome procedure, there is a strong de facto presumption against formal rulemaking. Thus, unless it is absolutely clear from the statutory language that formal rulemaking is required (usually through use of the formulation "on the record after agency hearing," or something very similar), courts will conclude that Congress intended that the agency be free to use informal procedures under §553. See *United States v. Florida East Coast Rwy. Co.*, 410 U.S. 224 (1973).

Many statutes require an agency to hold a **hearing**, and it has been argued that this means formal rulemaking or adjudication, depending on the context. The courts have not agreed: The word "hearing" in regulatory statutes is not usually interpreted as requiring formal procedures, or even oral hearings of any kind. Absent an unambiguous requirement that a hearing be conducted "on the record," the informal procedures of §553 are sufficient for rulemaking unless the statute clearly contemplates something more. For example, §1(14)(a) of the Interstate Commerce Act (ICA) gave the Interstate Commerce Commission (ICC) the power to make rules "after hearing." In *United States v. Allegheny-Ludlum Steel Corp.*, 406 U.S. 742 (1972), the Supreme Court held that this language, without a requirement that rules be made "on the record," was not sufficient to require formal rulemaking. In *United States v. Florida East Coast Ry. Co.*, 410 U.S. 224 (1973), a case arising under the same section of the ICA, the railway company made two arguments for procedures in addition to those specified in §553. First, it argued that because the ICA specified the factors that the ICC should take into account, formal rulemaking was required. Relying on *Allegheny-Ludlum*, the Court rejected this argument out of hand. Second, the railway company argued that the "after hearing" language, while not triggering full, formal procedures, required some kind of oral hearing in addition to §553 notice and comment procedures. The Court also rejected this argument, holding that absent evidence to the contrary, when Congress uses the term "hearing," it means the procedures mandated by the applicable APA provision—here §553's notice and comment procedures. Thus, in this context, the term "hearing" means the paper procedures of §553, not any sort of formal procedures.

(4) Agency Power to Make Policy by Adjudication

Some agencies, most notably the NLRB, make policy primarily through an adjudicatory process in which new rules of decision are announced in the course of deciding particular cases in formal adjudicatory hearings. Because the APA's definitions appear to contemplate rulemaking as the procedure for formulating general rules, promulgation of such rules in adjudication has been attacked as invalid due to the absence of a proper rulemaking procedure. The Supreme Court has rejected these challenges, although not definitively, stating that the choice between adjudication and rulemaking lies largely within the discretion of the agency.

The NLRB's practice of announcing new substantive rules in adjudicatory opinions arose with a twist in *Excelsior Underwear, Inc.*, 156 N.L.R.B. 1236 (1966). The NLRB held an adjudicatory hearing on a union's challenge to the fairness of a union representation election among Excelsior's workers. The union challenged the election as unfair because Excelsior had not provided the union with a list of the names and addresses of the employees eligible to vote in the election. Prior to *Excelsior*, the NLRB had ruled that employers were not required to provide unions with the list, and unions consistently complained that they were at a disadvantage when trying to communicate with the employees in the potential bargaining unit. The NLRB approved the Excelsior election but stated in its opinion that in all such elections beginning thirty days after the issuance of the opinion, employers must provide the list to the union. This **prospectivity** was the twist — not only did the NLRB announce what looks like a rule in an adjudicatory opinion, it did not even apply the new rule to the parties to the case, but rather stated that the requirement would apply only in the future to elections conducted at least thirty days after the decision.

Excelsior was attacked as improper because no "order" was issued requiring the employer in that case to provide the list. Therefore, since *Excelsior* does not appear to be an order, it was argued that it must be a rule, and thus the procedure was improper. The validity of the "rule" in *Excelsior Underwear* was addressed by the Supreme Court in *NLRB v. Wyman-Gordon Co.*, 394 U.S. 759 (1969). Unfortunately, although a majority on Court approved the rule, there was no majority opinion and thus the status of prospective rules made in the course of adjudication is still somewhat unclear.

In *Wyman-Gordon*, the NLRB ordered the employer to provide the union with a list of employees' names and addresses. The reasoning in the agency's order consisted mainly of a citation to *Excelsior*. The employer challenged the order in court, arguing that because the *Excelsior* rule had not been promulgated in a rulemaking proceeding, it was invalid and could therefore not be applied to *Wyman-Gordon* with a simple citation to the *Excelsior* opinion. A divided Supreme Court upheld the order in *Wyman-Gordon*, but a majority did not agree on the grounds.

Justice Fortas, joined by three other Justices, stated that the NLRB's order that *Wyman-Gordon* turn over the list in its election was a valid order and that the NLRB's reliance on *Excelsior* was irrelevant. Justice Fortas opined that agencies may, in the course of deciding particular cases, announce general rules and rely upon them as precedent, the way courts apply stare decisis. In his view, the prior decision in *Excelsior Underwear* was not important to the validity of the order in *Wyman-Gordon* because "the Board in an adjudicatory proceeding directed [Wyman-Gordon] itself to furnish the list." *Wyman-Gordon*, 394 U.S. at 766. In other words, so long as Wyman-Gordon was ordered to turn over the list pursuant to an adjudicatory proceeding, what the agency had done or said in *Excelsior Underwear* was not relevant to the validity of the order in *Wyman-Gordon*. Justice Fortas also stated that the procedure in *Excelsior* was invalid because the NLRB did not apply the new requirement to the parties in *Excelsior* itself. In such circumstances, the NLRB was legislating and should have used a rulemaking procedure.

Justice Black's opinion, joined by two others, disagreed with Justice Fortas and argued that the procedure in *Excelsior Underwear* was a proper adjudicatory proceeding because courts often announce new rules and make them prospective out of concerns for fairness or the orderly administration of justice. To Justice Black, the NLRB's decision was within the traditional bounds of the adjudicatory process and thus was included in the adjudicatory power Congress granted to the NLRB. Because the NLRB followed proper adjudicatory procedures, the NLRB did not violate the APA by announcing the new "rule" in the course

of adjudication. Given his view that the procedure in *Excelsior* was valid, it should not be surprising that Justice Black also concluded that it was proper for the NLRB to rely in *Wyman-Gordon* on *Excelsior*'s rule that employers furnish the list of employees.

Justice Black also disagreed strongly with Justice Fortas's argument that the order in *Wyman-Gordon* was proper regardless of the legality of the *Excelsior* decision. To Justice Black, this reasoning would free the NLRB from all procedural constraints in formulating policy. Under Justice Fortas's reasoning, the NLRB could simply write a press release stating that in future elections employers must provide the union with the list of employee names and address, and then in the first challenge to an election after the issuance of the press release, the agency could invalidate the election in an opinion that simply cited the press release. In Justice Black's view, the Fortas opinion would validate what Black viewed as an obviously defective procedure.

Two Justices dissented, disagreeing with the conclusion and reasoning in both the Fortas and Black opinions. Justices Douglas and Harlan both argued, in dissent, that the NLRB should have used a rulemaking procedure to announce the rule requiring employers to provide the list. Both argued that the NLRB's prospective rule in *Excelsior* was improper because prospective rulemaking is not within the APA's definition of adjudication. Rather, the only APA process for making prospective rules is rulemaking, and since the NLRB in *Wyman-Gordon* relied on the rule announced in *Excelsior*, the order in *Wyman-Gordon* was also invalid.

It is important to isolate the areas of agreement and disagreement in the *Wyman-Gordon* opinions. Apparently, the Justices in the majority are in agreement that it is proper for the NLRB to announce rules of general applicability and future effect in adjudicatory opinions. The controversy erupted only over the prospectivity of the rule in *Excelsior Underwear*. Thus, it appears that the agencies have the discretion to announce new rules in adjudicatory proceedings so long as the new rule is applied in the proceeding in which it is announced. In *NLRB v. Bell Aerospace Co.*, 416 U.S. 267 (1974), the Supreme Court unanimously upheld the NLRB's power in an adjudication to change its standard for determining whether certain employees (buyers) were managers. The Court stated that the choice between rulemaking and adjudication is a matter of agency discretion. The Court rejected the argument that because the new standard would be different from its prior rulings and because the new standard would be in the nature of a general rule, the NLRB was required to use rulemaking.

The Court noted that the question in *Bell Aerospace* was particularly suited to case-by-case adjudication because there is great variation among the degree to which buyers have management-type responsibilities. Thus, the Court did not clearly adopt, as a general matter, Justice Black's reasoning in *Wyman-Gordon* that all adjudicatory rules are valid as long as they are later applied pursuant to proper adjudicatory procedures. There may be cases in which the Court would invalidate case-by-case adjudication due to the lack of legally significant differences among the subjects being regulated. However, this seems unlikely considering that courts are likely to defer to agency judgments concerning the proper decisionmaking method in any particular case. It thus appears that agencies may authoritatively decide general issues in the course of resolving particular controversies in adjudication.

In summary, the decision whether to use rulemaking or adjudication lies largely within the discretion of the agency. However, the Supreme Court has never definitively approved the making of prospective general rules in an adjudicatory process. Because the opinion in *Bell Aerospace* stresses the fact-specific nature of the inquiry into whether the employees are managers, it is dangerous to generalize from the holding in *Bell Aerospace* to a principle that agencies are free to make general rules in adjudication. However, although the Court in *Bell Aerospace* specifically disavowed deciding the more general issue, it seems very likely that the Court would approve this longstanding and widespread agency practice of announcing general rules in the course of deciding particular cases in adjudication.

B. Informal Decisionmaking

There are many situations in which agencies make decisions without using either notice and comment rulemaking or adjudication. There are two general categories of informal decisionmaking. The first category involves rules made without notice and comment procedures either because the agency believes that the rule fits into an exception to §553's notice and comment requirements or because, for some reason, the agency believes that §553 does not apply at all. The second category involves what is called "informal adjudication." This category includes a wide array of informally made particular decisions such as the grant or denial of a permit or license when formal adjudicatory procedures do not apply. In both categories, important agency policies may be implicated, which provokes challenges on the basis that the agency should have employed a more formal procedure to make policy.

(1) Exceptions to the Applicability of §553

Under some circumstances, agency action in the nature of rulemaking falls within an exception to APA §553's notice and comment requirements. In other cases, by statute or traditional practice, agencies make what look like rules informally — making decisions without any formalized procedure. Under some circumstances, however, informal decisionmaking may violate the APA. In such cases, agencies must engage in a more formal decisionmaking process before their rules can be given legal effect.

There are two different types of exceptions to the rulemaking provisions of APA §553. The first set of exceptions, contained in APA §553(a), completely exempts certain categories of rules from the coverage of §553. Section 553(a) states that §553 does not apply to military or foreign affairs functions; to matters relating to agency management or personnel; or to public property, loans, grants, benefits, or contracts. The list of exempt rules has in common the notion that these are sensitive areas in which some privacy may be desirable. Certainly, military and foreign affairs functions would be harmed by public proceedings on many matters. In contracting and property matters, the government's economic interests could be prejudiced by too much openness. In these areas, agencies are free to make rules without regard to any of §553's requirements.

The second set of exceptions contained in APA §553 applies to "interpretative rules, general statements of policy [and] rules of agency organization, procedure or practice . . . [and when] the agency for good cause finds . . . that notice and public procedure . . . are impracticable, unnecessary, or contrary to the public interest." It is not a complete exemption from the section's requirements, but is rather an exemption from the provisions of subsection (b), the notice and comment provisions. This implies that the requirements of §553(a), (c), (d) and (e) still apply. However, this narrow view of exception does not really work in light of the structure of §553. As is analyzed in greater detail in Chapter 7, §553(b) requires agencies to publish notice of their proposed rules in the Federal Register.

F   A   Q

Q: From which of §553's procedural requirements are interpretive rules, policy statements, and organizational or procedural rules exempt?

A: This is a bit complicated. Section 553(b) states that such rules are exempt from the requirements of "this subsection." Subsection (c) begins by providing that "[a]fter notice required by this section, the agency shall give interested persons an opportunity to participate in the rulemaking through submission of written data, views, or arguments with or without the opportunity for oral presentation." If a rule is exempt from subsection (b)'s notice requirement, it makes no sense to require agencies to allow comments, because with no notice, no one will be able to comment. Therefore, §553(b)'s exemptions for interpretive rules and the like must exempt covered rules from all of the public aspects of the rulemaking proceedings except for §553(c)'s requirement of a concise general statement of basis and purpose.

As noted above, APA §553(b) exempts interpretive rules, general statements of policy, and rules of agency organization or practice from notice and comment requirements. These exempt rules are often referred to collectively as "**nonlegislative rules**" because they are not supposed to have actual legal effect. Further, §553(b) allows agencies to dispense with notice and comment procedures when it finds that such procedures are "impracticable, unnecessary or contrary to the public interest." In determining the reach of these exemptions, it is necessary to formulate an understanding of the difference between legislative and nonlegislative rules.

A **legislative rule** is a rule that has legal effects in the sense that it adds to or changes preexisting legal requirements. A legislative rule effects an actual change in existing law or policy, and it creates new rights or duties. Coming at the issue from a different perspective, a legislative rule has actual legal effect in subsequent agency and judicial proceedings. A nonlegislative rule can have no such effect. Interpretive rules and general statements of policy are the quintessential examples of nonlegislative rules. Because notice and comment procedures take time and can excite public opposition to agency proposals, agencies often attempt to avoid undertaking notice and comment on rules by characterizing them as interpretive or policy statements. Therefore, we need to understand the attributes of nonlegislative rules.

Interpretive rules are rules that interpret existing legal duties and do not change or add to those preexisting duties. For a rule to be considered an interpretive rule, it must not add anything to existing legal rules. Rather, it must merely inform the public of the agency's views of the meaning of existing statutes or regulations. Factors that courts look to in deciding whether a rule is interpretive include the agency's intent, whether the rule was codified in the Code of Federal Regulations (which indicates that it is legislative, not interpretive), whether it is inconsistent with or repudiates a prior legislative rule (same), whether it is based on a particular legislative provision (which indicates that it is interpretive), whether the rule appears to be have binding effect (which indicates that it is legislative), and whether the agency treats the rule as if it reduces its own discretion (which indicates that it is legislative). See *American Mining Congress v. Mine Safety & Health Administration*, 995 F.2d 1106 (D.C. Cir. 1993).

Many agency efforts to characterize rules as interpretive have been challenged on the ground that the rule was actually legislative and thus should have been subjected to notice and comment proceedings. For example, in 1988, the Department of Health and Human Services (HHS) promulgated (using notice and comment) a regulation known as the "gag rule," which prohibited health care professionals (including doctors) receiving federal family planning funds from mentioning abortion to their patients (even if abortion was potentially medically indicated). Violations could result in loss of federal funds. In 1991, the regulation was upheld on judicial review against constitutional and statutory challenges. See *Rust v. Sullivan*, 500 U.S. 173 (1991). At that time, the Supreme Court characterized the regulation as a complete prohibition on abortion counseling by covered professionals, including doctors.

After that decision, President Bush directed HHS not to apply the regulations in a manner that restricted the information a woman could receive from a doctor. An HHS undersecretary then issued, without notice and comment, a directive, characterized as an interpretive rule, instructing enforcement officers not to prevent doctors from discussing abortion with their patients. This directive was challenged as procedurally infirm and the D.C. Circuit held that it should have gone through notice and comment procedures. The court stated that because the directive substantially amended an existing regulation, it was a legislative rule and thus could only be effective after notice and comment rulemaking. The court emphasized that a rule amending an existing legislative rule is itself a legislative rule and must go through notice and comment. See *National Family Planning and Reproductive Health Association, Inc. v. Sullivan*, 979 F.2d 227 (D.C. Cir. 1992).

Interpretive rules can have substantial impact on regulated parties. Although this seems inconsistent with the definition of interpretive rules, by deferring to them, courts have allowed interpretive rules to have substantial impact. For example, the Postal Service, based on its interpretation of statutory standards, adopted (without notice and comment) a new method of calculating the retirement annuity benefits of certain substitute postal workers. Although this substantially changed the expected annuity payments for many workers, it was held to be an interpretive rule because the new method was based upon an interpretation of governing law. See *American Postal Workers Union v. United States Postal Service*, 707 F.2d 548 (D.C. Cir. 1983).

A **general statement of policy** informs the public of the agency's policy views, but does not purport to add to or alter existing legal rules. Agencies use policy statements to inform the public of their enforcement priorities, but by definition such a policy statement cannot create binding law. As one court has stated, an "agency cannot apply or rely upon a general statement of policy as law because a general statement of policy only announces what the agency seeks to establish as policy." *Pacific Gas & Electric v. Federal Power Comm'n*, 506 F.2d 33, 38 (D.C. Cir. 1974). When the agency attempts (through enforcement or other administrative action) to realize its policy, it must convince the relevant tribunal of its policy's legality — although a court will show appropriate deference to the views of the agency. The Indian Health Service, for example, had for many years operated a clinic in Albuquerque, New Mexico, to serve the health care needs of handicapped Indian children. In 1985, the service decided to close the clinic and spend its lump sum appropriation on a national program to serve such children. This decision was announced in a memorandum, and no notice and comment procedures were used. The Court of Appeals held that notice and comment procedures should have been used, but the Supreme Court reversed. The Court held that this decision was a general statement of policy because it stated the agency's intention on how it would spend its lump sum appropriation in the future. *Lincoln v. Vigil*, 508 U.S. 182 (1993). There was no preexisting legal right to the prior allocation of the funds, and thus the agency's announcement that the funds would be spent differently in the future was appropriately characterized as a policy statement.

In another case, the FDA promulgated rules specifying the levels ("action levels") of toxins in food products that would provoke FDA enforcement action against a product as "adulterated." The FDA argued that the action levels were general statements of policy because they described only when the FDA would bring enforcement actions and did not purport to establish binding rules on the permissible level of the toxins. The D.C. Circuit held that the action levels were not policy statements and that therefore notice and comment procedures should have been used. Contrary to the FDA's representations, the court found that in practice the FDA had treated the action levels as binding, for example, by requiring food producers to seek exceptions from action levels if they want to ship food with higher levels of toxins. See *Community Nutrition Institute v. Young*, 818 F.2d 943 (D.C. Cir. 1987). Judge Starr, in dissent, argued that the test for whether a rule is legislative should be whether it has the force of law in future proceedings. In this case, Judge Starr argued that because the FDA would have to prove in court (in an enforcement proceeding) that a product is

Sidebar

EFFECT OF NONLEGISLATIVE RULES

When a court finds that a rule is not genuinely interpretive or does not qualify as a "general statement of policy," the court typically holds the rule invalid for failing to follow required procedures. This is an odd result because if an agency characterizes a rule as interpretive or a general statement of policy, the agency is basically stating that the rule is not intended to have legal effect. Courts could, therefore, take the agency at its word and simply hold that interpretive rules and general statements of policy have no legal effect. This would mean that when enforcement issues arise, agencies must rely on statutes and legislative rules, not interpretive rules or policy statements. To achieve this result, courts would have to stop deferring to interpretive rules.

adulterated without regard to the action level documents, the action levels should not have been considered legislative rules.

Agencies have also attempted to avoid rulemaking procedures by issuing "guidance documents" without notice and comment. The agencies claim that these guidance documents merely advise regulated parties of agency policy without legal effects and thus are exempt from notice and comment as policy statements. The problem is that the agencies appear to treat these documents as if they are binding law, promising, for example, that no enforcement action will be taken against a party that follows a guidance document or that a party that follows a guidance document will be granted a permit. The courts have resisted these agency efforts to avoid notice and comment procedures when guidance documents actually alter legal rights. See *Appalachian Power Co. v. EPA*, 208 F.3d 1015 (D.C. Cir. 2005) (guidance document "significantly broadened" EPA rule and thus was invalid absent notice and comment); *General Electric Co. v. EPA*, 290 F.3d 377 (D.C. Cir. 2002) (guidance document invalid absent notice and comment because applicant following it was assured that it had satisfied requirements for a permit). However, courts may not be able to prevent agencies from using guidance documents informally as "arm-twisting" devices.

Rules of agency organization, such as rules establishing the distribution of authority within an agency, are also exempt from the notice and comment procedures of §553. Rules of agency organization may affect the interests of members of the public but are primarily concerned with the internal organization of the agency. In *Lincoln v. Vigil*, for example, the Supreme Court also suggested that the decision to spend the lump sum appropriation on a national program, rather than on the clinic in Albuquerque, might qualify as a rule of agency organization because it involved the "organization" of the agency's provision of services, not the alteration of anyone's legal rights or duties.

Rules of agency procedure, which inform the public how to proceed when presenting an application or claim to an agency, are also exempt from §553's notice and comment requirements. A rule that appears to be procedural will nonetheless be considered substantive if, in operation, it reflects a substantive judgment about particular conduct by substantially altering the rights or interests of parties engaging in disfavored conduct. For example, the Federal Aviation Administration (FAA), in compliance with legislatively mandated changes, and without notice and comment, amended its regulations to increase the maximum civil penalty in safety violation cases. The new rule also created an internal enforcement procedure that covered cases that previously could be prosecuted only in the United States District Courts. The agency claimed that the new rule was exempt as "procedural." In *Air Transport Association of*

Sidebar

AGENCY GUIDANCE PRACTICES

Concern that agencies were treating informally promulgated guidance documents as if they were binding rules led OMB in 2007 to issue a Bulletin on Agency Good Guidance Practices. The Bulletin noted that guidance documents can be issued without sufficient transparency or deliberation and that agencies sometimes use them as a substitute for more open rulemaking processes. Among other reforms, the Bulletin requires agencies to employ notice and comment before promulgating "significant guidance documents." See Office of Management and Budget, "Final Bulletin for Agency Good Guidance Practices," 72 Fed. Reg. 3432 (January 18, 2007).

Sidebar

PUBLICATION OF NONLEGISLATIVE RULES

Rules that are exempt from §553's notice and comment procedures must still be published in the Federal Register. APA §552(a)(1). If a rule is not properly published, it may not be used against any party not having actual notice of it. Id. The publication must also include a concise general statement of the basis and purpose of the rule.

America v. Department of Transportation, 900 F.2d 369 (D.C. Cir. 1990), the Court of Appeals held that although the rule appeared to be procedural, it did not fall within the §553 exemption because it affected the civil violators' rights, including the right to a hearing. Judge Silberman dissented, arguing that, in effect, the majority had mischaracterized the procedural right to a hearing as a substantive right.

(2) Policymaking by Manual or Other Internal Document: *Morton v. Ruiz*

Agencies often make policy internally — in operations manuals and other agency memoranda that are provided to agency personnel but are not made public or promulgated pursuant to any APA procedure. Perhaps surprisingly, the requirements of agency manuals are often not supported substantively by any statutory or regulatory provision but rather embody the agency's practices, often longstanding, that have never been codified. Because such manuals and internal memoranda are usually prepared without public input and are often not published, agencies encounter procedural problems when such internal documents are challenged by a member of the public. In *Morton v. Ruiz*, 415 U.S. 199 (1974), the Supreme Court addressed the procedural regularity of "**policymaking by manual**."

In *Morton*, the Bureau of Indian Affairs (BIA) denied welfare benefits under a BIA-administered program to the Ruizes, members of the Papago Indian Tribe. Mr. Ruiz worked at a copper mine and applied for benefits when a strike shut down the mine. The Ruizes lived fifteen miles away from the reservation in a largely Indian community of miners and their families. The BIA relied upon a provision of its manual stating that only Indians living on a reservation were entitled to benefits under the applicable program. However, no statute or regulation restricted benefits to Indians living on reservations. The BIA argued that although Congress never wrote the "on reservation" limitation into law, because the BIA requested funds only for Indians "on reservation," Congress intended to restrict benefits to such Indians. The Supreme Court rejected this argument, mainly on the ground that Congress was aware of BIA exceptions to the "on reservation" rule, especially those instances in which the BIA equated Indians living "near" reservations in nonurban areas with Indians living "on" reservations. The Court further noted that Congress had never written the restriction into law.

F	A	Q

Q: Did the decision in *Morton v. Ruiz* actually require the agency to use notice and comment rulemaking to promulgate the rule confining benefits to Indians living on reservations?

A: No. Although the decision has sometimes been interpreted that way, the opinion faulted the agency for not publishing the eligibility criterion either because the APA required publication or because the agency's own rules required publication. The Court also advanced a general argument in favor of administering benefits programs under clear rules, but it never explicitly mentioned notice and comment rulemaking.

The primary procedural problem with the eligibility rule in *Morton* was that it was not published. Rather, it was contained only in an internal agency manual that was used by agency employees to resolve benefits claims. The *Morton* Court noted that this presented three separate procedural problems. While the precise grounds for the decision are unclear, it is clear that the Court disapproved of nonpublic policymaking when the policy restricts the rights of members of the public.

The *Morton* Court's clearest holding is that the BIA's rule restricting eligibility for benefits to Indians living on the reservation should have been published in the Federal Register as required by APA §552(a)(1). It stated that the APA's procedural requirements were designed "to avoid the inherently arbitrary nature of unpublished ad hoc determinations." Without such publication, the rule could not be used against the Ruizes since they did not have advance notice of it.

The Court may have also viewed the publication requirement as emanating from general principles of administrative law rather than from the APA. The *Morton* Court was generally concerned with the absence of a properly promulgated rule defining the eligibility requirements for benefits. The Court acknowledged that an agency administering a benefits program must have the power to create eligibility criteria especially if there are not sufficient funds to provide benefits to all applicants who meet the statutory requirements. The Court stated, however, that such narrowing criteria are not valid unless they are published: "But in such a case the agency must, at a minimum, let the standard be generally known so as to assure that it is being applied consistently and so as to avoid both the reality and the appearance of arbitrary denial of benefits to potential beneficiaries."

Another procedural problem noted by the *Morton* Court is that the BIA should have followed its own procedural rule, which required it to publish any directives that inform the public of eligibility requirements. The Court stated that "where the rights of individuals are affected, it is incumbent upon agencies to follow their own procedures." *Morton*, 415 U.S. at 235.

The *Morton* Court also stated that the APA requires that "administrative policies affecting individual rights and obligations be promulgated pursuant to certain stated procedures" and that agencies must "employ procedures that conform to the law." The Court reasoned that proper procedure was necessary to avoid "ad hoc" decisionmaking. *Morton*, 415 U.S. at 232. This has been interpreted by some as a requirement that notice and comment rulemaking should be used in situations like *Morton*. However, the best reading of *Morton* is that the Court's "APA" reference meant §552's publication requirement, since matters relating to "benefits" are exempt from §553's notice and comment requirements. Nowhere does the Court state that the agency should have used notice and comment rulemaking.

As discussed in Chapter 5, agencies must also follow any procedural rules they have formally adopted through notice and comment procedures. If a rule was not formally adopted, courts may invalidate agency action taken in violation of such rules only when there is both detrimental reliance by a member of the public and agency intent to benefit the public with the informally adopted procedural rule. See *American Farm Lines v. Black Ball Freight Service*, 397 U.S. 532 (1970). Otherwise, agency violation of informally adopted procedural rules does not invalidate the agency's action. See *Schweiker v. Hansen*, 450 U.S. 785 (1981).

(3) Informal Decisionmaking More Generally: When May an Agency Act without Adjudication or Rulemaking?

Policy decisions are often embedded in informal agency action, for example when an agency grants or denies an application or petition informally, without using either a rulemaking or formal adjudicatory procedure. For instance, in *Overton Park*, the Secretary of Transportation approved a highway design without any particular procedure and without a formal explanation of the decision. While the Secretary's decision was only to approve the particular route, it doubtless embodied the Secretary's views on when parkland should be used for highway routing. The statutory basis for the widespread practice of using informal procedures is unclear because the APA appears to divide all agency action between rulemaking and adjudication — with no third, informal, category. See APA §551(4)-(7). Thus, the informal category is often referred to as **"informal adjudication"** and it is statutorily authorized by default, when the APA does not require more formal procedures. (Note that agencies must also satisfy constitutional due process norms, discussed below.)

Informal adjudication applies when an agency makes a particular decision that does not result in a rule (and it does not affect an individual in a way that requires formal adjudication). In essence, the agency is acting without following any APA procedural model. In *Overton Park*, for example, the Secretary's decision to approve the highway route and design was not an order directed at any particular member of the public, and it was not a rule that could be followed in other cases. The Court rejected the plaintiffs' argument that the Secretary was required to make formal findings, and there was no suggestion that the informal procedure used was inappropriate for that type of decision.

When an agency makes a decision informally, the only APA procedural requirements are notice of the decision and a brief statement of the reasons supporting it. See APA §555(e). This provision provides the best support for the agency practice of making some decisions informally because it appears to contemplate decisions without either a rulemaking or an adjudicatory process. In *Pension Benefit Guaranty Corp. v. LTV Corp.*, 496 U.S. 633 (1990), the Supreme Court, relying upon *Vermont Yankee*, discussed in Chapter 7, held that the only APA-mandated procedures for informal adjudication are those specified in APA §555. Courts may not impose additional procedures not required either by the agency's particular statute or the APA.

Sidebar

INFORMAL AGENCY ACTION

Although the APA's definitions divide all agency action into rulemaking and adjudication, agencies are not required to use a formal adjudicatory procedure for every decision not involving a rule. This definitional dichotomy has resulted in informal agency action being referred to as informal adjudication. It is more accurate, however, to state that the agency is doing neither rulemaking nor adjudication but is rather deciding a matter informally.

Sidebar

MEANING OF "HEARING"

There is not a great deal of law on when agencies are required by the APA to employ formal, as opposed to informal, adjudicatory procedures. We know in the rulemaking context from *Allegheny-Ludlum* and *Florida East Coast* that the word "hearing" is insufficient to require even an oral hearing. What about the use of the word "hearing" in a statute concerning adjudication? For a long time, the First Circuit presumed that any reference to a hearing in such a context meant formal adjudicatory procedures. *Seacoast Anti-Pollution League v. Costle*, 572 F.2d 872 (1st Cir. 1978). This presumption was attacked by commentators as inconsistent with the Court's views on the meaning of "hearing" in the rulemaking context. Recently, the First Circuit abandoned the presumption in favor of agency discretion to choose between formal and informal adjudication, not based on a changed view of the meaning of "hearing" but rather on the ground that agency constructions of procedural provisions in the statutes they administer are entitled to *Chevron* deference. See *Dominion Energy Brayton Point, LLC v. Johnson*, 443 F.3d 12 (1st Cir. 2006).

C. Constitutional Constraints on Choice of Decisionmaking Procedure

As we have seen, the APA leaves decisions concerning the form and level of agency procedure largely to the discretion of the agency. However, agencies are not completely free to employ informal procedures whenever they find it expedient. Rather, the choice between rulemaking and adjudication, and between formality and informality, is influenced heavily by constitutional **due process** concerns. Under certain circumstances, due process requires adjudication even at a relatively informal level of procedure. In most cases, however, the choice between rulemaking and adjudication is left to Congress or to the agency under delegation from Congress. The constitutional rules governing when adjudication is required and when legislative procedures are sufficient were developed in two Supreme Court decisions from the early twentieth century, *Londoner* and *Bi-Metallic*. As elaborated below, the Court has concluded that due process requires adjudication when individualized factual determinations lead to adverse governmental action, while a legislative process is sufficient for government to make an across-the-board determination regarding more generalized matters.

(1) The *Londoner* and *Bi-Metallic* Dichotomy

Londoner v. Denver, 210 U.S. 373 (1908), established the basic principle that when a government agency takes action based on the particular situation or circumstances related to a regulated party, due process requires notice and an opportunity for the party to be heard, i.e., adjudication. *Londoner* concerned the City of Denver's method of taxing property owners for street paving. This type of local improvement is often financed by what are called "special assessments," under which each property owner pays a pro rata share of the cost of the improvement based normally on an objective factor such as the number of feet of street frontage or the number of square feet of the lot or the building. In this case, however, Denver decided to tax property owners based on an individualized assessment of the benefit conferred upon each particular piece of property. Because the agency's decision was particularized to the situation of each property owner, the Court held that due process requires a hearing with the right to present arguments and evidence on the issue, i.e., the benefit to each particular parcel.

This decision stands for the general proposition that when an agency regulates a party based on the particular situation of that party, due process requires that the party be given an adjudicatory hearing to present its version of the facts. The particularized facts are referred to as adjudicative facts because they are found through an adjudicatory process that focuses on the particular situation of a single or small number of parties.

Sidebar

LEGISLATIVE AND ADJUDICATIVE FACTS

Kenneth Culp Davis, in his venerable Administrative Law treatise, first recognized the distinction between **legislative facts** and **adjudicative facts**. Legislative facts are the sort of general, sometimes predictive, judgments that legislative bodies rely on when formulating general rules. Adjudicative facts involve particularized determinations related to the situation of a specific party. See 1 Kenneth C. Davis, *Administrative Law Treatise* 702 (1958).

When a government agency makes a generalized decision, due process may be satisfied by a legislative process such as agency rulemaking. In *Bi-Metallic Investment Co. v. State Board of Equalization*, 239 U.S. 441 (1915), the Court held that when an agency imposes a tax on an across-the-board basis, without attention to the particulars of any taxpayer, due process does not require individualized hearings. In *Bi-Metallic*, an agency increased the value of all taxable property in the city of Denver by 40 percent. The Court rejected a due process challenge to the procedure, based on the lack of individualized, adjudicatory hearings, stating that when "more than a few people" are affected, legislative procedures are sufficient and the normal channels of government accountability provide the only practical safeguard.

> ### Sidebar
>
> **CONTINUED VITALITY OF *LONDONER* AND *BI-METALLIC***
>
> Although the *Londoner* and *Bi-Metallic* decisions are approximately a century old, they still govern the choice, as a matter of due process, between legislative and adjudicatory procedures. See *Gallo v. U.S. Dist. Court for Dist. of Arizona*, 349 F.3d 1169 (9th Cir. 2003) (applying *Londoner* and *Bi-Metallic* to determine whether attorney was entitled to individualized notice and hearing before new rule barring non-residents from practicing in U.S. District Court could be applied to him).

(2) Legislative Facts, Adjudicative Facts, and Due Process

Due process does not require hearings when agencies make across-the-board decisions based on general factual conditions and not the particular situation of any particular regulated party. The legislative fact determinations relevant to these sorts of across-the-board determinations are normally made legislatively.

For example, a Virginia statute gave the state Highway Commission the power to determine when public safety required railroads to remove a grade crossing and build a railroad bridge over a highway. This determination was made without notice or a hearing. The statute did not provide for judicial review, although the Virginia Supreme Court had stated that equity review for "arbitrary" action was available. In *Southern Railway v. Virginia*, 290 U.S. 190 (1933), the railway company challenged this statute as violating due process by not providing for a hearing on the safety of each crossing in advance of the order that the railroad remove a crossing and construct a bridge. The Court held that this procedure violated due process and it rejected the argument that administrative action without a hearing was constitutional because the Virginia legislature might have taken the same action without a hearing. The Court held that the fact that a legislature can act without an adjudicatory hearing does not mean that an administrative officer (without the fact-finding and deliberative procedures or electoral accountability of a legislature) was free to make such a determination without a hearing. The Court also found that the power of a court of equity to overturn the decision as "arbitrary" was too uncertain to provide due process.

A more recent counter-example can be found in the *Gallo* decision mentioned above. The federal District Court in Arizona promulgated a new rule imposing membership in the forum state's bar as a condition for membership in the District Court's bar. An attorney who was not admitted in Arizona, but had been admitted to the District Court's bar before the adoption of the rule, argued that this new rule in effect stripped him of his membership in the District Court's bar and that this could be done only after notice and an individualized hearing on his fitness to practice

ADMINISTRATIVE DECISIONS AND DUE PROCESS

Southern Railway moves beyond *Londoner* in one respect: It supports a claim that the argument for a hearing is strengthened by the fact that an administrator, as opposed to the state legislature itself, is making the decision. Thus, even if the removal of a particular grade crossing was a proper subject for the Virginia legislature employing a legislative process, an administrator making the same decision is required by due process to employ an adjudicative process.

before the District Court. The Court of Appeals rejected this argument, holding that the facts relevant to the amendment to the rules were legislative and thus could be determined in a legislative proceeding: "Since the amended rule affects a large number of people, as opposed to targeting a small number of individuals based on individual factual determinations, Gallo's claim that he is entitled to individual notice and an opportunity to be heard fails." *Gallo*, 349 F.3d at 1182. Whether a legislative process is sufficient to satisfy due process is also discussed in Chapter 8's unit on determining what process is due.

The distinction between adjudicative facts and legislative facts is both simple and elusive. It may help to keep the distinction clear by considering it in a practical sense. Adjudicative facts are usually testified to by witnesses or contained in documents or other exhibits related to a particular situation. For example, in a criminal trial, witnesses testify to the identity of the person they observed firing a gun, and ballistics experts testify to the scientific basis for concluding that a certain bullet was fired from a particular gun. Legislative facts are described by experts relying on statistics, studies, and policy generalizations. For example, in considering regulating handgun possession and use, experts may testify to the overall prevalence of handgun violence, the utility of handguns for self-protection, the availability of alternative means of protection, and the economic impact of the proposal on the manufacturers and sellers of handguns.

In sum, when agency action is based on adjudicative facts, i.e., particularized facts specific to one or a few parties, due process requires individual notice and hearings before the agency may act. However, when agency action is based on legislative facts, i.e., general factual issues common to more than a few affected parties, due process is satisfied by a legislative process that does not include individual notice and hearings.

SUMMARY

■ The main APA policymaking tools are rulemaking and adjudication. A great deal of agency action is done informally, and this informal action may have policy effects.

■ Agencies have a great deal of discretion over which mode to use, although adjudication may be required by the APA and due process before an agency may issue an order directed at a particular party.

■ Where no particular procedural model is statutorily or constitutionally required, agencies may make policy informally, i.e., without using either an adjudicatory or rulemaking process.

■ Agencies, like common law courts, often announce new rules in the course of deciding matters in adjudication. The Supreme Court approved this practice on two theories: first, that the practice is within the traditional adjudicatory process and second, that subsequent parties are ordered to follow the rule in a proper adjudication.

■ Rulemaking is the favored procedure for formulating general policy-oriented rules because of greater fairness and fact-finding ability.

■ The APA exempts several types of rules, such as policy statements and interpretive rules, from notice and comment procedures. For a rule to be exempt as a policy statement or interpretive rule, it must not add to or change existing legal obligations.

■ If an agency is required to make rules "on the record after opportunity for an agency hearing," the agency must employ formal rulemaking procedures under which rulemaking is conducted in an "on the record" adjudicatory-type proceeding. Otherwise, the agency is free to use informal, notice and comment, rulemaking.

■ Agencies must follow their own formally promulgated procedural rules, and they also must follow informally promulgated procedural rules when a member of the public has relied on the rule and has been prejudiced by the agency's failure to follow it.

■ Due process requires notice and an adjudicatory hearing when agency action affects a particular party and is based on facts specific to the situation of that party. These facts are referred to as "adjudicative facts."

■ Where agency action is based on conditions common to many parties, such as the value of all property in a city, or the effects of a widely used food additive, such general facts are referred to as "legislative facts" and a legislative process is constitutionally sufficient.

CONNECTIONS

Choice of Procedure

In considering the choice of procedure, it is important to be familiar with the features of each kind of procedure, rulemaking (Chapter 7) and adjudication (Chapter 8). For example, Chapter 7's discussion of rulemaking procedure is helpful for determining whether a rule is exempt from §553 notice and comment procedures.

Vermont Yankee and Choice of Procedure

The discussion of *Vermont Yankee* in Chapter 7 is relevant to the agency choice of procedures — courts cannot require agencies to add procedures beyond those required by rules and statutes unless there is a due process violation.

Agency Obligation to Follow Its Own Rules

On an agency's obligation to follow its own procedural rules, see Chapter 5.

Legislative Due Process

On when legislative procedures are sufficient to satisfy due process, see Chapter 8.

APA Rulemaking Procedures

7

This chapter examines the procedures required for rulemaking under the Administrative Procedure Act (APA). The focus is primarily on informal

(notice and comment) rulemaking under APA §553, including discussion of the judicial gloss on the most important provisions of §553. The primary process for promulgating rules under the APA is notice and comment rulemaking under APA §553, which is also referred to as informal rulemaking. This is a legislative process designed to allow agencies to formulate legislative rules after receiving input from the public. The principal requirements of informal rulemaking are notice, opportunity to comment, and publication of the decision together with a concise general statement of basis and purpose of any rules adopted. Agencies have discretion to supplement the APA's requirements to gather additional input.

The most common procedural challenge to rulemaking is that the notice of proposed rulemaking was not adequate. Section 553 requires notice of the terms or substance of the proposed rule or a description of the subjects and issues involved in the rulemaking. Out of concern for fairness to interested parties, and to produce a better rulemaking record, many courts require more notice than specified in the literal words of §553(b). Courts have required that the rule adopted be the logical outgrowth of the proposal and that the agency not materially or substantially depart from the proposal. Courts also have required that agencies provide advance notice of data or studies upon which the agency intends to rely. If notice is inadequate, the cure is a new notice and comment period. Interested parties must be afforded a meaningful opportunity to submit comments. In order for the opportunity to comment to be meaningful, parties must have notice of data or other information upon which the agency is relying.

Another procedural issue that arises with some frequency in notice and comment rulemaking is what, if anything, to do about ex parte comments, i.e., comments made to administrators outside the normal comment channels. Because ex parte contacts in notice and comment rulemaking are not explicitly prohibited by the APA, it is unclear whether and to what extent they are regulated by the APA. Most decisions do not invalidate rules based on ex parte comments, although there are several theories under which some courts have held that ex parte contacts are improper. As a remedy for ex parte comments, some courts have required that if an agency does receive ex parte comments, it should place such comments on the rulemaking record, especially if the ex parte comments turn out to be important to the agency's decision. A related issue concerns whether agencies may consider comments received after the official end of the comment period.

The political context of agency rulemaking raises issues about prejudgment and bias in rulemaking. Although the APA does not address the question, courts have held that an administrator must have an open mind in rulemaking and thus an administrator with an unalterably closed mind may be disqualified from participating in a rulemaking.

APA §553 requires that final rules must be accompanied by a "concise general statement of . . . basis and purpose." The concise general statement of basis and purpose must explain the agency's decision on major issues involved in the rulemaking and must provide answers to major concerns raised in the comments. Court decisions on this requirement have been criticized as requiring much more than the words "concise" and "general" normally imply.

Hybrid rulemaking is rulemaking to which some adjudicatory procedures, such as cross-examination of experts, are added. Some agency statutes require hybrid rule-making. Courts have required hybrid procedures when they found that notice and comment procedures were inadequate for the particular rulemaking. The Supreme Court, in *Vermont Yankee*, rejected judicial authority to impose procedures in addition to those specified in §553. This calls into question a great deal of the procedural elaborations courts have imposed in decisions applying §553.

There are two additional rulemaking procedures that should be noted. Formal rulemaking, or "on the record" rulemaking, is rulemaking pursuant to trial-type proce-dures akin to adjudication. Formal rulemaking is required when the agency is statutorily commanded to make rules "on the record after agency hearing." Negotiated rulemaking is a procedure under which a notice of proposed rulemaking is formulated through negotiations among interested parties. These negotiations are presided over by the agency. After negotiation produces a proposal, the proposal is subjected to a normal notice and comment rulemaking procedure.

A. APA §553 INFORMAL ("NOTICE AND COMMENT") RULEMAKING PROCEDURES

1. Basic Procedural Requirements for Informal Rulemaking
2. Notice

3. Opportunity to Submit Comments: The Opportunity to Participate
   Must Be Meaningful
4. The Problem of Ex Parte Contacts in Rulemaking
5. Prejudgment in Rulemaking: The "Unalterably Closed Mind" Standard
6. Explanation of the Decision: The Concise General Statement
7. Publication of Final Rules and Their Effective Date

B. HYBRID RULEMAKING AND *VERMONT YANKEE*: THE REJECTION OF JUDICIAL POWER TO REQUIRE MORE THAN §553 PROCEDURES IN INFORMAL RULEMAKING

C. FORMAL RULEMAKING PROCEDURES: THE ADDITIONAL REQUIREMENTS OF APA §§556 AND 557

1. When Is Formal Rulemaking Required?
2. Formal Rulemaking Procedures Resemble Adjudicatory Procedures

D. ALTERNATIVE PROCEDURAL MODELS FOR RULEMAKING

1. Negotiated Rulemaking
2. Direct Final Rulemaking
3. Interim Final Rules

A. APA §553 Informal ("Notice and Comment") Rulemaking Procedures

The bulk of agency rulemaking is done under (Administrative Procedure Act (APA) §553. This rulemaking is often referred to as "**notice and comment**" rulemaking or "**informal rulemaking**" and should be distinguished from "**formal rulemaking**," which is conducted under the formal adjudicatory procedures of APA §§556-557.

Section 553 appears to contemplate a fairly informal legislative procedure, not a highly constrained, overproceduralized process. Rulemaking procedures should be analyzed with three separate concerns in mind. The first is openness and democracy. Agency rulemaking often resolves important and controversial issues, and thus the process should be open to public scrutiny and influence. The second concern is agency expertise. Agency rulemaking often deals with technical matters that require agency expertise, and the process should allow for that expertise to play a significant role. The third concern is politics. Agency rulemaking often involves matters that are politically controversial, and the rulemaking process should accommodate political involvement in agency decisionmaking, but only to the extent that such involvement is consistent with democracy and the application of agency expertise as intended by Congress. The challenge in applying §553 is to accommodate these three disparate influences on agency rulemaking.

(1) Basic Procedural Requirements for Informal Rulemaking

The basic requirements of informal rulemaking are published **notice of the proposed rulemaking**; the **opportunity for public comment**; and (after agency consideration of the comments) publication of the final rule, together with a **concise general statement of the rule's basis and purpose**.

(2) Notice

Publication of the notice of proposed rulemaking (and of final rules and other agency action) in the Federal Register is central to the creation and maintenance of an open, democratic, and accountable system of administrative law. Publication of all important administrative documents in a central location allows the public, including all regulated parties, to monitor the activity of the administrative state and become aware of all possible administrative actions that might affect them. If an agency fails to publish notice as required, any rule adopted will be invalid. Further, if an agency fails to publish a final rule, the APA provides that unless the party has timely notice some other way, anything that is legally required to be published in the Federal Register but is not so published may not be used against that party. This eliminates the possibility of secret law, because any rules that have not been published as required cannot adversely affect someone without actual notice.

These five volumes constitute the Federal Register for one week during fall, 2010.

> The operative notice provision of §553 provides that "General notice of proposed rule making shall be published in the Federal Register[.] The notice shall include . . . either the terms or substance of the proposed rule or a description of the subjects and issues involved."

The two most common situations in which notice is challenged as inadequate are first, when the comments convince the agency to issue a final rule that is different from its proposal, and second, when the agency relies on material, such as studies or data, that were not publicly available as part of the rulemaking process.

The language of the APA does not require very detailed notice. While the notice require- ment can be fulfilled by publishing the text of the actual proposed regulation, the terms of §553 are also satisfied with as little as a descrip- tion of the subjects or issues involved in the rule- making. As one court has stated:

> [T]he statutory language makes clear that the notice need not identify every precise proposal which the agency may ultimately adopt; notice is adequate if it apprises interested parties of the issues to be addressed in the rule-making pro- ceeding with sufficient clarity and specificity to allow them to participate in the rulemaking in a meaningful and informed manner.

American Medical Association v. United States, 887 F.2d 760 (7th Cir. 1989). The key language here is that the notice must be sufficient "to allow them to participate in the rulemaking in a meaningful and informed manner." The D.C. Circuit has elaborated on the purposes that should animate notice analysis as follows:

Sidebar

NORMATIVE BASIS FOR STRICT NOTICE REQUIREMENT

The construction and application of the notice requirement is animated by the basic understanding that for interested parties to have a meaningful opportunity to participate in rulemaking through submission of comments, they need sufficient notice both to alert them in advance that their interests are at stake and to help them understand what is likely to influence the agency's ultimate decision. Sufficient notice is also necessary to ensure that the comments are informative enough to be useful to the agency in the decisionmaking process. Further, an agency's proposal may lead to political activity, such as an effort by an inter- ested party to enlist Congress or the President to become involved in the matter before the agency.

> The APA requires an agency to provide notice of a proposed rule, an opportunity for comment, and a statement of the basis and purpose of the final rule adopted. These requirements, which serve important purposes of agency accountability and reasoned decision-making, impose a significant duty on the agency. Notice of a proposed rule must include sufficient detail on its content and basis in law and evidence to allow for meaningful and informed comment: "the Administrative Procedure Act requires the agency to make available to the public, in a form that allows for meaningful comment, the data the agency used to develop the proposed rule." *Engine Mfrs. Ass'n v. EPA*, 20 F.3d 1177, 1181 (D.C. Cir. 1994); see also *Connecticut Light & Power Co. v. NRC*, 673 F.2d 525, 530-31 (D.C. Cir. 1982) ("An agency commits serious procedural error when it fails to reveal portions of the technical basis for a proposed rule in time to allow for meaningful commentary."); *Home Box Office, Inc. v. FCC*, 567 F.2d 9, 55 (D.C. Cir. 1977) (proposed rule must provide sufficient information to permit informed "adversarial critique").

American Medical Ass'n v. Reno, 57 F.3d 1129, 1132-33 (D.C. Cir. 1995).

The notice requirement creates tension between advance notice of an agency's intentions and the agency's ability to revise its proposal in light of the comments it receives. When an agency relies on comments to alter its proposal before adopting a rule, parties whose interests are affected by changes often complain that the original notice did not inform them of the damage that the adopted rule would do to their interests. The agency is caught between two values recognized in the APA. On the one hand, there are strong reasons for providing advance notice of the possibility that someone's interests may be affected by agency action. On the other hand, the whole premise of notice and comment rulemaking is that the agency should pay attention to the comments it receives and alter its plan when convinced by those comments.

The jurisprudence that has grown up around the notice requirement pays a great deal of heed to the unfairness that parties experience when they are surprised by an agency's changes between the notice and the final decision. Despite this unfairness, courts have no explicit statutory authority to require a second comment period whenever the comments convince the agency to promulgate a rule that differs from the proposal. (It should be noted that agencies often voluntarily provide multiple comment periods to allow comments on agencies' initial impressions or to allow commentors to reply to other comments.) As long as the agency honestly puts forward its proposed rule, or specifies the subjects and issues involved in the rulemaking, the language of §553 does not appear to be violated when the comments convince the agency to take an approach different from the proposal.

There must, however, be some standard that regulates the degree to which agencies can make changes between the proposal stage and the rule-promulgation stage. Otherwise, an agency can shield its true proposal from public scrutiny by proposing something that it has no intention of adopting and then promulgating a rule that has not been subjected to public comment. Although an agency is certainly free to make significant changes from proposals when promulgating final rules, an agency would violate the spirit of the notice requirement if it proposed, for example, a rule regulating lawnmowers and then promulgated a final rule about televisions. It is difficult to imagine how those interested in televisions would know to protect their interests by commenting on a rule about lawnmowers.

Sidebar

STRICT NOTICE AND *VERMONT YANKEE*

As courts stray further and further from the language of §553's notice requirement, they risk violating the *Vermont Yankee* rule, discussed below, which prohibits courts from adding to the procedures required by statute and rule. Does it violate *Vermont Yankee* for a court to require an agency to provide more than the terms of the proposed rule or the subjects and issues involved in the proposal?

To facilitate meaningful participation in the rulemaking process, courts have constructed a few different legal standards that govern the amount of change an agency can make between notice and promulgation without subjecting the final rule to a new round of notice and comment. The main standard that governs the degree to which final rules may deviate from the notice is the **"logical outgrowth"** test. Courts have required that the rules ultimately adopted be the logical outgrowth of the proposal. Courts have also stated that the final rule may not **materially alter** the issues involved in the rulemaking or **substantially depart** from the proposal. Courts have also required that the final rule be reasonably foreseeable from the proposal. While these courts are motivated by the concern that interested parties have a meaningful opportunity to participate in the rulemaking, some of the rulings may require greater notice than required under §553.

F A Q

Q: Are the notice decisions consistent with the APA's legislative notice and comment rulemaking model?

A: The more aggressive notice decisions can be rightly accused of imposing an adjudicatory model on what is designed as a legislative process. For example, the phrase "adversarial critique," drawn from the *HBO* decision cited with approval by the D.C. Circuit in the excerpt above, sounds like it belongs more in a discussion of adjudication than in a discussion of the legislative notice and comment rulemaking process. However, in more recent decisions, the D.C. Circuit seems to recognize that notice can be adequate even if significant changes based on the comments are made before the final rule is promulgated. See, e.g., *American Coke and Coal Chemicals Institute v. E.P.A.*, 452 F.3d 930 (D.C. Cir. 2006) (notice is adequate as long as agency disclosed data and gave interested parties opportunity to comment, even if analysis led to significant changes in final rule).

The Supreme Court has not weighed in definitively on the appropriate understanding of §553's notice requirement although it has recently expressed approval or at least acceptance of the "logical outgrowth" test, stating, "The Courts of Appeals have generally interpreted this to mean that the final rule the agency adopts must be "a 'logical outgrowth' of the rule proposed. *National Black Media Coalition v. FCC*, 791 F.2d 1016, 1022 (2d Cir. 1986). . . . The object, in short, is one of fair notice." *Long Island Care at Home, Ltd. v. Coke*, 551 U.S. 158, 174 (2007). The Court did not actually adopt the "logical outgrowth" test as its own. Rather it simply identified it as the test that has been applied by the lower courts. Perhaps the Court is leaving open the possibility that it might adopt some other test in a case in which the propriety of the "logical outgrowth" test is challenged. The Supreme Court also implied that notice is fair if the changes were reasonably foreseeable from the notice. Id. See also *Owner-Operator Independent Drivers Ass'n, Inc. v. Federal Motor Carrier Safety Administration*, 494 F.3d 188 (D.C. Cir. 2007) (citing *Long Island Care at Home* for "reasonably foreseeable" test).

The following decisions illustrate differing judicial approaches to the notice problem:

American Medical Association v. United States, 887 F.2d 760 (7th Cir. 1989), involved the IRS's method of accounting for the taxable activities of tax-exempt organizations, an issue that had proven to be difficult for the IRS to deal with. The agency proposed, in a notice and comment rulemaking, a seven-factor accounting test to be employed on a case-by-case basis. Several comments on the proposal claimed that the IRS's proposal was too vague and would leave organizations too uncertain of their potential tax liability. The IRS was convinced by the negative comments and, in place of the seven-factor test, it promulgated a rule requiring that organizations use one of three specific accounting methods. The American Medical Association (AMA), whose activities were directly affected by this rule, did not submit comments during the rulemaking but sought judicial review of the rule on the ground that the approach adopted by the agency was such a departure from the agency's proposal that notice of the proposal was inadequate in violation of APA §553. The Seventh Circuit upheld the adequacy of the notice. The court reasoned that since the rulemaking was about the activities of tax-exempt organizations, the AMA was on notice that its interests were at stake, and even if it was happy with the initial proposal, it could have submitted comments in support of that proposal. Thus, notice was adequate. While the court quoted the "logical outgrowth" test, its analysis stuck relatively close to the bare words of the APA notice requirement, which requires notice either of the terms or substance of the proposed rule, or a description of the subjects and issues involved.

Chocolate Manufacturing Association v. Block, 755 F.2d 1098 (4th Cir. 1985) involved the WIC program, which is a welfare program administered by the Department of Agriculture that provides food benefits to pregnant women, infants, and children.

The benefits are confined to a list of foods that is constructed via notice and comment rulemaking. In 1979, after a statutory revision, the agency published a notice of proposed rulemaking that included two elements: a list of all proposed permissible foods and a preamble that identified special concern in Congress about fat, sugar, and salt and that high-sugar cereals and juices were particular problems. The notice asked for comments on the issues mentioned in the preamble and comments "in favor of or in opposition to the proposed regulations" as a whole. Flavored milk, including chocolate milk, was not mentioned in the preamble and was on the list of permissible foods as it had been in the past. However, seventy-eight comments urged the agency to remove flavored milk from the list because of its high sugar content and increased cost. The agency agreed and in the final rule, flavored milk was not among the foods eligible for purchase under the WIC program. The Chocolate Manufacturers Association (CMA) did not comment on the proposed rule, but after the final rule was promulgated, it filed a petition for judicial review claiming inadequate notice. The Fourth Circuit held that because the preamble mentioned specific foods, such as sugared cereals and juices, and did not mention flavored milk, "there was insufficient notice that the deletion of flavored milk from the WIC program would be considered if adverse comments were received." The court thus concluded that the final rule was not the logical outgrowth of the proposal even though the notice asked for comments on all the foods on the list.

While both courts linked the notice requirement to the adequacy of the opportunity to participate in the rulemaking, the Seventh Circuit stuck more closely to the language of the APA in the *AMA* case than the Fourth Circuit did in the *CMA* case. Given that the APA approves notice even if it only contains "a description of the subjects or issues involved," it is difficult to see how the notice in *CMA*, which listed all the WIC foods, was deficient. However, the *CMA* court's approach may be closer to the Supreme Court's "fair notice" understanding, which evaluates the sufficiency of notice under §553 in light of the general concept of fair notice rather than under the language of §553.

The Supreme Court's opinion in *Long Island Care at Home* did clarify one problematic issue under the logical outgrowth approach. If an agency proposes a rule and then decides against promulgating that rule, or decides to promulgate the opposite rule, the final rule may not appear to be the logical outgrowth of the proposal. "No" is not normally thought of as the logical outgrowth of "yes." The *Chocolate Manufacturers* decision can be understood this way. The Fourth Circuit in that case held that because flavored milk was on the proposed list of foods that WIC recipients could purchase, deleting it from the list without specific advance warning is not the logical outgrowth of the proposal. In *Long Island Care at Home*, the Court clarified that by nature a proposed rule may or may not be adopted after the agency receives and considers comments: "Since the proposed rule was simply a proposal, its presence meant that the Department was *considering* the matter; after that consideration the Department might choose to adopt the proposal or to withdraw it." 551 U.S. at 160-61. This may relax somewhat on the application of the notice requirement in the lower courts.

Sidebar

DISCLOSURE OF STUDIES AND DATA

Agencies have also been required to disclose for public comment any studies, data, or other material that the agency intends to rely upon in formulating the final rule. This requirement is a notice requirement as well as an element of a meaningful opportunity to participate through comments, which is the purpose of the notice requirement. Participation would not be meaningful if the agency bases its final rule on information not available to the public for comment. See *United States v. Nova Scotia Food Prods. Corp.*, 568 F.2d 240 (2d Cir. 1977); *National Black Media Coalition v. FCC*, 791 F.2d 1016 (2d Cir. 1986). Note that there is no clear statutory mandate for this requirement.

The cure for inadequate notice is a new notice and a new comment period. If an agency is convinced by the comments it receives to make substantial changes from its original proposal, the agency must issue a new notice and hold a new comment period. The new notice must inform the public of the changes in the agency's views since the initial notice. Even if comments appearing on the public record suggested the changes between the notice and the final rule, substantial changes in an agency's views might render the initial notice inadequate to support the final rule. See *National Black Media Coalition v. FCC*, 791 F.2d 1016 (2d Cir. 1986).

Courts have recognized that requiring agencies to reopen the comment period whenever the agency makes changes presents the potential for a never-ending cycle of repeated notice and comment periods and significantly raises the cost to agencies of altering rules in response to comments. The entire democratic basis for the notice and comment process would be undermined if agencies faced strong disincentives to actually pay attention to the comments submitted by members of the public. Minor changes, or even substantial changes within the parameters of the initial proposal, do not justify a new comment period. Sometimes, this has been expressed in harmless error terms — if an agency's final rule should have been foreseen based on the notice, the failure to issue a new notice alerting people to possible changes is in effect harmless error because more or better notice would not have produced more comments and more comments would not have changed the agency's decision anyway. *American Coke and Coal Chemicals Institute v. E.P.A.*, 452 F.3d 930, 941 (D.C. Cir. 2006).

Courts should keep in mind that rulemaking is a legislative process and not a judicial one, and they should not impose adjudicatory notions of procedural fairness on the rulemaking process. Rather, they should recognize that interested parties have been treated fairly when they have been given an opportunity to comment on the subject matter of the agency's proposed rule, even if all the details of the final rule were not known until after the comment period was over. Arguably, it should be left to the agencies themselves to determine whether to provide a second notice and comment period.

RULEMAKING NOTICE CHECKLIST

1. Did the agency publish notice of its proposed rulemaking in the Federal Register, including notice of the proposed rule or the subjects and issues involved (and all other matters required by APA §553)? If so, the agency has satisfied the basic notice requirements for informal rulemaking.　　☑

2. Were any changes in the rule as adopted the logical outgrowth of the notice and comments? Stated differently, was the final rule not so materially different from the proposal such that affected parties had fair notice that their interests were at stake? If so, the agency has satisfied the APA's notice requirement for informal rulemaking.　　☑

3. Did the agency publish (as part of the notice) all studies and data upon which the final rule depended? If so, the agency has met the judicially imposed notice requirement that such material be published.　　☑

4. If any of the notice requirements is not met, the agency must publish a new notice and allow a new period for comment.　　☑

(3) Opportunity to Submit Comments: The Opportunity to Participate Must Be Meaningful

Section 553(c) provides that "the agency shall give interested persons an opportunity to participate in the rulemaking through submission of written data, views or arguments with or without opportunity for oral presentation." Section 553 thus contemplates paper proceedings, with comments submitted in writing. Further, the APA allows oral hearings at the discretion of the agency.

Some courts have interpreted §553(c) to require a "meaningful" opportunity to participate, holding that the APA requires more than merely the mechanical right to submit comments. These courts have read into §553 a number of procedural requirements designed to ensure that all interested persons have a meaningful opportunity to participate in rulemaking. For example, courts have required agencies to provide notice of any data or studies upon which the agency relies, reasoning that it is impossible to participate meaningfully in the rulemaking process without sufficient notice of the information the agency is considering. See *United States v. Nova Scotia Food Prods. Corp.; National Black Media Coalition v. FCC.* For example, in *National Black Media Coalition*, the Second Circuit held that the FCC violated the APA by relying on maps and internal studies that were not disclosed to the public for comment when it decided to abandon its minority preference in awarding broadcast licenses. The court stated:

> Further, the FCC's conclusions were, by its own admission in its report and order, based on maps which were appended to that order and internal studies. These maps and studies were not disclosed throughout the proceeding and thus parties had no opportunity to comment on their methodology or conclusions. It is clear that " '[i]t is not consonant with the purpose of a rulemaking proceeding to promulgate rules on the basis of inadequate data or on data that, [in] critical degree *is known only to the agency.*' " *Nova Scotia Food Prods.*, 568 F.2d at 251 (quoting *Portland Cement Ass'n v. Ruckelshaus*, 486 F.2d 375, 393 (D.C. Cir. 1973), *cert. denied*, 417 U.S. 921 (1974) (emphasis added in *Nova Scotia Food Prods.*)).

National Black Media Coalition v. FCC, 791 F.2d 1016, 1023 (2d Cir. 1986).

Although nothing in the APA explicitly requires it, courts have held that for the opportunity to participate to be meaningful, interested persons must be allowed to respond to opposing comments. This right is difficult to implement when comments are received late in the comment period or even after the comment period has ended. For example, in *Ober v. EPA*, 84 F.3d 304 (9th Cir. 1996), the court invalidated a rule because there was no opportunity for interested parties to comment on late comments that turned out to be important to the final rule. The case arose under a provision of the Clean Air Act that requires each state to submit a plan to the EPA for controlling particulate pollution. If the EPA approves the state's proposal, the plan becomes law. If not, penalties apply and a process for formulating a new plan is triggered. The EPA is required to conduct a §553 notice and comment rulemaking on whether to approve the state plan. Arizona submitted a plan for controlling particulate pollution in Phoenix. After the period for comments closed, the EPA requested (and Arizona submitted) additional data amounting to three hundred pages of information that was crucial to the EPA's approval decision. The Ninth Circuit held that the EPA violated the APA by not giving interested persons the opportunity to comment on the post-comment period submissions that were critical to the EPA's decision to approve the plan.

The *Ober* decision is subject to criticism for creating procedural rights in excess of those recognized in the APA. Suppose that Arizona had submitted its data on the last day of the comment period, and that the EPA refused to consider any comments submitted after the official end of the comment period. Would the EPA have violated the APA by not considering comments submitted after the end of the period? By considering comments submitted late in the comment period? If the answer to these questions is "no," it is difficult to see how the APA was violated in *Ober*. This decision appears, once again, to import concepts of fairness applicable to the adjudicatory process into the legislative notice and comment rulemaking process.

The effects of the *Ober* decision are tempered by the understanding that interested parties are not entitled to comment on every new bit of data that comes before the agency during or after the comment period. This would be an overly restrictive rule that would discourage agencies from learning anything during the comment period. Rather, agencies must allow comments on new data only when the data are truly new and do not merely supplement or reinforce data that are already available for comment. As the Ninth Circuit has stated:

> [T]he public is not entitled to review and comment on every piece of information utilized during rule making. Instead, an agency, without reopening the comment period, may use "supplementary data, unavailable during the notice and comment period, that expands on and confirms information contained in the proposed rulemaking and addresses alleged deficiencies in the pre-existing data, so long as no prejudice is shown." *Idaho Farm Bureau Fed'n* [*v. Babbitt*, 58 F.3d 1392, 1402 (9th Cir. 1995)] (quoting *Solite Corp.* [*v. EPA*, 952 F.2d 473, 484 (D.C. Cir. 1991)]) (internal quotations omitted).

Kern County Farm Bureau v. Allen, 450 F.3d 1072, 1076 (9th Cir. 2006).

Sidebar

RIGHT TO COMMENT ON OTHERS' COMMENTS

The requirement that parties be allowed to comment on other parties' comments is in tension with the informal, legislative nature of the rulemaking process. If, for example, an important comment arrives on the last day of the comment period, would the agency be required to reopen the comment period? In adjudicatory procedures, parties are normally allowed to respond to every bit of new evidence offered by the other side. Not so in the legislative arena, where the process is viewed as much less formal and presentations are not strictly constrained by procedural rules.

(4) The Problem of Ex Parte Contacts in Rulemaking

Another procedural issue that has been brought under the umbrella of the opportunity to comment is the problem of **ex parte contacts** that occur during the rulemaking proceeding. Ex parte contacts consist of communications from interested parties to administrators made outside the formalities of the normal comment process. For example, an interested party may present information or arguments in person in the administrator's office, place a telephone call to an administrator, or write a letter directly to an administrator without submitting the letter as a comment. Ex parte comments may also occur in social settings, when an interested party presents his or her views to an administrator over lunch or at some sort of social event. Ex parte contacts are made by private parties and, very often, by Members of Congress (or their staff) expressing their own interest or the interest of constituents.

Ex parte contacts are very common in rulemaking. Their prevalence in informal rulemaking raises the question whether such contacts violate the APA or some other principle of administrative law. No provision of the APA prohibits, or even explicitly addresses, ex parte contacts with administrators in informal rulemaking. See *Sierra Club v. Costle*, 657 F.2d 298 (D.C. Cir. 1981). By contrast, APA §554(d) prohibits most ex parte contacts in formal adjudication. By negative implication, it would appear that the APA does not prohibit ex parte contacts in §553 rulemaking, which would fit with the legislative model of informal rulemaking. It should also be noted that in most cases in which the issue has been raised, rules have not been invalidated due to the occurrence of ex parte contacts. Nonetheless, it has been argued (and some courts have been convinced) that ex parte contacts are inconsistent with APA informal rulemaking procedures.

Ex parte contacts can threaten the ability of other interested parties to participate meaningfully in the rulemaking process when the agency considers information or arguments presented in the ex parte contacts without giving other parties information on the content of those comments. Opposing interests may have no opportunity to comment on the content of an ex parte presentation.

Sidebar

CONCEPT OF EX PARTE CONTACTS

The entire concept of ex parte contacts comes from adjudication, where it is well understood that parties to a pending case, or their lawyers, should not communicate with the judge outside the procedural strictures of the adjudicatory process and without providing notice and an opportunity to appear to other parties to the adjudication. The concept does not fit into the legislative model very well, where traditionally legislators communicate privately with numerous interested parties before making a decision on a legislative matter.

F   A   Q

Q: Is there a statutory basis for prohibiting or regulating ex parte contacts in rulemaking?

A: APA §553(c) provides that the agency shall make and explain its decision "after consideration of the relevant matter presented" in the rulemaking. Based on this provision, it has been argued that the agency should only consider comments presented as part of the comment process and should not consider ex parte comments. Stated more strictly, it has been argued that the agency must base its rule only on matter that was part of the comment process, either received by the agency in comments or put forward by the agency as part of its notice. The problem with this reasoning is that if the rule adopted is supportable based on the public record, it would be difficult to prove that the agency was actually swayed by comments presented "off the record" in an ex parte fashion.

Because there is no explicit prohibition on ex parte comments in notice and comment rulemaking proceedings, the courts that are concerned over such comments have had to look elsewhere for statutory support to regulate the practice. It has been suggested, for example, that ex parte contacts violate the requirement (contained in APA §706 and *Overton Park*) that judicial review be based on the whole record before the agency, because the ex parte comments will not be part of the record before the court on judicial review. See *HBO v. FCC*, 567 F.2d 9

(D.C. Cir. 1977). The *HBO* court, in fact, went even further and appeared to presume that if ex parte contacts have occurred, there is a good chance that the agency's rule will be overturned as "arbitrary and capricious." While the *HBO* court's distaste for ex parte contacts in rulemaking has not been adopted by other courts, or even by different panels within the D.C. Circuit, its condemnation of ex parte contacts is worth reading, if only to provide context for the debate:

> Even the possibility that there is here one administrative record for the public and this court and another for the Commission and those "in the know" is intolerable. Whatever the law may have been in the past, there can now be no doubt that implicit in the decision to treat the promulgation of rules as a "final" event in an ongoing process of administration is an assumption that an act of reasoned judgment has occurred, an assumption which further contemplates the existence of a body of material documents, comments, transcripts, and statements in various forms declaring agency expertise or policy with reference to which such judgment was exercised. Against this material, "the full administrative record that was before (an agency official) at the time he made his decision," *Citizens to Preserve Overton Park, Inc. v. Volpe*, supra, 401 U.S. at 420, it is the obligation of this court to test the actions of the Commission for arbitrariness or inconsistency with delegated authority. See id. at 415-416, 567 F.2d at 34-36, supra. Yet here agency secrecy stands between us and fulfillment of our obligation. As a practical matter, *Overton Park*'s mandate means that the public record must reflect what representations were made to an agency so that relevant information supporting or refuting those representations may be brought to the attention of the reviewing courts by persons participating in agency proceedings. This course is obviously foreclosed if communications are made to the agency in secret and the agency itself does not disclose the information presented. Moreover, where, as here, an agency justifies its actions by reference only to information in the public file while failing to disclose the substance of other relevant information that has been presented to it, a reviewing court cannot presume that the agency has acted properly, *Citizens to Preserve Overton Park, Inc. v. Volpe*, supra, 401 U.S. at 415, 419-420 . . . but must treat the agency's justifications as a fictional account of the actual decisionmaking process and must perforce find its actions arbitrary.

HBO v. FCC, 567 F.2d at 54-55 (footnotes omitted).

In light of these concerns, the *HBO* court stated that agencies should resist attempts by interested parties to comment on a proposed rule outside the normal rulemaking procedure. In other words, agencies should not accept ex parte contacts. However, the *HBO* court also recognized that ex parte contacts in rulemaking are very common, and therefore it would be impractical to invalidate every rule in which ex parte contacts were made. Thus, the court held that although agencies should, whenever possible, just say "no" to ex parte contacts once the comment period has begun, if ex parte contacts do occur, documents and the substance of oral ex parte communications should be placed on the record for other interested parties to comment upon:

> Once a notice of proposed rulemaking has been issued, however, any agency official or employee who is or may reasonably be expected to be involved in the decisional process of the rulemaking proceeding, should "refus(e) to discuss matters relating to the disposition of a (rulemaking proceeding) with any interested private party, or an attorney or agent for any such party, prior to the (agency's) decision * * *," Executive Order 11920, §4, supra, at 1041. If ex parte contacts nonetheless occur, we think that any written document or a summary of any oral communication must be placed in the public file established for each rulemaking docket immediately after the communication is received so that interested parties may comment thereon.

HBO v. FCC, 567 F.2d at 57. The court also stated that if ex parte contacts occur after the close of the comment period, the agency may be required to reopen the comment period to allow other interested parties to comment upon the matters in the ex parte contact.

Despite the strength of the condemnation of ex parte contacts in the *HBO* opinion, the rule that officials should refuse such contacts during the pendency of a rulemaking has not been widely followed. In a subsequent D.C. Circuit opinion, a different panel adopted a much milder view, that absent a statutory prohibition, ex parte contacts are not forbidden and that only ex parte comments of "central relevance" to the rulemaking must be summarized and placed on the public record. See *Sierra Club v. Costle*, 657 F.2d 298 (D.C. Cir. 1981). Even this requirement was based on the particular statute under which the rulemaking in that case had been conducted. In general, the current consensus seems to be that ex parte communications are allowed in informal rulemaking but anything upon which an agency relies for its decision, including ex parte contacts, must be placed on the public record.

Ex parte contacts from within the government raise special concerns for several reasons. The great weight that input from Members of Congress or the President is likely to carry counsels caution in condoning ex parte contacts from those sources. Further, such input may be so powerful that it drowns out competing voices. However, there are also reasons to welcome contact from the President and Congress. As the head of the executive branch, the President arguably has a right to control, or at least influence, the conduct of all agencies. Additionally, the President has a constitutional obligation to "take care that the Laws are faithfully executed," which implies that the President must be able to communicate with agencies to perform this constitutional duty. Members of Congress are also highly interested in agency rules partly because they want to be sure that their statutes are enforced properly and partly to protect the interests of constituents. Ex parte contacts from Members of Congress are an informal method of congressional oversight of agencies, for better or for worse.

The courts have not been called upon often to address the special problem of ex parte contacts from executive branch officials and Members of Congress concerning pending rulemakings and other administrative action. As noted, the President, as chief executive, has a right to receive information from administrative officials regarding pending rulemakings, and he also has a right to give input on the substance of rulemakings. See *Sierra Club v. Costle*, 657 F.2d 298 (D.C. Cir. 1981). The *Sierra Club* court held that in rulemakings, presidential contact with an agency is allowed unless it violates due process. Nevertheless, Congress may require agencies to place the substance of contacts with the President on the public record. In fact, the statute at issue in *Sierra Club* required that all documents of "central relevance" to the rulemaking be placed on the public rulemaking docket. The court held that this requirement applied to oral communications also (summaries would have to be written) even those from the President if they were important to

Sidebar

PRE-RULEMAKING CONTACTS

It should be noted that because prior to the issuance of the notice of proposed rulemaking no proceeding is actually pending, it is understood that ex parte communications are allowed. Indeed, since there is no proceeding pending, it is a misnomer to characterize pre-notice communications as ex parte contacts. Agencies must be free to receive communications from the public before a rulemaking has been initiated because they rely to a great extent on input from the public to identify situations in need of regulation. However, if a pre-notice communication made to an agency is important to the agency's decision, that communication should be placed on the record for other parties to comment upon.

the outcome of the rulemaking. The court also implied that presidential prodding that influences an agency is not a ground for overturning a rule as long as the rule is supported by the record.

The *Sierra Club* court also approved congressional contacts with agencies during rulemakings. The court found it appropriate for members of Congress to vigorously represent the interests of their constituents, so long as the input remained focused on the merits of the pending rule and did not apply extraneous pressure on the agency to decide in a particular way. The court was concerned that if it prohibited inquiries and input from Congress during the pendency of rulemaking proposals, the validity of all rules would be questionable since such contacts are ubiquitous.

Ex parte contacts in adjudicatory proceedings are another matter. Even the President, as chief executive, does not have a right to attempt to influence the outcome of adjudicatory proceedings. Due process requires that formal adjudications be free of ex parte contacts except in limited, extraordinary circumstances. Further, in agency adjudicatory proceedings, the ban on ex parte contacts has always been strict and is based on the text of APA §554(d). Likewise, Members of Congress should not attempt to engage in ex parte contacts with adjudicators. In general, government officials have no special right to engage in ex parte contacts with adjudicators.

In some cases, courts have tightened up on the rules concerning ex parte contacts in rulemaking when the outcome of the rule has effects similar to the issuance of an order in adjudication. Sometimes, rulemaking is the procedure employed to resolve competing private claims to a valuable government privilege, and ex parte communications are improper and should not be accepted. In such cases, courts have viewed the rulemaking as more in the nature of adjudication and have held that due process concerns require greater procedural regularity. For example, in *Sangamon Valley Television Corp. v. United States*, 269 F.2d 221 (D.C. Cir. 1959), the court reviewed an FCC rulemaking that decided which of two licensees would receive the license to operate a VHF TV station with a favored channel designation. One licensee had several personal conversations with FCC commissioners, sent each commissioner a substantive letter after the close of the comment period, took commissioners to lunch, and bought them turkeys on Thanksgiving. The D.C. Circuit held that in this context, these ex parte contacts violated "basic fairness" and the rulemaking had to be redone. *Sangamon Valley Television Corp. v. United States*, 269 F.2d 221 (D.C. Cir. 1959). The stakes in the particular rulemaking were more like those involved in an adjudication, and therefore the ban on ex parte contacts was necessary to ensure fairness.

Later panels of the D.C. Circuit have disagreed over the reach of *Sangamon*. The *HBO* court relied upon it in support of an across-the-board ban on ex parte contacts in rulemaking.

Sidebar

GOVERNMENTAL EX PARTE CONTACTS

Ex parte contacts from Members of Congress and the executive branch are probably allowed in notice and comment rulemaking proceedings. However, the comments should remain on the merits of the rulemaking and not raise extraneous matters in an attempt to influence the outcome of the rulemaking. This is related to the requirement that agencies consider only those factors made relevant by applicable statute or rule.

Sidebar

EX PARTE CONTACTS AND *VERMONT YANKEE*

Later in this chapter, there is a discussion of the *Vermont Yankee* doctrine, which holds that absent unconstitutionality, courts may not require procedures in addition to those required by applicable statutes and rules. At least one court has held that the *Vermont Yankee* rule precludes courts from regulating ex parte contacts in rulemaking proceedings. This casts doubt on the *HBO* court's injunction to agencies to refuse ex parte contacts, but leaves intact the *Sangamon* rule insofar as agencies resolving competing private claims to a valuable privilege are required by due process to avoid ex parte contacts with interested parties.

Some panels of the D.C. Circuit have insisted that *Sangamon* applies only to the rare case of rulemaking that resolves competing private claims to a valuable privilege and that it has little relevance in normal legislative notice and comment rulemaking proceedings. See *Sierra Club v. Costle; Action for Children's Television (ACT) v. FCC*, 564 F.2d 458 (D.C. Cir. 1977).

(5) Prejudgment in Rulemaking: The "Unalterably Closed Mind" Standard

A major difference between adjudication and legislation is that we expect judges and others conducting adjudications to maintain an open mind until hearing the evidence and legal arguments in the matter before them. In an adjudication, due process dictates that the appearance of even a small measure of **prejudgment** may be sufficient to disqualify a decisionmaker from participating. The leading case on pre-judgment in administrative adjudication is *Cinderella Career & Finishing Schools, Inc. v. FTC*, 425 F.2d 583, 591 (D.C. Cir. 1970), in which the court held that an administrative official is disqualified from participating in an adjudication if it can be shown that the adjudicator "has in some measure adjudged the facts as well as the law of a particular case in advance of hearing it." By contrast, legislators are often chosen because of their ideological views on subjects they will vote on. Voters would be disappointed if a legislator did not vote as promised in the election campaign. In the rulemaking context, the issue has arisen over which, if any, model should apply to prejudgment by agency officials.

Informal rulemaking, being a legislative process, does not require the same neutrality as adjudication. However, the APA's notice and comment provision does contemplate that the agency will consider "the relevant matter presented" during the comment period. Although no statute specifically addresses the matter, courts have held that decisionmakers in rulemakings must be open to persuasion based on the comments received during the notice and comment process. Being part of the political system, administrators will naturally have opinions on regulatory matters. However, the D.C. Circuit has held they may not participate if it is shown by clear and convincing evidence that they have an **"unalterably closed mind"** on the subject of the rulemaking. See *Association of National Advertisers, Inc. v. FTC*, 627 F.2d 1151 (D.C. Cir. 1979), *cert. denied*, 447 U.S. 921 (1980).

As with all procedural issues, the question arises whether there is a legal basis for the "unalterably closed mind" standard. The APA does not specifically address the issue. Due process concerns over bias and prejudgment apply mainly to adjudication, in which a high standard of neutrality is expected of all decisionmakers. However, the APA's notice and comment procedure would be a sham if agencies had already made up their minds before issuing the notice of proposed rulemaking. The closest thing to a requirement of openmindedness comes in APA §553's provision requiring the concise general statement. That requirement begins with the phrase "after consideration of the relevant matter presented," suggesting that decisionmakers in rulemaking proceedings are required to consider the comments before promulgating the final rule. As we shall see in the next subsection, another way in which courts ensure that agencies pay attention to the comments is by requiring that agencies respond to major comments in the precise general statement of basis and purpose that the APA requires for every rule.

Proving that a rulemaking decisionmaker has an unalterably closed mind involves showing, from public or private statements made by the decisionmaker, that the decisionmaker is convinced that the proposed rule is necessary without regard to the substance of comments received. This standard is difficult to meet since general statements regarding the need for regulation in an area are not enough to prove an unalterably closed mind. The statements must show that the decisionmaker will not even pay attention to the comments. Although the issue has arisen in about a dozen cases that have been litigated in the courts of appeals, none has yet disqualified a decisionmaker in a rulemaking proceeding under the "unalterably closed mind" standard.

The case in which the "unalterably closed mind" standard was created provides a useful illustration of how unlikely it is that a court will ever disqualify a decisionmaker for prejudgment. In the late 1970s, FTC Chairman Michael Pertschuk made several public and private statements advocating restricting television advertising aimed at children. For example, in a television interview, he stated (in response to a question about "all the garbage that's advertised for the kiddies") that "it's an area of prime concern" and "I have some serious doubt as to whether any television advertising should be directed at a three or four or five year old, a preschooler." In a letter to the FDA Commissioner, he stated that "children's advertising is inherently unfair." He also wrote in that letter, on the topic of advertising for sugared cereals, that "we do not have to prove the health consequences of sugared cereals. What we do have to prove is that there is a substantial health controversy regarding the health consequences of sugar—a much lower burden of proof." This is pretty strong evidence of prejudgment, since what Pertschuk is apparently saying is that as long as there is evidence both ways, we can go ahead and regulate without having to fear being overturned on judicial review. He is apparently uninterested in what the weight of the evidence actually shows.

When the FTC proposed three different possible regulatory regimes regarding television advertising directed at children, opponents of regulation attempted to disqualify Pertschuk from participating in the rulemaking. The case ended up in the Court of Appeals for the D.C. Circuit, where the majority held that Pertschuk should not be disqualified. The court held that discussing and exploring possible regulatory options and expressing opinions is not enough to disqualify an administrator and that based on the totality of Pertschuk's statements, it had not been established by clear and convincing evidence that he had an unalterably closed mind. See *Association of National Advertisers, Inc. v. FTC*, 627 F.2d 1151 (D.C. Cir. 1979), *cert. denied*, 447 U.S. 921 (1980).

(6) Explanation of the Decision: The Concise General Statement

APA §553 requires the agency to "incorporate in the rules adopted a **concise general statement** of their basis and purpose." The statement must contain a reasoned explanation for the agency's decision. This is a safeguard against arbitrary agency decisionmaking because it requires the agency to give reasons for rules. The phrase "concise general statement" evokes a document much less detailed and of less depth than a judicial opinion. The APA maintains this distinction. While informal rulemaking requires a concise general statement, formal adjudication (and formal rulemaking) requires "findings and conclusions, and the reasons or basis therefore on all the material issues of fact, law, or discretion presented on the record; and . . . the appropriate rule, order, sanction, relief, or denial thereof." APA §557(c)(3)(A) and (B).

Courts have required that agencies, in their concise general statements, respond to substantial comments on important issues in the rulemaking. See *United States v. Nova Scotia Food Prods. Corp.*, 568 F.2d 240 (2d Cir. 1977). This ensures that agencies pay attention to the comments received during the comment period and is closely related to the requirements of the arbitrary, capricious test — an agency acts unreasonably if it cannot be discerned whether it considered alternatives or important challenges to the wisdom of its proposal. For example, the D.C. Circuit has approved an agency's concise general statement on the basis that it "demonstrate[d] that the agency considered and rejected petitioners' arguments (and cited support) for adopting [its model.] This is all that the APA requires." *City of Waukesha v. EPA*, 320 F.3d 228, 258 (D.C. Cir. 2003). Courts have recognized that requiring detailed comprehensive responses to everything put before the agency is inconsistent with the meaning of "concise general statement." As the D.C. Circuit recently stated, "This requirement is not meant to be particularly onerous. . . . It is enough if the agency's statement identifies the major policy issues raised in the rulemaking and coherently explains why the agency resolved the issues as it did." *National Mining Ass'n v. Mine Safety and Health Admin.*, 512 F.3d 696, 700 (D.C. Cir. 2008).

Agencies thus are not required to explain every factual, legal, or policy element of the decision. Nevertheless, agencies must inform the public of their views on the major issues that were decided in the rulemaking. The concise general statement should cite support in the record and should identify the policy considerations found to be persuasive. See *Industrial Union Department, AFL-CIO v. Hodgson*, 499 F.2d 467, 475 (D.C. Cir. 1974). The rule at issue in *Nova Scotia Food Prods. Corp.*, for example, dealt with the method for preparing smoked fish to avoid botulism. The processors of one species of smoked fish, in comments to the agency, stated that the commercial viability of their fish would be destroyed by the agency's proposed (and ultimately adopted) method. The same processors argued that the agency's method was not necessary to prevent botulism in their species of fish. The agency adopted its proposed method and did not address the two concerns raised by the processors regarding their particular species of fish. The Court of Appeals held that the rule could not be enforced against Nova Scotia Food Products because the concise general statement did not explain the agency's conclusions on these major issues raised in the comments.

(7) Publication of Final Rules and Their Effective Date

Agencies must publish final rules, substantive and procedural, in the Federal Register. APA §552(a)(1)(C) and (D). If a rule is not published in the Federal Register, the rule is ineffective as to any party without actual notice of the rule. APA §552(a)(1). Agency rules normally specify an effective date, and the APA provides that the effective date may not be sooner than thirty days after publication of the final rule unless the agency finds good cause to specify an earlier date. APA §553(d). In addition, the Congressional Review Act provides that for major rules, the effective date cannot be less than sixty days after publication, to allow Congress time to consider whether to reject the rule. See 5 U.S.C. §801(a)(3).

F　A　Q

Q: What explains the judicial inclination to impose procedures in addition to those explicitly required by APA §553 and other applicable statutes and rules?

A: The courts, concerned with fairness to interested parties, the veracity of the record on judicial review, and the quality of the rulemaking record, have sometimes applied the requirements of APA §553 rather strictly. In a sense, the courts have imported concepts from adjudication and superimposed them on the legislative rulemaking mode. In this vein, they have required the sort of notice viewed as fundamental to the litigation process in which parties are entitled to relatively precise information in advance on the issues and evidence likely to arise in the litigation process. They have imported the concept of ex parte contacts from the judicial process even though the APA appears to regulate them only with regard to formal adjudicatory procedures. And some courts have required a concise general statement more akin to the findings and conclusions that are required in formal adjudication. In general, it appears that courts reviewing procedures in legislative rulemaking have often worked within the judicial model that is familiar to them. The *Vermont Yankee* decision, discussed below, raises a general question regarding the propriety of the aggressive application on judicial review of the procedures in informal rulemaking under APA §553.

B. Hybrid Rulemaking and *Vermont Yankee*: The Rejection of Judicial Power to Require More Than §553 Procedures in Informal Rulemaking

Perhaps in reaction to the sparseness of the procedural requirements contained in APA §553, in the 1970s some federal courts began requiring agencies to employ procedures for informal rulemaking in addition to those specified in APA §553. This practice went beyond expansive applications of the text of §553 and involved imposition of procedures without any tie to the language of the APA, based on the importance or the complexity of the rulemaking.

The judicial instinct in these cases was similar to the instinct behind the aggressive procedural decisions discussed above — courts imposed elements of the adjudicatory model on the legislative rulemaking process. The resulting rulemaking process was referred to as **hybrid rulemaking** because it combined legislative rulemaking procedures with some elements drawn from formal adjudicatory procedures such as cross-examination of adverse experts and more precise notice coupled with additional comment periods so that interested parties could comment on adverse comments submitted. Because courts were imposing procedures in addition to those required by applicable statutes, judicially created hybrid rulemaking was always plagued by a question of legitimacy — what power do federal courts have to require procedures in addition to those prescribed by Congress?

Courts commonly added cross-examination of opposing witnesses, multiple comment periods, and opportunity for oral presentation to the procedures mandated by §553 because they viewed the APA's specified procedures as inadequate or unfair to the interested parties. These courts viewed the APA as setting the procedural floor, but not the ceiling, for informal rulemaking. In other words, these courts viewed the APA's provisions as establishing statutory minima, but in their view the courts retained a sort of common law power to require more in the way of procedure when policy concerns dictated.

There are two situations in which hybrid rulemaking does not pose a serious question of legitimacy, namely **statutory hybrids** and due process requirements. Statutory hybrids involve statutes that add some adjudicatory elements to §553 legislative rulemaking. These statutory hybrids add procedures such as cross-examination, multiple comment periods, and detailed agency explanatory memoranda to the more spare §553 process. Congress has also on occasion specified that the less deferential substantial evidence test applies to review of informal rules rather than the more deferential arbitrary and capricious standard. So long as courts are merely following the applicable statutes and rules, statutory hybrids do not present a question of legitimacy of judicial action. Congress is virtually always free to increase procedural requirements and prescribe less deferential judicial review.

The second situation in which hybrid rulemaking is less suspect is when due process norms militate in favor of procedures in addition to those required under §553. In situations in which rulemakings have a great impact on a small number of interested parties, courts have required increased procedures out of sensitivity to the due process interests of the affected parties, especially when the issues in the rulemaking focus on the behavior or situation of those interested parties. This is similar to the reasoning behind the ban on ex parte contacts in *Sangamon Valley Television Corp. v. United States*, 269 F.2d 221 (D.C. Cir. 1959). Judicial action here still faces some question of legitimacy because, unless there is an actual statutory or constitutional basis (such as a due process violation) for requiring greater procedures than required by §553, courts may lack the power to add to statutory procedural requirements. However, in many of these situations, a due process violation is lurking just below the surface, and courts are wise to require procedural protections greater than those specified in §553.

The *Vermont Yankee* decision arose out of litigation over the licensing of the Vermont Yankee nuclear power plant. In its decision, the Supreme Court held that absent unconstitutionality or extremely compelling circumstances, courts may not require procedures in addition to those specified in the APA or other applicable statutes. *Vermont Yankee Nuclear Power Corp. v. NRDC*, 435 U.S. 519 (1978). The Court held that the APA is both the procedural floor and ceiling as far as courts are concerned, although agencies remain free to voluntarily adopt procedures in addition to those specified in the APA.

The history of the *Vermont Yankee* litigation provides a good illustration of the complexity of the hybrid rulemaking issue. In *NRDC v. Nuclear Regulatory Comm'n*, 547 F.2d 633 (D.C. Cir. 1976), the Court of Appeals rejected a Nuclear Regulatory Commission (NRC) rulemaking on how the negative effects and costs of nuclear waste should be considered in individual NRC licensing decisions. The agency had adopted a rule providing that nuclear waste disposal would be counted in licensing decisions but only as a very small cost factor in the overall licensing decision. (The primary competing alternative in the rulemaking was to not count the cost of nuclear waste at all.) The rule was based primarily on a relatively brief statement by an agency scientist specifying a feasible method of nuclear waste disposal. This statement was attacked by the opponents of the rule (environmentalists who wanted the waste issue to count as much more of a negative in the licensing process) as too conclusory to support such an important rule. They wanted to be able to cross-examine the expert or employ some other method of probing the bases for his conclusions.

The Court of Appeals agreed with the challengers, but it is a bit difficult to pin down whether that court's problems with the agency decision were procedural or substantive. On the substantive side, the opinion seems to hold that the conclusory statement on waste disposal was substantively insufficient to support the rule, i.e., the rule was arbitrary and capricious because there was insufficient evidence in the record to support it. The principal problem seemed to be that without a sense of the underlying basis for the statement's conclusions, the statement was inadequate by itself for the agency to reasonably conclude that nuclear waste disposal would have only small negative effects. On the procedural side, the Court of Appeals suggested that the rule might be upheld if a better record were

Sidebar

LEGITIMACY OF STATUTORY HYBRIDS

The cases involving judicially imposed hybrids with no hint of unconstitutionality present the greatest problem for the legitimacy of judicial action, since there is no purported constitutional or strong statutory basis for the addition of procedures. This attitude toward the APA was rejected by the Supreme Court in the landmark *Vermont Yankee* decision.

Sidebar

NUCLEAR WASTE DISPOSAL

As of this writing, more than thirty years after the *Vermont Yankee* litigation, the problem of nuclear waste disposal has not been solved. For decades, the federal government planned to create a permanent disposal site in Nevada, but funding for continuing work on the disposal site was not included in the President's proposed 2009-2010 budget, due perhaps in large part to opposition from Nevada Senator Harry Reid, a powerful Democrat. It appears that the situation is back to the drawing board regarding permanent nuclear waste disposal.

made via the application of procedures such as discovery, cross-examination, and other forms of more direct interchange. These procedures would allow for probing of the underlying scientific bases of the statement and thus would provide a more reasonable basis for a conclusion on the impact of nuclear waste.

The Supreme Court resolved the ambiguity in the Court of Appeal's opinion by concluding that the lower court had decided that the procedures were inadequate due to the complexity and importance of the rule. Note that this is not the only or even the most textually accurate reading of the lower court's opinion. The opinion can be reasonably read as substantively rejecting the agency's conclusion as formed on too slender a scientific basis.

The Supreme Court, having characterized the Court of Appeal's decision as procedural, ruled in *Vermont Yankee* that courts may not require agencies to follow procedures in addition to those specified in the APA (or a statute specific to the agency) unless statutorily prescribed procedures are constitutionally inadequate or unless some other extraordinary circumstance requires additional procedures. The Court supported this rule with policy arguments that support confining judicial review as confined to enforcing the procedures specified in the APA and other applicable statutes. First, judicial imposition of procedures in a common law-like process based on the complexity or importance of the rulemaking would be unpredictable because the standards employed by courts in fashioning judicial hybrids are not very precise and it is often difficult to predict in advance just how complex or important a rule is likely to be. Second, because of this unpredictability, agencies would have a strong incentive to overproceduralize to avoid possible reversal on judicial review. Third, overproceduralization would eliminate the informality and flexibility Congress intended for the informal rulemaking process.

The Court also supported its rule against judicial imposition of additional procedures with observations related to the fundamental nature of the legislative rulemaking process that challenge the judicial tendency to impose adjudicatory norms on the legislative rulemaking process. The Supreme Court noted that the Court of Appeals "uncritically assumed that additional procedures will automatically result in a more adequate record." The Supreme Court observed that reviewing courts should not expect the substantive quality of the record to be what is normally produced in an adjudicatory or hybrid process. Rather, the record is adequate if it is the sort of record that is normally produced in the rulemaking process. "Thus, the adequacy of the 'record' in this type of proceeding is not correlated directly to the type of procedural devices employed, but rather turns on whether the agency has followed the statutory mandate of the Administrative Procedure Act or other relevant statutes." 435 U.S. at 547. The Supreme Court linked this aspect of its holding to the potential for overproceduralization if reviewing courts always demand a record that is unlikely to be produced in a rulemaking procedure: "If the agency is compelled to support the rule . . . with the type of record produced only after a full adjudicatory hearing, it simply will have no choice but to conduct a full adjudicatory hearing prior to promulgating every rule. . . . [T]his sort of unwarranted judicial examination of perceived procedural shortcomings of a rulemaking proceeding can do nothing but seriously interfere with that process prescribed by Congress." 435 U.S. at 548.

F   A   Q

Q: In addition to pure judicial hybrids, are any other APA decisions potentially inconsistent with _Vermont Yankee_?

A: _Vermont Yankee_ did not resolve the question whether judicial review under the APA was too aggressive. It may be useful to distinguish between the letter of _Vermont Yankee_, which disallows judicially created hybrids, and the spirit of _Vermont Yankee_, which expresses concern over unpredictability and overproceduralization. Under the letter of _Vermont Yankee_, any decision that relies on an APA provision is still good law in the sense that it does not violate the terms of the _Vermont Yankee_ decision. Thus, because _Chocolate Manufacturers_ is about the meaning of §553's notice requirement, it is not necessarily inconsistent with _Vermont Yankee_. The fact that the Supreme Court, in its recent _Long Island Care at Home_ opinion, quoted the "logical outgrowth" test for the adequacy of notice with apparent approval reinforces the sense that the Court does not understand its _Vermont Yankee_ decision to require a literalist application of the APA's procedural provisions. Other decisions, such as the D.C. Circuit's effort in the _HBO_ case to ban ex parte communications in §553 rulemakings (insofar as they do not rely on a provision of the APA) are cast into doubt by the letter of _Vermont Yankee_, which requires some statutory basis for procedural rulings. In _District No. 1, Pacific Coast Dist., Marine Engineers' Beneficial Assoc. v. Maritime Administration_, 215 F.3d 37, 42-43 (D.C. Cir. 2000), the D.C. Circuit held that under _Vermont Yankee_, courts may not impose a ban on ex parte contacts without a basis in a statute or rule.

It can be argued that a ban on ex parte contacts in rulemaking is based on the APA's requirements that interested parties have an opportunity to comment and that courts review the "whole record" on judicial review. However, the spirit of _Vermont Yankee_, which demands predictability and therefore adherence only to explicit statutory requirements, counsels against expansive readings of §553's provisions, and thus may cast doubt even on decisions like _Chocolate Manufacturers_ (where a strong argument exists that the agency complied with the explicit terms of §553). There is great unpredictability inherent in reading §553's requirement that interested parties have an opportunity to comment to ban ex parte communications or to require that decisionmakers have an open mind. These are specific requirements that Congress could easily impose in so many words, and allowing courts to impose them based on textually unrelated general provisions opens the door to numerous unpredictable procedural decisions. The spirit of _Vermont Yankee_ seeks to preserve §553's informality and to constrain courts from creating procedural rights that are difficult for agencies to predict. Note that statutory hybrids are unaffected by _Vermont Yankee_ because courts there are following Congress's instructions and are not imposing additional procedures on their own.

C. Formal Rulemaking Procedures: The Additional Requirements of APA §§556 and 557

(1) When Is Formal Rulemaking Required?

Formal rulemaking means rulemaking done through an adjudicatory process in which opposing interests present evidence, arguments, and cross-examine opposing witnesses and where a decision is made under the strict procedural requirements of adjudication. The situations in which agencies are required to use formal rulemaking are detailed in Chapter 6. In brief, §553 requires formal rulemaking only in those rare instances when an agency's statute requires that rules be made "on the record after a hearing," or explicitly states that formal rulemaking is required.

(2) Formal Rulemaking Procedures Resemble Adjudicatory Procedures

In the rare instance when rules are made formally ("on the record"), APA §§556 and 557 prescribe trial-type procedures with regard to the submission of evidence, the impartiality of the decisionmaker, the composition of the record, and the explanation of the decision. Unless the agency's statute provides otherwise, one or more of the agency heads or one or more Administrative Law Judges preside at the formal rule-making hearing. APA §556(b). The official or officials presiding at the hearing have similar powers, and are subject to constraints similar to those of a judge presiding over an adjudication. APA §556(c).

When presenting evidence in a formal rulemaking, parties are entitled to present their cases by oral or documentary evidence, they are entitled to conduct cross-examination when appropriate, and they are entitled to present rebuttal evidence. Nevertheless, an agency may adopt rules requiring written submission of evidence when it is not prejudicial to a party's ability to present the case. See APA §556(d). The record, including transcripts of oral proceedings and documents admitted into evidence, constitutes the exclusive record for decision in formal rulemaking. This is why formal rulemaking is also referred to as "on the record" rulemaking. APA §557(e).

Agency officials presiding at formal rulemaking hearings, and other agency officials expected to be involved in the decisionmaking process, are prohibited from engaging in ex parte communications regarding the formal rulemaking with any interested person. If such communications nevertheless take place, they must be placed on the public record; the party making such communications may suffer sanctions — including losing the case. APA §557(d). The decision in a formal rule-making must include findings and conclusions (with record support) on all issues of fact, law, and discretion. When the agency itself did not preside at the hearing, the parties are entitled to present proposed findings and conclusions and to take exception to any tentative or recommended decision. APA §557(b)-(c).

Formal rulemaking is almost never used, for the simple reason that conducting a formal rulemaking can be a nightmare for the agency. With numerous parties, the simplest procedural steps can go on interminably. For example, numerous parties may be entitled to cross-examine each witness or insist on proper authentication of every document or other item placed in evidence. The adjudicatory model does not provide a workable process for producing a legislative rule.

D. Alternative Procedural Models for Rulemaking

In addition to informal and formal rulemaking, alternative rulemaking models have been established, some established by Congress and others created by agencies. In this section, we consider three such models, one established by Congress and two fashioned by agencies. These three are **negotiated rulemaking**, which was established by Congress, **direct final rulemaking** and **interim final rulemaking**, the latter two of which were created by agencies without explicit approval by Congress.

(1) Negotiated Rulemaking

In 1990, Congress passed the Negotiated Rulemaking Act, which allows agencies to hold formal negotiations among interested parties to formulate rulemaking proposals that have the support of the interested parties. The idea behind negotiated rulemaking is that the process is likely to run more smoothly, and thus is less likely to result in rejection on judicial review, if the major stakeholders in the rulemaking process have agreed in advance to the rulemaking proposal. The Negotiated Rulemaking Act allows agencies, under circumstances in which negotiations are likely to be fruitful, to form negotiating committees composed of representatives of all interests in the potential rulemaking. The Act contains detailed requirements for the conduct of negotiated rulemaking. See 5 U.S.C. §§561-570. The goal of the committee is to reach consensus among all competing interests on the issues raised by the potential rulemaking, at which point the agency will issue a notice of proposed rulemaking embodying that consensus. Normal §553 procedures follow the negotiations.

An agency using negotiated rulemaking is not statutorily bound to propose the rule agreed upon by the parties to the negotiation, although there is obviously a strong incentive for the agency to do so if it expects parties in the future to participate in negotiated rulemaking. See *City of Portland, Oregon v. E.P.A.*, 507 F.3d 706 (D.C. Cir. 2007). However, courts have not required agencies to adopt the rule agreed to in negotiation. See *USA Group Loan Services, Inc. v. Riley*, 82 F.3d 708, 715 (7th Cir. 1996). If they did, the notice and comment rulemaking would be a sham because the agency would be required to adopt the proposal agreed to during the negotiation process.

> ### Sidebar
>
> **NEGOTIATION AND NOTICE AND COMMENT**
>
> Negotiated rulemaking does not replace notice and comment rulemaking under §553. If the negotiation process produces an agreement, the proposal still must go through normal notice and comment procedures. 5 U.S.C. §563(a). In other words, the negotiated rulemaking produces a rulemaking proposal for notice and comment, not a final rule.

The fact that a rule was first proposed through negotiated rulemaking under the Negotiated Rulemaking Act should not affect its status on judicial review. The Act precludes review of the conduct of the negotiated rulemaking, including the composition of the negotiating committee, and the Act provides that a rule proposed through negotiated rulemaking is not entitled to greater deference in court than any other rule. 5 U.S.C. §570. (The fact that a negotiated rulemaking was employed may be important in cases in which negotiations were conducted pursuant to a statute other than the Negotiated Rulemaking Act. See *Center for Law and Educ. v. Department of Educ.*, 396 F.3d 1152 (D.C. Cir. 2005).) In the very few cases in which negotiated rulemaking has arisen as an issue, the fact that a rule was proposed and promulgated after negotiation has not been important to reviewing courts. Any defects in the negotiation process are probably cured by the notice and comment process through which all such rules are ultimately promulgated.

(2) Direct Final Rulemaking

When an agency expects no comments in response to a rulemaking proposal it may issue what is called a "direct final rule." Under this process, which has been used mainly by the EPA, the agency publishes a final rule and specifies that it will go into effect on a certain date unless the agency receives adverse comments. This procedure speeds up the process of promulgating rules and collapses the notice and decision steps into one step of promulgation of a final rule (unless adverse comments are received). If the agency does receive adverse comments, the direct final rulemaking is canceled and the agency conducts a normal notice and comment process. While there is no statutory authorization for direct final rulemaking, as long as the receipt of adverse comments triggers a notice and comment process, the method is likely to be upheld since no one is prejudiced by the procedure. In fact, courts of appeals have reviewed at least two rules that were initially promulgated as direct final rules, and in neither case did the court comment unfavorably on the process. (In both cases, timely adverse comments led to a full-blown notice and comment procedure.) See *Southwestern Pennsylvania Growth Alliance v. Browner*, 144 F.3d 984 (6th Cir. 1998); *Sierra Club v. U.S. E.P.A.*, 99 F.3d 1551 (10th Cir. 1996).

(3) Interim Final Rules

In recent years, agencies have issued numerous "interim final rules." "Interim final rules" are final rules issued on a temporary basis, often because there are remaining areas of uncertainty and the agency wants to engage in additional notice and comment procedures before issuing a comprehensive permanent final rule. Sometimes interim final rules are issued when the agency must act quickly to administer an ongoing program but still wants the benefit of a full notice and comment period before issuing final, permanent rules. Agencies claim authority to issue interim final rules without notice and comment on APA §553(b)(3)(B), which allows agencies to dispense with notice and comment "for good cause." Agencies base good cause findings on factors such as a statutory deadline that must be met or the existence of an ongoing program that must continue during the pendency of rules that may have been necessitated by a new statute. Rules issued without notice and comment are invalid without a finding of good cause. This process is distinct from direct final rulemaking because even if negative post-promulgation comments are received, interim final rules remain in effect until the promulgation of the permanent final rule. Despite some discomfort with the process based on unjustified failure to hold notice and comment proceedings before issuing interim final rules, interim final rulemaking has become ubiquitous and courts have not viewed it with disfavor.

SUMMARY

■ The primary process for promulgating rules under the APA is notice and comment rulemaking under APA §553, which is also referred to as informal rulemaking.

■ The principal requirements of informal rulemaking are notice, opportunity to comment, and publication of the decision together with a concise general statement of basis and purpose of any rules adopted.

- Many courts require more notice than specified in the literal words of §553(b). Courts have required that the rule adopted be the logical outgrowth of the proposal and that the agency not materially or substantially depart from the proposal.

- Courts also have required that agencies provide notice of data or studies upon which the agency intends to rely. This is sometimes connected to the requirement that interested parties have an opportunity to comment: In order for the opportunity to comment to be meaningful, parties must have notice of data or other information upon which the agency is relying. If notice is inadequate, the cure is a new notice and comment period.

- Ex parte comments (comments made to administrators outside the normal comment channels) are a problem in informal rulemaking, although it is unclear whether and to what extent they are regulated by the APA. Some courts have required that if an agency does receive ex parte comments, it should place such comments on the rulemaking record, especially if the ex parte comments turn out to be important to the agency's decision. However, other courts have stated that because the APA does not regulate ex parte contacts in informal rulemaking, courts should not address them.

- An administrator must have an open mind in rulemaking, and if it is shown by clear and convincing evidence that an administrator had an unalterably closed mind, that administrator may be disqualified from participating in a rulemaking.

- The concise general statement of basis and purpose must explain the agency's decision on major issues in the rulemaking, including providing answers to major concerns raised in the comments.

- Hybrid rulemaking is rulemaking to which some adjudicatory procedures, such as cross-examination of experts, are added. Some agency statutes require hybrid rulemaking. At one time, courts required hybrid procedures when they found that notice and comment procedures were inadequate for the particular rulemaking. This practice came to an end when the Supreme Court, in *Vermont Yankee*, rejected judicial authority to impose procedures in addition to those specified in §553.

- Formal rulemaking, or "on the record" rulemaking, is rulemaking pursuant to trial-type procedures akin to adjudication. Formal rulemaking is required only in the rare case when the agency is statutorily commanded to make rules "on the record after agency hearing."

- Negotiated rulemaking is a procedure under which a notice of proposed rulemaking is formulated through negotiations among interested parties, presided over by the agency. After negotiation produces a proposal, the proposal is subjected to a normal notice and comment procedure.

- When agencies expect no adverse comments, they have sometimes used a procedure known as "direct final rulemaking" under which a final rule is announced without prior notice, with a promise that if adverse comments are received, the agency will withdraw the rule and subject it to notice and comment. Although some commentators have questioned the legality of this process, it has not been tested in court, probably because the rules made this way tend to be technical and noncontroversial.

■ Agencies have also promulgated interim final rules without notice and comment, often to meet a statutory deadline while continuing the notice and comment process toward promulgation of final rules.

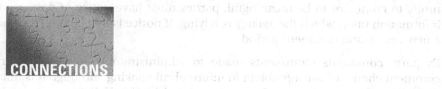

CONNECTIONS

Formal Rulemaking Required?

See Chapter 6 to learn more about when formal rulemaking procedures are required.

Due Process and APA Procedures

In some situations, due process may require more than APA §553 procedures. See Chapter 8.

Vermont Yankee and the Record

Before *Vermont Yankee*, courts sometimes required additional procedures because the record produced by §553 procedures was not adequate to support the rule. For more on the standard of judicial review applicable to rulemaking, see Chapter 4.

Prejudgment in Adjudication

The standard for disqualification for prejudgment in rulemaking is discussed in this chapter. The standard for disqualification in adjudication is discussed in Chapter 8. In adjudication, norms against prejudgment and bias are much stronger than in rulemaking.

Agency Adjudication and Due Process

8

This chapter examines a variety of questions relating to agency adjudication and due process. The topics include due process requirements for agency procedure, how substantive law affects the scope of an agency hearing, and the scope and enforcement of statutory rights to procedure. More specifically, the chapter covers identification of the interests protected by due process, the procedures required by due process, and statutorily required procedures that sometimes differ from those required by due process.

O V E R V I E W

The first area of attention in this chapter is the methodology for identifying those interests to which due process applies. The Due Process Clauses expressly apply to life, liberty, and property. In administrative law, our main concern is property, with some attention to liberty. Property interests protected by the Due Process Clauses are usually created by law external to the Constitution, such as state law. A party has a property interest in a government benefit, license, or job if that law creates an entitlement by prescribing criteria under which the benefit, job, or license will be granted or retained. Liberty interests protected by the Constitution are often created by the Constitution itself. These include the liberty interest in being free from bodily restraint or bodily harm. They can also be created by positive law, such as a statute governing the conditions under which prisoners are held or are entitled to early release for good behavior.

The next issue addressed by this chapter is the method for determining, once a protected interest is found, what procedures are required by due process. The primary methodology for making this determination is the *Mathews v. Eldridge* balancing test, which balances the strength of the private interest involved, the value in terms of accuracy of additional procedure, and the government's interest in proceeding without additional process. The chapter also looks at some procedural issues that seem to be determined outside of this framework.

The due process analysis addressed in this chapter builds on the traditional model of due process as an adjudicatory, trial-type hearing, usually in advance of the adverse action. As we shall see, in many situations, alternative procedural models apply that may involve less formality and hearings only after the adverse government action has been taken. Further, in some settings, due process may be provided through alternative models such as common law remedies and informal, consultative processes.

One of the principal due process rights this chapter examines is the basic right to a neutral decisionmaker. A decisionmaker is not neutral if he or she has a pecuniary or other personal interest in the outcome of the hearing or if he or she has prejudged the facts or law. Sometimes, bias results from the capture of an agency by one segment of an industry, which uses its power to harm its competitors.

In the area of statutory rights, this chapter looks at the requirements that arise from the statutory requirement of a "hearing." When a statute requires a hearing, the agency must provide a genuine hearing at which the applicant has a real opportunity to prevail. However, this does not necessarily mean that agencies must provide a full hearing on every issue. Agencies are free to use rulemaking to narrow the issues decided at a statutorily required hearing, as long as the rules made to do so are substantively valid.

A. DUE PROCESS AND THE ADJUDICATORY HEARING

1. Identifying Interests Protected by Due Process: Property
2. Identifying Interests Protected by Due Process: Liberty
3. Determining What Process Is Due
   a. Due Process Basics
   b. *Mathews v. Eldridge* Balancing
   c. Post-Deprivation Process and Government Torts
   d. Due Process Issues with a Reduced Role for the *Mathews* Factors

B. STATUTORY HEARING RIGHTS

1. Formal and Informal Adjudication
2. The Statutorily Required Hearing Must Be a Genuine Hearing — Not a Sham
3. Substantive Standards That Limit the Right to a Hearing
4. The Irrebuttable Presumption Doctrine and the Right to a Hearing

A. Due Process and the Adjudicatory Hearing

Due process is one of the most important and fundamental constraints on government action, dating back at least to the Magna Carta, the cornerstone document that was first promulgated in England in the year 1215. The Due Process

Clauses of the Fifth and Fourteenth Amendments to the Constitution of the United States provide that government may not deprive any person of life, liberty, or property without due process of law. State constitutions contain similar or identical provisions. In addition to the obvious procedural element of due process, the Due Process Clauses have been interpreted to create a host of substantive rights in areas such as economic freedom, personal privacy, and reproductive rights. In administrative law we are concerned with procedural due process, mainly how procedural due process affects administrative processes for resolving disputes between the government and private parties, including regulated entities, government employees, and recipients of, and applicants for, government benefits.

The original meaning of the concept of due process is not clear. Professor (now Judge) Frank Easterbrook concluded that the meaning of due process is something like this: Government must follow the procedures established by law, and in cases involving "fundamental natural liberties," the legislature may not abrogate well-established judicial procedures.[1] In other words, in most cases, due process did not mean that courts would evaluate the sufficiency of procedures in every interaction between government and citizen based on a standard of adequacy or fairness. Rather, the only issue, except in the rare case involving fundamental liberties, would be whether government had provided all the procedures required by the legislature. "Due" in due process meant something like "promised in advance."

In current law, due process has come to mean that courts review the sufficiency of procedures employed in all government actions affecting life, liberty, or property, as measured against a judicially created constitutional standard. Thus, in due process controversies, there are two key questions that must be answered. First is the question whether the government action affects an interest in life, liberty, or property. If this question is answered in the affirmative, the next question is what process is due, i.e., what procedures does due process require for a deprivation of the particular interest. Once it is determined that process, such as a hearing, is required, federal due process standards govern the contours of that hearing. This determination is made with sensitivity to the procedures already specified in the governing law, but the courts are not bound by the legislative determination of the appropriate level or form of procedure.

The material that follows discusses the two interests most often involved in administrative law controversies, property and liberty. As we shall see, the existence of a property interest is always determined with reference to a non-constitutional source of law, such as the statute creating a benefits program. By contrast, although liberty interests are also sometimes determined that way, there is also a core of constitutionally recognized liberty interests that exist regardless of positive law.

(1) Identifying Interests Protected by Due Process: Property

As discussed, due process hearing rights attach when the government deprives or threatens to deprive a person of life, **liberty**, or **property.** (In administrative law, we are concerned mainly with liberty and property interests.) The first step in due process analysis is to identify the **protected interest** — has the private party been subjected to a deprivation of a protected interest? While this inquiry is often simple, for example when government threatens to imprison or execute an alleged criminal,

---

[1]See Frank Easterbrook, *The Substance of Process*, 1982 Sup. Ct. Rev. 85, 98.

it frequently may be less clear. The difficulty usually arises in cases involving controversies over private parties' interests in things such as government benefits, licenses, permits, and employment. At one time, interests like these were thought of as privileges or gratuities that could be withdrawn at any time without any process, except perhaps whatever process the government had promised as part of the particular program.

This dichotomy between privileges and gratuities on the one hand and traditional property interests (real and personal property) on the other began to break down in the 1960s with the flowering of welfare programs enacted as part of President Lyndon Johnson's Great Society programs. Beginning with the landmark 1970 decision in *Goldberg v. Kelly*, the Supreme Court decided that government benefits, licenses, permits, and employment (collectively referred to below for convenience as "government benefits") have been recognized as property interests. The Court was influenced heavily by a series of law review articles by Charles Reich, including one entitled *The New Property*,[2] the title of which was adopted as the name of these nontraditional property interests to distinguish this novel form of property from the more established real and personal property interests that had long been protected by due process.

Sidebar

THE NEW PROPERTY

Charles Reich's articles advocated property status for government benefits, professional licenses, government jobs, and the like because they play the same social role today as traditional property played in the past. Although the Supreme Court recognized new property, it did not accept Reich's basis for doing so. Rather, the Court limited property interests to entitlements, discussed further below.

As noted, *Goldberg v. Kelly*, 397 U.S. 254 (1970), was the first Supreme Court decision to recognize due process rights in **new property**, in this case welfare benefits. In *Goldberg*, the Court held that welfare benefits could not be terminated without first holding a hearing to determine the recipient's continued eligibility. The statute provided that prior to termination, the recipient could object to termination in writing in addition to the informal give and take that would normally occur between the welfare recipient and the caseworker. Only after termination did the recipient have the right to request a full hearing to challenge termination. The Court held that in light of the grievous loss likely suffered by a person wrongly terminated from welfare, where eligibility is determined by extreme poverty, due process required some sort of oral hearing before termination.

The *Goldberg* decision was less revolutionary than it might appear because it did not actually focus on the issue of the status of welfare benefits as property. Rather, although some courts and commentators may have focused on the Court's reference to "grievous loss" and read *Goldberg* as holding that grievous loss was sufficient to create a protected interest, the opinion is clear that the status of welfare as a protected interest was conceded by the government and almost taken for granted by the Court: "Appellant does not contend that procedural due process is not applicable to the termination of welfare benefits. Such benefits are a matter of statutory **entitlement** for persons qualified to receive them." The Court's characterization of welfare benefits as a "matter of *statutory entitlement*" hints at the subsequent development of entitlement theory, but *Goldberg* itself did not analyze the issue of the

---

[2]Charles Reich, *Individual Rights and Social Welfare: The Emerging Legal Issues*, 74 Yale L.J. 1245 (1965); Charles Reich, *The New Property*, 73 Yale L.J. 733 (1964).

existence of a protected interest beyond this brief allusion. While, as discussed below, grievous loss may have some relevance in a small category of liberty cases in which government affirmatively acts to injure a private party, it is not relevant to the existence of a protected interest in cases involving government benefits, licenses, permits, and employment.

Whether a protected interest exists in most cases is determined by what can be referred to as "**entitlement theory**." Entitlement theory looks at whether law external to the Constitution creates an entitlement to the interest, by specifying the conditions under which the interest must be legally recognized. This standard was first applied by the Supreme Court in *Board of Regents v. Roth*, 408 U.S. 564 (1972). In that case, the Supreme Court rejected the grievous loss test for the existence of a property right and instead created a test that looks to positive law, usually state or federal statutes or regulations, or state common law, for the existence of property interests.

The plaintiff in *Roth* was a college professor who was not rehired after his contract expired. He claimed that the decision not to rehire him deprived him of his property interest in his employment, and that due process was violated because the state university failed to hold a hearing before making the decision. He argued, and the lower court held, that loss of government employment amounts to a deprivation of a property interest in the employment based on the weight of the employee's interest in continued employment. The lower court held that due process requires some sort of hearing to prevent arbitrary termination of government employment, in effect outlawing at-will government employment. The Supreme Court took a completely different approach to determining the existence of a property interest. Rather than look at categories of interests, the Court held that a property interest depends on whether some source external to the Constitution, such as state law, creates a "legitimate claim of entitlement" to the interest. *Roth*, 408 U.S. at 577. Conversely, if state law does not create a claim of entitlement to the interest, so that the claimant has only a unilateral expectation of receiving the government benefit, permit, or employment, no property interest exists and due process protections do not attach. Thus, in *Roth*, the Supreme Court held that there was no property interest because nothing in either state law or Roth's employment contract constrained the government's decision whether to continue the employment beyond the initial contractual term. Therefore, under entitlement theory, Roth had no property interest in his job.

F   A   Q

Q: What is a "legitimate claim of entitlement"?

A: A legitimate claim of entitlement exists when law, custom, or practice establishes that claims to the government benefit, job, or permit, etc., are evaluated under a definite set of criteria. For example, if state law, or an employment contract with the state, provides that a government employee may not be terminated absent good cause, the employee has a property interest in continued employment and due process must be followed before termination of employment. Government employees at will, by contrast, have no claim of entitlement and may be terminated without due process.

This exact reasoning is used across the entire spectrum of potential property interests. To determine whether a property interest exists, it must be determined whether some source of law specifies the criteria under which the claim must be evaluated. For example, virtually all welfare programs contain eligibility criteria in terms of income, assets, work history, and the like that create a property interest in receipt of the benefits. With government employment, a property interest exists when the employee may not be fired except for cause, i.e., for specified reasons, while an at-will employee has no property interest in the job.

Usually, the for-cause standard (if one exists) is explicit in either state law or the contract of employment. In the absence of an explicit entitlement, the Court has held that less formal assurances or state practices may create an entitlement and, therefore, a property interest. For example, in *Perry v. Sindermann*, 408 U.S. 593 (1972), the Court held that Sindermann, a teacher in a state junior college, might have a property interest in his job even though neither state law nor his contract explicitly created an entitlement to continued employment. Sindermann alleged that he had been assured by provisions in an employee handbook and by regulations promulgated by the state college system's governing board that he had de facto tenure, i.e., that his employment would be continued as long as his performance was satisfactory. The Supreme Court analogized to the law of implied contracts, and held that if Texas law would recognize the de facto tenure alleged by Sindermann, he would also have a property interest in his position, which would mean that he could not be fired without due process.

Sidebar

ONLY SUBSTANCE CREATES AN ENTITLEMENT

The entitlement doctrine focuses on substance, not procedure. If a statute provides procedural protections only, no entitlement exists. Entitlements are created by the substantive provisions of law. If an entitlement does exist, the federal courts will examine any applicable procedural provisions to determine whether they are sufficient to satisfy due process. However, procedural constraints on government action alone are insufficient to create an entitlement.

Note an important feature of entitlement theory, that whether a property interest exists in a government benefit can vary from benefit to benefit and from state to state even with regard to the exact same government benefit. For example, state college teachers in states with a tenure system have property interests in their jobs while teachers in a state without tenure do not. The particulars of state law creating and defining the government benefit determine whether a protected interest exists, not the nature of the benefit. Justice Marshall disagreed with entitlement theory because he thought that all government employees should receive due process protections, just as he thought that government should be required to provide due process with regard to all benefits decisions. Justice Marshall thus dissented in *Roth* because he thought that the lower court was correct that all government employees have a protected interest in continued employment. Justice Marshall's view is consistent with Charles Reich's law review articles that advocated recognizing the "new property" in things like government benefits and employment. The argument in those articles was based on the nature and importance of the interests and not on entitlement theory.

From the opposite perspective, the more conservative members of the Court are unhappy with entitlement theory's separation of substance from process. Professor

Easterbrook argued in the article discussed above that it makes no sense to trust the legislature to determine whether to create an entitlement, and then not trust the legislature to decide on the proper level of process. In *Arnett v. Kennedy*, 416 U.S. 134 (1974) (plurality opinion), Justice Rehnquist argued that if the statute that created an entitlement provided claimants with only minimal procedures for securing the entitlement, those procedures should limit the reach of the property interest. In *Arnett*, Justice Rehnquist was joined by two other members of the Court in arguing that a civil service employee (with a for-cause termination provision) should receive only the process specified in the statute granting the for-cause entitlement. He stated that claimants should have to take the "bitter with the sweet" and accept the procedural limitations (the bitter) in the statute that created the entitlement (the sweet). However, a majority of the Court rejected this argument, adhering to *Roth*'s separation of procedure from substance. Arnett lost his case not because he lacked a property interest in his employment, but rather because a majority of the Court found that even if he had a property interest, he had received all the process that was due.

F   A   Q

Q: Consider the following statute, which regulates employment within a government agency:

> Section A: No employee shall be terminated absent good cause, defined as lack of success in completing assigned tasks, inability to function in the work environment, or misconduct.
> Section B: The determination of whether good cause for termination exists shall be made by the personnel manager with no opportunity for input, either written or oral, from the affected employee.

Do employees in this agency have property interests? What role does Section B play in determining termination procedures?

A: Section A creates a property interest in continued employment. Once such an entitlement is created, federal due process governs what process is due. Section B is, in effect, unconstitutional because it provides for no hearing before the employee is deprived of a property interest. Under Justice Rehnquist's bitter with the sweet argument, Section B would limit any property interest created by Section A. However, this argument was rejected by a majority of the Court in *Arnett* and thus federal standards govern what process is due under the substantive standard contained in Section A.

Unhappiness on the Court with entitlement theory has led to some strained decisions finding no protected interest. Two examples should suffice to illustrate this tendency. In the first, *Bishop v. Wood*, 426 U.S. 341 (1976), the Court affirmed a finding of no property interest for a fired city policeman despite the existence of the following provision governing the employment:

> Dismissal. A permanent employee whose work is not satisfactory over a period of time shall be notified in what way his work is deficient and what he must do if his work is to be satisfactory. If a permanent employee fails to perform work up to the standard of the

classification held, or continues to be negligent, inefficient, or unfit to perform his duties, he may be dismissed by the City Manager. Any discharged employee shall be given written notice of his discharge setting forth the effective date and reasons for his discharge if he shall request such a notice.

Although this provision appears to create a for-cause requirement for dismissal from employment, the Supreme Court upheld the District Court's counter-textual determination that this statute creates at-will employment for city employees on the basis that, in the absence of an authoritative construction by a North Carolina state court, the District Court is more familiar with North Carolina law and thus its views on North Carolina law are entitled to respect.

Another decision denying a property interest that appears to be inconsistent with entitlement theory is *American Manufacturers Ins. Co. v. Sullivan*, 526 U.S. 40 (1999). In that case, employees who were receiving medical benefits under Pennsylvania's workers' compensation law sued when their benefits were suspended while the insurer conducted a "utilization review" to determine whether the treatment was "reasonable and necessary." The employees alleged that their due process rights were violated because their benefits were suspended without any opportunity for them to have input into the decision to suspend. The Court held that the employees had no property interest in the benefits because no determination had been made that the benefits were "reasonable and necessary."[3] Id. at 61.

This decision seems inconsistent with entitlement theory, which stands for the proposition that terms such as "reasonable and necessary" are sufficient to create property interests because they create an entitlement to the benefit assuming the claimant meets the standard. For example, a government employee who commits misconduct at work has a property interest in her employment if the governing law requires cause for termination. Whether cause exists is determined pursuant to the procedures required by due process, just as whether the medical expenses in *American Manufacturers* were "reasonable and necessary" should have been determined pursuant to the procedures required by due process. Under this logic, only a successful claimant has a property interest. This cannot be the test because it assumes the very conclusion that is supposed to be determined pursuant to the procedures required by due process.

Justice Rehnquist's opinion for the Court in *American Manufacturers* distinguished *Goldberg*, and other entitlement precedent, on the basis that in those cases, a determination had been made that the claimant was entitled to benefits, and the entitlement could not be halted without due process. But the exact same thing is true in *American Manufacturers* — the employees had been receiving medical benefits, and the benefits were halted pending a determination that further treatments were reasonable and necessary. Similarly, the welfare recipient in *Goldberg* had been receiving benefits, and it was held that he had a property interest in continued benefits even though it might later be determined that he had at some point lost eligibility. Perhaps the best explanation of the *American Manufacturers* decision is that Justice Rehnquist was not a fan of entitlement theory. He wrote the plurality opinion in *Arnett v. Kennedy* that advocated the "bitter with the sweet"

---

[3]The Court in *American Manufacturers* held first that the insurers were not state actors and thus could not have violated due process, 526 U.S. at 58, but then the Court went on to decide the merits of the constitutional question out of concern for the precedential effects of the lower court's finding of a due process violation.

approach, and in another case, he refused to join the majority opinion applying entitlement theory, but rather concurred on equal protection grounds.[4]

<table><tr><td>F</td><td>A</td><td>Q</td></tr></table>

Q: Does an initial applicant for a government benefit or government employment have a property interest in securing the benefit or position?

A: Surprisingly, this issue has not been resolved by the Supreme Court although the logic of entitlement theory would point to a positive answer. Lower courts have found that applicants have property interests in benefits. For example, in *Cushman v. Shineski*, 576 F.3d 1290 (Fed. Cir. 2009), the court concluded, with regard to veterans' disability benefits, that initial applicants have a property interest in benefits that are "nondiscretionary" and "statutorily mandated." Basically, the court found that if there is an entitlement, initial applicants have a property interest in receiving them. This means that applicants must receive due process before the application can be rejected. See also *National Assoc. of Radiation Survivors v. Derwinski*, 994 F.2d 583 (9th Cir. 1992). With regard to government employment, because it would be impractical for all rejected applicants to receive full hearings, courts are likely to require only minimal process, perhaps only a brief statement of reasons, in such cases.

Agencies may not impose legally binding orders on regulated parties without following due process. For example, an order to pay a fine or some other penalty is a deprivation of property, and thus the subject of the order must be afforded due process before the order can become final. For example, in *Tennessee Valley Authority [TVA] v. Whitman*, 336 F.3d 1236 (11th Cir. 2003), the Court held that the TVA must be given a chance to contest the basis of an "administrative compliance order" (ACO) issued by the EPA, because ACOs are issued without affording the alleged violator any right to a hearing. Note that the absence of advance process did not necessarily render the ACO invalid, it just meant that the ACO may not be enforced absent some opportunity to contest its basis. Here, the EPA could bring an action in federal district court to enforce the ACO, and the TVA would have a right to contest the basis for the order, i.e., that the alleged violation actually occurred. In effect, the ACO is treated in court like a complaint rather than a final determination that a violation has occurred.

(2) Identifying Interests Protected by Due Process: Liberty

Liberty interests are recognized under both entitlement theory and directly under the Constitution. In other words, some liberty interests are created by positive law while others are thought to fall under a purely constitutional definition of liberty. Traditional liberty interests, such as freedom from bodily restraint and freedom from unwarranted use of force by government officials such as police officers, are part of the Constitution's definition of liberty. These liberty interests exist regardless of the

---

[4]See *Logan v. Zimmerman Brush Co.*, 455 U.S. 422, 443 (1982) (Powell, J., joined by Rehnquist, J. concurring in the judgment).

provisions of state law, and due process must be afforded if the state wishes to deprive a person of one of these interests. Entitlement-based liberty interests are created in the same way as the property interests discussed above. We call some entitlement-based interests "liberty" because they are more like traditional liberty interests than traditional property interests. For example, if positive law contains criteria for early release from prison on parole, parole in that jurisdiction would be an entitlement-based liberty interest even though, as a constitutional matter, the prisoner does not have any liberty-based claim for release until the end of the sentence. In this section, constitutionally-based liberty interests are discussed first and then the discussion turns to entitlement-based liberty interests.

Sidebar

CREATION OF LIBERTY INTERESTS

Some liberty interests are created by entitlements while others are derived from the constitutional definition of "liberty."

The courts have recognized a variety of constitutionally-based liberty interests. Many liberty interests, such as those involved in criminal procedure disputes or fundamental rights cases, are beyond the scope of the study of administrative law. In administrative law we look at the more routine interactions between government and members of the public or government employees. A key difference between constitutional liberty and entitlement theory is that, in a constitutional liberty case, the court is much freer to shape the interest than in an entitlement-based liberty case because constitutional liberty interests are not created or constrained by positive law. In a constitutional liberty case, both the substance and procedure are creatures of federal constitutional law.

For example, in *Ingraham v. Wright*, 430 U.S. 651 (1977), although state law specifically allowed corporal punishment, the Supreme Court held that corporal punishment deprives paddled students of liberty, regardless of state law. The Court stated this conclusion as follows:

> While the contours of this historic liberty interest in the context of our federal system of government have not been defined precisely, they always have been thought to encompass freedom from bodily restraint and punishment. . . . It is fundamental that the state cannot hold and physically punish an individual except in accordance with due process of law.[5]

In *Parham v. J.R.*, 442 U.S. 584 (1979), the Court recognized that children's liberty is infringed when they are confined to a mental institution and labeled "mentally ill" at the instance of their parents or guardians (including the state). The Court stated that

> [i]t is not disputed that a child, in common with adults, has a substantial liberty interest in not being confined unnecessarily for medical treatment and that the state's involvement in the commitment decision constitutes state action under the Fourteenth Amendment. . . . We also recognize that commitment sometimes produces adverse social consequences for the child because of the reaction of some to the discovery that the child has received psychiatric care, even though state law did not recognize such an interest.

Id. at 600. In such cases, the Court looks to traditional understandings of liberty and normative understandings of what interests ought to be recognized rather than any

---

[5]*Ingraham v. Wright*, 430 U.S. 651, 673-74 (1977) (footnote and citation omitted).

aspect of state law that might purport to establish the limits of liberty and related interests.

These cases allow us to get a general sense of the sorts of interests that constitute liberty within constitutional meaning. Freedom from bodily restraint, physical injury and punishment, forced medical treatment, and branding as a criminal or mentally ill person are the sorts of state actions that can trigger due process protections as deprivations of liberty. However, the Court has not been altogether consistent or clear on exactly what sort of injury constitutes a deprivation of liberty, as the discussion that follows should reveal.

The Supreme Court has rejected the argument that merely branding someone as a criminal without more constitutes a deprivation of liberty. Support for that argument can be drawn from the Court's decision in *Wisconsin v. Constantineau*, 400 U.S. 433 (1971). In that case, state law authorized local officials, without notice or a hearing, to instruct merchants not to sell alcoholic beverages to excessive drinkers. After a local chief of police designated Constantineau an excessive drinker and instructed merchants in the city not to sell alcohol to her, she sued to have the Wisconsin statute declared void as violating due process for not allowing designees the opportunity, in advance, to contest their designation as excessive drinkers. The Supreme Court agreed with Constantineau, and it appeared to hold that simply branding a person as an excessive drinker amounts to a deprivation of liberty:[6] "[w]here a person's good name, reputation, honor, or integrity is at stake because of what the government is doing to him, notice and an opportunity to be heard are essential. . . . Only when the whole proceedings leading to the pinning of an unsavory label on a person are aired can oppressive results be prevented." 400 U.S. at 437.

Subsequently, the Court pulled back from this expansive language and limited *Constantineau*'s reach to cases in which the labeling entailed material consequences for the person branded as a criminal or excessive drinker or with some other odious label. In *Paul v. Davis*, 424 U.S. 693 (1976), a local chief of police circulated a list, with photographs, of active shoplifters in the area. Davis, who had been charged but not convicted, was included on the list of active shoplifters, and he sued the police chief for branding him a criminal without due process of law. The Court rejected Davis's claim on the ground that placing his name on the list did not deprive Davis of liberty because it did not alter his legal status by, for example, legally banning him from designated stores or rendering him ineligible for certain employment. The Court distinguished *Constantineau* on the basis that designation as an excessive drinker legally altered a person's status by making it illegal to sell alcohol to that person.

The Court in *Paul* rejected an entitlement-like theory for damage to reputation by stating that the "interest in reputation is simply one of a number which the State may protect against injury by virtue of its tort law, providing a forum for vindication of those interests by means of damages actions. And any harm or injury to that interest, even where, as here, inflicted by an officer of the State, does not result in a deprivation of any 'liberty' or 'property' recognized by state or federal law[.]" This basis for rejecting reputation as a protected interest under due process is somewhat

---

[6]The Court also appeared to hold that any grievous loss inflicted by government constitutes a deprivation of liberty: " '[T]he right to be heard before being condemned to suffer grievous loss of any kind, even though it may not involve the stigma and hardships of a criminal conviction, is a principle basic to our society.' " 400 U.S. at 437, quoting *Joint Anti-Fascist Refugee Committee v. McGrath*, 341 U.S. 123, 168 (Frankfurter, J., concurring). *Roth v. Board of Regents*, however, made clear that "grievous loss" goes to the amount of process required, not to the determination of whether a party has been deprived of an interest protected by due process.

doubtful. State law, through the common law of defamation, protects one's reputation by recognizing a damages claim for defamation. Under entitlement theory, this should be sufficient to create a property or liberty interest. After all, many property rights are created and protected by common law remedies for conversion and the like. The Court was apparently concerned, however, that such reasoning would convert every tort committed by a state or local official into a federal due process violation. Thus, the Court held that damage to reputation through defamation, without an actual alteration of the person's legal status, did not amount to a deprivation of liberty.

F   A   Q

Q: Does every grievous loss imposed by government implicate a liberty or property interest?

A: The Court has made it clear that the answer to this question is "no." Grievous loss is relevant to how much process is due, but the existence of a property or liberty interest must be established through entitlement theory or constitutional liberty analysis.

Another decision illustrates the rejection of the grievous loss argument, that all serious injuries inflicted by government amount to deprivations of liberty. In *O'Bannon v. Town Court Nursing Center*, 447 U.S. 773 (1980), the Court held that nursing home patients were not deprived of a liberty interest when they were forced to move because their home lost its certification to treat Medicare and Medicaid patients. They argued that they would suffer from transfer trauma, which could result in serious illness or even death, and that therefore the withdrawal of certification deprived them of liberty. In rejecting this claim, the Court relied in part on the fact that the administrative action was aimed at the home and not at the patients, but the Court also rejected the argument that a liberty interest was involved simply because government action caused potentially great harm.

In addition to the constitutionally-based liberty interests discussed above, liberty interests may also be created by positive law in the same way that positive law creates property interests. One area in which this has occurred is the prison context, although more recently the Supreme Court has cut back on liberty protections for convicted criminals. A good example of positive law creating a liberty interest is parole, the procedure under which prisoners are released before the end of their sentences based on factors such as good behavior and rehabilitation. Prisoners have no constitutionally-based liberty interest in being considered for parole because any interest in freedom has been extinguished for the duration of the sentence imposed by the criminal court. However, if state law creates an entitlement to parole, a liberty interest is created and due process standards govern the procedures employed at parole hearings. See *Morrissey v. Brewer*, 408 U.S. 471 (1972); *Board of Pardons v. Allen*, 482 U.S. 369 (1987) (liberty interest exists when state statute specifies that parole board "shall" grant parole under specified conditions). If, however, state law leaves parole to the discretion of the parole board, with no binding criteria, there is no liberty interest in parole and thus no due process scrutiny of the procedures employed at parole hearings. *Greenholtz v. Nebraska Penal Inmates*, 442 U.S. 1, 7 (1979).

More recent developments in entitlement theory establish that it is not always possible to apply pure logic to determine whether an entitlement has been created. Sometimes, the historical and legal context is relevant to whether the Court is likely to find an entitlement-based protected interest. For example, in *Town of Castle Rock v. Gonzales*, 545 U.S. 748 (2005), the Court rejected an entitlement-based claim of a liberty interest in the enforcement of a restraining order. The plaintiff brought a claim against the municipality in which she lived, claiming that she was deprived of liberty when town police failed to enforce a restraining order against her ex-husband, who murdered her three children. The Court stated that even though the order might appear to create an entitlement by stating that the police "shall use every reasonable means to enforce this

restraining order . . . [a] well established tradition of police discretion has long coexisted with apparently mandatory arrest statutes." 545 U.S. at 760. Thus, there was no legitimate claim of entitlement to protection under state law and no liberty interest under federal law.

Additional cases concerning prison confinement illuminate the standards for finding both entitlement and constitutional liberty interests. Liberty is implicated when the conditions or type of confinement are so altered that the nature of confinement is transformed. Constitutional liberty may be implicated when a change in prison conditions amounts to a change outside "the normal limits or range of custody" implicit in the fact of conviction. See *Meachum v. Fano*, 427 U.S. 215, 225 (1976). Positive law liberty interests may be implicated when the change in prison conditions involves an entitlement, such as state or federal law that governs when a prisoner should be moved into a higher security prison. State or federal law can create a liberty interest if standards govern the treatment of prisoners, such as decisions concerning the nature of confinement, level of security, or placement in punitive conditions.

In *Vitek v. Jones*, 445 U.S. 480 (1980), entitlement theory supported the finding of a deprivation of liberty when a prisoner was moved from prison to a mental hospital. The *Vitek* Court looked to state law governing the transfer and found a liberty interest, stating: "This 'objective expectation, firmly fixed in state law and official penal complex practice,' that a prisoner would not be transferred unless he suffered from a mental disease or defect that could not be adequately treated in the prison, gave Jones a liberty interest that entitled him to the benefits of appropriate procedures in connection with determining the conditions that warranted his transfer to a mental hospital." *Vitek*, 445 U.S. at 489-90.

The Supreme Court has more recently moved to cut back on entitlement theory liberty interests in the prison context. In *Sandin v. Connor*, 515 U.S. 472 (1995), the Supreme Court rejected an entitlement-based constitutional liberty claim brought by a prisoner who had been sentenced to solitary confinement for misconduct under a "substantial evidence" of misconduct standard. The Court, in an opinion by Chief Justice Rehnquist, criticized prior cases for encouraging prisoners to "comb regulations" for entitlement-creating language. Without overruling *Vitek*, the Court appeared to limit prisoner entitlement liberty cases to interests that are closely related to constitutional liberty interests, such as length of sentence or transfer to a different form of confinement such as a mental hospital. Concerning entitlement theory as applied to prison discipline, the Court stated:

> [W]e believe that the search for a negative implication from mandatory language in prisoner regulations has strayed from the real concerns undergirding the liberty protected by the Due Process Clause. The time has come to return to the due process principles we believe were correctly established and applied in [prior cases.] [W]e recognize that States may under certain circumstances create liberty interests which are protected by the Due Process Clause. . . . But these interests will be generally limited to freedom from restraint which, while not exceeding the sentence in such an unexpected manner as to give rise to protection by the Due Process Clause of its own force, . . . nonetheless imposes atypical and significant hardship on the inmate in relation to the ordinary incidents of prison life.

Sandin, 515 U.S. 483-84. Note that by acknowledging that state-created liberty need not "give rise to protection by the Due Process Clause of its own force," the Court is careful to preserve some measure of entitlement theory. However, the Court's opposition to extending entitlement theory to every aspect of prison life is clear.

The Court has also recognized constitutionally-based liberty interests in the prison setting, and these appear to be more viable after *Sandin*, although it is still difficult to establish a constitutional liberty interest in changed conditions of imprisonment. A prisoner (who after conviction and sentence has only a limited residuum of liberty) has been deprived of liberty only if a change in conditions or nature of confinement is beyond the normal range of the deprivation of liberty inherent in incarceration. Movement from a medium security prison to a higher level of security is not a deprivation of liberty. See *Meachum v. Fano*, 427 U.S. 215 (1976). Further, no liberty interest is implicated when a prisoner is transferred to an out-of-state prison. See *Olim v. Wakinekona*, 461 U.S. 238 (1983) (transfer from Hawaii to California was within the range of permissible incarceration implicit in the conviction). See also *Kentucky Dep't of Corrections v. Thompson*, 490 U.S. 454 (1989) (inmate has no liberty interest in the number and identity of visitors). However, in *Vitek v. Jones*, 445 U.S. 480 (1980), the Court did find that incarceration in a mental hospital, including being labeled as mentally ill and subjected to mandatory treatment, is qualitatively different from incarceration in a prison, and thus constitutional liberty (in addition to entitlement-based liberty) was implicated.

The continued viability of constitutionally-based liberty claims is most strongly evidenced by the Supreme Court's post-*Sandin* decision in *Wilkinson v. Austin*, 545 U.S. 209 (2005). In *Wilkinson*, the Court found that assignment of a prisoner to an Ohio "supermax" prison constituted a liberty deprivation, noting that inmates confined to the supermax prison were precluded from almost all human contact, subjected to having a light on in their cell at all times, permitted only one hour of exercise outside the cell per day, and disqualified from parole consideration. While noting that transfer to "more adverse conditions of confinement" does not automatically constitute a deprivation of liberty, the Court found that the conditions of confinement in the supermax prison "impose an atypical and significant hardship within the correctional context. It follows that respondents have a liberty interest in avoiding assignment to" the supermax prison. *Wilkinson*, 545 U.S. at 224.

A final issue that arises in understanding the limits of constitutional protection of liberty is the distinction between government action and government inaction. This goes more to the meaning of "deprive" in the Due Process Clauses — does the government deprive a person of life, liberty, or property by failing to take action to prevent privately inflicted injuries or suffering not directly inflicted by government? The Supreme Court has answered this question with a resounding "no." In *DeShaney v. Winnebago County Dep't of Social Servs.*, 489 U.S. 189 (1989), the Court held that social workers did not deprive a child of liberty when they failed to prevent his father from injuring him severely, even though the social workers knew that the child was in danger and had in fact returned the child to his father's custody after previous incidents of apparent child abuse. The Court concluded that "the Due Process Clauses generally confer no affirmative right to governmental aid, even where such aid may be necessary to secure life, liberty, or property interests of which the government itself may not deprive the individual." Id. at 196. The Court did acknowledge that if a private person is in a special relationship with the government, for example in government custody, the government may owe a duty to take affirmative steps to preserve the person's well-being. This means that government may be required to protect prisoners and involuntarily committed patients in state hospitals, among others. But in the ordinary case of people living in free society, due process does not require the government to affirmatively protect the well-being of the people.

(3) Determining What Process Is Due

Once it is determined that a person has been deprived of an interest protected by due process, the next issue is whether the procedures that have been provided are sufficient to satisfy due process. In other words, the issue becomes "what process is due?" The determination of what process is due is made by applying federal due process standards to the procedures already provided and asking whether those procedures are adequate. If they are not, federal due process law mandates supplementing those procedures to bring them up to constitutional standards.

The discussion that follows is in three parts. The first part briefly discusses some basic due process principles. The second part sets out and elaborates the general balancing test that has come to govern the determination of how much process is due. The third part discusses some situations in which a categorical approach is taken instead of the more general balancing test.

(a) Due Process Basics

When due process applies, it requires process, usually a hearing, at a meaningful time. By meaningful, what is meant is that the hearing must be at a time when there is still a

Sidebar

FEDERAL DUE PROCESS PRINCIPLES

A property or liberty interest is created by a state or federal entitlement or by constitutionally recognized liberty. Federal due process principles determine what procedures are required before government may deprive a person of a protected interest.

realistic chance that the deprivation can be prevented or reversed. Sometimes this hearing must be before adverse government action is taken, although under certain conditions, the hearing can occur after government action is taken. The procedural rights that are most often associated with due process include notice of the time and place of the hearing and the subjects and issues involved, opportunity for a hearing in advance of adverse government action, the right to present evidence and testimony at the hearing, the right to confront adverse evidence and witnesses, the right to be represented by counsel at the hearing, the right to a neutral decisionmaker, and the right to an explanation of any adverse decision.

(b) *Mathews v. Eldridge* Balancing

Whether due process requires procedures in addition to those already provided in the particular program is determined under the three-part **Mathews v. Eldridge balancing test**. *Mathews v. Eldridge*, 424 U.S. 319 (1976), involved the termination of disability benefits. The process for terminating disability benefits includes written submissions in advance of termination and, if the recipient disagrees with termination, the terminated recipient can request an oral hearing. At the time *Mathews* was decided, the wait for the full post-termination hearing was about a year. The claimant argued that under *Goldberg v. Kelly*, due process requires a pre-termination hearing for disability benefits just as the *Goldberg* Court required a pre-termination hearing for welfare benefits. The Supreme Court distinguished *Goldberg* on two bases and held that the process provided under the disability benefits program, including an oral hearing only after the termination of benefits, was sufficient to satisfy due process. The opinion in *Mathews* also established a balancing test for determining what process is due.

Sidebar

PRE-DEPRIVATION PROCESS

Although *Goldberg* was the case that signaled the beginning of the due process revolution, the Court has not in any other situation required as much pre-deprivation process as it did in *Goldberg*. It has come the closest in cases involving government employment, where it requires a pre-termination oral hearing.

The two bases upon which the *Mathews* Court distinguished *Goldberg* involve the relative importance of disability benefits to the claimant and the relative value of written versus oral procedures in the two situations. On the first basis, the *Mathews* Court noted that disability benefits are not necessarily as important to the claimant as welfare benefits. Eligibility for disability benefits is based on work history and medical condition, not on wealth or income. Eligibility for welfare benefits, by contrast, is based purely on lack of wealth and income. Therefore, while it is certain that a wrongfully terminated welfare recipient is immediately placed in a desperate situation ("grievous loss" in the language of *Goldberg*), a wrongfully terminated disability recipient may have assets to fall back on while waiting for the hearing, and can also apply for welfare benefits if the financial situation becomes desperate. On the second basis, the *Mathews* Court stated that continued eligibility for disability benefits is well suited to determination without an oral hearing. Much of the evidence comes from medical reports written by professionals such as doctors. Further, disability recipients, who must have a substantial work history to qualify in the first place, are much more likely than welfare recipients to be able to communicate effectively in writing. Further, the issues in a disability case are less likely to turn on witness credibility than in a welfare case.

Instead of simply deciding the *Mathews* case based on the factors discussed above, the Court used the case as a vehicle to specify a standard to govern the determination of what process is due. The Court stated that once it is determined that government action will deprive a person of a protected interest, three factors must be considered to determine the level of process that must be afforded:

1. the strength of the private interest affected by the government action;
2. the risk of an erroneous deprivation if additional procedure is not afforded; and
3. the government's interest in proceeding with no more process than already afforded.

While there is no mathematical formula to determine how much process is due, these factors are intended to provide guidance in making the determination.

On the first factor, the stronger the private interest, the more process is required by due process. This factor explains why the Court found more process required in *Goldberg v. Kelly* than in *Mathews v. Eldridge*. Because *Goldberg* involved welfare benefits that by definition implicate the claimant's very survival, the importance level of the interest was very high, and the Court held that due process requires an oral hearing before such benefits are terminated. By contrast, in *Mathews* itself, the Court held that because eligibility for disability benefits is not based on need, it does not implicate subsistence, and an oral pre-termination hearing is not required.

In addition to welfare, the Court has found the private interest in continued government employment to be very strong, strong enough to require at least limited pre-termination process, even if a full hearing is available after termination. As the Court put it, "the significance of the private interest in retaining employment cannot be gainsaid. We have frequently recognized the severity of depriving a person of the means of livelihood. . . . While a fired worker may find employment elsewhere, doing so will take some time and is likely to be burdened by the questionable circumstances under which he left his previous job." *Cleveland Board of Education v. Loudermill*, 470 U.S. 532, 544 (1985). Note that this may be in tension with *Mathews*: Insofar as disability benefits are a substitute for wages, "the severity of depriving a person" of disability benefits is likely to be similar to the severity of terminating employment.

The *Loudermill* decision did not require a full adversary hearing before termination of government employment for cause. Rather, as the Court explained, "the essential requirements of due process, and all that respondents seek or the Court of Appeals required, are notice and an opportunity to respond. The opportunity to present reasons, either in person or in writing, why proposed action should not be taken is a fundamental due process requirement. . . . The tenured public employee is entitled to oral or written notice of the charges against him, an explanation of the employer's evidence, and an opportunity to present his side of the story." Id. at 546.

Sidebar

THE STRENGTH OF THE PRIVATE INTEREST

It is very important to be precise about the interest involved. The interests in *Goldberg* and *Mathews* were not the permanent interests in the welfare and disability benefits because each program offered an oral hearing at some point in the future at which the final determination would be made. Rather, the interest at stake was the interest in receiving benefits during the period between the initial determination of ineligibility and the hearing. Sometimes, this will not be the case. For example, if a business applies for a permit and the permit is denied with no further appeal available, the interest would be the entire interest in the permit. But an initial denial followed by a later full hearing would involve only the interest in having the permit between the initial denial and the later full hearing. In general, the interest involved in a final deprivation is stronger than a temporary deprivation of the same interest.

The Court noted that it may have required more had state law not provided for a full post-termination hearing.

F A Q

Q: Why are government employees with property interests entitled to pre-termination hearings?

A: Although the Court has not put it in these exact terms, the Court apparently believes that the *Mathews v. Eldridge* balance always points to pre-termination hearings in the employment context. It is not clear why a meaningful post-termination hearing, with backpay and reinstatement available to the employee, is not sufficient to protect the property interest in government employment, especially in light of the prevalence of at-will employment in the United States.

The second *Mathews* factor is the value of additional process to an accurate determination. The greater the risk of an erroneous deprivation, the stronger the claim is to additional procedures. As noted above, in *Goldberg v. Kelly*, one reason for requiring an oral pre-termination hearing was that welfare recipients might be unable to state their claims effectively in writing, thus increasing the risk of an erroneous deprivation. By contrast, in *Mathews v. Eldridge*, the Court reasoned that no advance oral hearing was required, in part because the objective, medical nature of the relevant evidence meant that an erroneous determination was less likely than in *Goldberg*.

Sidebar

FOCUS ON ACCURACY

The second *Mathews* factor considered together with entitlement theory reveals that due process law in the United States is primarily concerned with accuracy. The reason no hearing is required when there is no entitlement is that absent a set of binding criteria, the hearing is legally meaningless since the government would be legally free to decide any way it chooses. In the presence of an entitlement, a hearing is meaningful because it can be judged on whether it is consistent with the terms of the entitlement.

The third and most controversial factor in *Mathews* is the consideration of the government's interest in not increasing process beyond that already afforded. The government's fiscal and administrative interests almost always favor minimizing process and thus factoring in the cost of process could seriously undercut the value of due process. This factor should have the greatest impact when reasons unrelated to the pure costs of the hearing point toward minimizing process. For example, with regard to disability benefits, the *Mathews* Court noted that if the government were required to continue disability benefits until after an oral hearing, it would be very difficult if not impossible for the government to recover benefits paid between the determination that disability benefits should be terminated and the hearing. Further, due process has also been flexible enough in emergencies such as the discovery of poisonous or rotten food to allow government to act first and hold the hearing later.

The best example of adjusting the timing of process in light of a special need for quick action is *Gilbert v. Homar*, 520 U.S. 924 (1997). In that case, a state university police officer was arrested and charged with a felony drug crime. Upon learning of the arrest, university officials suspended him immediately, without a pre-suspension hearing. Although the drug charges were subsequently dismissed, the officer remained suspended and he was not allowed to tell his side of the story until weeks after the suspension. Ultimately, he was demoted to groundskeeper and he sued, claiming that due process required a hearing before the suspension. The Supreme Court held that the state's interest in acting quickly to remove a campus police officer charged with a drug crime justified departing from the classic model of a hearing before an adverse employment action is taken. While reaffirming *Loudermill*'s general rule in favor of pre-termination hearings, the Court explained that due process allows flexibility when important state interests favor quick action. Thus, *Gilbert* presented an ideal case for minimizing process under the third *Mathews* factor without threatening due process values in the typical case. The state's interest in *Gilbert* was not simply the general fiscal and administrative preference for less procedure, but was rather that government interests would be threatened if additional procedures were required.

Another similar example is the prison placement case discussed above, *Wilkinson v. Austin*, 549 U.S. 209 (2005). In that case, the Court held that the government's interest in minimizing process was the primary reason for not requiring a full adversary hearing as part of the process for determining whether a prison inmate should be sent to a supermax prison. The state needs to be able to control difficult inmates immediately, and other inmates may be very reluctant to testify concerning the behavior of an inmate whose conduct has been so bad that supermax incarceration is a likely result. Full adversary hearings may hamper the state's ability to make necessary adjustments to the level of incarceration. The Court in *Wilkinson* also relied on the state's general fiscal interest in minimizing costs of process, establishing that as a legitimate factor, although it should not override factors pointing in favor of additional process when there is no special reason, such as an emergency, for minimizing process.

(c) Post-Deprivation Process and Government Torts

Until now, the analysis has focused on the traditional model of pre-deprivation process involving advance notice and adjudicatory hearings. There are, however, many situations in which other procedures may satisfy due process. For example, recall that in *Ingraham v. Wright*, although the Court recognized a liberty interest in being free from corporal punishment, the Court found that post-punishment common law remedies under Florida law were sufficient to satisfy due process. The common law of Florida limited a teacher's privilege to inflict the punishment, and the Court held that the existence of the common law remedies, coupled with the low incidence of abuse, meant that due process did not require a hearing in advance of inflicting the punishment.

> **Sidebar**
>
> **THE GOVERNMENT INTEREST IN LESS PROCESS**
>
> The third *Mathews* factor is at its most legitimate when it considers special reasons why more process would be contrary to important government interests. It is at its least legitimate when it considers the simple cost of holding hearings. The cost of providing due process is a questionable basis for denying it.

This brings up the general problem of torts committed by government officials. Victims of torts committed by government officials often try to turn them into constitutional claims to take advantage of better remedies available in such cases or to avoid state law immunities that might prevent victims from winning any damages at all. Tortious conduct by government officials can destroy or damage property or affect liberty interests in freedom from physical injury. The Supreme Court has resisted turning all official torts into due process violations, first by holding that post-deprivation tort remedies can satisfy due process and later by holding that negligent conduct does not constitute a "deprivation" of a protected interest.

Post-deprivation remedies have been most strongly approved when random and unauthorized tortious conduct by a government official damages the victim's property or liberty. In the first in this line of cases, a state prisoner sued after his mail-order hobby materials were lost somewhere in the prison before he received them. See *Parratt v. Taylor*, 451 U.S. 527 (1981), *overruled in part by Daniels v. Williams*, 474 U.S. 327 (1986). He claimed that he had been deprived of property without due process of law, since no hearing was held before his property was lost. The Supreme Court realized that because the state could not, as a practical matter, hold a hearing before tortious conduct by a state employee, accepting this reasoning would transform virtually all state official torts into federal due process violations. To prevent this result, the Court held that in the case of random and unauthorized tortious conduct by a government employee, adequate post-deprivation remedies satisfy the *Mathews v. Eldridge* due process requirements. 451 U.S. at 542-44. In other words, in the case of such torts, post-deprivation tort remedies provide all the process that is due.

Even the rule in *Parratt* allowing post-deprivation tort remedies to satisfy due process threatened to turn many state official torts into federal due process cases because some states immunize government employees, rendering state remedies inadequate. For example, in *Daniels v. Williams*, 474 U.S. 327 (1986), a Virginia state prisoner was injured when he slipped and fell on a pillow negligently left on the stairs by a prison guard. Virginia granted immunity from damages in negligence cases to prison guards, and the state itself also enjoyed sovereign immunity. The prisoner thus had a strong claim that there was no adequate state remedy and therefore he had been deprived of liberty without due process. The Court, recognizing that agreeing with the prisoner would essentially void state tort immunities for state employees, held, contrary to *Parratt*, that something more than negligence is required for conduct to deprive someone of liberty or property.

Daniels means that the *Parratt* "adequate state remedies" requirement does not apply in negligence cases, but it still applies in intentional tort cases. For example, in *Hudson v. Palmer*, 468 U.S. 517 (1984), a prison guard allegedly stole property from a prisoner's cell during a routine search. The prisoner sued for damages, claiming that the property was taken without due process of law. Because the prison guard's theft was random and unauthorized, an adequate post-deprivation remedy (such as an administrative claims procedure) satisfies due process. However, had no post-deprivation remedy been available, due process would have been violated and the federal court could have awarded damages against the guard. And when the challenge is to the statutory deprivation procedures themselves, the availability of post-deprivation remedies may not be adequate to satisfy due process. See *Zinermon v. Burch*, 494 U.S. 113 (1990).

In addition to state tort remedies, due process may also be satisfied in some contexts with an informal, consultative procedure. For example, in *Board of Curators of the University of Missouri v. Horowitz*, 435 U.S. 78 (1978), the Court held that due process was not violated when a medical student at a state school was dismissed for academic reasons without a formal, advance hearing. The Court held that the consultative review process employed (which included normal academic monitoring and review by several area physicians) was sufficient.

The academic context and reasons for dismissal were important to the Court's acceptance of the informal consultative process. Injecting traditional due process requirements into the academic setting would interfere with the ability of academic institutions to control their core academic programs as they saw fit. Academic institutions are better able to design academically oriented procedures than are judges. In *Horowitz*, the Court appeared particularly reluctant to judicialize the academic review process at state universities and did not feel that judges should second-guess whether a student's academic performance was up to par. The Court distinguished dismissal for academic reasons from dismissal for disciplinary reasons where an adversarial process might be more appropriate. Even there, however, the Court noted a formal, advance hearing was not necessary as long as there was some opportunity for an advance, informal oral discussion of the disciplinary matter. See *Goss v. Lopez*, 419 U.S. 565 (1975).

It should be pretty clear that the overwhelming consideration in the due process law of the United States is accuracy, balanced against government interests in minimizing process. This is exemplified best by the dominance of entitlement theory and the second *Mathews* factor, which measures the value of additional process in terms of its contribution to accuracy. The essence of an entitlement is the existence of criteria under which the applicable determination is supposed to be made. The purpose of the hearing required by due process is to determine whether the criteria governing the matter are met. Without an entitlement, the determination is left to the discretion of the agency, and no matter what evidence is produced at the hearing, the agency would be free to rule as it saw fit. Without an entitlement, there is simply no such thing as an inaccurate decision, and thus in our system, due process does not apply. It is possible to imagine a different understanding of due process that places a higher value on the dignity and sense of fairness of the subject of adverse government action and recognizes that even without an entitlement, an agency may be persuaded by evidence and arguments presented at a hearing. In the United States, however, absent a rule that raises the strong possibility of winning, due process does not grant the right to a hearing.

(d) Due Process Issues with a Reduced Role for the *Mathews* Factors

Some due process issues have been decided without much attention to the *Mathews v. Eldridge* balancing test. For example, in *Loudermill*, the Court established a bright line rule requiring that government employees with a property interest in their employment normally receive a hearing of some sort before they are deprived of that employment. Although the Court did apply the *Mathews v. Eldridge* balancing test in *Loudermill*, the discussion was cursory and seemed more like a categorical decision that employment terminations should not occur without a hearing.

Similarly, the Court has analyzed cases involving challenges to the neutrality of the decisionmaker without applying the balancing test. The right to a neutral decisionmaker is one of the most important rights protected by due process. Neutrality is an acute problem in the modern administrative agency because investigation, prosecution, adjudication, and legislation are often conducted within a single agency. While the courts have not objected in principle to the combination of functions within a single agency, they have developed legal doctrines to safeguard the due process right to neutrality. The Administrative Procedures Act's (APA) formal adjudication provisions, APA §§554, 556, and 557, also contemplate a measure of independence for Administrative Law Judges (ALJs) to avoid bias and prejudgment, at least in formal hearings.

Due process is violated if the decisionmaker is **biased**. Bias means that the decisionmaker favors one side over the other for reasons unconnected to the merits. For example, if a decisionmaker has a pecuniary interest in the outcome of the adjudication, the decisionmaker would be biased. An obvious violation would be a judge presiding over a case involving a corporation in which the judge owns shares of stock. However, less direct pecuniary interests may also violate due process.

Sidebar

BIAS AND PREJUDGMENT

The two most common bases for challenging the propriety of a particular decisionmaker hearing a case are bias and prejudgment. It is important to distinguish the two. Bias, discussed in this section, involves reasons for questioning the decisionmaker's impartiality, such as pecuniary interest in the outcome or a relationship with a party or attorney. Prejudgment, discussed in the following section, exists when there is reason to believe that a decisionmaker has decided one or more issues before hearing the case. Proof of prejudgment usually involves statements made by the decisionmaker.

A pair of classic cases illustrates the fundamental due process requirement of neutrality. In *Tumey v. Ohio*, 273 U.S. 510 (1927), the village mayor was the official who would hear certain cases involving violations of Prohibition's ban on the possession of alcoholic beverages. The mayor was allowed to keep a portion of any fine paid by convicted defendants, and would not be paid if the defendant was found not guilty. In Tumey's case, Tumey was fined $100 and ordered to pay costs, $12 of which went to the mayor. The Court held that allowing the mayor to assess costs against guilty defendants but not against acquitted defendants gave the mayor a direct pecuniary interest in the outcome of the cases, in violation of due process. The Court stated that it "violates the Fourteenth Amendment, and deprives a defendant in a criminal case of due process of law, to subject his liberty or property to the judgment of a court the judge of which has a direct, personal, substantial, pecuniary interest in reaching a conclusion against him in his case." *Tumey*, 273 U.S. at 523. The government argued that the small amount of the costs should be viewed as insufficient to destroy the mayor's impartiality, but the Court disagreed, stating the test as whether this situation "would offer a possible temptation to the average man as a judge to forget the burden of proof required to convict the defendant, or which might lead him not to hold the balance nice, clear, and true between the state and the accused[.]" Id. at 532.

In *Ward v. Village of Monroeville*, 409 U.S. 57 (1972), the Court extended *Tumey* to cover a case in which the mayor's pecuniary interest in the outcome of cases he was authorized to adjudicate was less direct. In *Monroeville*, the village mayor sat as judge on traffic cases, and fines assessed in such cases accounted for more than a third — sometimes more than half — of the village's total annual revenues. Given the magnitude of the fines in comparison with the village budget, it is not hard to imagine that the town budget was constructed around successful operation of a speed trap at a curve in the road. Relying on the test set forth in *Tumey*, the Court held that the mayor could not be viewed as an impartial adjudicator in this situation. As the Court stated, "Plainly that 'possible temptation' may also exist when the mayor's executive responsibilities for village finances may make him partisan to maintain the high level of contribution from the mayor's court. This, too, is a 'situation in which an official perforce occupies two practically and seriously inconsistent positions, one partisan and the other judicial, (and) necessarily involves a lack of due process of law in the trial of defendants charged with crimes before him.'" *Ward*, 409 U.S. at 60, quoting *Tumey*, 273 U.S. at 534.

The Court also rejected the argument that trial de novo before a higher court cured the due process violation in the initial tribunal. The Court stated that "there is nothing to suggest that the incentive to convict would be diminished by the possibility of reversal on appeal. Nor, in any event, may the State's trial court procedure be deemed constitutionally acceptable simply because the State eventually offers a defendant an impartial adjudication. Petitioner is entitled to a neutral and detached judge in the first instance." *Ward*, 409 U.S. at 61-62.

Although the Court in *Ward* found a due process violation with a less direct interest in the outcome of the cases than in *Tumey*, the Court subsequently made it clear that the decisionmaker's interest must be substantial enough to raise a significant probability of bias for a due process violation to be found. In *Marshall v. Jerrico, Inc.*, 446 U.S. 238 (1980), the Court held that an ALJ is not disqualified from hearing a case when the agency is allowed to retain fines and use the funds to support its enforcement program. The Court noted that the fines accounted for only 1 percent of the agency's budget, and the salary and working conditions of ALJs were not related to the amount of fines collected. Thus, the ALJ did not have a substantial pecuniary interest in the outcome of the case and the arrangement did not violate due process. Whether or not the Court was correct about the degree of interest in *Marshall*, some limit like it is required or all defendants subject to a fine could complain that it is unfair for judges employed by the state to hear their cases when the fines are paid into the state treasury.

The Court has gone even further in recognizing potential due process problems with interested adjudicators. **Capture** of a regulatory agency by one segment of a regulated industry can make agency proceedings seem predetermined and unfair. In a controversy that culminated in the Supreme Court's decision in *Gibson v. Berryhill*, 411 U.S. 564 (1973), the Alabama Board of Optometry came to be dominated by independent optometrists who would benefit if they could eliminate competition from optometrists practicing in a corporate setting such as optical departments in department stores. After state law was amended to eliminate express permission for optometrists to practice in the corporate setting, the Board filed a complaint in court alleging that corporate optometrists were in violation of state statutes and rules regulating the practice. The Board also began agency proceedings to penalize optometrists for practicing in the corporate form.

The corporate optometrists challenged the Board's proceedings on due process grounds, alleging that the Board was biased due to pecuniary interest and also that the Board had prejudged the cases against corporate optometrists as evidenced by the allegations contained in the complaint against corporate optometrists filed in state court. The Supreme Court held that due to pecuniary interest in the outcome, the Alabama Board of Optometry could not constitutionally adjudicate whether optometrists violated state law by practicing in the corporate form. Because all board members were independent optometrists, the Court held that the independent optometrists' desire to eliminate competition from department store optometrists was a sufficient pecuniary interest to violate due process. The Court did not reach the prejudgment allegation, perhaps because finding prejudgment based on the filing of a complaint would place the procedures of numerous federal and state agencies in doubt. Many agencies do not completely separate prosecutorial and adjudicatory functions.

GIBSON AND NON-DISCIPLINARY MATTERS

It should be noted that the *Gibson* analysis may not ban non-disciplinary agency administration by one segment of a profession, such as rulemaking. In *Friedman v. Rogers*, 440 U.S. 1 (1979), the Court held that a similarly constituted group could administer the non-disciplinary aspects of a licensing scheme for optometrists. For more on this, see Chapter 10.

Due process and other notions of procedural fairness may be violated if it appears that the decisionmaker is under pressure from superiors to decide cases in a particular way. Pressure from supervisors can bias adjudicators. While they are somewhat protected, Administrative Law Judges do not have the high degree of insulation from external pressure that Article III judges have. Sometimes, agencies put pressure on ALJs to decide their cases in line with agency priorities not reflected in statutes or regulations. In *Association of Administrative Law Judges v. Heckler*, 594 F. Supp. 1132 (D.D.C. 1984), the court held it was improper to subject the decisions of particular ALJs to closer scrutiny because they ruled in favor of social security claimants more often than other ALJs. The court did not find a due process violation or even a violation of any section of the APA. However, the court disapproved of review of ALJ performance based upon allowance rates because of the pressure this would put on ALJs to allow fewer claims.

APA PROTECTIONS OF ALJ INDEPENDENCE

The APA attempts to protect the independence of adjudicatory decisionmakers including ALJs by prohibiting ex parte contacts and by providing that adjudicatory decisionmakers may not be supervised by an agency employee involved in "investigative or prosecuting functions of an agency." APA §554(d). "Ex parte contacts" are communications between a party to a dispute or another person interested in the outcome with the decisionmaker outside the proceedings, often in private. In very rare circumstances, usually involving extreme emergencies, ex parte proceedings are allowed in adjudication.

A decisionmaker may also be considered biased due to a familial, social, or business relationship with one of the parties or their attorneys or even a witness. However, judges and other decisionmakers often have professional relationships with government officials named as parties or who participate in the presentation of the government's case, and such decisionmakers have discretion over whether to step aside due to the appearance of impropriety. A notorious example is *Cheney v. U.S. Dist. Court for Dist. of Columbia*, 542 U.S. 367 (2004), in which Justice Scalia was asked to recuse himself from hearing a case involving the Vice President of the United States after Justice Scalia accepted a free ride on the Vice President's airplane to a duck hunting trip they went on together with a large group. The case concerned the public's right of access to information concerning President Bush's National Energy Policy Development Group, over which Vice President Cheney presided. Justice Scalia's main reason for refusing to recuse himself was that the case concerned Vice President Cheney's official functions and thus the pair's personal friendship had no bearing on Justice Scalia's ability to participate fairly in deciding the case.

Another threat to the neutrality of the decisionmaker, which can also violate due process, is **prejudgment**. Prejudgment in adjudication exists when the decisionmaker has, in some measure, adjudged the facts or law of a particular case prior to hearing it. *Cinderella Career and Finishing Schools, Inc. v. FTC*, 425 F.2d 583 (D.C. Cir. 1970). This test is well suited to measuring prejudgment in adjudication, but would not work in rulemaking where officials are expected to have strong views when making legislative decisions. They are disqualified only if it is shown that they have an unalterably closed mind and thus will not consider the comments presented in the rulemaking procedure. In adjudication, by contrast, decisionmakers are expected, perhaps naively, to come to the hearing with a completely open mind.

The standard for disqualification for prejudgment of an administrative adjudicator was announced by the D.C. Circuit in *Cinderella Career and Finishing Schools, Inc. v. FTC*, 425 F.2d 583 (D.C. Cir. 1970). In that case, a Federal Trade Commissioner had publicly criticized certain business practices and referred to them as "deceptive" while a case was pending before the FTC that would determine whether those practices were legally deceptive under the FTC Act. The D.C. Circuit held that this commissioner could not participate in the adjudication due to apparent prejudgment. The court stated that the test for disqualification is "whether a disinterested observer may conclude that the agency has in some measure adjudged the facts as well as the law of a particular case in advance of hearing it." *Cinderella*, 425 F.2d at 591. The court held that the commissioner's public reference to the practice at issue as "deceptive" met this test.

The disqualification of this particular FTC commissioner raises broader questions concerning the interaction between due process and the combination of various functions within a single agency that is common in the administrative state. Many agencies perform investigatory, prosecutorial, adjudicatory, educational, and legislative functions, and the agency heads often participate in all of these functions. If, for example, the FTC issues a complaint against a business alleging unfair and deceptive practices, and also publishes literature to educate the public on avoiding such practices, it may seem unfair that the very same commissioners who preside over those aspects of the agency's work will also preside at the ultimate adjudicatory hearing within the agency.

As noted, the APA separates lower-level adjudicators such as ALJs from the agency's prosecutorial function by prohibiting the official hearing a case from being responsible to, or under the supervision of, an agency official involved in the investigation or prosecution of the case. APA §554(d). This prohibition does not apply, however, to agency heads such as FTC commissioners who may participate in the decision to bring a charge and then sit as the adjudicator of the case. This combination has been held not to violate due process per se, although the commissioners must be careful about making public statements while the case is pending before them. For example, in an earlier ruling in the *Cinderella* case, the Court of Appeals held that the FTC had the power to issue a press release alerting the public to suspected illegal practices in advance of the hearing, and subsequent FTC adjudication to determine if the practices were illegal would not violate due process. See *FTC v. Cinderella Career and Finishing Schools*, 404 F.2d 1308 (D.C. Cir. 1968). However, as discussed, when a commissioner publicly stated that the practices involved in the case were deceptive, he went too far and was disqualified from further participation.

An agency's role in initiating charges was challenged in *Withrow v. Larkin*, 421 U.S. 35 (1975). In *Withrow*, a state medical board initiated an investigation of Larkin, a doctor, after he began performing abortions. The board later charged Larkin with licensing violations and set a date for a hearing at which the board would preside. At the same time, the board also referred the matter to the local prosecutor after finding probable cause that Larkin had committed criminal acts. Larkin sued to enjoin the board from hearing the case on the ground that, given the board's prejudgment as evidenced by its prior actions, it would violate due process for the board to hear the case.

The Supreme Court held in *Larkin* that it would not violate due process for the board to hear the case after its investigation and referral to the prosecutor. The Court held that the combination of these functions did not constitute a per se violation of due process. As noted with reference to *Gibson v. Berryhill*, had the Court held otherwise, it would have amounted to a constitutional rejection of the combination of prosecutorial and adjudicatory functions that is common in many regulatory agencies. The Court suggested that a due process violation would be found only when some additional evidence existed that the board had prejudged the ultimate outcome of the case. The Court analogized to judges in criminal cases in which the same judge who issues a warrant or finds probable cause to go forward after a preliminary hearing may ultimately preside over a jury trial or even a bench trial. The *Withrow* decision validates the structure of many administrative agencies under which the agency heads (e.g., FTC commissioners) take part in deciding which prosecutions to bring and then sit as ultimate adjudicators within the agency.

F   A   Q

Q: Why don't these due process cases use the *Mathews v. Eldridge* balancing test?

A: It appears that bias and prejudgment violate due process in and of themselves, and thus are not subject to balancing under *Mathews v. Eldridge* for the ultimate fairness of the proceedings. Perhaps this is because bias and prejudgment make any hearing fundamentally unfair, regardless of whatever additional procedural protections are followed. For example, all the cross-examination and access to evidence in the world will not matter if the decisionmaker is not paying attention. The one innovation that could possibly ameliorate bias or prejudgment is trial de novo in a higher tribunal, but even then the Supreme Court has stated that a hearing de novo before an unbiased decisionmaker does not cure unfairness at the initial hearing.

B. Statutory Hearing Rights

In addition to procedural rights required by due process, agencies must follow the procedures required by statutes and regulations. We are going to look at four issues that arise under procedural statutes and rules. First, we will look at the distinction between formal and informal adjudication and analyze when a statute should be construed to require formal adjudication. Second, we will look at case law that requires that statutory hearings be genuine in that the private party must have a real opportunity to prevail at the hearing. Third, we will look at the relationship between agency rulemaking and adjudication, specifically how the existence of substantive legislative rules affects the scope of the adjudicatory hearing required by statute. Finally, we will look at a related constitutional issue, the irrebuttable presumption doctrine that, when it existed, might have restricted the ability of agencies or legislatures to limit the scope of hearings by blanket rules.

(1) Formal and Informal Adjudication

In general, hearings under the APA can be divided into two types, formal adjudication and informal adjudication. Formal adjudication resembles the judicial trial, and is conducted under APA §§554, 556, and 557. These APA sections contain detailed provisions governing trial-type hearings, including comprehensive notice of the nature of the hearing; the opportunity to present evidence; arguments and offers of settlement; the opportunity to present rebuttal evidence and cross-examine opposing witnesses; the opportunity to review a transcript of the proceedings; and the opportunity to submit proposed findings, conclusions of law, and exceptions to the agency's proposed findings and conclusions. There are also provisions assigning the burden of proof to the proponent of any order and requiring the agency to place the transcript and all pleadings and exhibits on a public record.

As noted above, the APA also contains provisions that grant a degree of independence to ALJs and other agency officials presiding over formal adjudicatory hearings. The APA imposes a strict ban on ex parte communications during the proceedings and parties are specifically allowed to file affidavits of bias or other grounds for disqualifying a presiding official. Other provisions relating to the independence of the presiding officer include a requirement that the official presiding at the hearing make the initial or recommended decision and not be involved in, or under the supervision of any agency official involved in, an investigative or legislative function for the agency. Further, other provisions remove ALJs from internal agency merit pay systems, provide that ALJs should be assigned cases in rotation, and prohibit ALJs from performing functions "inconsistent with their duties and responsibilities as administrative law judges." 5 U.S.C. §3105. The goal is to ensure that formal agency adjudication is fair to the subjects of regulation involved in the hearings.

As discussed in Chapter 6, the APA is understood as recognizing a very broad category of **informal adjudication**, which comprises basically every procedure an agency might use to formulate an order that is not within the category of formal adjudication. The APA says very little about the procedures required for informal adjudication. APA §555 contains some procedural requirements that apply to all agency action. Those include a right to be accompanied by counsel if summoned to appear before an agency, and prompt notice of the denial of any petition or other application made "in connection with any agency proceeding." See APA §555(e). The notice of denial must normally "be accompanied by a brief statement of reasons of the grounds for denial." Id. Unless an applicable statute, rule, or due process requires additional procedures, the Supreme Court has firmly held in reliance on *Vermont Yankee* that courts may not add to the procedures provided by the agency in cases of informal adjudication. In other words, there is no review for the overall reasonableness of informal procedures.

F A Q

Q: When is formal adjudication the required procedural model?

A: APA §554 specifies that formal adjudication is required, subject to exceptions, "in every case of adjudication required by statute to be determined on the record after opportunity for an agency hearing." "On the record after opportunity for an agency hearing" is the same language that governs the choice between formal and informal rulemaking. This is similar to the analysis that governs the circumstances under which the APA requires an agency to employ formal adjudicatory procedures. In that context, the Supreme Court has held that formal rulemaking is not required without very clear language requiring that proceedings be on the record of an agency hearing. However, the case law has not determined whether formal adjudication is required only when the governing statute is absolutely clear, as in the case of formal rulemaking.

Sidebar

"HEARING" IS AMBIGUOUS

Unless and until the Supreme Court speaks, the consensus seems to be that the simple word "hearing" or the phrase "public hearing" is ambiguous and thus a court on judicial review should defer, under *Chevron*, to the agency's determination of whether to conduct a formal APA adjudicatory hearing or a less formal proceeding. Under this analysis, only very clear language will require formal adjudication, such as an explicit statutory reference to "an on the record" agency hearing.

The federal courts of appeals have been divided on whether the term "**hearing**" in a statute referring to adjudication means formal or informal adjudication. Most notably, the First Circuit for a long time presumed that "hearing" means formal adjudication. *Seacoast Anti-Pollution League v. Costle*, 572 F.2d 872 (1978). In distinguishing adjudication from rulemaking, where the Supreme Court requires more than the word "hearing" to invoke formal proceedings, the First Circuit reasoned that adjudications are more likely than rulemakings to involve particularized fact finding that lends itself well to quasi-judicial procedures, and thus the court was "willing to presume that, unless a statute otherwise specifies, an adjudicatory hearing subject to judicial review must be on the record." Id. at 876.

This is a relatively slender reed to support such an important procedural presumption, especially if the agency disagrees, and more recently the First Circuit has pulled back from the presumption by agreeing with the D.C. Circuit that courts should defer under *Chevron* to reasonable agency interpretations of statutes referring to "hearings." *Dominion Energy Brayton Point, LLC v. Johnson*, 443 F.3d 12, 17-18 (1st Cir. 2006) citing, inter alia, *Chem. Waste Mgmt., Inc. v. U.S. EPA*, 873 F.2d 1477, 1480-82

(D.C. Cir. 1989) (deferring, under *Chevron*, to agency interpretation of phrase "public hearing"). The First Circuit did not really abandon its understanding of the word "hearing" in adjudication statutes. Rather, it found that the word is ambiguous enough to justify deference to contrary agency understandings.

(2) The Statutorily Required Hearing Must Be a Genuine Hearing — Not a Sham

When a statute grants an applicant a hearing on an application for a government benefit or license, the hearing must provide the applicant with a genuine opportunity to prevail. The agency does not satisfy the hearing requirement by going through the motions of a hearing process when, as a practical matter, the applicant has no chance of prevailing at the hearing.

The best example of this is the Supreme Court's implementation of the licensing process under the Telecommunications Act. The Act requires the Federal Communications Commission (FCC) to provide an applicant with a full adjudicatory hearing before an application can be denied. The FCC is allowed to grant an application without holding an adjudicatory hearing. In *Ashbacker Radio Corp. v. FCC*, 326 U.S. 327 (1945), two parties applied for a license to construct radio stations that would operate on the same frequency in nearby communities. Because of potential frequency interference, these two applications were mutually exclusive. Following the letter of the statute, the FCC granted one application and set the other (Ashbacker's) for a hearing. Ashbacker sued, claiming that the hearing would not be genuine because its application could not be granted without violating an FCC policy against interference with the signal of the previously granted station in the nearby community. The Court agreed with Ashbacker, holding that as a practical matter, by granting the competitor's license, the FCC had deprived Ashbacker of the statutorily required hearing. The Court rejected the FCC's argument that it could make adjustments to the previously granted license if it decided to grant Ashbacker's after the hearing on the ground that for all intents and purposes, the grant of the competing application amounted to a denial of Ashbacker's right to a hearing before its application could be denied.

Sidebar

COMPARATIVE HEARINGS ARE UNCOMMON

The precise problem of *Ashbacker*—that the results of a hearing have been effectively predetermined by other regulatory events — is not very common. However, the *Ashbacker* doctrine was interpreted to require comparative hearings in a variety of contexts including airline route licensing and such and thus was important when the federal government was more involved in the licensing of scarce regulatory resources.

(3) Substantive Standards That Limit the Right to a Hearing

Another issue regarding statutorily required hearings is the relationship between hearing procedures and substantive rulemaking. As is discussed in Chapter 6, agencies often use notice and comment rulemaking to make new law on issues that would otherwise be determined in a hearing process. These substantive rules effectively narrow the issues to be decided at statutorily required hearings, which are referred to in the remainder of this discussion as "narrowing rules." This narrowing leads to legal arguments that the agency cannot rely on the rule, but rather must re-determine the issue at the statutory hearing. The challenger points out that notice and comment rulemaking is much less formal and provides a lower level of procedural protection to the private party than the adjudicatory hearing required by the statute.

In general, courts have resolved this apparent conflict between agency creation of narrowing rules and statutorily required adjudication in favor of agency authority to use rulemaking to limit the issues decided at the hearing. The agency must still hold the hearing, but the scope of the hearing is tailored to the remaining substantive standards governing the decision to be made. However, although the courts have upheld agency power to make narrowing rules, the courts recognize that narrowing rules are in tension with a party's statutory right to a full hearing on all issues. Thus, courts have required that agencies provide an opportunity for parties to argue that the rule does not, or should not, apply to the particular case. We can call this the "safety valve" requirement. If an agency does not respond to an argument for a safety valve in a particular case, a reviewing court may remand the case to the agency for an explanation to make sure that the agency actually entertained the argument.

F   A   Q

Q: Why do courts require agencies to entertain arguments that a substantive rule should not apply in a particular case?

A: This seems to be a way of resolving the apparent contradiction between statutory hearing requirements and agency rulemaking authority. It is open to question, however. If the agency has the authority to make substantive rules, those rules should be conclusive within their domains. For example, if a valid FCC rule bans the ownership of more than five radio stations, the FCC should not be required to entertain an argument that this requirement should be waived for a particular licensee. The contrary view essentially denies the FCC the power to make binding substantive rules.

The following example illustrates the law concerning narrowing rules and safety valves. Suppose a statute allows an agency to suspend the license of any licensed gambling business for employing persons in certain positions who "lack good moral character," and requires a formal adjudicatory hearing before the agency may impose a fine. Suppose further that the agency, using §553 notice and comment rulemaking, promulgates a narrowing rule specifying several criteria that establish an employee's lack of good moral character, including a dishonorable discharge from the armed services and conviction of any crime for which the maximum sentence is six months or greater. Suppose further that a licensed casino employs Smith, who everyone involved acknowledges received a dishonorable discharge from the Army and was later convicted of misdemeanor assault, a crime with a maximum nine-month sentence. The agency then issues a notice that it intends to suspend the Casino's license for employing Smith. In this situation, the law is clear on the following issues.

1. In order to impose the penalty, the agency must still provide the Casino with the statutorily required hearing. (If the narrowing rule concerned an application for a benefit or license, the agency might not be required to hold the hearing, unless an issue under number 3 below is raised.)

2. The agency has the power to decide the case based on Smith's dishonorable discharge and misdemeanor conviction and need not make findings under the more general statutory standard except as explained below.

3. If the Casino makes a safety valve argument, for instance a claim of extenuating circumstances, and offers other evidence of Smith's good moral character, the agency must entertain and answer the argument that the regulation should not be applied to him, although it is unclear whether a court would ever actually require an agency to grant the application in the face of a valid narrowing rule.

It should be apparent that disallowing narrowing rules undermines agency authority to make substantive rules. This is especially important with regard to vague statutes that Congress expects will be given content through agency rulemaking. Thus, a key to the rule allowing agencies to make narrowing rules is that the agency must have the statutory authority to engage in substantive rulemaking. Otherwise, a statutory hearing requirement would point toward congressional intent that the regulated parties receive an adjudicatory hearing on all issues. (In fact, no agency may engage in rulemaking without statutory authority to do so.) Further, a narrowing rule must be substantively valid under the standards of judicial review of agency rules. In other words, a narrowing rule that is contrary to the governing statute or arbitrary and capricious is invalid and thus cannot limit the issues to be determined at an adjudicatory hearing.

To illuminate these issues further, we now discuss a few of the more important cases that have arisen concerning narrowing rules. The first case is another dispute involving broadcast licensing. As discussed above, the Communications Act has long required that applicants be given hearings on their applications for broadcast licenses before the FCC may deny an application for a license. The statutory standard governing licensing is "public interest, convenience and necessity," an exceptionally vague standard that is made more definite through extensive FCC rulemaking. The FCC made a narrowing rule that limited the total number of broadcast licenses that any licensee could hold.

Storer Broadcasting Company applied for a license in addition to those it already held, and the application was denied without a hearing because Storer owned more than the maximum allowable number of broadcast licenses under the rule. Storer challenged this denial on two grounds, first that denial without a hearing is inconsistent with the statutory right to a hearing and second that the limit on the number of licenses is inconsistent with the more general statutory standard for determining license applications. In *United States v. Storer Broadcasting Co.*, 351 U.S. 192 (1956), the Supreme Court ruled in favor of the agency on both grounds. The Court held that the FCC is free to deny an application without a hearing when, from the application itself, it is apparent that the license would be denied under a substantively valid statute or regulation. Here, because it was clear that Storer could not meet the FCC's criteria for an additional license, the FCC could deny the application without holding a hearing. This is analogous to judgment on the pleadings or on a motion to dismiss. The Court also held that the FCC has the power to make substantive narrowing rules. Although the Court did allow that the applicant has the right to contest the application of the narrowing rule in the particular case, the Court in *Storer* made it clear that the burden was on the applicant to come forward with reasons not to apply the FCC's rules to the application.

The D.C. Circuit was skeptical of a different FCC narrowing rule involving the FCC's longstanding practice of favoring incumbent licensees over new applicants seeking to take licenses away from incumbents when the licenses come up for renewal. Until the passage of the 1996 revisions, nothing in the Communications Act indicated a preference for incumbent licensees at renewal time. Nonetheless, in a policy statement, the FCC attempted to grant a preference to incumbents. The policy statement provided that, in a contest between a renewing incumbent and a new applicant, the incumbent would receive a controlling preference if it were shown that the incumbent had rendered "substantial past performance without serious deficiencies." This is, in effect, a narrowing rule, specifying the meaning of "public interest, convenience and necessity" in the context of license renewal. The D.C. Circuit, in *Citizens Communication Center v. FCC*, 447 F.2d 1201 (D.C. Cir. 1971), held this policy unlawful under *Ashbacker* because, in effect, it deprived the challenger of a meaningful hearing on the application. This illustrates *Ashbacker*'s substantive element — if the preference for incumbents had been lawful, it would be proper for the FCC to tailor the scope of the hearing to that substantive standard. In order to hold the FCC's action improper, the court necessarily disapproved of the FCC's substantive preference for incumbents.

Another notable area in which narrowing rules have been used is in the context of social security disability benefits. Two principal issues govern eligibility for social security disability benefits: the applicant's medical condition and whether the applicant is employable in the national economy. The volume of social security disability hearings is very high, giving the agency an incentive to use narrowing rules. It is difficult to imagine how a narrowing rule could limit the claimant's ability to present evidence of his or her medical condition, but the Social Security Administration did conduct a rulemaking to create a narrowing rule on the availability of jobs in the national economy for each level of disability and skills. A rule, in the form of a grid, was promulgated that specified whether jobs existed for each level of disability and skills. Under the grid rule, entitlement to disability benefits is determined by quantifying the applicant's condition and skills and then plugging that information into the grid. This rule was challenged as depriving applicants of the hearing required by the Social Security Act.

In *Heckler v. Campbell*, 461 U.S. 458 (1983), the Supreme Court upheld the grid rule as a valid narrowing rule under the Social Security Act. The grid rule is different from other narrowing rules because the availability of employment for a person with a potential disability seems like a more individualized determination than the others that have been made under narrowing rules. However, the Supreme Court did not see any such problem. The Court reasoned that whether jobs existed for each particular skill level and medical condition presented an issue of legislative fact that could be decided in a rulemaking and that once the (narrowing) rule was promulgated, the hearing could be limited to the remaining issues of the applicant's exact condition and skill level. The Court explicitly stated that this applies "even where an agency's enabling statute expressly requires it to hold a hearing." *Heckler*, 461 U.S. at 467. The Court also noted that the applicant was free to make a safety valve argument at the hearing and attempt to persuade the agency that the guidelines did not fairly reflect the particular applicant's situation and thus should not be applied.

The normative bases for the courts' acceptance of narrowing rules is perhaps best exemplified by the D.C. Circuit's decision in the Octane Posting case, *National Petroleum Refiners Assoc. v. FTC*, 482 F.2d 672 (D.C. Cir. 1973), *cert. denied*, 415 U.S. 951 (1974). That case involved an FTC rule requiring all retail gasoline stations to post on the pumps the octane rating of their gasoline. The FTC has the power, after a full adjudicatory hearing, to order a business to cease and desist from "unfair or deceptive acts or practices," and the narrowing rule in this case defined the failure to post octane ratings as an "unfair or deceptive act or practice." The D.C. Circuit upheld this narrowing rule against the familiar challenge that it deprived the subject of the cease and desist proceeding of an adjudicatory hearing on all the issues.

In the course of upholding the rule against a strong argument that Congress had not granted the FTC the power to make substantive narrowing rules, the D.C. Circuit praised narrowing rules on several bases. First, narrowing rules save agency resources because the agency is not required to litigate the same issue repeatedly. Second, regulated parties receive clearer notice of what is expected of them than they would get by reading a series of adjudicatory decisions. Third, the rulemaking process allows all interested parties a better opportunity to provide input to the agency. Fourth, narrowing rules are actually fairer to all regulated parties because everyone is expected to obey them upon promulgation. This reduces the unfairness of being singled out in the cease and desist process while competitors remain free to continue the allegedly unfair or deceptive practice. Finally, the agency can accomplish its regulatory goals more quickly than if it had to go through multiple adjudicatory hearings to specify the contours of the regulatory prohibition. For these reasons and perhaps more, narrowing rules are a favored creature in the law despite the tension with statutory hearing requirements.

(4) The Irrebuttable Presumption Doctrine and the Right to a Hearing

Narrowing rules have a constitutional counterpart because some regulatory subjects have argued that if a narrowing rule affects a hearing involving a constitutionally protected interest such as liberty or property, the rule violates due process. For a short while, the Supreme Court agreed with this argument in certain contexts and constructed a constitutional rule that it referred to as the "**irrebuttable presumption doctrine.**" This doctrine held that where there was a constitutionally protected interest at stake (such as liberty or property), due process required a hearing on all issues and neither legislation nor administrative rules could constitutionally narrow the issues to be determined at the hearing. This doctrine was abandoned a few years after its genesis because of its potential for striking down numerous classifications in statutes and regulations.

The Supreme Court decision that represents the height of the irrebuttable presumption doctrine is probably *Bell v. Burson*, 402 U.S. 535 (1971). In *Bell*, the Court struck down a state statute that suspended the licenses of uninsured drivers involved in automobile accidents unless they posted security to cover the cost of any damages claimed against them or obtained a judicial ruling that they were not at fault in the accident. The Court held that this statute created an irrebutable presumption that the uninsured driver was at fault or would not pay any damages assessed, and the Court held that due process required a hearing before the state could make this determination.

In another irrebuttable presumption decision, in *Stanley v. Illinois*, 405 U.S. 645 (1972), the Court struck down a statute that excluded unwed fathers from eligibility for custody of their children upon the death of the mother. Since married fathers and unwed mothers would be awarded custody unless their unfitness as parents was established at a hearing, the Court ruled that the statute created an unconstitutional irrebuttable presumption that unwed fathers were unfit parents. This case involves more than normal due process concerns because the statute implicates the fundamental right to parent one's children. However, the decision was written in the language of due process and irrebuttable presumptions.

The irrebuttable presumption doctrine was doomed because it threatened the constitutionality of numerous statutory standards drawing somewhat arbitrary substantive lines and was thus actually substantive constitutional law, mainly equal protection, in a procedural disguise. For example, if it had been substantively valid to exclude unwed fathers from those eligible to take custody of the children of a deceased mother, there would be no colorable due process claim to a hearing on fitness. It was only because the Court perceived a substantive constitutional problem with excluding unwed fathers that it could go on to hold that they have a due process right to a hearing on their fitness. This is essentially an equal protection holding, not a due process decision.

CONSEQUENCES OF IRREBUTTABLE PRESUMPTION DOCTRINE

The irrebuttable presumption doctrine was essentially a constitutional attack on legislative rules in statutes and regulations that limit the issues addressed in adjudicatory hearings. Taken to its logical extremes, the irrebuttable presumption doctrine could have severely limited the ability of legislatures and agencies to enact bright line rules that would be applied in agency adjudication.

The Court recognized these problems with the irrebuttable presumption doctrine, and the doctrine died a somewhat sudden death when the Court rejected a challenge to a provision of the Social Security Act that excluded widows who were married to deceased workers for shorter than nine months from eligibility for survivors' benefits. *Weinberger v. Salfi*, 422 U.S. 749 (1975). The widow challenging the statute claimed that the nine-month rule was an invalid irrebuttable presumption that marriages lasting less than nine months were shams entered into to procure survivors' benefits. There are, of course, many marriages shorter than nine months that are not shams, but the statute represented Congress's judgment that no benefits should be paid to the surviving partner of a marriage shorter than nine months, perhaps because many are shams and perhaps also because in a short marriage, the surviving partner is less likely to have been dependent on the deceased spouse. In *Weinberger*, the Court held that the nine-month durational rule was a valid substantive eligibility requirement, and Congress was free to employ such a requirement as a prophylactic, easy-to-administer rule against sham marriages that might be difficult to prove. The nine-month rule would easily survive equal protection scrutiny. In its opinion, the Court rejected the irrebuttable presumption doctrine, holding, in effect, that requirements such as those rejected in *Bell* and *Stanley* should be upheld unless the regulatory classification itself is substantively unconstitutional.

SUMMARY

■ Although due process may have originally meant simply that government must provide whatever process has been promised in applicable statutes and rules, today due process is understood as requiring procedures considered adequate in light of the interests and issues involved in the adjudication.

■ Due process protects life, liberty, and property interests. Property interests protected by the Due Process Clauses are usually created by law external to the Constitution, such as state law. A party has a property interest in a government benefit, license, or job if that law creates an entitlement by prescribing criteria under which the benefit, job, or license will be granted or retained.

■ Liberty interests protected by the Constitution are often created by the Constitution itself. These include the liberty interest in being free from bodily restraint or bodily harm. Positive law can also create a liberty interest, for example by prescribing criteria the government must follow before applying a particular form of restraint, such as transfer from a minimum security prison to a substantially more restrictive environment.

■ Once a protected interest is found, federal constitutional law determines what process is due. Under the *Mathews v. Eldridge* balancing test, this determination is made by balancing the strength of the private interest, the accuracy value of additional procedure, and the government's interest in proceeding without additional process.

■ The traditional model of due process is an adjudicatory hearing, usually in advance of the adverse action. In many situations, however, it is constitutionally permissible to hold the hearing after the adverse government action has been taken. Further, in some settings due process may be provided through alternative models such as common law remedies and informal, consultative processes.

■ A basic right under due process is the right to a neutral decisionmaker. A decisionmaker is not neutral if he or she has a pecuniary interest in the outcome of the case or if he or she has prejudged the facts or law of the case.

■ The standard for disqualification for prejudgment in formal adjudication is much stricter than in rulemaking. An adjudicator is disqualified if a disinterested observer may conclude that the decisionmaker has in some measure adjudged the facts as well as the law of a particular case in advance of hearing it.

■ In the administrative setting, bias may exist when one segment of an industry has captured an agency and uses its influence over the agency to harm its competitors.

■ When a statute requires a hearing, the agency must provide a genuine hearing at which the applicant has an opportunity to prevail. However, agencies are free to use rulemaking to narrow the issues decided at a statutorily required hearing as long as the rules made to do so are substantively valid.

CONNECTIONS

Agency Adjudication and Separation of Powers

In addition to due process concerns, agency adjudication raises separation of powers questions because Article III vests the federal judicial power in the federal courts. See Chapter 2 for discussion of this aspect of agency adjudication.

Rulemaking and Hearings

On the issue of rulemaking that by rule determines some of the issues that would otherwise be decided in adjudication, see also Chapter 6.

Regulatory Capture and Due Process

For further discussion of the problems that arise when a regulatory agency is captured by one segment of a regulated industry or profession, see Chapter 10's discussion of *Gibson v. Berryhill* and *Friedman v. Rogers.*

Formal and Informal Adjudication

For further discussion of the distinction between formal and informal adjudication, and the circumstances in which formal procedures are required, see Chapter 6.

Agency and Private Enforcement

9

This chapter addresses the methods agencies and private parties use to enforce regulatory requirements. The chapter examines agency

prosecutorial discretion, discriminatory enforcement, and due process issues that have arisen when agencies impose penalties. It also looks at private enforcement including citizens' suits, private rights of action, and liability of agency employees and officials.

Agencies have a great deal of discretion over whether to regulate and over the choice of targets for enforcement action. However, clear statutory standards that prescribe enforcement under certain circumstances can narrow that discretion. Discriminatory enforcement claims, alleging that an agency has unfairly singled out one violator from among many, are unlikely to succeed absent proof of invidious discrimination. The standard for evaluating discriminatory enforcement claims is "patent abuse of discretion," which is a standard that is almost never met given that courts are extremely deferential to agency discretion in this area and accept almost any agency explanation for not prosecuting other violators along with the party raising the challenge. The courts also have been very deferential to agency choices regarding the severity of sanctions in a particular case.

Many relatively recent regulatory statutes, especially in the environmental area, contain citizens' suit provisions that allow private citizens, under prescribed circumstances, to sue government and regulatory violators. This essentially allows private actors to enforce regulatory requirements when the agency has not acted. Typically, agency officials can be compelled, under citizens' suit provisions, to take nondiscretionary actions. Further, private regulated parties and the government can be enjoined from violating regulatory requirements. However, citizens' suit provisions are not a substitute for judicial review. Discretionary regulatory actions can be challenged only under traditional judicial review provisions.

Even in the absence of a citizens' suit provision, a federal court may imply a private right of action from a federal regulatory statute. Originally, federal courts liberally recognized private rights under federal regulatory statutes based on the view that private rights of action would advance Congress's purposes by picking up the slack when agencies were unable or unwilling to take enforcement action. More recently, however, the Supreme Court has concluded that only Congress ought to decide whether to create a new federal regulatory claim, and it has stated that implied private rights of action should be recognized only when Congress clearly intended the courts to do so.

A. AGENCY ENFORCEMENT AND DISCRETION

1. Overview of Agency Enforcement
2. Agency Enforcement Discretion
3. Discriminatory Enforcement
4. Constitutionally-Based Claims of Discriminatory Enforcement
5. Due Process and Enforcement

B. PRIVATE LIABILITY SUITS TO ENFORCE REGULATORY REQUIREMENTS

1. The Citizens' Suit
2. Implied Private Rights of Action

A. Agency Enforcement and Discretion

Just like traditional criminal prosecutors, agencies normally have a great deal of discretion over their choice of enforcement targets. This discretion can be challenged in two ways. Competitors or victims (including public interest groups) of alleged violators of regulatory requirements may complain that an agency is not bringing enforcement action when it should. They may attempt to compel the agency to bring the enforcement action. The other potential challenge to agency discretion involves claims of discriminatory enforcement. An alleged or proven violator of regulatory requirements may complain about being singled out for enforcement while others, usually competitors, are allowed to continue with the exact same illegal conduct. In most circumstances, as the reviewability discussion in Chapter 3 revealed, agency decisions not to bring enforcement action are either not reviewable or are reviewed on an extremely deferential standard with courts rarely if ever requiring an agency to take enforcement action.

(1) Overview of Agency Enforcement

The creation of governing legal rules, either legislatively by Congress or administratively by agencies, is only the first step in accomplishing regulatory goals. The next step is to actually **enforce** those rules. Although some regulatory provisions are enforced through civil and criminal litigation, agencies themselves engage in a great deal of enforcement of regulatory norms. Agency enforcement takes many forms and employs multiple methodologies. In this chapter, we look at some general issues that arise in agency enforcement, such as discriminatory enforcement, and the circumstances under which private parties can employ civil litigation to enforce regulatory requirements. In other chapters, we look at enforcement methods such as inspections (Chapter 11), licensing (Chapter 10), and liability of government and government officials (Chapter 13). We also looked at some due process constraints on agency enforcement in Chapter 6.

The paradigmatic structure of agency enforcement is what is known as "**command and control**." In command and control enforcement, an agency issues commands, monitors compliance with those commands, and then imposes orders such as compliance orders and sanctions when the commands are violated. Enforcement tools in such situations include **inspections**, **complaint procedures**, and **self-reporting requirements**. The agency may also adjudicate complaints itself, subject to judicial review, sometimes with a requirement that an agency order is effective only if enforced by a court. Judicial review of the order is then built into the enforcement process. There are other methods of enforcement that may operate within an overall command and control regime, some of which are more market-based such as cap and trade regulation of pollutants.

Enforcement strategy and resources have significant, even overwhelming, effects on the level of enforcement. While the goal may be complete obedience or enforcement, attaining that goal is usually unrealistic. Society is unlikely to be willing to expend the resources or live under the constant supervision that would be necessary to achieve 100 percent compliance with regulatory norms.

In a realistic sense, the level of enforcement is an indication of the strength of the underlying norm — if an agency promulgates a rule but then decides not to spend any resources enforcing the rule, it is probably inaccurate to say that the rule is actually in force in any meaningful way. The behavior of enforcement targets is also important to this calculation. If it is valuable to violate the rule (for example because it substantially increases a company's profits) and violations are difficult to detect, society will have to devote more resources to enforcement than if violation is not valuable and violations are easy to detect. The various enforcement structures we

S i d e b a r

THE IMPORTANCE OF ENFORCEMENT

It is not possible to overstate the importance of enforcement to administrative law. Statutes and regulations are worth less if they are not enforced, and they are worth less if they are difficult or expensive to enforce. Therefore, it is important to consider enforcement issues on their own and as important to the original design of regulatory norms.

see throughout administrative law are often designed to increase the incentive to comply with regulatory norms by making violation less attractive and easier to detect. This can include more monitoring, increased penalties, or providing for private enforcement by victims of the regulatory violation.

Regulatory requirements are often designed with enforcement issues in mind. Going back to the idea of command and control, the more precise a regulatory requirement is, the easier it may be to enforce using traditional methods including inspections or advance regulatory approvals. The problem is that precision in requirements reduces flexibility for the regulated party, which can make compliance needlessly expensive and difficult. This raises the distinction between design standards and performance standards. Let's use a hypothetical example of regulatory requirements for the safe construction of scaffolds used in the workplace. **Design standards** would specify the materials and design of scaffolds. **Performance standards** would mandate that scaffolds be capable of holding a certain amount of weight and maintain stability under the conditions of use, etc. The advantage of performance standards is that they allow flexibility that could lead to better and less expensive scaffolds. Their drawback is that agency enforcement is much more complicated because each scaffold, being potentially unique, would have to be tested for compliance. Design standards may be much easier to enforce because compliance can be detected through a simple inspection. As a general matter, the choice between design and performance standards should be made by comparing the value of flexibility with the increased cost of enforcement.

In recent years, scholars have extolled the virtues of a more cooperative form of enforcement under which agencies and regulated parties work together to achieve regulatory goals.[1] The underlying normative premise is that the quality of enforcement would improve if cooperation were to replace the usually adversarial relationship between agencies and enforcement subjects. With better communication and more cooperation, agencies could better understand the concerns of regulated parties and optimize the design of enforcement programs. Additionally, regulated parties would better understand agency priorities and might be more willing to cooperate if they felt that agencies were listening to their concerns.

Sidebar

JUDICIAL REVIEW OF ENFORCEMENT DECISIONS

We have seen two enforcement areas in which the arbitrary and capricious standard is applied more leniently than in other contexts. These are judicial review of the denial of a rulemaking petition and judicial review of the refusal to bring enforcement action (in the rare case in which clear standards make the latter type of case reviewable). This reflects the general sense that enforcement decisions are not well suited to judicial review.

Agency exercise of enforcement power differs in many respects from agency formulation of substantive policy. Unlike substantive rulemaking or policymaking in formal adjudication, agency enforcement may proceed without the formulation of rules or standards guiding the exercise of discretion. Further, agency discretion over enforcement policy and priorities is usually even greater than over other aspects of agency policy. Courts barely scrutinize agency decisions over when and how to enforce regulatory requirements, and when they do, judicial review is usually much more lenient than review under the usual understanding of the arbitrary and capricious standard. The reasons for this leniency, as is discussed more fully below, lie in the view that Congress has entrusted agencies with discretion over how to allocate scarce enforcement resources and that the exercise of this discretion involves agency expertise that is not shared by courts.

Agencies sometimes use informal enforcement methods to avoid procedural constraints, including due process on the exercise of their enforcement powers. Agency officials can threaten enforcement action or other unfavorable consequences, such as stepped up inspections, to convince regulated parties to modify their behavior even if it is clear that no statute or rule has been violated. Regulated parties must weigh the costs, including reputational effects, of fighting the agency against the value of continuing their prior course of conduct. This is often termed "raised eyebrow" regulation, and it is surprisingly common. Often, the most

---

[1]See, e.g., Jody Freeman, *Collaborative Governance in the Administrative State*, 45 UCLA L. Rev. 1 (1997).

pervasive and effective agency enforcement arises from daily contact with regulated parties rather than formal proceedings brought by agencies against alleged violators.

(2) Agency Enforcement Discretion

Agency discretion over enforcement is founded upon several considerations revolving around resources and expertise. Agencies often have broad regulatory missions and insufficient resources to bring enforcement actions against every violator of regulatory requirements. Agencies must therefore choose among numerous potential enforcement targets, in much the same way that prosecutors decide whether to prosecute for criminal violations. Courts have generally concluded that agencies should be left to decide, in their expert judgment, which enforcement actions present the best use of agency resources in light of the myriad policies agencies must take into account. Further, like the criminal prosecutor, there may be some viola-

> ### Sidebar
>
> **ENFORCEMENT AND COMBINED FUNCTIONS**
>
> The **combination of functions** in agencies sometimes becomes relevant in review of enforcement decisions. As we saw in Chapter 8, if members of one segment of a profession dominate an occupational licensing agency, and they take disciplinary action to eliminate competition from another segment of the profession, the bias due to self-interest in the outcome of the disciplinary action may violate due process. However, outside the context of a particular disciplinary action, domination of a licensing agency by one segment of a profession does not automatically violate due process.

tions that agencies find, in their expert judgment, are better left unremedied because the violations are de minimis or because the agency does not believe that enforcement would serve the goals of the relevant regulatory norms.

Despite these reasons in favor of agency enforcement discretion, virtually unreviewable discretion to choose enforcement targets has serious drawbacks. There is a widespread perception that agency enforcement decisions are not made on any rational basis, that agencies have not done a good job of prioritizing and directing their resources where they can have the greatest positive impact. There are three related aspects to this criticism.

First, enforcement discretion can allow an agency to subvert congressional intent by applying different priorities from those that led Congress to pass the agency's enabling act. The agency may not select what Congress would consider the highest value targets but may apply different criteria or no criterion at all.

Second, agency prosecutorial discretion allows agencies to play political favorites. With no judicial review and ineffective congressional oversight, agencies may shape enforcement strategy to meet political goals rather than policy goals. Agencies may enforce their norms only against businesses or individuals identified with political opponents or without sufficient political power to resist enforcement through political channels. Politically connected violators may get a free pass. Of course, the political power of the regulated party is presumably irrelevant to whether enforcement would advance the policies embodied in the regulatory program.

Third, agency prosecutorial discretion may lead agencies to select only easy targets for prosecution — smaller businesses or individuals who may lack the resources to challenge the agency effectively. An agency might justify this strategy as cost effective, but it may be unfair to enforcement targets and subversive of public policy since the largest violators are left untouched.

Although extreme judicial deference to agency enforcement decisions may be worrisome, Congress can remedy the situation at least to a degree by legislating greater constraints on enforcement discretion. As we saw in Chapter 3, if Congress specifies circumstances under which an agency must take enforcement action, the agency's failure to act is subject to judicial review, albeit on a relatively deferential standard. If an agency's statute requires the agency to prosecute all known violators or if the statute sets a standard that the agency must follow when deciding whether to prosecute, the agency has less prosecutorial discretion. Presumably, Congress has the power to reduce agency discretion substantially. Another remedy, which we will examine below, is for Congress to legislatively provide for a private right of action in a citizens' suit or similar provision, under which victims of regulatory violations become "private attorneys general" and enforce regulatory requirements through private lawsuits. However, no matter what Congress does, the separation of powers is likely to leave agencies with substantial room to maneuver in making their enforcement decisions.

(3) Discriminatory Enforcement

Subjects of agency enforcement sometimes claim that although they may have violated regulatory norms, the agency should not issue an enforcement order against them unless and until the agency issues enforcement orders against others engaged in the same or a very similar practice. While there are some suggestions of pure equal treatment concerns, most of these cases are not the typical case of one criminal arguing that prosecution is unfair because others are committing the same crime. Rather, these cases typically involve competitors, and there are two reasons for special concern when administrative agencies appear to be singling out enforcement targets from a group of competitors. First, enforcement subjects argue that they will suffer a competitive disadvantage if they are ordered to halt a practice while their competitors are free to continue the very same practice. For example, in the antitrust area, if the enforcement action involves price discrimination that includes discounts to preferred customers, the first enforcement subject will argue that it will lose business if ordered to stop giving discounts if others are still allowed to give them. Second, there is a suggestion that enforcement is skewed toward weaker, less politically powerful, targets. In some of these cases, enforcement is brought against one of the smaller competitors in the group alleged to be engaged in the same potentially illegal practice. This raises the possibility of arbitrary selection of enforcement targets. However, regardless of the normative appeal of allegations of discriminatory enforcement, such claims rarely succeed because courts are loath to upset decisions implicating agencies' enforcement discretion, which courts analogize to the discretion possessed by a criminal prosecutor.

The typical discriminatory enforcement claim involving a federal agency has several elements. The regulated party resisting enforcement argues some or all of the following: The practice that the agency has ordered to be stopped is widespread in the industry; the agency has not ordered the party's competitors to halt the same practice, and the competitors will continue to engage in it; requiring the party to halt the practice without ordering competitors to do so as well will place the party at a severe competitive disadvantage; the party is a minor player in the industry compared with its competitors; and there is no rational basis for singling out the party ordered to halt the practice from others in the industry who are also engaged in the practice.

The Supreme Court has created a very deferential standard for deciding whether an agency has engaged in discriminatory enforcement, and it has applied the standard in a manner even more deferential than suggested by the bare words of the legal standard. The standard for deciding whether a court should preclude an agency from enforcing an order until the agency orders others in the industry to halt the same practice is "patent abuse of discretion." See *Moog Industries, Inc. v. FTC*, 355 U.S. 411 (1958). The reasons the Court gave for this highly deferential standard are spelled out in detail in the *Moog Industries* opinion, mainly agency expertise and Congress's delegation of discretion to the agency, not the courts:

> ### Sidebar
>
> **DISCRIMINATORY ENFORCEMENT CLAIMS**
>
> Most discriminatory enforcement claims are not made simply on the basis that the agency has chosen one subject for enforcement while allowing others to continue the same practice. Rather, these claims typically include an allegation that singling out the enforcement target will have special harm, for example by making it difficult for the target to compete with others who are still free to engage in the unlawful conduct.

[I]n the shaping of its remedies within the framework of regulatory legislation, an agency is called upon to exercise its specialized, experienced judgment. Thus, the decision as to whether or not an order against one firm to cease and desist from engaging in illegal price discrimination should go into effect before others are similarly prohibited depends on a variety of factors peculiarly within the expert understanding of the Commission. Only the Commission, for example, is competent to make an initial determination as to whether and to what extent there is a relevant "industry" within which the particular respondent competes and whether or not the nature of that competition is such as to indicate identical treatment of the entire industry by an enforcement agency. Moreover, . . . whether all firms in the industry should be dealt with in a single proceeding or should receive individualized treatment are questions that call for discretionary determination by the administrative agency. . . . Furthermore, the Commission alone is empowered to develop that enforcement policy best calculated to achieve the ends contemplated by Congress and to allocate its available funds and personnel in such a way as to execute its policy efficiently and economically.

355 U.S. at 314.

The patent abuse of discretion standard is intended to make it very difficult for a regulated party to prevail on a discriminatory enforcement claim. The Court has not stated with clarity what facts might lead to a finding of improper discriminatory enforcement. In its single decision applying the standard subsequent to *Moog Industries*, the Court rejected a claim without requiring much of an explanation from the agency. In *FTC v. Universal Rundle Corp.*, 387 U.S. 244 (1967), for example, the Court rejected Universal Rundle's attempt to meet the "patent abuse of discretion" standard. The Federal Trade Commission (FTC) had ordered Universal Rundle to cease and desist from offering its customers truckload discounts on plumbing supplies because, according to the FTC, the discounts had an anticompetitive effect since customers receiving the discount were in competition with customers not receiving the discount. Universal Rundle argued that (1) all major plumbing manufacturers offered the same truckload discounts; (2) it had only 5.75 percent of the market while its competitors' market shares ranged from 6 percent to 32 percent; and (3) it would be forced out of business if it could not offer the truckload discounts while its competitors continued to do so. The Supreme Court rejected the claim, relying primarily on the ground that Universal Rundle's evidence did not conclusively show that the discounts offered by competitors had the same anticompetitive effect as those offered by Universal Rundle. However, the Court also stated that even if Universal Rundle had shown that its competitors were engaged in illegal conduct, the FTC might still have discretion to enforce its order against Universal Rundle without also prosecuting the other companies. The patent abuse of discretion standard appears to require only that the agency articulate some rational basis for not proceeding against all competitors simultaneously.

Discriminatory enforcement claims have also not succeeded when focused on the stringency of sanctions for regulatory violations. Parties have argued that agencies have imposed overly harsh sanctions for violations — either compared to sanctions imposed on others or under agency policy regarding sanctions. The Supreme Court is not sympathetic to such claims and has held that, absent statutory restrictions, an agency is free to impose whatever sanctions are within its statutory power: "[A] sanction within the authority of an administrative agency is . . . not rendered invalid . . . because it is more severe than sanctions imposed in other cases." *Butz v. Glover Livestock Commission Co.*, 411 U.S. 182 (1973). This holding effectively rejects any consistency requirement regarding the severity of sanctions. The governing principle appears to be that agencies may impose any sanction within their statutory authority without regard to how the sanction compares to that imposed on others.

F   A   Q

Q: Why are discriminatory enforcement claims even reviewable?

A: Because the party raising a discriminatory enforcement or discriminatory sanctions claim is resisting enforcement of an agency order, the claim does not present the same reviewability problems as a claim that an agency has improperly failed to bring an enforcement action against a third party. However, the same policies of deferring to agency expertise and discretion in setting enforcement priorities that typically make non-enforcement claims unreviewable are behind the very deferential standards of review applied to discriminatory enforcement and discriminatory sanctions claims.

(4) Constitutionally Based Claims of Discriminatory Enforcement

The law is less deferential to agency discretion when an enforcement target raises a credible claim of unconstitutional **discrimination**. The landmark case of *Yick Wo v. Hopkins*, 118 U.S. 356 (1886), established the principle that an agency may not engage in invidious discrimination. In other words, an agency, whether it is a municipal government or an administrative agency, may not base its choice of enforcement subjects on a suspect classification. In *Yick Wo*, the Court held a municipality violated equal protection when it enforced a ban on wooden laundry buildings against Chinese-owned laundries only and not against other laundries.

Enforcement targets sometimes raise free speech concerns. For example, when outspoken criticism of an agency or the program the agency administers appears to trigger enforcement, the regulated party may claim that the prosecution punishes or chills speech in violation of the First Amendment. This claim has not been as successful as constitutional claims based on invidious discrimination.

The First Amendment issues are best illustrated by a case involving draft registration. The Selective Service System adopted a policy of "passive enforcement" under which it would refer for prosecution only the cases of people who openly identified themselves as having failed to register and those who were reported by third parties. When Wayte, an outspoken critic of the military who publicly identified himself as not having registered, was prosecuted, he claimed that the prosecution was in retaliation for speaking out against the draft — in violation of his free speech rights. The Supreme Court, in *Wayte v. United States*, 470 U.S. 598 (1985), rejected this claim, holding that the defendant was prosecuted not because he spoke out against the draft but rather because he identified himself to the Service as a non-registrant. The decision does not clarify, however, the circumstances under which a claim based on agency prosecution as retaliation for criticism of the agency would succeed.

In some circumstances, invidious discrimination may not be necessary to make out a claim of discriminatory denial of a permit or license (as distinguished from enforcement). There are numerous cases involving mainly local permitting agencies in which reviewing courts enforce a non-discrimination norm. In the typical case, a private party applies for a permit such as a building permit or business license, and after the permit or license is denied, the party alleges on judicial review that other similar applications had been granted and that the permitting agency had not articulated a basis for distinguishing the denied application from those that had been granted. In many state courts reviewing local government permitting decisions, an agency's inability to explain why one application was denied while another was granted is a strong basis for overturning the denial.

Sometimes, applicants cast these claims as allegations of equal protection violations. These have been referred to as **"classification of one"** claims because in effect the complainant is alleging that he or she has been singled out for negative treatment as compared to everyone else. The Supreme Court accepted such a claim in *Village of Willowbrook v. Olech*, 528 U.S. 562 (2000). In that case, the Village of Willowbrook determined that it would deny Olech a permit to connect to the municipal water system unless Olech granted the village a thirty-three-foot easement when it had required others to grant only a fifteen-foot easement. The Court stated that "[o]ur cases have recognized successful equal protection claims brought by a 'class of one,' where the plaintiff alleges that she has been intentionally treated differently from others similarly situated and that there is no rational basis for the difference in treatment." Id. at 564.

Justice Breyer, in a concurring opinion, raised the concern that the decision would convert routine violations of local land use rules into constitutional violations. He would have based the decision on the lower court's finding that the village's actions were motivated by subjective ill will toward the plaintiffs. The majority, however, disclaimed that rationale and held that the village violated equal protection by treating Olech differently than other similarly situated applicants. It remains to be seen whether Justice Breyer's fears will be borne out.

F   A   Q

Q: Why did the majority in *Olech* not adopt Justice Breyer's subjective ill-will standard for "class of one" equal protection claims?

A: The majority may have viewed the subjective ill-will standard as potentially converting even more routine cases into constitutional violations than its irrationality standard for classification-of-one cases. Enforcement subjects often get into verbal disputes with government enforcement agents, and thus many enforcement subjects may find it relatively easy to support allegations of subjective ill will with facts drawn from heated conversations and the like. It could expand the reach of the equal protection clause enormously if a violation is found every time it is shown that there is ill will between government officials and subjects of regulation.

(5) Due Process and Enforcement

In their zeal to enforce regulatory rules, agencies may threaten the due process interests of regulated parties. In the criminal context, a party charged with a crime is entitled to a jury trial on all the elements of the crime. Due process places similar constraints on agency enforcement action. A regulated party charged with violating regulatory requirements must be provided with a hearing at some point to contest any penalty imposed. This principle was at work in *Tennessee Valley Authority v. Whitman*, 336 F.3d 1236 (D.C. Cir. 2003). In that case, after finding that the TVA had violated the Clean Air Act by renovating nine coal-fired power plants without permits, the EPA issued an "administrative compliance order" (ACO) that required the TVA to undertake expensive compliance efforts as punishment for the violations. Under the applicable statutes and regulations, the EPA argued that ACOs had the force of law and could be appealed only within the agency to an appeals board employing informal adjudicatory procedures and without real power to reject the agency's factual determinations. The D.C. Circuit interpreted the applicable statutes and regulations to not give the ACOs the force of law, because in its view that would violate due process.

The court presented the issue as whether:

> an executive branch agency can (a) make a finding, on the basis of "any information available," that the law has been violated and (b) issue a compliance order which, if ignored, leads automatically to the imposition of severe civil penalties and perhaps imprisonment.

336 F.3d at 1256. The Court found the answer to this question pretty simple:

> The statutory scheme established by Congress — in which the head of an executive branch agency has the power to issue an order that has the status of law after finding, "on the basis of any information available," that a CAA violation has been committed — is repugnant to the Due Process Clause of the Fifth Amendment. Before the Government can impose severe civil and criminal penalties, the defendant is entitled to a full and fair hearing before an impartial tribunal "at a meaningful time and in a meaningful manner." *Armstrong v. Manzo*, 380 U.S. 545, 552 (1965). . . . [T]he scheme enacted by Congress deprives the

regulated party of a "reasonable opportunity to be heard and present evidence" on the two most crucial issues: (a) whether the conduct underlying the issuance of the ACO actually took place and (b) whether the alleged conduct amounts to a CAA violation.

336 F.3d at 1258 (footnotes omitted). The basic principle can be stated quite simply: Before an agency penalty can become final, the regulated party is entitled to a hearing on whether the party did what the agency says it did and whether the conduct proven violates applicable law. Due process prohibits the imposition of penalties without a hearing on these issues.

B. Private Liability Suits to Enforce Regulatory Requirements

Private litigation is also a method of enforcing regulatory requirements. In the non-administrative law context, victims of criminal conduct often bring tort suits against alleged criminals. In the infamous murder case involving O.J. Simpson, for example, despite Simpson's acquittal in the criminal proceeding, the families of the victims secured large civil verdicts against Simpson, predicated on a finding that he had committed the murders, albeit on the lower civil standard of proof. In the context of federal administrative law, federalism complicates this analysis, because federal jurisdiction over cases based on violation of federal regulations would displace the primacy of state law over liability in tort and contract. Some federal statutes explicitly provide for private litigation to enforce regulatory requirements. These statutory provisions are known as "citizens' suits," and they are discussed in subsection (1) below. In other cases, federal courts may imply a private right of action from a federal regulatory statute that does not contain a citizens' suit provision. Implied private rights of action are discussed in subsection (2) below.

(1) The Citizens' Suit

Many regulatory statutes, especially in the environmental area, include citizens' suit provisions under which private parties are authorized to bring suit against other private parties and government officials for violating statutes and regulations. Citizens' suits can be viewed as a supplement to agency enforcement. The sometimes slow and sporadic pace of agency enforcement provokes constant complaining from the proponents of enforcement. The citizens' suit takes the matter partially out of the agency's hands by allowing parties injured by regulatory violations to bring their own civil enforcement actions against the alleged violators. Citizens' suits bypass both the politics of the agency and limitations on agency resources, but they also may result in enforcement that is inconsistent with the judgment of the agency concerning the timing and contours of enforcement.

Citizens' suit provisions typically authorize two separate types of litigation, one directed at the agency and the other directed at violators. The provisions aimed at the agency authorize a mandamus-like remedy, allowing private individuals to bring suit to compel agency officials to take regulatory actions that they are legally required to take. For example, one subsection of the Endangered Species Act's citizens' suit provision authorizes an action by any person "against the Secretary where there is alleged a failure of the Secretary to perform any act or duty under section 1533 of this title which is not discretionary with the Secretary." 16 U.S.C. §1540(g)(1)(C). The key feature of this provision is that it addresses only nondiscretionary action such as the failure to take a required procedural step by a statutory deadline. As is explained below, it cannot be used to challenge the substance of regulations but rather only to compel the agency to take required procedural steps. The substance of agency action can be challenged only via traditional judicial review.

The citizens' suit provisions aimed at violators typically authorize "any citizen" or "any person" to seek damages, an injunction, or both against violations of the relevant statute. For example, the Endangered Species Act also provides that "any person may commence a civil suit . . . to enjoin any person, including the United States and any other governmental instrumentality or agency . . . who is alleged to be in violation of any provision of this Act or regulation issued under the authority thereof." 16 U.S.C. §1540(g)(1)(A). This type of provision authorizes injunctive suits against violators, including government agencies, when their activities violate the substantive provisions of the relevant statute, for example if the defendant's activities result in harm to an endangered species. If government agencies themselves are polluting the environment or harming endangered species, citizens' suit provisions like this apply to them just as they apply to private entities. This provision cannot be used to challenge the government's actions as a regulator. It is not a "violation" under a citizens' suit provision addressed at violators for a government agency to act improperly as a regulator—for example by adopting overly harsh or overly lenient regulations. See *Bennett v. Spear*, 520 U.S. 154 (1997). Unless a nondiscretionary duty is involved, which can be compelled under the citizens' suit provisions discussed above, challenges to government's role as regulator are typically available only through traditional judicial review.

As should be clear from this discussion, the citizens' suit can overcome agency recalcitrance both by forcing agencies to act when governing law is mandatory and by allowing private parties to enforce regulatory provisions themselves. Citizens' suits are not a complete cure for perceived defects in agency enforcement because most enforcement involves discretion and because private parties lack the resources and investigatory powers of government.

Citizens' suits do not displace traditional judicial review of agency action. Neither of the two typical citizens' suit provisions can be used to attack the substance of rules. The action to compel the performance of a mandatory agency duty essentially allows suit only when the regulator has failed to fulfill a mandatory duty, such as promulgating a regulation by a statutory deadline. Because agencies normally have a great deal of discretion over the choice of enforcement targets, it cannot be used to force an agency to enforce regulatory requirements against a violator. It can be used to compel agency enforcement only in the rare case in which a statute requires agency enforcement under stated circumstances, and then only if the existence of the stated circumstances can be discerned without threatening agency discretion.

Sidebar

QUI TAM ACTIONS

Another private enforcement method involving privately initiated litigation is the qui tam action authorized under the Federal False Claims Act. 31 U.S.C. §§3729-3733. The False Claims Act allows private citizens to assert claims on behalf of the United States government against a defendant who allegedly presented the government with a false or fraudulent claim. Private plaintiffs receive a portion of any damages recovered by the United States. The Supreme Court has held that the injury to the United States confers standing in these cases on the private plaintiffs who bring them. See *Vermont Agency of Natural Resources v. United States ex rel. Stevens*, 529 U.S. 765 (2000).

Thus, in *City of Hammond*, the Court of Appeals held that an allegation that the Clean Water Act imposes on the EPA "a nondiscretionary duty to ensure that water quality standards . . . protect the public health and welfare" was in reality a claim for judicial review of the standards adopted and not proper for a citizens' suit. *City of Hammond*, 741 F.2d at 995.

The distinction between discretionary and nondiscretionary agency duties may not always be crystal clear. For example, in *Bennett v. Spear*, 520 U.S. 154 (1997), the Court unanimously concluded that the plaintiffs could bring a citizens' suit to challenge an agency Biological Opinion on the basis that the agency had refused to take economic considerations into account. The Court noted that the ESA provides that the agency "shall designate critical habitat . . . on the basis of the best scientific data available and after taking into consideration the economic impact, and any other relevant impact." Id. at 172, quoting 16 U.S.C. §1533(b)(2). The Court concluded that the agency does not have discretion to ignore economic impact. The agency's weighing of the impacts may be discretionary, but not the determination of whether to consider the economic impact. Whether the agency has discretion over the determination of what other impacts are "relevant" remains to be seen.

In *Bennett v. Spear*, the Court provided several reasons for the conclusion that citizens' suit "violation" provisions do not address regulatory failures. First, the contrary reading would

S i d e b a r

CITIZENS' SUITS AND JUDICIAL REVIEW

Citizens' suit provisions cannot be used as a substitute for judicial review. The action to compel nondiscretionary government action does not work because the regulator normally has discretion over the content of regulations. See *Scott v. City of Hammond*, 741 F.2d 992 (7th Cir. 1984). The citizens' suit to enjoin a violation of a regulatory action cannot be used to challenge the substance of regulations because government is not "in violation" of a regulatory statute within the meaning of the citizens' suit provision even if it promulgates regulations that are contrary to the language or intent of the regulatory statute. *Bennett v. Spear*, 520 U.S. 154 (1997). "Violation" in this context means taking the action addressed by the statute, such as discharging pollutants into the air or water or taking an endangered species, not failing to fulfill obligations of a regulator.

render the mandatory duty citizens' suit provisions of the ESA "superfluous" because any failure to perform a nondiscretionary duty would also be a violation of the relevant regulatory statute. Second, the enforcement provisions of regulatory statutes such as the ESA provide for fines and other penalties against violators. It is beyond reason to imagine that Congress intended to assess fines against the EPA if its regulations under the ESA turn out to be legally insufficient. Finally, reading "violation" to include regulatory failure would allow litigants to avoid the APA's finality requirement and allow interested parties to challenge every regulatory failure in court immediately. Thus, a challenge to the substance of regulatory action cannot be raised under a citizens' suit provision directed at "violations" of a regulatory statute but rather may be brought only under judicial review procedures.

One area of consistent difficulty has been the use of citizens' suits to compel agency regulation, for example when an agency fails to meet a statutory deadline, or when an agency fails to act where Congress has statutorily required it to act. If the duty to act is mandatory, the citizens' suit provision for nondiscretionary duty may be an appropriate vehicle for compelling agency action. However, given judicial reluctance to compel agencies to act, it must be clear that the agency had no discretion for the citizens' suit to apply. A more promising avenue to compel agency regulation is judicial review of the denial of a petition for regulation. APA §553(e) requires agencies to receive petitions for the issuance of a rule. The Supreme Court recently held that the denial of a petition to make a rule is subject to judicial review, albeit on a highly deferential version of the arbitrary and capricious standard of review. See *Massachusetts v. EPA*, 549 U.S. 497 (2007). For further discussion, see Chapter 3.

F   A   Q

Q: What effect do citizens' suit provisions have on the application of standing rules?

A: Standing rules limit the utility of the citizens' suit. Although citizens' suit provisions appear to grant everyone the right to sue over violations of the relevant statute, the Supreme Court has made it clear that normal standing rules apply to citizens' suits. This is discussed further in Chapter 3. Congress may not authorize federal court jurisdiction over claims that do not meet Article III's case or controversy requirements. Citizens' suit plaintiffs must meet Article III standing requirements, including the requirement that they be among those actually injured by the alleged violation or agency failure that is the subject of the lawsuit. See *Lujan v. Defenders of Wildlife*, 504 U.S. 555 (1992). For citizens' suit plaintiffs to have standing to seek injunctive relief, they must show that they will benefit from the injunction in some concrete way.

However, citizens' suit provisions expand standing by overruling prudential limits that typically deny standing to interested third parties. For example, the Supreme Court has held that citizens' suit provisions override the zone of interests test by bringing all potential plaintiffs identified by the citizens' suit provisions within the zone of interests. See *Bennett v. Spear*, 520 U.S. 154 (1997). See Chapter 3. However, if a citizens' suit provision is more narrowly drawn, so that only a particular class of citizens is granted the right to sue, prudential limitations still apply to those outside the favored class.

Sidebar

IMPLIED RIGHTS OF ACTION AND CITIZENS' SUITS

Implied private rights of action overlap with citizens' suits but only partially. Citizens' suit provisions usually provide for actions against violators and against government for failure to properly enforce the law. Implied private rights of action normally involve only the former situation — one private party suing another private party based on the violation of regulatory requirements.

(2) Implied Private Rights of Action

Even in the absence of a citizens' suit or other provision authorizing a private claim, victims of regulatory violations can sometimes bring suit in federal court for damages or injunctive relief. Because there is no explicit right of action, these situations are referred to as "implied rights of action." An implied private right of action under a regulatory statute is a claim brought by an injured private party against another private party based on the defendant's violation of the regulatory statute. The action may be for damages or injunctive relief, depending on normal rules regarding appropriate remedies. The necessity of implying the right of action arises because many regulatory statutes provide for enforcement only by the relevant federal agency or by the Department of Justice through a criminal prosecution. If the federal regulatory statute contains a citizens' suit provision, the private action is available according to that provision and there is no reason to imply one.

Over the years, the test for whether a federal court should imply the right of action has evolved. At one time, federal courts liberally recognized private rights of action whenever doing so would advance the purposes of the underlying regulatory provision. Now, the inquiry focuses almost exclusively on Congress's intent regarding the private right of action.

Implied rights of action are controversial primarily because they provide federal jurisdiction and a federal claim in areas of traditional state authority. For example, if a private right of action is implied under federal laws regulating securities fraud, the federal action runs parallel to the traditional state common law action for fraud. Implied rights of action are also controversial because they involve judicial creation of a federal claim when Congress has not created a federal claim in a citizens' suit provision. Unlike state courts with common law powers, the general view is that federal courts should not create causes of action but should rather leave that task to Congress. The federalism concern discussed above reinforces this view — Congress, with representatives drawn from the states, should decide whether to create federal claims and federal jurisdiction over claims similar to those traditionally heard in state court under state law.

The implied private right of action is similar to state tort law's use of regulatory statutes to provide the standard of care in a tort action. However, there are important differences that make the federal implied right of action less well established than the use of regulatory standards in state tort law. In the state law case, the cause of action is established by the relevant branch of state law (usually tort law) and the state courts have general jurisdiction over all such claims. The only issue in state court is whether the regulatory statute should supply the standard of care to be applied to that preexisting cause of action. The issue in the implied right of action cases is *whether there should be a cause of action at all*. Because an implied right of action under a federal statute results in federal jurisdiction under the general federal question jurisdiction provision of the federal judicial code, recognizing the cause of action also results in federal jurisdiction over a claim that would otherwise be heard in state court. Without the private right of action, the plaintiff would be left to whatever remedies, if any, exist under state law and the case would be heard in state court.

In the 1960s, the federal courts took an expansive view of federal jurisdiction mainly in the area of civil rights enforcement, but also toward implying rights of action under regulatory statutes. At first, the federal courts analogized to state doctrines that used regulatory statutes to supply standards of conduct and held that a private right of action would be implied whenever the private right of action was "necessary to make effective the congressional purpose." See *J.I.*

Sidebar

SECURITIES LAW PRIVATE RIGHTS OF ACTION

Implied rights of action under federal regulatory statutes are well established under some federal securities laws. For example, §10(b) of the Securities Exchange Act of 1934, 15 U.S.C. §78j, prohibits, "in connection with the purchase or sale of any [registered] security" the use of "manipulative or deceptive" devices "in contravention of [the] rules and regulations" of the Securities Exchange Commission (SEC). An SEC rule, known as Rule 10b-5, prohibits fraudulent and deceitful devices in connection with the purchase and sale of registered securities. The Supreme Court has upheld private rights of action under the SEC's rule. See *Superintendent of Insurance of New York v. Bankers Life & Casualty Co.*, 404 U.S. 6 (1971). Had the Court not so ruled, the plaintiffs would have had only state law fraud claims, which might not be as easy to prove as the federal claims under §10b and Rule 10b-5. Because the implied private right of action was implied under a federal regulatory statute, the federal courts had jurisdiction to hear the claims.

Case v. Borak, 377 U.S. 426, 430 (1964). By "necessary" the Court did not mean essential or absolutely necessary, but rather something more akin to the use of the word "necessary" in the Constitution's Necessary and Proper Clause — i.e., tending to advance the purposes of the federal law. This test allowed private rights of action under a broad range of federal regulatory statutes that did not explicitly provide a private right of action.

The *J.I. Case* test was criticized for allowing private rights of action in situations that Congress may not have intended and for federalizing claims in areas that had previously been under state control. The Court attempted to tighten up on implied private rights of action in *Cort v. Ash*, 422 U.S. 66 (1975). In *Cort*, the Court of Appeals had implied a private right of action brought by shareholders on behalf of a corporation against officers who had violated a federal criminal prohibition against making campaign donations out of corporate funds. (Without a private right of action, the federal criminal statute would be enforced only if the Department of Justice initiated a criminal prosecution.) The Court stated that henceforth, claims that a private right of action should be implied from a regulatory statute would be judged on four factors:

1. whether the plaintiff is a member of a class intended to benefit from the statute;
2. whether Congress intended a right of action to exist;
3. whether implying a private right of action would advance Congress's purposes in enacting the regulatory statute; and
4. whether the implied right of action would address matters traditionally regulated by states.

While these factors do not appear to be much, if at all, more restrictive than the test applied in *J.I. Case*, the *Cort* opinion applied them in a very restrictive manner to deny the implied right of action in that case. On the first factor, the Supreme Court stated that the criminal prohibition on using corporate funds to make campaign contributions was meant primarily to protect voters from corporate influence — not to protect corporations and stockholders from depletion of corporate funds. On the second factor, the Supreme Court could find no evidence of congressional intent either way. To the Court, this meant that the expectation probably was that state law would continue to govern the relationship among the corporation, its shareholders, and its officers. On the third factor, the Supreme Court observed that forcing the officers of the corporation to repay the funds would not undo the impact those funds had on the election, and thus the private right would not advance the congressional purpose. This conclusion seems wrong. A personal obligation of corporate officers to repay the funds would certainly deter violations in the future, and thus would provide some protection to the electoral process. The fourth factor, according to the Supreme Court, weighed against recognizing the right of action because corporate law has traditionally been the province of state regulation.

Although *Cort v. Ash* was intended to tighten up on allowing implied private rights of action, it was widely perceived as a failure because the four factors still allowed federal courts to imply rights of action when Congress may not have intended them. Thus, *Cort* was followed by a strong movement toward further tightening of the standard for recognizing a private right of action, influenced heavily by Justice Powell's dissenting opinion in *Cannon v. University of Chicago*, 441 U.S. 677 (1979). In *Cannon*, the Court implied a private right of action under a statute that prohibits sex discrimination by institutions that receive federal educational subsidies. The only enforcement method provided in the statute itself is that the

Department of Education can cut off federal funds to violators. Justice Powell, in dissent, argued forcefully that federal courts should never allow private rights of action under regulatory or criminal statutes without compelling evidence that Congress intended to recognize private actions. Implicit in his analysis is the notion that the absence of a citizens' suit provision is strong evidence that Congress did not intend a private right of action, because if it did it could easily have written it into the statute. As a political reality, Justice Powell noted that whenever Congress fails to include a private right of action in the legislation itself, it must mean that any such proposal would have been voted down.

Although Justice Powell was in the minority in *Cannon*, the Supreme Court subsequently adopted Justice Powell's general skepticism about private rights of action. In *Karahalios v. National Federation of Federal Employees*, 489 U.S. 527 (1989), the Court rejected a fairly strong claim in favor of an implied private right of action, and stated that in the future, federal courts should not imply a private right of action under a federal regulatory statute unless it is clear that, although Congress failed to write the private action into the statute, it intended that the courts recognize it. The Court did not explicitly overrule *Cort v. Ash*, but instead recharacterized it in a way that is inconsistent with *Cort*'s language, stating, "Congress was undoubtedly aware from our cases such as *Cort v. Ash* . . . that the Court had departed from its prior standard for resolving a claim urging that an implied statutory cause of action should be recognized, and that such issues were being resolved by a straightforward inquiry into whether Congress intended to provide a private cause of action." *Karahalios*, 489 U.S. at 536. Thus, if the other three *Cort* factors are still relevant, it is only as aids for determining congressional intent. At bottom, the opinion in *Karahalios* stands for the proposition that Congress, and not the federal courts, should determine whether to create a private cause of action based on violation of a regulatory statute.

> ## Sidebar
>
> **IMPLIED RIGHTS OF ACTION AND SEPARATION OF POWERS**
>
> In his *Cannon* dissent, Justice Powell argued that judicial implication of a private right of action violated separation of powers because it placed the federal courts in a legislative role. This argument reflects the understanding that federal courts are not supposed to exercise the high degree of creativity of typical state common law courts.

SUMMARY

- Enforcement through command and control regulation involves agencies promulgating and enforcing specific commands. More specific commands, such as precise engineering standards, may be easier to enforce, but they are potentially costly in terms of lost flexibility and innovation.

- Agencies usually have a great deal of discretion in choosing enforcement targets. This allows agencies to prioritize, but it also has the potential for abuse in the form of favoritism based on factors such as political loyalty that are unrelated to regulatory goals.

- Agencies have a great deal of discretion over whether to regulate and over the choice of targets for enforcement action. Clear statutory standards that define when an agency must act and how an agency must choose its enforcement targets can narrow that discretion.

■ Agency enforcement targets sometimes argue against enforcement on the ground that their competitors are committing the same violation that they have been found guilty of, and it is unfair for the agency to single them out for enforcement without bringing enforcement actions against their competitors also. The standard for evaluating such discriminatory enforcement claims is "patent abuse of discretion." This standard is highly deferential and challengers rarely prevail.

■ The courts also have been very deferential to agency choices regarding the severity of sanctions in a particular case. In general, courts will approve the imposition of any sanction within statutory limits.

■ Due process requires a hearing before an agency can finally impose a penalty.

■ Citizens' suit provisions in many regulatory statutes allow injunctive actions against violators (including the government) and mandamus-like actions against the government when the claims involve the government as regulator.

■ The citizens' suit cannot be used as a substitute for judicial review of regulations. The government is not considered a "violator" of a regulatory statute if it allegedly fails to regulate properly. Citizens' suit provisions for suing government officials over their regulatory actions normally address only nondiscretionary duties, and there is usually discretion regarding the content of regulations.

■ Agency regulatory failings not involving the failure to perform a nondiscretionary duty are addressed on judicial review, not in the context of a citizens' suit.

■ Citizens' suit provisions override prudential standing limitations and bring all statutorily identified plaintiffs within the zone of interests but they cannot override Article III standing requirements such as injury, traceability, and remediability.

■ If there is no citizens' suit provision in a regulatory statute, a private right of action against a violator for damages may be implied. At one time, federal courts did this liberally, whenever the purposes of the statute would be advanced by allowing the private damages action. Because of separation of powers concerns over judicial creation of a cause of action, under current law, federal courts imply the private right of action only when it appears that Congress intended for the private right of action to be available. Implication of rights of action should be rare because if Congress really wants there to be a private right of action, it can easily include a citizens' suit provision in the regulatory statute.

CONNECTIONS

Reviewability and Enforcement Discretion
For more discussion of issues surrounding the reviewability of the exercise of enforcement discretion, see Chapter 3.

Particular Enforcement Methods

Particular enforcement methods are discussed in other chapters, including inspections, which are discussed in Chapter 13, licensing and ratemaking, which is discussed in Chapter 11, and liability of government and government officials, which is discussed in Chapter 13.

Due Process and Agency Enforcement

The due process rights of an enforcement subject may be violated if the state enforcement agency is dominated by individuals who have pecuniary interests in punishing the subject, for example to eliminate competition. This is discussed more fully in Chapter 8.

Standing and Citizens' Suits

The standing rules that apply to citizens' suits are discussed in Chapter 3. These include the basic constitutional requirements and the zone of interests test, which is usually not an issue when there is a citizens' suit provision.

Licensing and Ratemaking

10

OVERVIEW

Licensing and ratemaking are important enforcement methods that government uses to regulate industries. Licensing schemes condition entrance into an industry or profession on procuring a license from a government agency. Ratemaking schemes employ an administrative process to set prices and other terms of doing business.

The most prominent licensing scheme in the history of U.S. federal administrative law is broadcast licensing. The "public interest, convenience, and necessity" standard for awarding broadcast licenses gives the Federal Communications Commission (FCC) a great deal of discretion in licensing proceedings. The FCC cannot deny a license without offering the applicant a "full hearing" unless, as the *Storer* decision makes clear, it is apparent from the application or other pleadings that the applicant does not meet a statutory or valid regulatory standard. When there are competing applications for a new frequency, the *Ashbacker* decision holds that the FCC may not grant one application without holding a hearing on both, because the Court views the grant of one as effectively denying the other. The FCC may narrow the scope of its licensing hearings by promulgating regulations that make its general licensing standard more concrete and particular.

Comparative hearings are now very rare. Until 1996, the Communications Act did not distinguish between initial licensing standards and renewal standards. Thus, the FCC was required to hold comparative hearings between the incumbent and a competing applicant when a renewal was challenged. Under the 1996 Act, if the incumbent's past service is sufficient, and there have been no major violations of the Act or regulations, the FCC should grant renewal without a comparative hearing.

> Ratemaking is the process for establishing rates and terms of service in a regulated industry. Ratemaking agencies also often manage competition by restricting entry into an industry. Most ratemaking procedures begin with the filing of a tariff containing a schedule of proposed rates with the ratemaking agency. Ratemaking agencies normally must offer hearings before finally setting rates, although in recent years, with deregulation, tariffs may go into effect automatically unless the agency rejects them.

A. LICENSING

    1. Occupational Licensing
    2. Broadcast Licensing Procedures

B. RATEMAKING AND FILED TARIFFS

A. Licensing

Licenses are needed to engage in many professions and to operate in many industries. In such cases, licenses are obtained from administrative agencies whose actions are subject to judicial review. Most **occupational** and **business licensing** is done by states, and federal involvement in state licensing occurs only when a federal issue arises, such as a due process problem with licensing procedures. However, there are federal licensing schemes, most prominently Federal Communications Commission (FCC) broadcast licensing, and thus federal licensing norms have developed.

(1) Occupational Licensing

A common form of state licensing is occupational and professional licensing. Doctors, lawyers, optometrists, pharmacists, hair stylists, truck drivers, and dozens of additional professionals must obtain licenses from the state in order to engage in their professions. Business licensing is similar to occupational licensing but applies to a business entity. For example, a company operating a restaurant needs a license to serve alcoholic beverages and a company operating a casino needs a gambling license to operate the casino. While the substance and procedures for licenses vary from state to state, some common factors can be discerned. Occupational and professional licensing schemes typically impose minimum educational requirements, such as a law degree for lawyers or a certain number of hours of training for hair stylists. Usually, the education must be received at an accredited educational institution. They often require the applicant to pass an examination such as the bar examination for lawyers. The licensing schemes frequently include ethical standards administered by the licensing board, and provide that the board can impose discipline and even license suspension or revocation for disciplinary violations. It is widely accepted that occupational and professional licensing is well within the police powers of the state.

    Because legal standards normally govern the grant, denial, renewal, and revocation of professional licenses, such licenses are considered property under the

Roth test (see Chapter 8) and are protected by due process. In many situations, licensing boards make final determinations in formal adjudication governed by the entire range of due process rights. In addition to common issues concerning the fairness of procedures at particular hearings, licensing boards tend to present special due process issues concerning bias and prejudgment because of the combination of various functions within a single agency and because licensing boards are sometimes dominated by a particular segment of the regulated profession.

The combination of functions within licensing agencies can raise due process concerns. Licensing boards, like many agencies, often combine several functions in one body. For example, the same agency may accept and evaluate applications, investigate allegations of misconduct by licensed professionals, and adjudicate disciplinary cases and challenges to denials of applications. It should be noted that this structure is common in other regulatory agencies as well. The Supreme Court has found no per se due process violation in this combination of functions. Note that a contrary decision would invalidate numerous state and federal regulatory and licensing agencies.

Withrow v. Larkin, 421 U.S. 35 (1975), is a decision that approved in principle, against a due process challenge, the combination of functions typical of modern regulatory agencies. The case involved a state medical board proceeding against a doctor who was alleged to be performing abortions, which were illegal at the time. The Wisconsin State Medical Examining Board, which licenses doctors in Wisconsin, investigated whether Larkin was performing abortions and ultimately filed formal charges against Larkin. It set a date for a hearing at which it would preside. Although the federal district court had twice refused to enjoin the Board's investigative proceedings, which included hearings at which evidence was taken, it did issue a preliminary injunction against the holding of a disciplinary hearing after the investigative proceedings resulted in the filing of charges.

After the preliminary injunction against the disciplinary hearing was issued, the Board reconvened the investigative hearing, and then issued a formal finding of probable cause to believe that Larkin had violated state criminal law. The Board referred the matter to the state prosecutor. However, a three judge district court issued a preliminary injunction on due process grounds against the Board holding its disciplinary hearing against Dr. Larkin, stating that "[i]nsofar as §448.18(7) authorizes a procedure wherein a physician stands to lose his liberty or property, absent the intervention of an independent, neutral and detached decision maker, we concluded that it was unconstitutional and unenforceable." *Larkin v. Withrow*, 368 F. Supp. 796, 797 (E.D. Wis. 1973). Although the District Court did not elaborate very much on the basis of its decision, it appears that the court was most concerned that at the hearing the Board would be evaluating its own charges based on its own investigation. The court apparently did not believe that it would be reasonable to expect the Board to conduct a fair hearing on its own charges and investigation.

The Board appealed the preliminary injunction to the Supreme Court. The Supreme Court reversed, finding that the Board would not violate due process by

PREJUDGMENT AND COMBINATION OF FUNCTIONS

In adjudication, as discussed in Chapter 8, a decisionmaker is disqualified if to a reasonable observer it appears that the decisionmaker has in some measure prejudged the facts or the law in advance of hearing the case. The big question for administrative law is whether prejudgment inheres in the combination of investigatory, prosecutorial, and adjudicatory functions.

holding the hearing, and that it is not unfair for the same body to investigate, find probable cause, and preside over an adjudication of the charges. The Court noted that this is a common structure in state and federal agencies and that absent specific evidence of bias, the law presumes that administrators act fairly. It was also noted that in criminal cases, judges often preside at trials after issuing arrest warrants and finding probable cause at preliminary hearings in the same case.

The decision in *Withrow v. Larkin* should be understood as general approval of the combination of investigatory, prosecutorial, and adjudicatory functions in a single agency.

The *Withrow* Court did leave open the possibility that bias in a particular case would violate due process. Occupational licensing often presents the potential for bias due to self-interest because the licensing board may be dominated by one segment of a profession seeking to avoid competition from another segment. The ability to eliminate competition could give the members of a licensing board an interest in the outcome of a proceeding before it. If so, due process considerations may preclude the board from hearing it.

In *Gibson v. Berryhill*, 411 U.S. 564 (1973), the capture of a state licensing board by one segment of a business led the Court to invalidate that board's actions on due process grounds. The Alabama Board of Optometry, which had licensing and disciplinary authority over optometrists in the state, was composed solely of independent optometrists. After the governing state statute was amended, removing all references to optometrists practicing under trade names and as employees of corporations (referred to in what follows as "non-independent optometrists"), the Board initiated an investigation and other proceedings against non-independent optometrists. Ultimately, the Board brought charges in court against non-independent optometrists and also issued an administrative complaint, which would be heard by the Board itself against optometrists working for a corporation. The complaint set out violations of state law bans on, inter alia, practicing under a trade name and sharing fees with a non-optometrist employer. These provisions were typical of state law restrictions on professions like optometry and still exist in many states for other professionals, such as lawyers.

The non-independent optometrists brought suit in federal court to enjoin the proceedings in the Board on the ground that the Board was biased because it was composed exclusively of independent optometrists and had prejudged the case since it had issued the complaint against the non-independent optometrists. The Supreme Court ruled against the Board, but only on the basis of bias. The Court held that because the Board members were in competition with the subjects of the hearing, the Board's self-interest in the outcome of the case meant that board adjudication of the disciplinary proceeding violated due process.

The decision in *Gibson* is not as far reaching as it may seem for two reasons. First, the Court did not reach the claim that by issuing the complaint, the agency had prejudged the proceeding. This is understandable because had the Court reached this claim and ruled against the agency, it would have threatened the structure of the countless state and federal agencies that issue complaints and preside at the hearings on whether the allegations in the complaint are true.

Second, in a subsequent decision, the Court confined its holding in *Gibson* to disciplinary proceedings, holding that it did not necessarily violate the Constitution for a state to hand over non-disciplinary enforcement of a regulatory scheme to an agency dominated by one segment of a profession. See *Friedman v. Rogers*, 440 U.S. 1 (1979). In *Friedman*, the Court held that the Texas legislature did not violate equal protection when it required that two-thirds of the members of the Texas Optometry Board (created to enforce newly legislated restrictions on non-independent optometrists) be independent optometrists. The plaintiff claimed the requirement violated equal protection because, as a non-independent optometrist, it made him ineligible for two-thirds of the seats. The Court also upheld, against a First Amendment challenge, Texas's newly enacted ban on practicing optometry under a trade name. On the main issue of the perceived unfairness of being subject to regulation by an agency dominated by the other segment of the profession, the Court held that there was nothing unconstitutional about handing over general regulatory power to the agency as constituted. The Court did point out that, under *Gibson*, subjects of disciplinary proceedings "have a constitutional right to a fair and impartial hearing in any disciplinary proceeding conducted . . . by the Board." 440 U.S. at 18. While the Court did not come out and say it in so many words, it appears that it would violate due process for the agency as constituted to preside over disciplinary proceedings against non-independent optometrists.

F   A   Q

Q: Why would the Court allow an agency that is too biased to hold disciplinary hearings to write substantive rules that may be part of the effort to eliminate competition?

A: The answer to this question involves fundamental understandings in the distinction between legislative and adjudicatory functions. The law expects a much higher degree of neutrality and independence from those conducting adjudications than it does from officials engaged in legislative functions. Recall from Chapter 7 that an administrator will not be disqualified from participating in a rulemaking based on prejudgment unless it is clear that the administrator has a closed mind on the matter, a much more lenient standard than that applied to claims of prejudgment in adjudication. This difference in treatment may be based on the fear that a stricter standard could lead to numerous challenges to regulations based on perceived biases of the decisionmakers, who are often placed into policymaking roles in order to accomplish preconceived policy goals. While we expect neutrality in adjudication, it may be unrealistic, and in fact counterproductive, to expect it in pure policymaking activities. This may not, however, be a satisfactory answer to the concern that agencies often seem to be promoting the interests of one private group over those of another private group.

(2) Broadcast Licensing Procedures

The federal government has, since World War I, regulated the use of broadcasting frequencies. On the theory that the airwaves are publicly owned, federal law has required for many years that broadcasters (and other users of the airwaves) procure licenses in order to operate. The Telecommunications Act of 1996 significantly altered some aspects of federal broadcast licensing. However, broadcast licensing disputes have often helped develop important administrative law principles. Therefore, it is useful to look at broadcast licensing controversies even though much of what follows may be more representative of legal history than current doctrine.

Broadcast licensing, as well as many other communications areas including interstate and international telephone communications, is administered by the FCC, an independent agency composed of five commissioners appointed by the President for five-year terms, no more than three of whom may be of the same political party. On the basic standard for granting a broadcast license, the Communications Act provides that "if the Commission . . . shall find that public interest, convenience, and necessity would be served by the granting thereof, it shall grant such application." 47 U.S.C. §309(a). "Public interest, convenience, and necessity" is obviously not a very clear standard, which means that the FCC has a great deal of discretion over the decision whether to grant a broadcast license. This, coupled with the FCC's administration of the procedural requirements attached to the licensing process, and the high monetary value of broadcast licenses, has led to a great deal of litigation over broadcast licensing.

Sidebar

THE LENIENT NONDELEGATION DOCTRINE

The leniency of the nondelegation doctrine is best illustrated by the acceptance of the standard "public interest, convenience, and necessity" for granting broadcast licenses. If that standard satisfies the intelligible principle standard, it seems that any standard Congress is likely to enact will also pass nondelegation muster.

The process for deciding on an application for a broadcast license is also specified in §309 of the Communications Act. The decisionmaking model is formal adjudication. Once an application is filed, the Act specifies several steps — the most important of which are detailed below. The Act grants "any party in interest" the right to file a petition opposing an application. 47 U.S.C. §309(d). The petition is treated like a pleading and must allege facts, supported by affidavits, to make a prima facie case that granting the license would not be in the "public interest, convenience, and necessity." The applicant has the right to reply to the petition. If an application and the pleadings and other matters before the Commission do not raise any "substantial and material questions of fact," the Commission may grant the application and deny any contrary petitions in a summary judgment-like proceeding without holding a hearing. 47 U.S.C. §309(d)(2).

Formal adjudication actually occurs when the Commission's initial decision is not to grant the application. When the Commission does not find, on the pleadings, that the application should be granted (either because it does not find that granting the application would be in the "public interest, convenience, and necessity" or because there are contested material issues), the Commission is required to hold "a full hearing in which the applicant and all other parties in interest shall be permitted to participate." 47 U.S.C. §309(e). The "full hearing" specified has been interpreted to mean a formal, adjudicatory hearing. The statute also specifies that "[t]he burden of proceeding with the introduction of evidence and the burden of proof shall be on the applicant, except that with respect to any issue presented by a petition to deny or a petition to enlarge the issues, such burdens shall be as determined by the Commission." 47 U.S.C. §309(e).

The entitlement to a "full hearing" before an application is denied has been interpreted to require the FCC to provide each applicant with a genuine hearing, not a pro forma observance of statutory formalities. The best illustration of this is the *Ashbacker* decision, which holds that when two applicants file competing applications at around the same time (both of which cannot be granted because they are either for the same frequency or frequencies too close together to broadcast without interference), the Commission may not grant one of the applications without holding a hearing on the other. See *Ashbacker Radio Corp. v. FCC*, 326 U.S. 327 (1945). In March 1944, the Fetzer Broadcasting Company filed an application to construct a radio station in Grand Rapids, Michigan, to operate at 1230 am, with 250 watts of power. In May of the same year, Ashbacker Radio Corp. filed an application to change the frequency of its Muskegon, Michigan, station to 1230 am, also with 250 watts of power. The FCC determined that the applications were "actually exclusive" because simultaneous operation would result in "intolerable interference" with each other.

Recall that the statute requires the "full hearing" only when the Commission determines that it cannot grant an application on the pleadings. Thus, as the Communications Act on its face allows, the FCC granted the Fetzer application on the pleadings (without a hearing) in June 1944. On the same day, the Commission set Ashbacker's application for a hearing. Ashbacker, fearing that the Fetzer grant effectively precluded the FCC from granting its application, petitioned the FCC for a hearing regarding the Fetzer application. The FCC denied this petition, stating that its grant of the Fetzer application "does not preclude the Commission, at a later date, from taking any action which it may find will serve the public interest." *Ashbacker*, 326 U.S. at 331.

F A Q

Q: What legal provisions did the FCC violate when it granted the Fetzer application and set the Ashbacker application for a hearing?

A: The FCC, by granting the Fetzer application and setting the Ashbacker application for a hearing, followed the letter of the Communications Act. Nothing in the Act states that the Commission may not grant an application on the pleadings while a competing application is still pending. The FCC's statement (in response to Ashbacker's petition) that it remained free to take any action it found in the public interest, promised Ashbacker that it would change its decision in Fetzer if it was convinced that doing so would serve the public interest.

Despite the fact that the FCC's treatment of the Fetzer and Ashbacker applications appeared to follow the letter of the law, the Supreme Court held that the Commission violated the Act by granting Fetzer's application without first holding a hearing on Ashbacker's application. The Court held that when two mutually exclusive applications have been filed, "if the grant of one effectively precludes the other, the statutory right to a hearing which Congress has accorded applicants before denial of their applications becomes an empty thing." *Ashbacker*, 326 U.S. at 330. In the Court's view, the hearing that the Commission promised Ashbacker was no longer statutorily adequate once the Commission granted Fetzer's application.

As the Court stated, "[W]here two bona fide applications are mutually exclusive the grant of one without a hearing to both deprives the loser of the opportunity which Congress chose to give him." *Ashbacker*, 326 U.S. at 333.

In order to follow the rule in *Ashbacker*, when multiple competing applications are filed, the FCC must hold a **comparative hearing** in which the relative merits of each application are compared so that the license can be awarded to the applicant who, in the eyes of the FCC, will best serve the "public interest, convenience, and necessity." Although the comparative hearing process meets the Supreme Court's requirements in *Ashbacker*, it was often criticized as not being governed by any discernible standards. In order to bring some order to the process, in 1965 the FCC issued a Policy Statement on Comparative Broadcast Hearings, which set forth the factors that the FCC would apply to comparative hearings. Even though comparative hearings are not required in many of the circumstances in which they once were, it is still interesting to consider the factors that the FCC found were relevant in such proceedings.

The FCC's policy statement on comparative hearings spells out several factors that the FCC says it considers in evaluating the merits of competing applications:

1. *Diversification of ownership of media.* The FCC's policy favors diversified ownership of mass media and thus disfavors applicants who already own media outlets including newspapers and other broadcast stations.

2. *Integration of ownership and control.* The FCC's policy favors applicants whose owners intend to participate in the management of the station and disfavors applicants who have no management role.

3. *Local ownership.* Local owners and owners who have participated in civic affairs are also favored.

4. *Superior programming that meets local needs.* The FCC's policy favors owners who propose substantially better programming than the competition. The most important indication of superior service is programming designed to meet local needs arrived at in consultation with local civic groups and other local interests.

5. *Broadcast experience.* The FCC's policy favors an applicant with broadcast experience.

6. *Unusually good past service.* The FCC views "unusually good or unusually poor" past service as important factors in comparative hearings.

7. *Efficient use of frequencies.* The FCC's policy favors efficient uses of frequencies. In other words, an application that allows greater use of the broadcast spectrum is favored over an application that tends to minimize the ability of others to use the spectrum.

8. *Good character.* The FCC's policy, and the Act itself, disfavors applicants with past conduct indicating bad character. However, the FCC's policy statement says that it will not inquire into character evidence unless the pleadings create an issue of character.

9. *Other factors not excluded.* As with many legal standards, the FCC's policy statement allows it to consider other factors not specified but that it finds relevant to determining which application would best serve "the public interest, convenience, and necessity."

While this policy statement may have been an improvement over prior practice, in which the FCC conducted comparative hearings without any advance indication of what factors were relevant to the outcome, the FCC's critics were not satisfied. They viewed the factors contained in the statement as sufficiently pliable to allow the FCC to reach whatever result it would have reached without the policy statement, especially because it reserved the right to consider factors other than those listed. This dissatisfaction reflects, at least in part, a general distrust of the FCC, which was viewed by some as influenced by political factors and illegitimate favoritism not consistent with neutral decisionmaking under the "public interest, convenience, and necessity" standard.

Just as in other areas of the law, the promise of a "full hearing" does not necessarily preclude creation and enforcement of legal rules that operate to restrict the scope of the hearing or even allow the agency to avoid the hearing altogether in some circumstances. As we saw in Chapter 6, a principle of administrative law allows agencies, by substantive rule, to restrict the scope of statutorily required hearings. A related principle holds that, in such cases, the agency must allow the regulated party to present arguments for waiving or modifying the rule in a particular case to better meet statutory concerns. This principle applies to FCC broadcast licensing regulation. The FCC may make substantive rules specifying the meaning of "public interest, convenience, and necessity" and apply those rules in subsequent licensing proceedings to restrict the issues decided at the "full hearing." *United States v. Storer Broadcasting Co.*, 351 U.S. 192 (1956).

> ### Sidebar
>
> **DISSATISFACTION WITH FCC BROADCAST LICENSING**
>
> Throughout its entire history, there has been great dissatisfaction with the FCC's regulation of television broadcasting. This may be due to a perception that the FCC is overly political and seems to favor powerful licensees over the more general public interest. Given the amount of money at stake in the industries the FCC regulates, perhaps the FCC will always receive criticism from the losers in the regulatory process.

In *Storer*, the Court addressed whether the FCC's multiple ownership rules could be applied against Storer Broadcasting to effectively preclude it from obtaining an additional broadcast license. The FCC has long preferred diversification in the ownership of broadcast stations. To prevent overconcentration of media ownership, in 1953 the FCC (in its multiple ownership rules) placed restrictions on the number of television and radio licenses that a single licensee could hold. Storer applied for a television station license in Miami and the FCC denied the application without a hearing because another license would have put Storer over the limit for station ownership established in the recently promulgated multiple ownership rules. Storer challenged the multiple ownership rules on two grounds, one substantive and one procedural. The substantive ground was that the rules violated the Communications Act by precluding the grant of a license to Storer, even if the grant was in the "public interest, convenience, and necessity." The procedural ground was that the rules denied Storer its statutorily required "full hearing" by allowing the Commission to deny the application without a hearing whenever granting a new license would violate the rules.

The Court ruled in favor of the rules and against Storer on both arguments. On the substantive argument, the Court held that the Commission is free to enact regulations making the general "public interest" standard more specific. As long as the regulations are valid under the statute and applicable standard of judicial review, they become the definition of the "public interest," and the FCC can judge the application for compliance with them, not with the more general statutory standard. On the procedural ground, the Court held that if the application reveals that the applicant would exceed the maximum allowed ownership under the rules, the Commission is free to deny the application on the pleadings without holding a full hearing. As the Court stated, "[W]e do not think Congress intended the Commission to waste time on applications that do not state a valid basis for a hearing." *Storer*, 351 U.S. at 250. In other words, the right to a "full hearing" applies only to those issues that the applicant has a legitimate basis to contest at the hearing. This is similar to judicial practice in which many issues, even entire cases, are disposed of on the pleadings or based on pre-trial summary judgment motions. The Court's only caveat was that if an application presents valid reasons for waiving the rules in a particular case, the Commission must hold a hearing on whether to waive the rules.

License renewal has long been one of the most controversial elements of broadcast licensing. Although the Act long provided that licensees have no property rights in their licenses and that licenses may be revoked or not renewed whenever such action would be in the public interest, broadcast licenses have become very valuable and for a long time, the FCC treated licensees as having a presumptive renewal right. Although the effective presumption in favor of renewal was criticized for illegitimately favoring existing license holders, one reason for a presumption in favor of renewal is that it would encourage licensees to invest in improvements to their stations.

Sidebar

AGENCY RULES AND WAIVERS

The opportunity to argue for a waiver is a common requirement whenever an agency rule limits the issues that will be addressed at a statutorily provided hearing. The requirement appears to be an effort by the Court to resolve the conflict between agency rulemaking and hearing requirements. Thus, even after *Storer*, an applicant must be given the opportunity to show that an FCC rule (like the multiple ownership rules) should not be applied for some reason in the particular case. This means, in effect, that the FCC does not have the power to place an absolutely firm limit on the number of stations each licensee may own.

F A Q

Q: If the law explicitly states that licensees have no property interests in their broadcast licenses, what entitles them to formal hearings before a license application can be denied or an existing license can be revoked?

A: The right to hearings in the broadcast licensing area is derived from governing statutes. Even if due process does not require a hearing, a statute like the Telecommunications Act can create procedural requirements that will be enforced on judicial review.

The 1996 Telecommunications Act, as discussed below, created for the first time a legal presumption in favor of renewal. Before 1996, the Act did not distinguish between an initial license determination and a renewal application. If a competitor sought to displace an incumbent license holder at renewal time, the understanding was that the FCC was required to hold a comparative hearing with the same procedures and standards as comparative hearings for new or vacant licenses. See *Ashbacker*, 326 U.S. at 332 ("licenses . . . are limited to three years, the renewals being subject to the same considerations and practices which affect the granting of initial applications").

Despite the lack of statutory support, FCC practice favored incumbent license holders that filed renewal applications. In 1970, the FCC issued a policy statement providing that it would grant renewal applications if the incumbent licensee had provided service "substantially attuned to the needs and interests of its area and [whose] operation ha[d] not otherwise been characterized by serious deficiencies." Policy Statement Concerning Comparative Hearings Involving Regular Renewal Applicants, 22 F.C.C.2d 424, 425 (1970). Because the Act at that time did not favor incumbents at renewal time, this policy statement was invalidated as inconsistent with governing law by the D.C. Circuit. *Citizens Communications Center v. FCC*, 447 F.2d 1201 (D.C. Cir. 1971). The court held that the policy statement violated the Act because, by allowing renewal based only upon the incumbent's past service, it deprived competing applicants the "full hearing" required by §309(e) and *Ashbacker*.

The FCC remained very reluctant to deny renewal in favor of competing applicants. The best example of this is a 1976 renewal controversy over a station in Florida. Cowles Florida Broadcasting, Inc., operator of a television station in Daytona Beach, Florida, faced a competing application at renewal time from Central Florida Enterprises, Inc. The FCC conducted a comparative hearing between the two applicants and in *Cowles Florida Broadcasting, Inc.*, 60 F.C.C.2d 372 (1976), the FCC granted Cowles's renewal application even though most of the comparative factors favored the competing applicant. It looked like the FCC had applied its invalidated policy statement. The primary factor relied upon by the FCC was Cowles's past service, which the ALJ had characterized as "thoroughly acceptable" but which the FCC, on review of the ALJ's decision, called "superior, meriting a plus of major significance."

Not surprisingly, on judicial review the D.C. Circuit reversed the FCC's decision, concluding that the FCC had, despite the invalidation of the 1970 policy statement, created a de facto presumption in favor of renewal. See *Central Florida Enterprises, Inc. v. FCC*, 598 F.2d 37 (D.C. Cir. 1978), *cert. dismissed*, 441 U.S. 957 (1979). The D.C. Circuit observed that Central Florida had a clear advantage on the comparative factors and noted that when the FCC looked at Cowles's past service it had shifted into a non-comparative mode, concluding only that Cowles's record was superior without comparing it to Central Florida's proposed service. As is the usual practice, the D.C. Circuit remanded the case to the FCC, and on remand, the agency reaffirmed the renewal of Cowles's license but under a reformulated renewal policy, discarding any presumption in favor of renewal, but making a renewal expectancy one factor to be considered in comparative renewal hearings. The D.C. Circuit affirmed this policy and the result in *Cowles*, but not without expressing reservations regarding the fact that no television licensee had ever lost a license in a comparative renewal hearing.

F A Q

Q: Why was the FCC so determined to prefer incumbents in the license renewal process?

A: There are two contradictory possibilities. From a cynical perspective, it might be that the FCC was basically playing favorites, finding great benefit for itself in terms of post-agency career prospects in currying favor with licensees. However, it may also be that on the merits, the FCC found that licensees with an expectation of renewal are likely to make long-term investments that would improve service to the public. Congress apparently has seen the merit in the FCC's view that a renewal expectancy encourages quality service. As noted above, the 1996 Telecommunications Act, for the first time, statutorily recognizes the incumbent license holder's renewal expectation. It provides that the FCC should grant renewal applications if the station has served the public interest and the licensee has neither committed any serious violations of the Act or FCC rules nor engaged in a pattern of less serious violations. 47 U.S.C. §309(k)(1). The FCC is no longer required to hold a comparative hearing on a contested renewal application unless the Commission first finds that the incumbent has not satisfied the standards specified above.

Even during the term for which a license has been granted, the Communications Act grants the FCC the power to revoke a broadcast license as a sanction for a wide variety of misconduct. 47 U.S.C. §312. The Commission also has the power to order a license holder to live up to promises made during the licensing process. The FCC has almost never exercised the power to revoke a license. In one renewal case, involving television stations owned by RKO General, Inc., the FCC decided not to renew licenses because of a wide range of misconduct by RKO and its parent company, General Tire, Inc. See *RKO General, Inc. (WNAC-TV)*, 78 F.C.C.2d 1 (1980). Although RKO was actually a renewal controversy, its focus on misconduct provides insight into the circumstances that might lead to license revocation or other disciplinary action.

The RKO General renewal controversy involved several possible grounds for license revocation including the following: RKO allegedly filed false financial statements with the FCC. RKO and General Tire used General Tire's market power in the tire business to increase advertising on RKO stations. General Tire engaged in a pattern of improper conduct involving fraud and payoffs to political candidates and officials of foreign governments. Most important to the Commission, RKO engaged in a persistent lack of candor in the renewal proceedings involving non-disclosure of the misconduct and nondisclosure of proceedings against General Tire in another federal agency.

The Commission listed the following issues as relevant to deciding whether misconduct should lead to nonrenewal, which are similar to issues the agency might look at relative to revocation. First, nature of the misconduct — nonrenewal is more likely if the misconduct is related to broadcast operations or if the misconduct indicates how the applicant will operate a broadcast station. Second, frequency of the misconduct — nonrenewal is more likely if the misconduct appears to be a pattern and less likely if the misconduct is an isolated incident. Third, time of the misconduct — nonrenewal is more likely for recent misconduct and less likely for misconduct completed long before the proceedings. The FCC found against RKO on all three factors. The FCC noted that RKO and its parent had engaged in substantial serious misconduct over a long period of time, continuing through the renewal proceedings. The FCC found that RKO withheld material information regarding its misconduct and the misconduct of General Tire from the FCC during the renewal proceedings on the Boston license. The FCC held that both RKO's and General Tire's conduct indicated a lack of trustworthiness and that because General Tire and RKO worked closely together, it was appropriate to attribute General Tire's misconduct to RKO. The FCC disqualified RKO from holding any broadcast licenses, which resulted in nonrenewal of the licenses involved in the proceeding and potential revocation of all other RKO licenses.

On judicial review, the D.C. Circuit was sharply critical of the substance and process of the FCC's nonrenewal decision. The court found that some of the misconduct was very old and that the agency had not paid sufficient attention to evidence that the misconduct was not willful. Most important, the court held that only the Boston license was properly subject to nonrenewal because RKO withheld information only in the specific proceeding regarding that license. This saved most of RKO's licenses from nonrenewal or revocation, although the Boston station was held subject to nonrenewal for misconduct. *RKO General Inc. v. FCC*, 670 F.2d 215 (D.C. Cir. 1981), *cert. denied*, 456 U.S. 927 (1982).

The court found that the other grounds for nonrenewal of RKO stations were inadequate for the following reasons. First, the D.C. Circuit found that RKO could not be disqualified for using General Tire's market power to gain advertising because the FCC had, in a prior case, decided that such conduct was irrelevant to fitness to hold a license, and the FCC did not explain the change in policy. Second, the court rejected the FCC's finding that RKO had knowingly falsely certified that certain financial reports were complete and accurate because, although RKO claimed in affidavits that it did not know of any inaccuracies, the FCC did not hold a hearing on the issue. Third, the court found that General Tire's non-broadcast misconduct could not justify disqualification. The court noted that the Commission itself had stated that this misconduct was not an independent ground for nonrenewal of RKO's licenses but merely supported the ultimate decision that was based primarily on other grounds. In addition to the particulars of the case, the D.C. Circuit's decision demonstrates that reviewing courts are likely to review very carefully any FCC decision that results in the nonrenewal or revocation of a broadcast license.

As the use of the airwaves has expanded into multiple communications technologies, and as technology has developed to allow more intensive use of the spectrum, the FCC's allocation of the spectrum has adapted to business realities. With spectrum used in competitive realms such as cellular telephones, the market, and not the agency, is in the best position to determine whether the quality of service is in the public interest. Over the years, the FCC increasingly allocated the use of non-broadcast frequencies by **lottery** and by **auction**. It used lotteries beginning in 1983, but they proved to be lengthy and expensive processes and were subject to arbitrary manipulation so much so that Congress has since prohibited the FCC from using lotteries to allocate spectrum. The FCC has had statutory authority to use auctions since 1993. This procedure raises revenue for the U.S. Treasury, but it does not allow the FCC to pursue its goals of diversifying and dispersing ownership of communications companies. The FCC prefers these procedures to the comparative hearing process when there are large numbers of qualified applicants, and the public interest would be best served by getting the service started quickly and in a competitive environment. These procedures avoid the delay inherent in comparative hearings and judicial review. The services for which these alternative procedures have been used include low-power television and cellular telephony.

> **Sidebar**
>
> **SALE OF FREQUENCIES**
>
> For many business uses of the broadcast spectrum, such as communications services, it makes sense for the FCC to sell the right to use the spectrum rather than allocate it in competition based on promises of superior service. The market will determine whether the licensee is making good use of the spectrum, and the agency will no longer be able to show favoritism and bias in the licensing process.

B. Ratemaking and Filed Tariffs

One of the earliest forms of regulation is **ratemaking**, in which an agency sets the rates that may be charged for a product or service. An early example of rate regulation is shipping of goods on railroads. Railroads were often built with public subsidies, and it was the norm for there to be only one railroad serving a particular route. Rate regulation was used to make sure that railroads did not charge monopoly rates for shipping goods. Similar reasoning underlies traditional ratemaking in public utilities such as electricity and natural gas service.

Related to ratemaking is regulation of competition, in which the agency restricts entry into a field and allocates areas of service among regulated businesses. For example, during the later stages of the Civil Aeronautics Board's (CAB) regulation of airline fares and routes, the CAB rejected all applications to provide service from new airlines. Although the volume of ratemaking may not be as high as it once was, there are still industries in which administrative agencies set rates or in which companies must file tariffs in an agency with power to disapprove the tariff and require different rates.

Rate regulation takes many different forms. While the three most common ratemaking procedures are discussed below, it is important to recognize that there are variations on these and many ratemaking agencies combine more than one of the models.

The first model involves **ex post challenges** to rates as unreasonable. In some industries, like common carriers such as railroads, rates for services such as shipping were subject to challenge as unreasonable after the fact. The shipper would ship the goods, perhaps even pay for the service, and then go to an agency and claim that the carrier's rates were unreasonable. If the agency with jurisdiction found the rates unreasonable, the agency would prescribe a maximum reasonable rate. For example, railroad shipping rates were set by the Interstate Commerce Commission (ICC) only after a shipper complained that a carrier was charging an "unreasonable" rate. The ICC would, after a hearing, prescribe the maximum lawful rate and order a refund of payments made in excess of the reasonable rate.

The second model involves **comprehensive analysis** resulting in ex ante rate setting. This is the model that was used in traditionally regulated utility monopolies like the electric company, the gas company, and the local telephone company. The agency sets all rates based on comprehensive analyses of the relevant markets, costs, and service needs. Usually, the regulated business proposes a rate structure, and representatives of consumers, and perhaps the state, propose alternatives. The ratemaking agency would then hold a formal adjudicatory hearing with the business and opponents participating. The process would culminate in a comprehensive order establishing rates.

The third model involves **filed tariffs** in which the regulated businesses file tariffs with an agency, and those tariffs become effective automatically unless the agency finds unlawful discrimination or some other defect. This is the model used, for example, in the long-distance telephone industry. In many cases, the agency barely looks at the filed tariff, and the principal regulatory requirement is that the regulated businesses charge their customers only the rates specified in the filed tariff. However, most filed tariff systems allow the agency to reject unreasonable rates and allow customers to challenge filed rates as unreasonable.

Typically, agencies conduct ratemaking in a hearing process, and sometimes formal hearing procedures have been prescribed. When formal hearings are required, the parties must be given the opportunity to confront the other side's evidence and contentions, and the decision-maker should not engage in ex parte contacts with other government officials.

> ## Sidebar
>
> ### THE FILED RATE DOCTRINE
>
> Under the **"filed rate doctrine,"** valid tariffs have the status of law, and with regard to federal tariffs this means that state law cannot require or even allow regulated businesses to charge rates different from those listed in the tariff.

The epic *Morgan* litigation provides an example of the stakes involved in ratemaking processes and the procedural and substantive issues that can arise. The *Morgan* cases involved a lengthy dispute over maximum rates, essentially commissions on sales, charged by market agencies engaged in the livestock market in Kansas City. The Packers and Stockyards Act allowed the Secretary of Agriculture to set the rates after a "full hearing." The Secretary of Agriculture issued an order reducing rates after consolidated hearings regarding conduct by numerous market agencies. The evidence was heard by a trial examiner. The trial examiner issued no tentative report. An acting Secretary of Agriculture heard oral arguments in the case, and only the market agencies, not the government, submitted a brief. The market agencies challenged this procedure on several grounds, including: (1) that the Secretary who was planning to make the decision had not heard or read any of the evidence and had not heard the oral arguments; (2) that the hearing examiner's findings were not subject to challenge since he did not submit a public report; and (3) that the decision was unlawfully delegated to an acting Secretary.

In *Morgan v. United States*, 298 U.S. 468 (1936) (*Morgan I*), the Court held that the statutory "full hearing" requirement meant that the Secretary must act like an adjudicator in a judicial proceeding, i.e., consider only the record evidence, and that the Act required the Secretary himself to consider the evidence on the record. The question then arose as to how a reviewing court could ensure that the Secretary of Agriculture assumed the proper role in the decisionmaking process.

On remand, the district court allowed the Secretary to be interrogated about his role in the decision. The Secretary admitted that he looked at the record only slightly and that he made his decision based primarily on the briefs, the transcript of oral argument, conferences with other agency officials, and on proposed findings prepared by the agency. The Supreme Court found the agency's process unacceptable for several reasons: (1) because the Secretary had not considered the evidence; (2) because the Secretary relied upon the views of agency officials that the regulated parties had no opportunity to rebut; and (3) because the regulated parties were not given an opportunity to rebut the proposed findings since they were not published. Although the Supreme Court held that the hearing provided was not adequate, the Court was not happy that the District Court had allowed the Secretary to be questioned about the decisionmaking process. The Court stated that "it was not the function of the court to probe the mental processes of the Secretary." *Morgan v. United States*, 304 U.S. 1, 18 (1938) (*Morgan II*). The Court stated this rule more emphatically in a subsequent decision arising out of the same controversy. *United States v. Morgan*, 313 U.S. 409 (1941) (*Morgan IV*). Although the *Morgan* decisions stand for the proposition that when Congress specifies that ratemaking is to be conducted in a "full hearing," the agency must observe proper adjudicatory procedures, they also place limits on the courts' ability to examine whether the proper officials actually examined the record and made the decision independently.

In recent years, ratemaking has fallen into disfavor as a method of regulation. This is because ratemaking has been used as a device to keep prices artificially high by restricting competition. Other times, the fast pace of changing market conditions has rendered the hearing process too slow, and the complexity of the industry has made it impossible to take into account all relevant factors in any rational way. The trend has been away from ratemaking and toward deregulation to encourage price competition. Prime examples of deregulated rates include air fares, rates for shipping goods by truck, and legal fees. The advent of competition has also substantially changed the rate structure of long-distance telephone service, which operates under a filed tariff system.

However, ratemaking agencies may not deregulate without statutory authority even if the agency finds that deregulation would best serve the public interest by resulting in better service, lower rates, or both. The FCC tried to eliminate the requirement of tariff filing for most long-distance carriers, but this attempt was rebuffed by the Supreme Court. Section 203 of the Communications Act requires long-distance telephone carriers to file tariffs with the FCC, and carriers must charge their customers the rates specified in those tariffs. The Act also allows the FCC to "modify" any requirement of §203. In a series of orders, the FCC eliminated the tariff-filing requirement for all non-dominant long-distance carriers, (i.e., all carriers except AT&T, which at one time had a monopoly on long-distance service and maintained dominance after losing its legal monopoly). AT&T sought judicial review of this order. In *MCI v. AT&T*, 512 U.S. 218 (1994), the Supreme Court in an opinion by Justice Scalia, held that the word "modify" does not include the authority to eliminate a requirement of the Act. Thus, the FCC lacked legal authority to cease to require tariffs from non-dominant carriers. The Court noted that "rate filings are, in fact, the essential characteristic of a rate-regulated industry" and that it would be impossible to enforce the FCC Act's prohibitions of overcharges and unreasonable rates without filed tariffs. 512 U.S. at 230. The Court concluded that the agency could not eliminate the rate regulation without more explicit congressional authorization.

The FCC is allowed to deregulate within statutory limits. In *National Cable & Telecommunications Ass'n v. Brand X Internet Services*, 545 U.S. 967 (2005), the Court upheld an FCC rule that characterized cable television company-supplied internet services via cable modem as "information services" rather than "telecommunications services." This classification meant that cable-supplied internet was not subject to stringent regulation as a common carrier of telecommunications. Employing the *Chevron* framework, the Court found the governing statute ambiguous and the agency's construction of the statute reasonable. Justice Scalia, in dissent, charged that the FCC had once again abused its regulatory authority by radically altering its regulatory scheme in the guise of statutory interpretation.

SUMMARY

■ Practitioners of many occupations are regulated by state authorities through licensing and disciplinary processes. These include doctors, lawyers, hairdressers, and many more occupations. Subjects of disciplinary proceedings involving professional licenses are entitled to due process, but it does not violate due process for legislative, prosecutorial, and adjudicatory functions to be combined in a single agency.

■ Due process is not violated by the combination of investigatory, prosecutorial, legislative, and adjudicative functions that is common in agencies generally and licensing agencies in particular. However, proof of bias in a particular case may violate due process.

■ If members of one segment of a profession dominate an occupational licensing agency, and they take disciplinary action to eliminate competition from another segment of the profession, the bias due to self-interest in the outcome of the disciplinary action may violate due process.

■ However, outside the context of a particular disciplinary action, domination of a licensing agency by one segment of a profession does not automatically violate due process.

■ The most prominent federal licensing scheme is broadcast licensing administered by the FCC. The "public interest, convenience, and necessity" standard for awarding broadcast licenses gives the FCC a great deal of discretion in licensing proceedings.

■ The FCC cannot deny a license without offering the applicant a "full hearing" unless it is apparent from the application or other pleadings that the applicant does not meet a statutory or valid regulatory standard.

■ When there are competing applications for a new frequency, the *Ashbacker* decision holds that the FCC may not grant one application without holding a hearing on both, because the Court views the grant of one as effectively denying the other.

■ As with other agencies, the FCC may narrow the scope of its licensing hearings by promulgating regulations that make its general licensing standard more concrete and particular. Under the *Storer* decision, the FCC may deny a hearing to an applicant whose application clearly does not satisfy a requirement of a valid regulation.

■ Until 1996, the Communications Act did not distinguish between initial licensing standards and renewal standards. Thus, before 1996, the FCC was required to hold comparative hearings between the incumbent and a competing applicant when a renewal was challenged. Under the 1996 Act, if the incumbent's past service is sufficient, and there have been no major violations of the Act or regulations, the FCC should grant renewal without a comparative hearing.

■ Ratemaking is the process for establishing prices and other terms of service in a regulated industry. Ratemaking agencies also often manage competition by restricting entry into an industry.

■ Ratemaking agencies normally must offer hearings before finally setting rates. The *Morgan* decisions hold that the official making the decision must review the evidence in the case and not merely consult with other agency officials who have considered the evidence.

■ The central feature of a ratemaking regime is the filing of a tariff, or rate schedule, by the regulated business. The filed rate doctrine holds that once filed and approved, filed rates have the status of binding law. In recent years, deregulation of markets has meant a general disfavoring of ratemaking as a form of regulation.

CONNECTIONS

Due Process and Licensing

See Chapter 8 for due process aspects of licensing and ratemaking in terms of whether there is a property or liberty interest at stake and if so what process must be provided in licensing and disciplinary proceedings.

Capture of Licensing Agencies

Capture of agencies is a big problem in licensing and ratemaking. More on disqualification is contained in Chapter 8 (adjudication) and Chapter 7 (rulemaking).

Rules in Licensing Hearings

The use of substantive rules to limit the issues in licensing hearings is similar to the general power of agencies to make rules that apply in subsequent adjudications. See Chapter 6.

Public Choice and Licensing

On capture of licensing and ratemaking agencies by a segment of the regulated industry or profession, the public choice understandings discussed in Chapter 1 are relevant.

Agency Inspections and Information Gathering

11

This chapter examines how agencies gather information and the doctrines that restrict agency information gathering. The two methods agen-

O V E R V I E W

cies use most often to gather information are inspections and requests for information or documents. Agencies may inspect the premises of regulated businesses only if they have legal authority to do so. Further, under normal circumstances, the Fourth Amendment's Warrant Clause requires an agency to obtain a search warrant to conduct an inspection without the regulated party's consent. However, probable cause that violations are occurring is not necessary to obtain a warrant for an administrative inspection. Rather, agencies may obtain warrants merely by showing that the proposed inspection is pursuant to normal, reasonable, agency standards for conducting inspections.

Pervasively regulated businesses may be inspected without warrants and recipients of government benefits may be required to consent to home inspections as a condition for continuation of benefits.

Corporations and other businesses do not have a Fifth Amendment right to withhold business records that may be incriminating.

Drug testing of government employees is allowed when public safety dictates, but it may not be applied across the board to all government employees.

Agencies have broad power to require regulated parties to produce documents and provide information as long as the information is related to an area within agency jurisdiction. The Paperwork Reduction Act requires that agencies seek the approval of the Office of Management and Budget to collect information from private parties.

A. INSPECTIONS

1. Administrative Authority to Inspect Regulated Businesses
2. Constitutional Constraints on Agency Inspection
3. The Special Case of Inspections of Homes Relating to Regulatory Schemes
4. Drug Testing

B. PRODUCTION OF INFORMATION AND DOCUMENTS

1. The Paperwork Reduction Act
2. Agency Requests for Information or Documents
3. Disclosure of Privileged Information or Trade Secrets

A. Inspections

Many agencies monitor compliance with regulatory requirements by inspecting the subjects of regulation. Commonplace examples include inspections of food processing facilities and restaurants for proper food handling practices and sanitation, inspections of workplaces for proper worker safety practices, inspections of pollution-emitting facilities for compliance with environmental requirements, and inspections of residential properties for compliance with fire and building codes. Two legal issues are relevant to inspections. First, the agency must have authority to inspect. Second, inspections are subject to constitutional constraints.

Sidebar

EXPLOSION OF GOVERNMENT REGULATION

The explosion of government regulation in recent decades means that many activities that may have once been private are now subject to government scrutiny. If it is easy for government to conduct regulatory inspections, the range of private activity that is subject to direct government scrutiny will also explode.

(1) Administrative Authority to Inspect Regulated Businesses

Agencies may not conduct inspections, or otherwise gather information, without legal authority. This is a basic principle of all government action, i.e., that government agencies may act only pursuant to legal authorization. The Administrative Procedure Act (APA) confirms this as applied to federal agencies. The APA, §555(c), provides that "[p]rocess, requirement of a report, inspection, or other investigative act or demand may not be issued, made, or enforced except as authorized by law." Thus, in addition to any other restrictions that may exist on agency information gathering, the agency must always be prepared to make the affirmative case that it has legal authority to inspect or require the production of information, documents, or reports. However, as we shall see, if the agency has statutory authorization, courts are generally very deferential to agency information-gathering efforts.

(2) Constitutional Constraints on Agency Inspection

Business premises are protected by the Fourth Amendment's restrictions on searches. *See v. Seattle*, 387 U.S. 541 (1967). Searches must be reasonable, and under most circumstances, they may be conducted only pursuant to a **warrant**. However, the Supreme Court has recognized exceptions to normal Fourth

Amendment requirements for many administrative searches. **Probable cause** in the criminal law sense is not required for warrants to conduct inspections. Further, in "pervasively regulated businesses" warrants may be unnecessary.

Under normal circumstances, a warrant is required before government agents may enter and inspect a home or business in order to monitor compliance with regulatory requirements. See *Camara v. Municipal Court*, 387 U.S. 523 (1967). In *Marshall v. Barlow's Inc.*, 436 U.S. 307 (1978), the Supreme Court held that OSHA inspectors may not enter the non-public areas of a business without permission from the business owner unless they have a warrant. OSHA had argued that they did not need a warrant because programmed administrative searches of regulated businesses are inherently reasonable. In deciding that the warrant requirement applies to regulatory inspections, the Court may have feared that had it ruled otherwise, OSHA's broad jurisdiction over workplace safety would have made almost every business in the United States subject to administrative, warrantless searches.

In recognition of the preventative nature of many administrative inspections, the Court in *Camara* and *Marshall* stated that probable cause, as required for a warrant in a criminal case, is not required to obtain a warrant for an administrative inspection. (Probable cause in criminal cases means that authorities have reason to believe that a search will reveal evidence of a crime.) Rather, an agency may obtain a warrant merely by showing that normal legislative or administrative standards for conducting an inspection are met. Thus, if an agency conducts inspections periodically or when certain predetermined circumstances are present, such as the use of a particularly dangerous process or the occurrence of a specified incident, the agency can obtain a warrant merely by showing that the regular time for an inspection has arrived or the circumstances leading to an inspection are present.

There is an important exception to the warrant requirement derived from a longstanding tradition mainly at the state level. No warrant is required to inspect the premises of a business that is subject to pervasive regulation. This departure from the warrant requirement is justified by the presumed awareness of the operator of a facility under pervasive regulation that inspections are routine and thus it has a lowered expectation of privacy, and also by the fact that the pervasive regulatory scheme provides a substitute for the safeguards provided by the Fourth Amendment's warrant requirement. See *Donovan v. Dewey*, 452 U.S. 594 (1981). Examples of pervasively regulated businesses include establishments that serve alcoholic beverages, pawnshops, junkyards and mines, and other similar establishments.

> **Sidebar**
>
> **AGENCY WARRANTS**
>
> The lenient standard under which agencies can procure warrants to conduct regulatory inspections is attuned to the realities of the administrative process but it seems to be in tension with the concern over the general warrant that led to the Fourth Amendment's requirement that "no Warrants shall issue, but upon probable cause."

The Court has imposed three requirements for dispensing with the warrant requirement for inspecting pervasively regulated businesses. First, there must be a substantial government interest underlying the regulatory scheme. Second, warrantless searches must be necessary to advance the government interest. Third, the regulatory scheme must supply standards regarding the occurrence and scope of inspections that provide an adequate substitute for the safeguards of the warrant procedure. *Donovan*, 452 U.S. at 602-04.

Two examples illustrate the application of these principles, one involving a quarry, which is pervasively regulated under standards applicable to quarries and mines, and the other involving a junkyard, which is heavily regulated due to fears about receiving stolen property. In *Donovan v. Dewey*, 452 U.S. 594 (1981), the Supreme Court upheld the right of the Department of Labor to inspect a stone quarry without a warrant. The quarry was subject to regulation and periodic inspection under the Federal Mine Safety and Health Act. The Court reasoned that no warrant was required because "the certainty and regularity of [the] application [of the inspection program] provides an adequate substitute for a warrant." *Donovan*, 452 U.S. at 603. The Court found that the Fourth Amendment interest in preventing arbitrary and oppressive searches was satisfied by the Act's specific requirements regarding the timing and scope of inspections.

In *New York v. Burger*, 482 U.S. 691 (1987), the Court upheld a warrantless inspection of an automobile junkyard. The interesting thing about this decision is that the regulation was designed to find evidence of criminal conduct, where one would think that the warrant requirement would apply. A New York statute, designed to combat auto theft, required junkyards to be licensed, required owners of junkyards to maintain a "police book" containing records of the automobiles and parts in the junkyard, and required junkyard owners to permit police to inspect automobiles and parts in the junkyard. This regulatory scheme was designed to combat trade in stolen autos and auto parts. The junkyard involved in *Burger* was not licensed and the owners had not maintained the required "police book." After an inspection turned up stolen autos and auto parts, Burger was convicted of possession of stolen property.

Burger argued that the inspection system for junkyards was not a true regulatory scheme but was, in fact, a disguised criminal enforcement effort. The Court rejected this argument, holding that the statutory licensing, recordkeeping, and inspection requirements established that junkyards in New York are closely regulated businesses within the exception to the warrant requirement. The dissent disagreed, arguing that the regulatory scheme was not extensive enough to place junkyards in the category of closely regulated businesses, that the statute lacked criteria under which Burger's junkyard was selected for inspection, and that the regulatory scheme was a pretext for criminal enforcement of the sort that should require a warrant.

(3) The Special Case of Inspections of Homes Relating to Regulatory Schemes

The private home receives a higher degree of protection from government intrusion than businesses and other nonresidential premises. Yet, even with regard to regulatory inspections of private homes, requirements for obtaining warrants have been relaxed, and some searches may be conducted without a warrant. The Supreme Court has held that homes may not be searched for compliance with building codes and the like, without a warrant. See *Camara v. Municipal Court*, 387 U.S. 523 (1967). However, warrants to conduct such searches do not require probable cause in the criminal sense but may issue if the agency establishes that the inspection is part of its normal regulatory scheme to monitor compliance with the relevant code.

Further, somewhat analogous to pervasively regulated businesses, some people's lives are pervasively involved with government in a way that requires them to consent to inspections of their homes. For example, recipients of government benefits may be required to allow welfare caseworkers to inspect their homes as a condition of continued benefits. Although private homes normally receive the most Fourth Amendment protection, the Court held in *Wyman v. James*, 400 U.S. 309 (1971), that the state of New York could require that permission for a caseworker to perform quarterly inspections of the home was a condition that had to be met before the state would provide welfare benefits to the child. The only consequence of not consenting to the search was that benefits would be cut off. To the Court, this reinforced the rehabilitative, non-punitive nature of the inspections.

Another category of "pervasively regulated persons" are people who are on probation or have been released from jail on parole or on bail awaiting trial. The Supreme Court has held that probation officers may, without a warrant or probable cause, search the homes of convicted criminals who have been placed on probation. See *Griffin v. Wisconsin*, 483 U.S. 868 (1987). In *Griffin*, the Court approved searches of probationers' homes when the probation officer had "reasonable grounds" to believe that contraband was present. The Court is likely to extend this reasoning to convicted criminals who have been released from prison on parole and to people awaiting trial, where inspection might be necessary to ensure that the people are obeying conditions of release.

(4) Drug Testing

An increasingly common form of governmental information gathering is drug testing, under which individuals are tested for the presence of alcohol and illegal drugs. In the criminal context, under normal circumstances a warrant is required to force a suspect to submit to blood testing for the presence of illegal drugs or alcohol. With regard to regulatory uses of drug testing, for example for eligibility for government employment or for student athletes, the Court evaluates drug testing programs according to several factors including the subject's expectation of privacy, the degree to which the testing program invades that privacy, the importance of the governmental interest underlying the testing program, and the degree to which the testing program's standards ameliorate the potential for arbitrary selection of individuals to be tested. Although several testing programs have been challenged, most have been upheld.

In the employment context, the Court has approved drug testing of applicants for positions in the Customs Service involving drug interdiction, carrying firearms, or access to classified information. See *National Treasury Employees Union v. Von Raab*, 489 U.S. 656 (1989). The Court found a substantial government interest in conducting the testing, relying heavily on the sensitive nature of the duties of the covered employees and the fact that employees knew that they would be drug tested when they applied for employment in the covered positions, which lowers the expectation of privacy. The government may also require warrantless drug testing of railroad crew members after major accidents. See *Skinner v. Railway Labor Executives Association*, 489 U.S. 602 (1989). The Court found a strong government interest in the testing program and relied heavily on the high numbers of drug- and alcohol-related accidents in the railroad industry and the need for quick testing after an accident.

The Supreme Court has also approved mandatory, random drug testing of high school student athletes. The Court reasoned that schoolchildren's expectations of privacy are reduced, that urinalysis is not highly invasive of privacy, and that the government interest in preventing drug abuse among schoolchildren is very strong. See *Vernonia School Dist. 47J v. Acton*, 515 U.S. 646 (1995). When it comes to candidates for public office, however, the Supreme Court rejected a Georgia statute requiring all candidates for state-wide office to submit to drug testing. See *Chandler v. Miller*, 520 U.S. at 305 (1997). The Court stated that the lack of evidence in the record that Georgia has had problems with drug-abusing state officeholders meant that the invasion of privacy inherent in the drug testing program was not justified by a substantial state interest.

B. Production of Information and Documents

Agencies monitor compliance with regulatory requirements by requiring parties to provide information and/or documents to the government. A great deal of information reporting is routine, such as the requirement that taxpayers file annual tax returns. In addition to requiring the subjects of regulation to provide information, an agency may subpoena documents. If the custodian of the documents does not comply, the agency may ask a court to enforce the subpoena. In general, assuming statutory authority to issue subpoenas or otherwise collect information, agencies may require the provision of information or the production of documents whenever the information or documents relate to a proper subject of agency concern.

(1) The Paperwork Reduction Act

Federal agency information collection is subject to the requirements of the **Paperwork Reduction Act of 1980** (PRA), 44 U.S.C. §§3501 et seq. The PRA grants the Office of Information and Regulatory Affairs (OIRA), within the Office of Management and Budget (OMB), authority to review agency requests for information from members of the public. Under the PRA, before an agency may promulgate a new request for information, the agency must submit a proposal to OIRA with a justification as to its need for the information. OIRA may reject the agency's proposal if it finds that the agency does not have a legitimate need for the information, and OIRA may also approve the agency's proposal subject to conditions. Because OMB is an agency subject to direct supervision by the President, this gives the President a great deal of control over agency information requests.

The PRA has limits. The PRA does not apply to information requests pursuant to a rule promulgated under the APA specifying that the agency will collect information. This makes sense because OIRA would have already had an opportunity to review the regulation. Further, the PRA applies only to agency requests for information, not requirements that one regulated party disclose information directly to another party. See *Dole v. United Steelworkers*, 494 U.S. 26 (1990) (rule requiring employer to disclose workplace safety information to employees not subject to PRA). In *Dole*, the Court viewed the disclosure requirement as a substantive regulation, not an instance of agency information gathering. It also noted that the entire structure of the PRA relates to agency collection of information, not to regulations requiring private parties to disclose information to other private parties.

(2) Agency Requests for Information or Documents

Assuming PRA requirements are met, and the agency has statutory authority to issue subpoenas or otherwise collect information, an agency may require regulated parties to provide information or documents as long as the information sought is related to matters within the legal authority of the agency, the demand is not too indefinite or burdensome, and the information sought is reasonably relevant to a matter of legitimate agency concern. See *United States v. Morton Salt Co.*, 338 U.S. 632 (1950).

While at one time courts were reluctant to recognize broad agency power to require regulated parties to provide information or documents, courts today rarely refuse to enforce agency subpoenas. The basic rule is that the regulatory jurisdiction of the agency, and the issue of whether there is sufficient evidence that a regulatory violation may have occurred, should not be tested in a subpoena enforcement proceeding. As long as the information sought involves matters within the regulatory authority of the agency, a very lenient standard, the court should enforce an agency subpoena. However, courts occasionally refuse to enforce agency subpoenas on the ground that the information sought is outside any area of agency authority or production is too burdensome or detrimental to the subject. See, e.g., *Dow Chemical Co. v. Allen*, 672 F.2d 1626 (7th Cir. 1982) (court refused to enforce EPA subpoena of university research that the court found would impede research and chill academic freedom).

F	A	Q

Q: Why do courts seem to be so lenient about agency information collection, basically allowing agencies to collect any information that is even remotely relevant to their missions?

A: There are at least two probable explanations. First, courts may not want to question agency expertise and unduly hamper agencies' ability to carry out their missions. Second, given the high volume of agency information collection, courts may fear that if they make it easier for parties to resist agency information collection in court, an enormous number of new cases will be brought challenging information collection.

In general, courts liberally enforce agency information-gathering processes. Courts have enforced agency requests for information that are extremely broad and where compliance is extremely costly. Nevertheless, courts, including the Supreme Court in *Morton Salt*, have indicated that there are limits to the breadth and scope of agency subpoena power. Courts have been willing to issue protective orders to protect against the burden of disclosure of sensitive or valuable information. Agencies may only seek information that is reasonably relevant to a legitimate matter of agency concern. However, courts have generally deferred to agencies' assessments of relevance and have required only that the information be relevant to the general purposes of an agency investigation—a standard that agencies normally find very easy to meet.

(3) Disclosure of Privileged Information or Trade Secrets

It is unclear whether federal agencies must respect recognized privileges, mostly under state law, including (but not limited to) attorney-client privilege, doctor-patient privilege, and spousal privilege. The Fifth Amendment privilege against self-incrimination may apply to regulatory information collection, although its requirements are relaxed in the business setting. Further, the government may be required, under the Takings Clause, to compensate a regulated party whose trade secret information is disclosed to third parties as part of a regulatory scheme. These issues are discussed in more detail in what follows.

The limits of state law privileges have not been tested in federal agencies. The Supreme Court unanimously rejected arguments that it recognize a privilege based on academic freedom against disclosure of peer review documents in a case alleging discrimination in the denial of tenure to a professor. See *University of Pennsylvania v. EEOC*, 493 U.S. 182 (1990). In its opinion, the Court stated that it was not free to recognize the privilege since Congress had statutorily authorized the EEOC to obtain all relevant evidence. This implies that federal agencies are free to ignore state law privileges, such as the attorney-client privilege, when seeking information from regulated parties. Congressional authorization of agency information collection may override state law protections.

The Fifth Amendment protection against self-incrimination has only limited applicability to agency requests for information or production of documents. Corporations, and other entities such as labor unions and partnerships, have no Fifth Amendment privilege against providing government with information or documents. For example, in *Bellis v. United States*, 417 U.S. 85 (1974), the Court held that the Fifth Amendment did not entitle a partner in a small law firm to refuse to produce partnership records. Natural persons who have custody of entity records may not assert a Fifth Amendment right against production of such records. See *Braswell v. United States*, 487 U.S. 99 (1988). In *Braswell*, the custodian of corporate records argued that compulsory production of entity documents would violate his Fifth Amendment right against self-incrimination because the act of producing the records might be incriminatory. The Court (split 5-4) rejected this argument, reasoning that allowing the custodian to assert his or her own Fifth Amendment rights concerning the act of production would effectively recognize an entity privilege against self-incrimination since all entities act only through agents.

Even sole proprietors of businesses may not assert the Fifth Amendment right against self-incrimination to resist the production of business records required to be kept under a legitimate regulatory program. For example, in *Shapiro v. United States*,

335 U.S. 1 (1948), the Court upheld a requirement of the Price Control Act, applied to a sole proprietorship, that sellers of goods keep records of their transactions and make those records available to agency inspection. Shapiro argued that the records would incriminate him, but the Court held that as long as the records were the subject of legitimate regulation (i.e., regulation within the government's constitutional power and within the agency's statutory authority), the Fifth Amendment does not protect against production of records required to be kept by the regulatory program.

However, the government may not avoid the Fifth Amendment right against self-incrimination by requiring criminals to keep records of their illegal activities and then subjecting those records to government inspection. In *Marchetti v. United States*, 390 U.S. 39 (1968), the Court rejected applying the lenient standard of government agency information collection to records required to document compliance with a tax imposed on the business of accepting wagers, i.e., illegal bookmaking. Bookies were also required to register with the IRS. Marchetti argued that these requirements amounted to forced self-incrimination and that the regulatory scheme focused only on people suspected of criminal activities. The Court accepted Marchetti's arguments, distinguishing *Shapiro* on the grounds that registering as a bookie provided information beyond that contained in business records, that the information sought in *Marchetti* was essentially private, and that the records sought in *Shapiro* were created in a noncriminal setting while those sought in *Marchetti* were created in a criminal setting.

If an agency requires disclosure of information that is considered a trade secret under state law and then requires that the information be disclosed to third parties (thereby destroying the value of the trade secret), the Takings Clause of the Fifth Amendment may require that the government pay compensation to the party whose information has been disclosed. This principle was applied in *Ruckelshaus v. Monsanto Co.*, 467 U.S. 986 (1984), which held that applicants for permission to market pesticides who were required to disclose their formulas to the public must be compensated when their trade secrets were used by another applicant seeking approval of a similar pesticide. This seems somewhat inconsistent with the notion that constitutional requirements are relaxed with regard to pervasively regulated businesses, but the fact that the subsequent applicant was using the information for commercial purposes, not for government regulatory purposes, means that compensation is justified. Note that an injunction against a taking is not normally available. Rather, the party must disclose the information and then seek compensation for any property taken. Therefore, it does not affect the agency's legal authority to require the disclosure of the information.

SUMMARY

■ Agencies may inspect the premises of regulated businesses only if they have legal authority to conduct inspections. Under normal circumstances, the Fourth Amendment's Warrant Clause requires an agency to obtain a search warrant to conduct an inspection without the regulated party's consent. However, probable cause that violations are occurring is not necessary to obtain a warrant for an administrative inspection. Rather, agencies may obtain warrants merely by showing that the proposed inspection is pursuant to reasonable agency standards for conducting inspections.

■ Pervasively regulated businesses, such as establishments serving alcohol and automobile junkyards, may be inspected without warrants as long as the regulatory scheme is supported by a substantial government interest, warrantless searches are necessary to advance the government interest, and the standards governing inspections under the regulatory scheme provide an adequate substitute for the warrant procedure.

■ Warrants are required for inspections of homes for compliance with building codes and the like. However, welfare recipients and convicted criminals on probation or parole may be required to consent to home inspections as part of government supervision over them.

■ Across-the-board drug testing of government employees is not constitutionally permissible. However, drug testing of employees engaged in sensitive functions such as law enforcement is allowed, as is drug testing as part of the investigation of an accident, such as testing of the driver of a locomotive involved in an accident.

■ The Paperwork Reduction Act requires that agencies obtain the approval of the Office of Management and Budget before they may initiate new requirements that parties provide information to the agency. This requirement does not apply to agency rules that require one private party to disclose information directly to another private party.

■ Agencies have broad power to require regulated parties to produce documents and provide information. The information sought must be related to an area of proper agency concern. However, courts normally will not test the agency's jurisdiction in a proceeding to enforce a subpoena.

■ It is unclear whether federal agencies must respect state law privileges, such as the attorney-client privilege, that protect the confidentiality of information or documents.

■ If government seeks to reveal trade secrets or other valuable information, the Takings Clause may require it to provide compensation to the party whose information it reveals.

■ Corporations and other collective entities such as labor unions and partnerships do not have a Fifth Amendment right to withhold incriminating information, and individual business operators may not use the Fifth Amendment to resist providing documents or information related to a legitimate regulatory program. Further, individual custodians of the information of collective entities do not have a Fifth Amendment right to resist producing entity documents they control.

CONNECTIONS

Inspections and Enforcement

Inspections and information gathering are important enforcement tools that should be understood in light of the general issues surrounding enforcement discussed in Chapter 9.

Seeking Government Information

Chapter 14 discusses how private parties can obtain information from the government.

The Paperwork Reduction Act and *Chevron*

The *Dole* case, which involved an interpretation of the Paperwork Reduction Act, is a great example of "traditional tools of *Chevron*" discussed in Chapter 4.

Preemption and Primary Jurisdiction

12

OVERVIEW

This chapter concerns preemption of state law by federal law and the primary jurisdiction doctrine under which certain claims must be brought to an agency rather than to a court.

Before regulatory agencies were created, the primary method of regulation of private conduct was through common law litigation. State common law continues to provide remedies in areas that are also addressed by federal regulation. State common law often provides parallel remedies that survive the enactment of a federal scheme, but based on the Constitution's Supremacy Clause, federal law may preempt state law expressly or implicitly.

Express preemption arises from a federal statute identifying the preemptive effect of federal law. Implicit preemption exists when federal law occupies the field, when state and federal law conflict, and when state law presents an obstacle to the accomplishment of the purposes of federal law.

Related to preemption, federal agencies often have primary jurisdiction over disputes arising within their regulatory fields. Primary jurisdiction may not exist when a savings clause preserves parallel judicial remedies, but agency jurisdiction may overcome a savings clause if the parallel claim is inconsistent with the federal scheme.

313

A. STATE REMEDIES AND REGULATORY PREEMPTION

B. PRIMARY JURISDICTION

A. State Remedies and Regulatory Preemption

Before the dawn of the administrative state, the primary regulatory institution in the United States was the system of common law litigation and criminal prosecution, both conducted largely in state courts. Tort, contract, property, and criminal law regulated a wide range of conduct that is addressed today by administrative agencies. However, this parallel system of regulation has not disappeared. Rather, it continues to exist, and sometimes it comes into conflict with federal statutory and administrative regulation. Further, states have their own administrative agencies, which may regulate conduct that is also subject to regulation under federal law. Thus, conduct subject to federal regulatory standards may also be regulated under state law, including state administrative law and the general provisions of state common law, such as tort law. This creates the potential for conflict between state and federal law, and the doctrines of preemption and primary jurisdiction aid in determining whether state and federal standards can coexist. If not, federal law may preempt state law under the Supremacy Clause.

Preemption exists only when there are two levels of government such as federal-state, state-local, or even international-national. The preemption doctrine determines when the law of the higher level of government supersedes the law of the lower level of government. However, even if there is only one level of government, issues may arise concerning the relationship between agency regulation and traditional common law litigation. This relationship is determined under the primary jurisdiction doctrine, and also pursuant to questions of statutory interpretation regarding whether a regulatory statute has overridden features of the common law.

(1) State Remedies and the Presumption Against Preemption

Congress has the power to preempt state law under the **Supremacy Clause**, Art. VI, cl. 2 of the Constitution. The Clause provides, "This Constitution, and the Laws of the United States which shall be made in Pursuance thereof; and all Treaties made, or which shall be made, under the Authority of the United States, shall be the supreme Law of the Land; and the Judges in every State shall be bound thereby, any Thing in the Constitution or Laws of any State to the Contrary notwithstanding." The federal courts do not possess authority to preempt state law whenever it makes sense for federal law to displace state law. Rather, because preemption arises out of laws passed by Congress, it is understood as depending on congressional intent. Further, there is a presumption, rooted in federalism concerns and the historical understanding that states have the primary responsibility for regulating matters concerning the health, safety, and morals of society, that state law is not preempted unless Congress's intent to do so is clear. See *Wisconsin Public Intervenor v. Mortier*, 501 U.S. 597 (1991).

Agency action may also result in preemption of state law. If an agency rule conflicts with state law, the agency rule will preempt state law. Because agencies act only pursuant to authority delegated by Congress, as long as the agency rule is valid, the law treats the rule the same as it treats a statute passed by Congress, i.e., with full preemptive effect.

Preemption has been a very controversial issue, and many important preemption cases have resulted in 5-4 Supreme Court decisions. In recent years, the pro-preemption view has been ascendant. However, very recently, the Supreme Court ruled that FDA approval of a drug does not bar state liability for failure to warn of dangers beyond those on the federally approved label, mainly because under federal law the manufacturer is free to strengthen the warnings on the label. See *Wyeth v. Levine*, 129 S. Ct. 1187 (2009). This decision did not change the basic structure of preemption jurisprudence, which allows for extensive federal preemption of state products liability law. Justice Thomas, in a concurring opinion in *Wyeth*, criticized current preemption doctrine for making it too easy for a court to find preemption. See below.

> ### Sidebar
>
> **PREEMPTION AND TWO LEVELS OF GOVERNMENT**
>
> Preemption does not exist unless there are two levels of government with one having the power to override the other. The primary jurisdiction doctrine is similar to preemption but operates within a single level of government to allocate matters between agencies and courts.

F A Q

Q: Why is preemption so controversial?

A: The roots of the controversy lie in two fundamentally conflicting views of the appropriate relationship between state and federal law. On the pro-preemption side, the basic understanding is that once the federal government has acted, for example to approve the marketing of a prescription drug as safe and effective, state products liability law has no business declaring that same drug as defective. On the anti-preemption side, federal approval is viewed as a floor for allowing the product to be marketed in interstate commerce while state products liability is necessary to ensure that products meeting minimal federal standards are actually safe.

(2) Standards for Federal Preemption of State Law

While Congress's intent to preempt state law must be clear, it is not always necessary for Congress to announce explicitly that it intends to preempt state law. Rather, courts determine whether preemption has occurred using a variety of standards — all designed to shed light on Congress's intent. As noted above, there are two basic forms of preemption, express preemption and implied preemption.

Express preemption exists when a federal statute explicitly addresses the circumstances under which federal law displaces state law. **Implied preemption** exists when, even though no express preemption provision applies, state law conflicts somehow with federal law so that Congress must have intended for federal law to preempt state law. **Conflict** has been found in three ways: first, when state and federal law are in direct, irreconcilable conflict (this is referred to as "**conflict preemption**"); second, when federal law is so comprehensive that it appears inconsistent with congressional intent to preserve any state law in the relevant field (this is referred to as "**field preemption**"); and third, when state law presents an obstacle to the accomplishment of the purposes behind federal law (this is known as "**obstacle preemption**").

Express Preemption

The simplest form of preemption is express preemption. In many regulatory statutes, Congress expressly preempts state law by providing in a statute that state law is preempted. For example, the Cigarette Labeling Act (under which warning labels are required to appear on cigarette packages and cigarette advertising) provides that states may not impose any "requirement or prohibition based on smoking or health . . . with respect to the advertising or promotion of any cigarettes the packages of which are labeled in conformity with the provisions of this chapter." 15 U.S.C. §1334(b). This provision preempts state law claims based, for example, on failure to warn of the dangers of smoking, even if it is alleged that the cigarette company diluted the warning labels by minimizing health risks in other advertising and promotion. See *Cipollone v. Liggett Group, Inc.*, 505 U.S. 504 (1992).

Express preemption provisions usually provide for partial preemption, i.e., preempting certain aspects of state law while preserving others. For example, the Cigarette Labeling Act preempts state law only if it is related to smoking or health, and then only if the state law is directed at advertising or promotion of cigarettes. This statute does not on its face reach cigarette regulation directed at matters other than advertising or promotion, and thus does not preempt, for example, local bans on smoking in public places or state taxation of cigarettes.

Preemption controversies involving express preemption provisions often present complex and difficult issues of statutory interpretation, requiring courts to differentiate carefully between preempted and non-preempted claims. For example, in a controversy arising out of a partial preemption provision in the area of pesticide regulation, *Bates v. Dow Agrosciences LLC*, 544 U.S. 431 (2005), the Supreme Court held that the Federal Insecticide, Fungicide and Rodenticide Act (FIFRA) may preempt fraud and failure to warn claims if they conflict with federal labeling and marketing requirements, but the Act did not preempt state law claims for defective design, defective manufacture, negligent testing, breach of express warranty, and violation of a state deceptive trade practices act. FIFRA's preemption provision provided, in part, that states "shall not impose or continue in effect any requirements for labeling or packaging in addition to or different from those required under this subchapter." 7 U.S.C. §136v. The Court concluded that this provision required the courts to examine FIFRA and compare the federal provisions to each of the state law claims raised to determine whether any of the state claims were preempted. (The Court left it to the lower courts to determine whether any conflict exists.) Partial preemption provisions, like the one at issue in *Bates*, allow state law to fill gaps in federal law and regulate in areas not directly covered by federal law. Others explicitly preserve state law that is more stringent than federal law, so that federal law, in effect, supplies a regulatory floor that state law may raise.

The recent move toward greater preemption under express preemption principles is best illustrated by two cases that arose under federal regulation of medical devices. The federal government began regulating medical devices in 1976 when Congress passed the Medical Device Amendments of 1976 (the Act). The Act's express preemption provision prohibits state and local governments from maintaining any "requirement" that is "different from, or in addition to, any requirement applicable under this chapter to [a medical] device . . . which relates to the safety or effectiveness of the device or to any other matter included in a requirement applicable to the device under this chapter." 21 U.S.C. §360k. In the first case to reach the Supreme Court under this provision, *Medtronic Inc. v. Lohr*, 528 U.S. 470 (1996), the Court found that the process under which the FDA approved a particular medical device was not a federal "requirement applicable to the device" but was rather a general process designed to determine whether the device met statutory standards. The particular device involved in the case was approved by the FDA under a relaxed safety review that is applied to medical devices that are substantially equivalent to one that was on the market before the Act was passed, and was therefore allowed to remain on the market without going through any approval process. The Court ruled against preemption by a vote of 5-4, with the dissenters arguing that federal approval does constitute a requirement that can have preemptive effect.

The Court was also sharply divided over whether common law liability is a state requirement subject to preemption. The plurality opinion for four Justices found that state common law is not a requirement under the Act because the word "requirement" refers to positive law specific to the particular device, such as statutes or regulations, and not to general common law standards. The other five Justices, including four dissenters and Justice Breyer, who concurred in the result finding against preemption on other grounds, thought that state common law was a requirement subject to preemption.

In support of its decision in *Medtronic v. Lohr*, the plurality opinion pointed out that the Act's legislative history contains no suggestion that Congress intended the Act to foreclose common law liability. In fact, Congress was provoked to pass the Act at least in part because the State of California had established a regulatory approval process for medical devices, and device manufacturers feared the cost and delay that would occur if other states followed California's example. The statute's express preemption provision was apparently designed to preclude states from establishing their own systems of medical device regulation. State products liability litigation was not part of the agenda of proponents of the Act.

Despite this legislative history and background, the next major test of the scope of the Act's preemption provision resulted in a finding of broad preemptive scope. Medical devices that are not "substantially equivalent" to devices already on the market may not be marketed without going through a rigorous Pre-Market Approval (PMA) process designed to establish, to the FDA's satisfaction, the device's safety and effectiveness. See 21 U.S.C. §360c(a)(1)(C)(ii). In *Riegel v. Medtronic, Inc.*, 552 U.S. 312 (2008), the Court held that once a device has gone through the FDA's PMA process, federal law preempts state tort liability because the FDA has determined, as a matter of federal law, that the device is safe as designed and manufactured. Further, the Court found that the PMA process is a federal requirement with preemptive effect because once the FDA grants PMA, the manufacturer is prohibited from altering the design or labeling of the device without FDA permission. This decision was 8-1, with only Justice Ruth Bader Ginsburg dissenting. Her dissent stressed the absence of legislative history of congressional intent to take the major step of eliminating "all judicial recourse" for injuries caused by approved medical devices, but the majority held that the lack of legislative history was not important given what it found to be the clear import of the statutory language.

EXPRESS AND IMPLIED PREEMPTION

The *Riegel* decision illustrates the sea change in the Court's preemption jurisprudence over time. In earlier times, the operative presumptions concerning the relationship between federal regulation and state tort law, and concerning Congress's intent, weighed heavily against preemption. Federal regulation was thought to ensure a minimum level of safety, with state tort law doing most of the work to ensure that unsafe products did not remain on the market. Congress's intent in enacting safety regulation was to provide that regulatory floor, not to fully occupy the field of health and safety regulation that has been traditionally within the authority of the states. Today, state tort liability is viewed as a threat to the sanctity of federal regulatory schemes, and Congress's intent is viewed as favoring comprehensive federal regulation to allow approved products to be marketed. Federal law now provides both the floor and the ceiling for safety regulation.

Implied Preemption

In implied preemption cases, courts imply congressional intent to preempt from the circumstances, even when no express preemption provision applies. Because there is often little or no evidence of congressional intent to preempt, implied preemption sometimes appears to be created by the courts rather than based on Congress's intent. As noted above, there are three main categories of implied preemption.

First, comprehensive federal law that occupies an entire "field" of regulation preempts any state law within the field. The theory is that when federal law is so comprehensive, and the area is of such pressing federal concern, Congress must have intended to displace state law that is within the "field" occupied by Congress. Here, congressional intent to preempt is inferred from the comprehensiveness of federal regulation. Under field preemption, federal law occupies an entire area and state law within the field is displaced.

Second, state law that is in actual conflict with federal law is preempted. If, for example, federal law commands a particular course of conduct and state law prohibits the very same conduct, the state law is preempted because of the actual conflict between the two legal regimes. It is presumed that Congress intends such preemption. Note that if state law is merely somewhat more restrictive than federal law, conflict preemption does not necessarily exist because it would not violate federal law to obey the more stringent state standard.

Third, federal law also preempts state law when a court concludes that state law poses an obstacle to the accomplishment of Congress's purposes in enacting the federal law. For example, although no actual conflict exists, sometimes when Congress enacts relatively permissive regulation, it means to allow regulated parties to act up to the limits of federal law and thus intends to preempt more stringent state requirements. In such cases, the more stringent state law would pose an obstacle to the accomplishment of Congress's intent, and it would be preempted. However, it is often very difficult to distinguish between cases in which Congress meant to displace more stringent state regulation and cases in which Congress meant to leave states free to impose more stringent regulation. This difficulty means that many preemption cases become very controversial, with anti-preemption forces charging that pro-preemption forces are going beyond Congress's intent and imposing their own vision of tort law policy.

Justice Thomas identified a fundamental problem with implied obstacle pre-emption in his concurring opinion in *Wyeth v. Levine*, 129 S. Ct. 1187 (2009), when he stated:

Under this approach, the Court routinely invalidates state laws based on perceived con-flicts with broad federal policy objectives, legislative history, or generalized notions of congressional purposes that are not embodied within the text of federal law. . . . This, in turn, leads to decisions giving improperly broad pre-emptive effect to judicially manufactured policies, rather than to the statutory text enacted by Congress pursuant to the Constitution and the agency actions authorized thereby.

Id. at 1205, 1217 (Thomas, J., concurring in the judgment). Justice Thomas was especially critical of implied preemption in the face of a **savings clause**, which he thinks evidences congressional intent to preserve state tort liability.

Similar issues arise when a federal statute contains an express preemption provision that does not apply in the particular case. At one time, the Supreme Court held that when a federal statute contains an express preemption provision, implied preemption cannot exist because it is presumed that Congress expressed the limits of its preemptive intent in the express preemption provision within the federal statute. However, more recently, the Court has stated that express and implied pre-emption can coexist. See *Geier v. American Honda Motor Co.*, 529 U.S. 861 (2000). The strongest argument in favor of this change is that even when an express preemption provision exists but does not apply, Congress must intend to preempt state law that actually conflicts with provisions of federal law. However, when actual conflict does not exist, it appears that the Court goes beyond Congress's intent when it finds implied preemption after determining that an express preemption provision does not reach the particular case.

Another common feature of federal regulatory statutes is that many of them contain "savings clauses" under which parallel remedies, whether state or federal, explicitly survive the enactment of a new federal regulatory statute. When a savings clause exists, state tort and other remedies are not expressly preempted. However, it is sometimes necessary to determine the reach of a savings clause. Further, the Supreme Court has held that when a state law claim would frustrate Congress's purposes or cause a conflict with a provision of federal law, preemption may occur despite the existence of the savings clause. See, e.g., *Geier v. American Honda Motor Co.*, 529 U.S. 861 (2000). In *Geier*, even though the express preemption provision did not apply because a savings clause explicitly preserved common law remedies, the Court found implied preemption based on conflict between federal and state law.

The *Geier* decision, involving an automobile without an airbag, illustrates the interaction between express and implied preemption. The requirement that new cars be equipped with passive restraints such as airbags was phased in by the federal National Highway Transportation Safety Administration (NHTSA) over a period of years. After Geier was severely injured in an accident involving a 1987 car without an airbag, she sued under state law claiming that the car was negligently and defectively designed because it should have been equipped with a driver's side airbag. The Supreme Court held that this state law claim was implicitly preempted by the NHTSA's regulation requiring that only 10 percent of cars from that model year be so equipped. The Court first held that the Federal Motor Vehicle Safety Act's express preemption provision did not apply, mainly because of a savings clause that states that compliance with a federal safety standard " 'does not exempt any person from any liability under common law.' " *Geier*, 529 U.S. at 868, quoting 15 U.S.C. §1397(k). However, the Court went on to find implied preemption because the "no airbag" suit brought by Geier would conflict with the phase-in aspect of the federal regulation requiring airbags or other passive restraints. The Court found that the agency deliberately chose the gradual phase-in approach to preserve flexibility so that carmakers might invent cheaper and better alternatives to airbags. See *Geier*, 529 U.S. at 881. While the Court may be correct about the agency's reasons for phasing in the passive restraint requirement, its conclusion that state tort law claims are preempted by that regulation seems directly inconsistent with Congress's pronouncement that compliance with federal standards "does not exempt any person from any liability under common law." The best reading of Congress's intent seems to be that whatever might be preempted by federal automobile safety standards, state common law liability is not.

The *Geier* decision is best understood as an example of "obstacle preemption" under which state law is preempted when it poses an obstacle to the accomplishment of federal goals. There was no actual conflict between federal and state law — an automobile manufacturer would have been in compliance with both state and federal law by installing airbags in all of its cars. However, the federal purpose behind the phase-in requirement was to encourage the development of alternative methods of passive restraint. This would not happen if state law required all cars to be equipped with airbags. Arguably the Court should not have allowed the general purpose to encourage development to override the language of the savings clause. As Justice Thomas recently stated, "With text that allowed state actions like the one at issue in *Geier*, the Court had no authority to comb through agency commentaries to find a basis for an alternative conclusion." *Wyeth v. Levine*, 129 S. Ct. 1187, 1215 (2009) (Thomas, J., concurring in the judgment).

In *Wyeth*, the Supreme Court addressed whether federal prescription drug law preempts state tort claims. Levine was injured when a clinician injected an anti-nausea medication directly into her vein. In her suit, she alleged that the drug company did not provide adequate warnings concerning that method of administering the drug. The defendant drug company argued for preemption because federal law mandated that it provide only the labeling that had been approved by the Federal Food and Drug Administration (FDA). The Court disagreed with Wyeth's characterization of federal law, stating that drug companies are free to add warnings to their labeling without FDA approval. The Court also examined the history of federal drug laws and concluded that "Congress did not intend FDA oversight to be the exclusive means of ensuring drug safety and effectiveness." *Wyeth*, 129 S. Ct. at 1200.

In the course of determining that federal law did not preempt the tort suit in *Wyeth*, the Court engaged in an extensive review of Congress's purposes in creating the system of federal approval of drugs, including a look at the historical interaction between state and federal law on the subject and related areas dating back to the initial federal statute passed in 1938. Justice Thomas wrote a concurring opinion in which he was highly critical of the Court's implied preemption jurisprudence, especially the "obstacle preemption" variety. Justice Thomas stated, "Under this approach, the Court routinely invalidates state laws based on perceived conflicts with broad federal policy objectives, legislative history, or generalized notions of congressional purposes that are not embodied within the text of federal law. Because implied pre-emption doctrines that wander far from the statutory text are inconsistent with the Constitution, I concur only in the judgment." Id. at 1205 (Thomas, J., concurring in the judgment).

Justice Thomas offered two criticisms of implied "obstacle" preemption, both flowing from the fact that obstacle preemption is not grounded in the language of the allegedly preemptive federal statute. The first problem is constitutional — under the Supremacy Clause, only the Constitution, treaties, and *statutes* have preemptive effect. Judicial implication of preemptive intent usurps Congress's role in establishing the domain of federal law over state law. The second problem is more practical — the loose "obstacle preemption" standard allows federal judges to impose their own policy preferences to prevent the operation of state law in areas that are traditionally entrusted to the states. Time will tell if Justice Thomas's call for reevaluation of implied preemption doctrine is heeded by his colleagues on the Court.

F A Q

Q: If the federal government decides not to institute safety regulation, does that implicitly preempt state regulation in the same area?

A: The mere fact that a federal agency has decided not to regulate in an area is not usually sufficient to implicitly preempt state regulation in the same area. Congress or federal agencies may decline to regulate for a variety of reasons, including the conclusion that state tort law is adequate, that principles of federalism militate in favor of leaving the matter to state law, or that more time or more observation of various state regulatory schemes is needed to decide on the best regulatory strategy. Thus, in *Sprietsma v. Mercury Marine*, 537 U.S. 51 (2002), the Supreme Court held that the U.S. Coast Guard's rejection of a requirement that boats be equipped with propeller guards did not preempt state tort law claims based on boat manufacturers' failure to include propeller guards in the design of boats.

(3) Punitive Damages and Regulatory Preemption

Even when general tort liability litigation is not preempted, punitive damages under state tort law can present a stronger case for preemption than compensatory damages because they are designed to punish and deter and thus have a more regulatory focus than compensatory damages. In the famous *Silkwood* case, for example, it was argued that punitive damages should be preempted by federal law because the punitive damages were aimed at conduct that was allowed under federal law. *Silkwood v. Kerr-McGee Corp.*, 464 U.S. 238 (1984). The argument in favor of preemption was that state law should not deter conduct expressly permitted under federal law. This would conflict with, or at least frustrate the purpose of, federal law. However, in *Silkwood*, a narrow majority of the Court held that punitive damages should be treated like other common law remedies; if common law remedies generally are not preempted, punitive damages are also not preempted.

B. Primary Jurisdiction

The **primary jurisdiction** doctrine requires that certain claims be heard in an agency either before, or instead of, an action in a court. This doctrine is related to preemption since, as applied to a state law claim, primary jurisdiction in a federal agency may preempt a parallel state law claim if it is held that the substantive claim may be litigated only within a federal agency under federal standards. However, primary jurisdiction is different from preemption because it operates even within a single level of government to allocate issues between courts and agencies, rather than as a doctrine enforcing the superiority of a higher level of government. For example, primary jurisdiction may preclude or delay litigation of federal issues in federal courts in favor of presentation of the issues to the appropriate federal agency.

The primary jurisdiction doctrine serves three related purposes. First, it ensures that courts respect the assignment of regulatory matters to the agency created to administer the particular area of law. Second, it advances uniformity of interpretation and administration by assigning initial decisionmaking power to a single entity. See *Marquez v. Screen Actors Guild, Inc.*, 525 U.S. 33 (1998) (NLRB has primary jurisdiction over challenge to operation of union security clause in labor contract). Third, it facilitates the application of agency expertise to regulatory matters.

At its most basic, the primary jurisdiction doctrine provides that a claim that is within the substantive jurisdiction of an agency must be heard first by that agency, even if the facts give rise to a claim otherwise cognizable in a court. For an example of a federal issue that was held to be in the primary jurisdiction of a federal agency, consider *United States v. Western Pacific Rwy. Co.*, 352 U.S. 59 (1956). This case involved litigation over the proper rate the federal government was required to pay for shipping napalm. The government shipped unfused napalm bombs by rail and refused to pay the tariff rate for "incendiary bombs." The government argued that since the bombs were unfused, the lower rate for "gasoline in steel drums" applied. The railroad sued the government for the higher rate in the Court of Claims, and the Supreme Court held that the controversy should have been presented to the Interstate Commerce Commission (ICC) since the Commission had established the categories at issue and would therefore be in a better position to decide which category applied. Although the Court mentioned both uniformity and expertise, the principal basis for primary jurisdiction in this case was that proper categorization of the shipments implicated the expertise of the agency.

Savings clauses usually defeat arguments for primary jurisdiction because they state that regulatory jurisdiction is in addition to, and does not displace, preexisting remedies. This normally means that the primary jurisdiction doctrine does not bar a claim in court. However, if the judicial remedy would destroy the jurisdiction of the agency, even a savings clause will not prevent the preemption of alternative remedies. For example, under state common law, shippers may sue common carriers if they believe the carrier charges "unreasonable" rates. The federal Interstate Commerce Act (ICA) also prohibited carriers from charging unreasonable rates. Congress placed jurisdiction to decide whether rates were reasonable in the now-defunct Interstate Commerce Commission, but the Interstate Commerce Act also explicitly preserved shippers' common law remedies. When a manufacturer of cotton oil sued a railroad over allegedly unreasonable rates, the railroad defended on the basis of the Interstate Commerce Commission's control over rates. Despite the presence of the savings clause, the Supreme Court held for the railroad, ruling that the claim that the rates were unreasonable was within the primary jurisdiction of the Interstate Commerce

Commission. To allow the common law remedy, reasoned the Court, would effectively destroy the jurisdiction of the Commission since the courts of all the states would be able to declare federally approved rates "unreasonable." See *Texas & Pacific Rwy. Co. v. Abilene Cotton Oil Co.*, 204 U.S. 426 (1907). While the Court's reasoning makes sense, it does seem inconsistent with the statute, which was apparently designed to preserve traditional state authority over the reasonableness of shipping rates.

Another interesting controversy illustrates the primary jurisdiction doctrine and its relationship to savings clauses. Consumer activist Ralph Nader had a speaking engagement in Connecticut. He had a confirmed reservation on a flight from Washington, D.C. to Hartford, but the airline overbooked the flight and when Nader arrived only five minutes before the scheduled departure, he was bumped from the flight. Nader refused the airline's offer of compensation, and he and the group for whom he was scheduled to speak sued for damages under state tort law. (He was able to get to the engagement by taking a flight to Boston and driving to Connecticut.) The airline, perhaps realizing its misfortune in choosing Nader as one of the passengers to bump, claimed that federal regulation of the airline industry under the Federal Aviation Act placed primary jurisdiction over the claim in the Civil Aeronautics Board. The court of appeals agreed with the airline, relying primarily on the heavy regulation of the airline industry, including the Board's close supervision of fares and competition.

The airline's problem was that the relevant chapter of the Act contained the following savings clause: "[n]othing contained in this chapter shall in any way abridge or alter the remedies now existing at common law or by statute, but the provisions of this chapter are in addition to such remedies." 49 U.S.C. §1506 (repealed). Given this very broad savings clause, and the fact that Nader did not claim that the airline had violated any provision of the Act, or its tariff filed with the Board under the Act, the Supreme Court held that the claim was not within the Board's primary jurisdiction and could be brought directly in a court. See *Nader v. Allegheny Airlines, Inc.*, 426 U.S. 290 (1976).

Finally, it should also be noted that the primary jurisdiction doctrine is often easier to apply than this analysis might suggest simply because many regulatory statutes spell out in detail those cases in the exclusive or primary jurisdiction of the agency. For example, state workers' compensation statutes specify that claims under the workers' compensation laws must be brought in a particular agency. If a claimant for workers' compensation benefits attempted to bring a claim directly in court, the claim would be dismissed based on clear statutory jurisdictional provisions. It is the rare case in which there is uncertainty over the allocation of jurisdiction between an agency and a court.

Sidebar

FEDERAL AND STATE PRIMARY JURISDICTION

Primary jurisdiction operates within the federal system and within the state system. In other words, a federal court claim that relates to a federal agency's jurisdiction might be directed to a federal agency, and a state court claim that relates to a state agency's jurisdiction might be directed to a state agency. Sometimes, primary jurisdiction will work together with preemption to direct a state court claim to a federal agency.

SUMMARY

- State law often provides a remedy for conduct that is also addressed by federal regulation. Often, state law provides parallel remedies that survive the enactment of a federal scheme, but sometimes, under the Supremacy Clause, federal law preempts state law either expressly or implicitly.

■ Express preemption arises from a federal statute that specifies the preemptive effect of federal law.

■ Implied preemption exists when federal law is inconsistent with state law but does not specifically address preemption. There are three kinds of implied preemption: field preemption, conflict preemption, and obstacle preemption. Obstacle preemption can be controversial, because it is based on an understanding of often vague and conflicting congressional purposes.

■ Savings clauses express congressional intent to preserve state common law remedies, but even then some federal courts, including the Supreme Court, find implied preemption when there is an apparent conflict between federal and state law.

■ Agencies often have primary jurisdiction over disputes arising within their regulatory fields. Primary jurisdiction means that a dispute must be presented to an agency, either first or sometimes exclusively. Primary jurisdiction may not exist where a savings clause preserves parallel judicial remedies, but agency jurisdiction may overcome a savings clause if the parallel claim is inconsistent with the federal scheme.

CONNECTIONS

Express Preemption and *Chevron*

Express preemption disputes turn on the interpretation of a federal statute, the review of which may be governed by the *Chevron* doctrine, Chapter 4.

Preemption and Enforcement

Regulatory preemption is, in a sense, a method of enforcement and thus should be understood in light of general enforcement principles discussed in Chapter 9.

Preemption and Federalism

The federalism arguments that counsel against preemption are similar to the federalism arguments that counsel against implied rights of action, discussed in Chapter 9. Basically, federalism points toward state authority over civil liability.

Liability of Agencies and Officials

13

OVERVIEW

This chapter looks at damages liability of government entities and officials. Damages liability is an alternative to judicial review as a method for controlling government officials, although usually the liability rules are derived from a source external to the administrative system such as tort law or constitutional law. Sovereign immunity in the United States has traditionally protected government and government officials from tort liability. The federal government, in the Federal Tort Claims Act (FTCA) and related statutes, has, to a limited extent, waived its sovereign immunity. Under the FTCA, the government is liable for the negligent torts of federal officials if a private party would be liable in tort under state law. The FTCA bars suit against the officials themselves. Liability under the FTCA is limited by many exceptions and limiting doctrines, the most important of which is the statutory bar on liability for discretionary functions. The discretionary function exception disallows liability for official choices involving the exercise of policy judgment.

Federal officials can be held liable for their constitutional violations under the *Bivens* action, which is a judicially created damages action against individual federal government officials for constitutional violations. The *Bivens* action is available for constitutional violations unless Congress has designated a substitute *Bivens* action or special factors counsel hesitation in the absence of congressional recognition of the *Bivens* action. Defendants in *Bivens* actions enjoy traditional common law immunities from damages awards. Officials performing judicial, legislative, and prosecutorial functions are absolutely immune from damages. Other officials have a qualified immunity under which they may be held liable only if they violate a clearly established constitutional right.

State officials violating the Constitution or federal statutory law may be sued by parties injured under 42 U.S.C. §1983, which provides a damages action against officials who violate federal constitutional and legal rights under color of state law. State officials enjoy the same immunities as federal officials sued under *Bivens*. State governments and state agencies may not be sued under §1983 but municipalities may be held liable under §1983, but only when a constitutional violation is caused by a municipal policy or custom. Municipalities may not be held vicariously liable for the constitutional torts of their employees.

A. SOVEREIGN IMMUNITY AND SUITS AGAINST FEDERAL AGENTS AND AGENCIES

1. Common Law Sovereign Immunity
2. The Federal Torts Claim Act

B. LIABILITY OF FEDERAL OFFICIALS FOR CONSTITUTIONAL VIOLATIONS

C. LIABILITY OF STATE AND LOCAL GOVERNMENT OFFICIALS AND ENTITIES

1. The Eleventh Amendment and Sovereign Immunity
2. "And Laws" Actions
3. Municipal Liability

A. Sovereign Immunity and Suits Against Federal Agents and Agencies

(1) Common Law Sovereign Immunity

When errors, tortious conduct, or other misconduct by government officials causes damage to the property or person of private parties, the victim may attempt to sue for damages rather than merely seek judicial review of the official action. Traditionally, **sovereign immunity** barred suits against the government and government officials unless the government consented to be sued. For example, in *Spalding v. Vilas*, 161 U.S. 483 (1896), the Supreme Court held that the Postmaster General of the United States could not be sued for libel allegedly contained in official communications. The Court stated:

> We are of opinion that the same general considerations of public policy and convenience which demand for judges of courts of superior jurisdiction immunity from civil suits for damages arising from acts done by them in the course of the performance of their judicial functions apply to a large extent to official communications made by heads of executive departments when engaged in the discharge of duties imposed upon them by law.

Id. at 498. The Court found that the private interest in compensation for officially inflicted injuries was outweighed by the public interest in effective administration of the laws, which the Court thought would be threatened if government officials had to worry about personal liability.

Barr v. Matteo, 360 U.S. 564 (1959), extended this reasoning to libel suits brought against lower-level federal officials. In *Barr*, the plurality opinion posed the issue as requiring the Court to weigh in a particular context two considerations of high importance that now and again come into sharp conflict. On the one hand, the protection of the individual citizen against pecuniary damage caused by oppressive or malicious action on the part of officials of the federal government, and, on the other, the protection of the public interest by shielding responsible governmental officers against the harassment and inevitable hazards of vindictive or ill-founded damage suits brought on account of action taken in the exercise of their official responsibilities. Id. at 564-65. Once again, the Court found that the public interest outweighed the private interest.

Federal government officials sued for common law torts allegedly committed while performing official duties have a variety of immunities from liability. In many situations, government officials are privileged to engage in conduct that, if performed by a private party, would be tortious. For example, police officers have a good faith defense to false-arrest claims that is not available to private parties. The courts have also recognized immunity from tort liability for federal government officials acting within the scope of their duties. At first this immunity protected only high-ranking officials but was later extended to all officials acting within the "outer perimeter" of their duties. See *Barr v. Matteo*, 360 U.S. 564 (1959).

In *Barr v. Matteo*, 360 U.S. 564 (1959), a federal official issued a press release naming two of his employees as the officials responsible for a questionable practice that had been characterized as a conspiracy to defraud the federal government. The employees brought a defamation action, alleging that their supervisor acted with malice and defamed them. The Supreme Court sustained a plea of "absolute privilege," holding that as long as the action taken is within the "outer perimeter" of the official's duties, the official is immune from damages for defamation. The Court further held that it is within an executive official's discretion to publish a press release on a matter of public interest. The Court stated that the immunity is necessary to ensure that officials exercise their discretion free from the fear of damage suits.

Sidebar

CLAIMS AGAINST GOVERNMENT OFFICIALS

Most claims against government officials arise under tort law or constitutional law and do not involve enforcement of regulatory norms against the government officials. However, administrative law issues can arise if, for example, it is alleged that the defendant government official lacked legal authority to take the actions over which the plaintiff is suing.

Sidebar

SCOPE OF OFFICIAL IMMUNITY

Official immunity from tort actions is very broad, extending to the "outer perimeter" of official duties.

Sidebar

DECLINE OF SOVEREIGN IMMUNITY

In recent decades, state and federal courts and legislatures have whittled away at sovereign immunity. In most jurisdictions, there has been a steady erosion of sovereign immunity, especially with regard to immunity from tort actions. In most states, state and local governments are liable in tort on pretty much the same basis as private defendants, although sometimes with special procedures and limits on the size of damage awards. Officials are still likely to be immune or at least indemnified by their government employers. At the federal level, sovereign immunity in tort and contract has been statutorily waived, as discussed below.

(2) The Federal Torts Claim Act

The two major waivers of the sovereign immunity of the government of the United States are the Tucker Act, which in 1887 waived the government's immunity in contract, admiralty, and other non-tort matters and the Federal Tort Claims Act (FTCA), which, in 1947, waived the sovereign immunity of the federal government over a large area of tort actions. In administrative law, our focus is on the FTCA because it is often used to pursue damages when the conduct of administrators is allegedly tortious.

The FTCA waives the sovereign immunity of the United States for negligent or otherwise wrongful acts or omissions by the United States government or its employees. It creates federal government liability for "tort claims . . . in the same manner and to the same extent as a private individual under like circumstances." 28 U.S.C. §2674. The liability is for "negligent or wrongful acts or omissions of any employee of the Government." 28 U.S.C. §1346(b). The Act grants jurisdiction over FTCA claims to the federal district courts, and instructs the district courts to assess the liability of the government "in accordance with the law of the place where the act or omission occurred." 28 U.S.C. §1346(b). This means that liability under the FTCA is usually determined under state law.

Government liability is a substitute for individual liability. The FTCA displaces all other liability of federal officials for torts committed in the scope of their federal employment. Whether or not the government is liable under the FTCA, federal officials involved are individually immune from tort damages for acts done within the scope of their federal employment. 28 U.S.C. §2679(d)(1). If, for example, the individual government official's conduct would give rise to strict liability under state law, even though the government is not liable under a strict liability theory, the FTCA immunizes the official from liability as well.

Sidebar

NO STRICT LIABILITY UNDER FTCA

Because the FTCA's language refers to "negligent" and "wrongful" conduct, the Supreme Court has held that strict liability is not allowed under the FTCA even if the conduct involved would result in strict liability under state law. See *Laird v. Nelms*, 406 U.S. 797 (1972).

F A Q

Q: Is FTCA liability as favorable to plaintiffs as normal tort liability?

A: No, for procedural and substantive reasons. The FTCA does not provide for jury trial or punitive damages, there are strict requirements that claims be presented to administrative agencies, and administrative remedies must be exhausted before bringing suit. These procedural features of FTCA claims are typical of procedural aspects of state tort claims acts (in which states waive their sovereign immunity in state court) throughout the United States. Further, as discussed below, there are exceptions to FTCA liability that make it much more limited than traditional tort liability.

One issue that has come up under the FTCA is whether the government should be liable for torts with no clear analog in the private sector. The government has often argued in defending FTCA claims that the government is not liable when the conduct giving rise to the claim has no private analog, because in such cases the plaintiff cannot establish that a private person would be liable under state law for the same conduct. The Supreme Court has consistently rejected this argument, except with regard to military activities. In the military context, the Court has rejected FTCA liability on the ground that there is no private law analog to allowing a soldier to sue his superior officers or the government for damages. See *Feres v. United States*, 340 U.S. 135 (1950). The Feres doctrine, which in essence creates a non-statutory exception to FTCA liability, is discussed below in more detail.

A good example of a case in which the government unsuccessfully argued that the FTCA should not be read to create liability when the government acts as a regulator is *Berkovitz v. United States*, 486 U.S. 531 (1988). In that case, an FTCA suit was brought alleging that the government negligently approved an oral polio vaccine that actually caused an infant who received the vaccine to contract polio. The government argued that the FTCA's analogy to private liability precluded liability for regulatory conduct such as the approval of a vaccine. The Court rejected this argument, noting that it had twice before rejected a regulatory-function exception to the FTCA. The claim was thus allowed to go forward.

The FTCA contains numerous exceptions and limitations, the most important of which is the **discretionary function exception**, which is discussed in detail below. Other exceptions include no liability for negligence in delivering the mail, no liability for negligence in the collection of taxes or customs duties, no liability for intentional torts, no liability for combatant activities of the armed forces, and no liability for claims arising in a foreign country.

> ## Sidebar
>
> ### FTCA LIABILITY IS EXCLUSIVE
>
> If a claim against a federal government official falls within the scope of the FTCA, the government is substituted as the defendant and the official is released from liability. Any action against an individual federal employee for actions within the scope of the employment is deemed a suit against the federal government. 28 U.S.C. §2679(d)(1). Even if the government prevails based on an exception to FTCA liability, the official retains his or her immunity. The plaintiff cannot bring the official back into the case as a defendant simply because government liability is foreclosed. In essence, for officials this preserves the ancient common law sovereign immunity recognized in cases like *Spalding v. Vilas* and *Barr v. Matteo*.

The most widely litigated exception to liability under the FTCA is the exception for "the exercise or performance or the failure to exercise or perform a discretionary function or duty." 28 U.S.C. §2680(a). This exception has been defined as follows: "The exception, properly construed, therefore protects only governmental actions and decisions based on considerations of public policy. . . . In sum, the discretionary function exception insulates the Government from liability if the action challenged in the case involves the permissible exercise of policy judgment." *Berkovitz v. United States*, 486 U.S. 531, 537 (1988). Although this definition may appear narrow, exempting only policy decisions, in application the Supreme Court has exempted a great deal of the operations of the government from the coverage of the FTCA.

The decision that set the tone for broad application of the discretionary function exception is *Dalehite v. United States*, 346 U.S. 15 (1953). In that case, the government's negligence in manufacturing, labeling, and shipping fertilizer caused a massive explosion while the fertilizer was being loaded onto a ship for shipment overseas as part of post–World War II aid to foreign countries. Hundreds of people were killed, thousands injured, and massive property damage resulted. Although it would seem that operational decisions concerning the execution of the policy of providing the fertilizer would not be considered "discretionary functions" within the FTCA exception, the Court held that the discretionary function exception barred liability for the negligence that caused the explosion. The Court relied on several factors for this conclusion: The acts involved furthered "governmental functions"; the acts were initiated by a high-level government official; the acts involved choices among different methods of production, packing, and shipment; and the acts followed from planning-level (as opposed to operational-level) decisions.

Soon after *Dalehite*, a narrow majority of the Court adopted a definition of the discretionary function exception under which the key distinction was between planning-level decisions (which were exempt from FTCA liability) and operational-level activities (which were not exempt). In *Indian Towing Co. v. United States*, 350 U.S. 61 (1955), the owners of a ship that ran aground sued over the Coast Guard's failure to maintain or repair a lighthouse and to warn that the lighthouse was not operating. The Court found liability in this case, distinguishing between the decision whether to have a lighthouse (which was a planning decision that could not give rise to FTCA liability) and the maintenance of the existing lighthouse (which, being an operational activity, was not a discretionary function within the meaning of the FTCA exemption). This does not seem completely consistent with *Dalehite*—the decision to ship the fertilizer could be seen as planning, while the method of manufacturing, packing, and shipping could be seen as operational. However, the Court has not disavowed *Dalehite* and it still influences the development of the discretionary function exception.

Sidebar

FTCA IN FOREIGN COUNTRIES

For an application of the exception for activities in foreign countries, see *Sosa v. Alvarez-Machain*, 542 U.S. 692 (2004). In that case, the U.S. Drug Enforcement Agency (DEA) suspected that Alvarez-Machain had participated in the murder of a DEA agent in Mexico. After Mexico refused to arrest and extradite Alvarez-Machain, the DEA had him kidnapped and brought to the United States for prosecution. After he was acquitted of the charges in federal court, Alvarez-Machain sued the Mexican Nationals under the Alien Tort Statute, 28 U.S.C. §1350, and the United States government under the FTCA. The Supreme Court held that the Alien Tort Statute does not create a cause of action in these circumstances and that the FTCA did not create tort liability against the United States because the kidnapping occurred in a foreign country.

The most difficult questions under the discretionary function exception arise when government negligence occurs in the course of government regulation. Although, as discussed above, the Court has rejected a blanket rule of no liability for regulatory actions, the Court has still been skeptical of claims that the government should be held liable for negligence in performing inspections and similar regulatory functions. For example, in *United States v. S.A. Empresa De Viacao Aerea Rio Grandense (Varig Airlines)*, 467 U.S. 797 (1984), the Court rejected an FTCA claim that attributed a fire in an airplane to the FAA's negligent certification of the airplane even though the towel disposal area, where the fire started, did not meet FAA fire-resistance standards. The Court stated that the FAA's administration of the certification procedure is within the discretionary function exception to FTCA liability. The Court held that both the FAA's decision to implement its safety standards through "spot checks" and the application of the spot-check program to the particular airplane involved discretionary decisionmaking regarding the best method for implementing the standards.

Another important case that involved the discretionary function exception is *Berkovitz v. United States*, 486 U.S. 531 (1988). Berkovitz sued the government over alleged negligence in licensing a private company to produce a polio vaccine and in approving the release of the batch of vaccine that contained the dose that gave the Berkovitzs' child polio. Although the *Berkovitz* Court rejected a blanket exception for regulatory functions and allowed the particular claims to proceed beyond the pleading stage, the Court appeared to approve a rather broad reading of the discretionary function exception under which all conduct involving "choice" and "policy judgment" within the bounds of legally granted discretion would be exempt from FTCA liability. In *Berkovitz* itself, the claim involving licensing the firm to produce the vaccine was not barred because the plaintiffs alleged that the officials granted the license without receiving statutorily required data from the company. The Court held that there is no discretion to violate mandatory provisions of governing law. The Court left it to the district court to determine whether the plaintiffs were attacking further failures to follow established licensing procedures or whether the plaintiffs were attacking discretionary activity regarding the conduct of regulatory oversight.

The *Berkovitz* Court allowed the claim alleging negligent release of the batch of vaccine to go forward because the plaintiffs alleged that the government officials allowed the vaccine to be released without testing it, despite a regulation requiring testing of all lots of vaccine before release. Once again, this conduct would not involve discretion because the testing policy was alleged to be mandatory. Thus, it appears that the discretionary function exception should not bar claims that the government violated a clear statutory command.

In *Gaubert v. United States*, 499 U.S. 315 (1991), the Supreme Court held that the discretionary function exception barred FTCA claims based on negligent government management of the day-to-day operation of a savings and loan institution. The government became involved in the operation of the institution under federal programs that insure deposits and require institutions to meet certain financial requirements. Insolvent savings and loans cost the government billions of dollars in the 1980s and 1990s. The *Gaubert* decision applied the broad understanding of the discretionary function exception and held that claims based on negligent bank operation, and claims based on negligent selection of bank officers and directors, were barred because the activities of the regulators involved "choice or judgment" and "the exercise of discretion in furtherance of public policy goals." 499 U.S. at 325, 334. Although the language defining the exception comes from *Berkovitz*, the application of the exception in *Gaubert* seems broader than in *Berkovitz*. However, it is true that the government officials in *Gaubert* had a great deal of choice over how to best pursue their goal of limiting the government's losses when the savings and loan became insolvent, whereas in *Berkovitz* it was alleged that the government violated clear statutory commands over which they had no choice. Thus the application of the exception in the two cases may be consistent.

Related to the liability of government is the liability of government contractors. Suppose the government had hired a private contractor to produce, pack, and ship the fertilizer in *Dalehite* under precise specifications provided by the government. Should the victims of that disaster be able to sue the private contractor even though they cannot sue the government itself? In a series of cases related to the discretionary function exception, federal courts have accorded government contractors a defense (known as the "**government contractor defense**") to state tort liability when a government contractor is sued for design defects when the government prescribed or approved the design specifications. See *Boyle v. United Technologies Corp.*, 487 U.S. 500 (1988). The logic underlying this doctrine is that if the government is shielded from liability because approval of the design specifications is a discretionary function, the private company that follows the specifications approved by the government should also be shielded from liability. Otherwise, the government will indirectly bear the liability costs in the price of the product. The government contractor defense does not apply if the government was not involved in the design, and it does not apply to manufacturing defect claims in which the problem is departure from proper manufacturing practices.

As noted above, the FTCA contains an exception for military combat activities. The precise language of the exception is relatively narrow, exempting from liability "[a]ny claim arising out of the combatant activities of the military or naval forces, or the Coast Guard, during time of war." 28 U.S.C. §2680(j). The exemption thus applies only to "combatant activities" during "time of war." However, the Supreme Court has exempted a much broader area of military activities from FTCA liability by creating a non-statutory exception, known as the "**Feres doctrine**," to FTCA liability for all claims that are "incident to service" in the armed forces. *Feres v. United States*, 340 U.S. 135 (1950). Given the explicit narrow statutory exception for combat activities in wartime, it might be argued that other military claims are implicitly allowed by the FTCA and that the Supreme Court has no business creating a non-statutory exception so closely related to a statutory one. However, in *Feres*, the Court held that injuries to persons on active military duty (but not in combat or during wartime) were not covered by the FTCA because there is "no liability of a 'private individual' even remotely analogous to . . . permitt[ing] a soldier to recover for negligence, against either his superior officers or the Government he is serving." *Feres*, 340 U.S. at 141. The Feres doctrine grants broad discretion to federal courts to exempt military-related activities from potential FTCA liability.

The Feres doctrine bars most claims against the United States by members of the armed forces arising out of their service. *Feres* itself barred medical malpractice claims by active-duty servicemen against allegedly negligent military doctors and barred a claim for injuries caused by unsafe military barracks. The Feres doctrine has been held not to bar a medical malpractice claim brought by a veteran alleging negligent care in a veterans' hospital or a claim by a member of the military arising from negligent driving by a civilian employee of the military. However, the Feres doctrine did bar a claim based on the Navy's decision not to erect lights on a road leading to a naval base. See *Lauer v. United States*, 968 F.2d 1428 (1st Cir.) *cert. denied*, 506 U.S. 1033 (1992).

COVERAGE OF THE FEDERAL TORT CLAIMS ACT CHECKLIST

1. Does the claim allege injuries caused by a federal government official within the scope of federal employment? If so, the claim may fall within the scope of the FTCA. ☑

2. Does the plaintiff allege negligence or recklessness by the federal government official? If so, the claim may fall within the scope of the FTCA. Note: Strict liability claims are not allowed under the FTCA. ☑

3. Is the suit brought against an individual official? If so, and if the claim falls within the scope of the FTCA, the federal government should be substituted as the defendant. The individual defendant will not be liable even if the federal government successfully defends the suit. ☑

4. Does the suit allege negligence in the formulation of policy or plans? If so, the suit may fall within the discretionary function exception to the FTCA, and the federal government may prevail. ☑

5. Does the suit allege negligence in the execution of policy or plans? If so, the suit may not be barred by the discretionary function exception and the federal government may be liable.   ☑

Note: There are numerous additional defenses to FTCA claims including claims brought challenging actions taken in the military context and actions conducted in a foreign country.

B. Liability of Federal Officials for Constitutional Violations

The Supreme Court has recognized another avenue for seeking damages against individual government officials who violate private parties' constitutional rights and cause injuries. In 1971, the Supreme Court, in *Bivens v. Six Unknown Named Agents of Federal Bureau of Narcotics*, 403 U.S. 388 (1971), created a damages action, known as the ***Bivens* action**, against federal officials for constitutional torts, i.e., injury-causing conduct that violates the Constitution.

In reaction to the Court's *Bivens* decision and subsequent developments, Congress amended the FTCA to include claims such as false imprisonment and malicious prosecution against federal law enforcement officials. The FTCA does not create liability for all constitutional violations. Rather, it covers only certain law enforcement–related violations and only against law enforcement officers. Further, this is an area in which the FTCA is not exclusive. Congress explicitly provided, in 28 U.S.C. §2679(b)(2), that the exclusivity provision of the FTCA does not apply to constitutional claims brought against federal officials. Thus, even if the FTCA is also available, liability under *Bivens* is assessed against the individual official, not against the government. The federal government, including federal agencies, may not be sued under *Bivens*.

The availability of the *Bivens* remedy has ebbed and flowed in a common law process. While *Bivens* itself involved only Fourth Amendment claims, the Supreme Court subsequently appeared to hold that the *Bivens* action presumptively exists whenever a constitutional right is violated and causes injury. See *Carlson v. Green*, 446 U.S. 14 (1980). However, there are several important defenses to *Bivens* actions and more recently the Court has reined in the recognition of *Bivens* actions in new contexts.

In *Bivens* and subsequent cases, the Supreme Court recognized two broad categories of cases in which the *Bivens* action would not be available. The first is, as the Court stated in *Bivens* itself, that the *Bivens* action is not available when there are "**special factors counseling hesitation** in the absence of affirmative action by Congress." *Bivens*, 403 U.S. at 396. In other words, there are some situations in which a court should not create a damages remedy without support from Congress. For example, in *Chappell v. Wallace*, 462 U.S. 296 (1983), the Court rejected a *Bivens* claim brought by five Navy enlisted men alleging racial discrimination by their superior officers in work assignments, performance evaluations, and disciplinary penalties. The Court refused to create a *Bivens* remedy in that case because of the unique situation and internal disciplinary structure of the military.

The *Bivens* Court also stated that it would not create a remedy when Congress had provided an **alternative remedy that Congress viewed as equally effective** to liability under the Constitution. As reformulated in *Carlson v. Green*, 446 U.S. 14 (1980), this exception bars the *Bivens* remedy when "Congress has provided an alternative remedy which it explicitly declared to be a *substitute* for recovery directly under the Constitution and viewed as equally effective." *Carlson*, 446 U.S. at 18-19 (emphasis in original). This standard is very difficult to meet because it requires an express declaration from Congress that the alternative remedy is a substitute for *Bivens*, which obviously will not apply to statutes that predate *Bivens*. It does not appear that Congress has ever explicitly declared a remedy as a substitute for *Bivens*. See also *Castaneda v. United States*, 546 F.3d 682 (9th Cir. 2008) (reaffirming that the FTCA is not a substitute for *Bivens*).

Government liability under the FTCA does not displace the *Bivens* remedy. We have already seen that the statute contemplates continued individual liability for constitutional violations. In *Carlson v. Green*, the survivor of a federal prisoner (who died in prison) brought an Eighth Amendment claim based on the circumstances of the prisoner's death. The government argued that the FTCA provided an alternative remedy that should displace the *Bivens* action. The Court rejected this argument because, in the Court's view, the FTCA remedy was not as effective as *Bivens* (because it did not allow, inter alia, jury trials and punitive damages) and because the FTCA did not explicitly preempt the *Bivens* remedy as it did with some other remedies that had been available before passage of the FTCA. Although it might seem redundant to allow a *Bivens* action when an FTCA remedy is also available, the Court was reluctant to hold that the FTCA is a substitute for *Bivens*. Because many constitutional torts also involve common law tortious conduct, the contrary holding would eliminate a large number of *Bivens* actions. The Court also viewed the FTCA as insufficiently protective of constitutional rights and thus a poor substitute for *Bivens* liability.

Sidebar

ALTERNATIVE REMEDIES UNDER *BIVENS*

It may seem odd that an alternative remedy that does not meet the Court's standard for displacing the *Bivens* remedy as a substitute can qualify as a special factor counseling hesitation. The *Bush* Court appeared trapped by its narrow formulation in earlier cases of the situations in which an alternative remedy can serve to bar the *Bivens* action. Therefore, it held, as it has on a few additional occasions, that the existence of an alternative remedy is a "special factor." It might be simpler for the Court to reformulate its "substitute remedy" test and declare that the *Bivens* remedy is not available when Congress has provided an adequate alternative, even if that alternative is not quite up to *Bivens* standards.

Subsequent to *Carlson*, the Court appears to be more willing to allow alternative remedies to displace the *Bivens* remedy, on the ground that the existence of an alternative remedy can be a "special factor counseling hesitation" in the absence of congressional action creating the *Bivens* remedy in the particular context. This seems counter to the strict requirements for recognizing a "substitute" remedy, but the logic is that the existence of a statutory remedial scheme should make courts cautious to create another one. For example, in *Bush v. Lucas*, 462 U.S. 367 (1983), Bush, a federal employee, sued his supervisor, Lucas, when Lucas demoted Bush and reduced Bush's pay—allegedly because Bush made statements critical of the operation of the federal agency where both worked. Bush alleged a violation of his First Amendment rights. Bush succeeded in having the demotion reversed through civil service appeals, but he later brought a *Bivens* suit for damages not recoverable in the civil service system. Bush argued that the civil service remedies were not as effective as *Bivens* because punitive damages, attorney's fees, and jury trials are not available in the civil service system. The Court agreed with the plaintiff that Congress had not explicitly declared the civil service system a substitute for the *Bivens* action, but the Court held that the existence of the complex system of civil service remedies was a special factor counseling hesitation and thus precluded the assertion of a *Bivens* claim.

More recently, the methodology for deciding whether to recognize a *Bivens* claim in a new context appears to have shifted toward great reluctance to do so coupled with an individualized examination of the propriety of the *Bivens* remedy in each particular context. After *Carlson v. Green*, it appeared that the *Bivens* action was presumptively available for all constitutional claims unless there were strong reasons (special factors) to not apply *Bivens* in the particular context. More recent cases appear to proceed from the opposite presumption, asking whether there are good reasons to extend *Bivens* to cover a new context. In light of the Court's greater willingness to find "special factors counseling hesitation," it is not surprising that the Court could say in 2001 that

> [i]n 30 years of *Bivens* jurisprudence we have extended its holding only twice, to provide an otherwise nonexistent cause of action against individual officers alleged to have acted unconstitutionally, or to provide a cause of action for a plaintiff who lacked any alternative remedy for harms caused by an individual officer's unconstitutional conduct.

Correctional Servs. Corp. v. Malesko, 534 U.S. 61, 70 (2001). Thus, when it was asked to approve a *Bivens* action brought by a foreigner who was allegedly sent by U.S. officials to a foreign country for torture, the Second Circuit said that to do so would be "to disregard the clear instructions of the Supreme Court by extending *Bivens* not only to a new context, but to a new context requiring the courts to intrude deeply into the national security policies and foreign relations of the United States." *Arar v. Ashcroft*, 532 F.3d 157, 177 (2d Cir. 2008) vacated, 585 F.3d 559 (2d Cir. 2009) (en banc).

A further limitation on the *Bivens* remedy is that the Supreme Court has applied the **immunities** developed in civil rights actions against state and local government officials under 42 U.S.C. §1983 to *Bivens* actions against federal officials as well. Under the official immunities, which are based on the longstanding common law tradition of official immunity, some officials are **absolutely immune** from damages remedies and others have a **qualified immunity**, under which they may be held liable only if they violate a clearly established constitutional right. There are two main policy bases for official immunities. The first is to protect the public interest in uninhibited official conduct by allowing public officials to make decisions free from concerns over potential liability. The fear is that the public interest in effective government will suffer if the potential for liability makes officials timid in carrying out their responsibilities. The second basis for the immunities is to free officials from the distraction and drain on their time and energy entailed in defending *Bivens* actions.

Absolute immunity attaches to the legislative, judicial, and prosecutorial functions. Whether an official is entitled to absolute immunity (or the less-protective qualified immunity) is determined by the function that the official was performing when the alleged constitutional violation occurred. See *Butz v. Economou*, 438 U.S. 478 (1978). This **functional approach** is derived from the common law background of the immunities as they were developed in §1983 actions. Thus, under *Butz*, even though all officials in administrative agencies are technically in the executive branch of the government, agency officials performing functions that were protected by absolute immunity under the common law receive that immunity, while remaining officials receive a qualified immunity. Because many officials perform more than one function, the immunity any particular official enjoys will vary based on the function being challenged.

Administrative officials performing judicial, legislative, and prosecutorial functions are absolutely immune from damages because at common law, judges, legislators, and prosecutors were absolutely immune from damages. See *Supreme Court of Virginia v. Consumers Union of the United States, Inc.*, 446 U.S. 719 (1980). Thus, administrative law judges and other agency officials engaged in adjudication are absolutely immune from damages, as are agency officials engaged in rulemaking (a legislative function) and prosecution. *Butz, supra.* Prosecutorial immunity is based on its close connection to the judicial process. *Imbler v. Pachtman*, 424 U.S. 409, 430 (1976). Officials performing functions not traditionally accorded an absolute immunity are protected by qualified immunity.

Officials are protected by absolute immunity only when they are performing the function to which the absolute immunity attaches. For example, Administrative Law Judges (ALJs) are absolutely immune if they violate someone's constitutional rights in the course of adjudicating a case, but they do not receive absolute immunity for administrative functions such as hiring and firing employees. Even the absolute immunity of actual judges and prosecutors is limited by the functional approach in this way.

To understand the operation of the functional approach, consider this scenario. A hypothetical federal agency is composed of three commissioners. The commissioners have the power to make rules and regulations, they sit as adjudicators on appeals from decisions of ALJs on whether the rules or statutes have been violated, and they issue reports concerning the practices of the parties they regulate. They also hire, discipline, and fire numerous agency employees. Under the functional approach, they are absolutely immune from damages in *Bivens* actions challenging the constitutionality of rules they promulgate and in *Bivens* actions that challenge the constitutionality of their conduct in the course of adjudicating violations. However, in their more purely administrative capacities in the hiring, disciplining, and firing of employees (as well as in their investigative function under which they issue reports), they would only receive a qualified immunity and could be held liable for damages if they violated clearly established constitutional rights in the course of carrying out those functions.

F   A   Q

Q: Do officials who do not qualify for absolute immunity enjoy any immunity from damages relief in *Bivens* cases?

A: Yes, they receive qualified immunity under which they are not liable unless they violated clearly established constitutional rights of which a reasonable official should have known.

The qualified immunity is the same regardless of the function, but it has evolved into a much more protective doctrine than it once was. Originally, qualified immunity protected the government official unless the official violated a clearly established constitutional right of which a reasonable official should have known (the objective prong) or if the defendant acted with ill will or malice against the plaintiff (the subjective prong). In other words, there were two ways the plaintiff could overcome the immunity, either by convincing the court the defendant violated a clearly established right or by proving that the defendant acted with ill will. In *Harlow v. Fitzgerald*, 457 U.S. 800 (1982), the Court abolished the subjective prong of qualified immunity because, in the Court's view, the subjective prong was allowing too many insubstantial claims to proceed to trial. This was because the factual issues regarding the defendant's state of mind could not be resolved on summary judgment, even though ultimately the defendant would convince the trier of fact that there was no malice or ill will. Thus, under the current, purely objective, standard for qualified immunity, the only way a plaintiff can overcome the immunity is to show that the defendant violated a clearly established constitutional right. The defendant's state of mind is irrelevant, and proof of malice or ill will does not help overcome the immunity.

For example, suppose an agency official enters a private business without a warrant to search for evidence that the company is engaged in conduct violating regulatory norms. The official tells the business owner that the search is to get back at her for firing his cousin from the company. Under the old standard for qualified immunity, the official's ill will directed at the business owner would be relevant in determining whether the qualified immunity defense would protect the official from an award of damages in a *Bivens* action for a warrantless search in violation of the Fourth Amendment. Now, under the purely objective standard, the only issue is whether a reasonable official, based on clearly established law, should have known that the particular search violated the Fourth Amendment. Thus, it is now more difficult for the plaintiff to overcome the qualified immunity defense. It should be noted that there are many issues concerning the contours of the *Bivens* action and the immunities that are beyond the scope of a study of administrative law.

C. Liability of State and Local Government Officials and Entities

The *Bivens* action making federal officials personally liable for their constitutional violations was modeled after a federal statute, 42 U.S.C. §1983, that provides a federal cause of action in federal court for damages and injunctive relief against state and local officials (and, in some circumstances, local governments) who violate the federal Constitution and laws.[1] Section 1983, with amendments, provides:

> Every person who, under color of any statute, ordinance, regulation, custom, or usage, of any State or Territory or the District of Columbia, subjects, or causes

---

[1] Each state has its own system of judicial review of agency action, its own tort claims laws, and its own sovereign and official immunity doctrines. The §1983 action is in addition to any state remedies that might be available against state and local officials and local government entities.

to be subjected, any citizen of the United States or other person within the jurisdiction thereof to the deprivation of any rights, privileges, or immunities secured by the Constitution and laws, shall be liable to the party injured in an action at law, suit in equity, or other proper proceeding for redress, except that in any action brought against a judicial officer for an act or omission taken in such officer's judicial capacity, injunctive relief shall not be granted unless a declaratory decree was violated or declaratory relief was unavailable. For the purposes of this section, any Act of Congress applicable exclusively to the District of Columbia shall be considered to be a statute of the District of Columbia.

Section 1983 was passed after the Civil War to enforce the Fourteenth Amendment against state and local officials, but it covers violations of all federal constitutional rights and some federal statutory violations committed by state and local officials. There are, however, significant limitations on the availability of the §1983 action.

(1) The Eleventh Amendment and Sovereign Immunity

The **Eleventh Amendment**, as interpreted and applied by the Supreme Court, prohibits the federal courts from awarding damages against states and state government agencies. State officials can be held liable for damages, but the plaintiff must look to the individual defendant, and not the state treasury, for damages. While at one time it was thought that this limitation on federal court jurisdiction could be avoided by suing in state court, more recently the Court has held that states and state officials, when damages are sought from the state treasury, are not "persons" subject to suit under §1983. Similar to *Bivens*, damages are not available from the state itself, although the Court has allowed for damages against local government entities, as explained below.

(2) "And Laws" Actions

While most §1983 actions attack constitutional violations, the statute refers to deprivations of "rights, privileges, or immunities secured by the Constitution *and laws*," which means that it also provides a cause of action against state officials who violate federal statutory law. Because there are many federal programs that are jointly administered with state agencies, many §1983 actions brought under the "and laws" provision allege that state administrators have failed to follow federal standards in administering such programs. For example, in *Maine v. Thiboutot*, 448 U.S. 1 (1980), the plaintiffs successfully sued state officials under §1983 for violating their rights under federal Social Security statutes. The §1983 "and laws" action thus potentially provides a remedy when a state official violates federal regulatory standards.

The Supreme Court has recognized two broad categories of exceptions to the availability of the §1983 "and laws" action. The first involves alternative remedies contained in the federal law itself. When the federal regulatory statute allegedly violated by the defendant state official contains a **comprehensive remedial scheme** that includes its own private right of action to redress violations, the Supreme Court has held that plaintiffs must use the particular statutory remedy and not the more general §1983 action. See, e.g., *Middlesex County Sewerage Authority v. National Sea*

Clammers Association, 453 U.S. 1 (1981); *City of Rancho Palos Verdes v. Abrams,* 544 U.S. 113 (2005) (no "and laws" claim against local government for violating federal telecommunications law's requirements regarding siting of communications towers because the federal act contains its own remedial scheme). The theory underlying this exception is the conclusion that when Congress includes a remedial scheme in a federal statute, it means for litigants to use that scheme and not the more general §1983 cause of action. Claimants should not be able to avoid procedural and substantive limits contained in the remedial provision of the statute by using §1983 instead.

The second category of exceptions to the availability of "and laws" actions involves federal statutes that, in the Court's view, create **no enforceable rights.** For example, in *Suter v. Artist M.,* 503 U.S. 347 (1992), the Court held that a §1983 suit was not available to enforce a federal law requiring state officials to make "reasonable efforts" to keep families together and return children placed in foster care to their parents. The Court held that the "reasonable efforts" standard was too vague to create enforceable legal rights. This is, in essence, a decision on the merits of the claim. If a statute does not create enforceable legal rights, the defendant obviously did not violate the plaintiff's rights. Provisions requiring reasonable or best efforts are often found in federal statutes providing funds for state agencies, and the Court has decided that normally the only remedy when a state violates a funding statute is for the state to lose the funding. Section 1983 should not be used to turn a statute conditioning the use of federal funds on state compliance with federal standards into a statute creating liability under §1983. See *Gonzaga University v. Doe,* 536 U.S. 273 (2002) (no "and laws" liability against university that violated federal statute prohibiting funding of schools that did not observe statutory standards regarding privacy of student records).

(3) Municipal Liability

After first deciding that cities were not "persons" subject to suit under §1983, see *Monroe v. Pape,* 365 U.S. 167 (1963), the Supreme Court later reversed itself and held that municipalities are "persons" under §1983, but it has also held that municipalities may be held liable only for **municipal policy or custom** and may not be held liable on a vicarious liability theory for the constitutional violations of their employees. See *Monell v. City of New York Department of Social Services,* 436 U.S. 658 (1978).

The simplest case for municipal liability is when the municipal lawmaking body, such as a

Sidebar

THE ORIGINS OF "AND LAWS" ACTIONS

The statutory provision that created the §1983 "and laws" action is of doubtful historical provenance. As originally passed, §1983 did not contain the words "and laws." In 1874, when all federal statutes were reorganized and recodified into the Revised Statutes, the revisers inserted the words "and laws" into §1983, but they claimed, consistent with their mission, that they did not intend to change the meaning of the statutes they were recodifying. Contrary to this claim, the insertion of the words "and laws" into §1983 significantly expanded the scope of the statute.

Sidebar

IMMUNITIES UNDER §1983

Defendants in §1983 actions are protected by the same immunities that the courts have applied in *Bivens* actions. In fact, the immunities were developed in §1983 actions on the theory that, because the immunities were very well established under the common law, Congress must have intended to preserve them since it did not expressly overrule them when it passed §1983. See *Pierson v. Ray,* 386 U.S. 547 (1967).

city council, has adopted an unconstitutional statute or ordinance. When a city ordinance is unconstitutional, the municipality is liable under §1983 for damages and other appropriate relief. However, a formal, unconstitutional policy is not necessary to hold a city liable. Municipalities are also liable for policies made by municipal officials with final authority to make policy in an area, even if the policy has not been adopted by the municipality's legislative body. For example, in *Pembaur v. City of Cincinnati*, 475 U.S. 469 (1986), the Court held that a county could be held liable for the decision of the county prosecutor to advise county sheriff's police to execute a warrant in an unconstitutional manner. The Court reasoned that the county prosecutor had, under both state law and county policy, final authority to establish policy over the execution of warrants by sheriff's police. Thus, whatever the prosecutor decided constituted the county's policy.

Section 1983 plaintiffs often attempt to avoid the ban on municipal vicarious liability by alleging that a constitutional violation was caused by the municipality's failure to train its employees or the municipality's failure to screen employees for past conduct, such as the commission of crimes. Recognizing that such allegations have the potential to effectively impose vicarious liability, the Court has made it very difficult for plaintiffs to prevail on such claims. A municipality may be held liable for grossly inadequate training of its employees, but the training must be so inadequate that the city's failure to train must imply deliberate indifference to the constitutional rights violated. A single incident of excessive force by a police officer is ordinarily inadequate to infer that the municipality's training is so inadequate as to exhibit deliberate indifference to the safety of citizens injured in such encounters with police. See *Oklahoma City v. Tuttle*, 471 U.S. 808 (1985). In other words, it must be so obvious that insufficient training will lead to constitutional violations that the local government has in effect chosen to take the risk that the violations will occur.

For example, in *Canton v. Harris*, 489 U.S. 378 (1989), the plaintiff alleged that she was injured when the police failed to seek medical attention for her when she became emotionally ill while she was in custody at the police station. She alleged that the municipality was liable because the officers in charge of deciding whether medical care was necessary were not trained to recognize when a person in custody needed treatment for emotional illnesses. The Court held that these allegations were sufficient to raise the possibility that the municipality's training decisions exhibited deliberate indifference to the constitutional rights of detainees to receive adequate medical care.

It is even more difficult to hold a municipality liable for failing to screen employees who later commit constitutional violations. The Court has held that inadequate screening can be the basis for municipal liability only if the candidate's background indicates that the failure to screen exhibits deliberate indifference to a high probability that the municipal employee will commit the constitutional violation alleged. The Court has said that a high standard of causation and culpability is necessary to prevent failure to screen cases from becoming, in effect, vicarious liability. See *Board of Commissioners of Bryant County v. Brown*, 520 U.S. 397 (1997).

In *Bryant County*, for example, the county sheriff (with final authority to hire officers) failed to examine the criminal record of his nephew before he hired him as a police officer. His nephew's criminal record included misdemeanor assault convictions and several serious traffic infractions. Later the nephew seriously injured a passenger in a car that had been involved in a police chase; and the injured passenger attempted to hold the county liable. The Court held that the county could be held liable only if the candidate's actual background indicated a high probability that the candidate would commit the constitutional violation alleged. Only then, the Court held, would it be appropriate to conclude that the county was deliberately indifferent to the plaintiff's constitutional rights. The Court also expressed doubts that the failure to screen the employee actually caused the constitutional violation. The Court's analysis appears better suited to a case in which the municipal policymaker was aware of the candidate's background and decided to hire him anyway. Then it might be concluded that the municipality knew of the probability that the candidate would violate constitutional rights and was deliberately indifferent. When the policymaker is unaware of the candidate's background and decides to go ahead and hire the candidate, the candidate's actual background should be irrelevant to whether the policymaker exhibited deliberate indifference to the possibility that the candidate may commit constitutional violations. More relevant is how important it is to hire only those with clean backgrounds for the particular position. Imagine, for example, hiring city youth counselors without checking for crimes involving sexual assault on minors. The candidate's actual background seems irrelevant to whether it was deliberately indifferent to the possibility that the counselors hired will commit crimes on the job. It is only dumb luck if the backgrounds of the applicants were actually clean. However, the *Bryant County* case is the law, and it is thus very difficult to hold a municipal government liable for constitutional violations traceable to the failure to screen municipal employees.

SUMMARY

- Sovereign immunity in the United States has traditionally barred liability actions against government and government officials for official misconduct that causes damages to private parties.

- The federal government, in the Federal Tort Claims Act (FTCA) and related statutes, has, to a limited extent, waived its sovereign immunity. Under the FTCA, the government is liable for negligence torts of government officials if a private party would be liable in tort under state law. The government becomes the defendant and the official is immune even if ultimately the government prevails based on an exception to liability or other defense.

- Liability under the FTCA is limited by many exceptions and limiting doctrines, the most important of which is the statutory bar on liability for discretionary functions. The discretionary function exception disallows liability for official choices involving the exercise of policy judgment.

- The Feres doctrine is a non-statutory exception that bars FTCA liability for conduct involving military matters, such as damages claims brought by members of the armed forces for injuries while on duty.

- The *Bivens* action is a judicially created damages action against individual federal government officials for constitutional violations. The *Bivens* action is available unless Congress has designated a substitute for the *Bivens* action or special factors counsel hesitation in the absence of congressional creation of a federal remedy. In recent years, the Court has been very hesitant to recognize *Bivens* claims in new areas.

■ Defendants in *Bivens* actions enjoy immunities from damages awards. Officials performing judicial, legislative, and prosecutorial functions are absolutely immune from damages. Other officials have a qualified immunity under which they may be held liable only if they violate a clearly established constitutional right.

■ State and local officials who violate the Constitution or federal statutory law may be sued by parties injured under 42 U.S.C. §1983, which provides a damages action against officials who violate federal constitutional and legal rights under color of state law.

■ If a federal statute contains its own comprehensive remedial scheme, it may not provide the basis for a §1983 action against a state official who violates it. Rather, the plaintiff must seek a remedy under the federal statute's own remedial scheme.

■ State officials enjoy the same immunities as federal officials sued under *Bivens.*

■ State governments and state agencies may not be sued under §1983 because of Eleventh Amendment immunity and because the Court has held that Congress did not intend for states to be §1983 defendants.

■ Local government entities may be held liable under §1983, but only for government policy. Local governments may not be held vicariously liable for the constitutional violations of their employees.

CONNECTIONS

Bivens and Separation of Powers

Judicial creation of the *Bivens* remedy raises the same separation of powers issues that counsel against judicial implication of private rights of action from regulatory statutes. See Chapter 9.

Liability and Judicial Review

Liability can be viewed as an alternative method of judicial review, see Chapter 4, although liability is for torts and constitutional violations not for violations of regulatory standards.

Functional Approach and Integration of Functions

The functional approach to immunities from damages relief recalls the integration of functions within administrative agencies. See Chapters 9 and 10.

Freedom of Information and Open Meetings

14

This chapter is about public access to information held by the government and requirements regarding the conduct of government business in public,

such as open meetings requirements. The Freedom of Information Act (FOIA), codified as part of 5 U.S.C. §552, grants the public access to most agency records. As defined in FOIA, "agency records" are those records created or obtained by the agency in the course of doing the agency's work and in the control of the agency at the time of the FOIA request.

There are several exemptions to FOIA's disclosure requirement. The exemptions fall roughly into three categories: protection of proprietary business information, protection of personal privacy, and protection of internal government functions. The Supreme Court has stated repeatedly that the exemptions should be narrowly read so as not to frustrate FOIA's pro-disclosure purpose. FOIA exemptions do not prevent the government from releasing information voluntarily. However, the Trade Secrets Act and the Privacy Act protect suppliers of covered information from government disclosure.

Government documents also are subject to disclosure through discovery in litigation. In addition to the usual doctrines governing discovery, the federal government has two sets of defenses to discovery, the evidentiary privileges, which protect sensitive information such as military secrets and foreign affairs information, and executive immunity, also known as executive privilege, which allows the executive branch, in limited circumstances, to claim immunity from disclosure of information.

The Government in the Sunshine Act requires that agency meetings be open to the public. The Sunshine Act does not apply to agencies with only one person at the top.

343

"Meeting of an agency" means a gathering of agency members where business is conducted. An agency may meet in private if one of the exceptions to the Sunshine Act is met. These exceptions are similar to the FOIA exemptions.

The Federal Advisory Committee Act (FACA) requires that nongovernmental bodies established to provide advice to the President or a federal agency follow the open meetings requirements of the Sunshine Act and the open information requirements of FOIA. Serious constitutional questions exist regarding whether FACA unduly interferes with the President's ability to seek advice from private citizens or groups regarding matters within the President's constitutional powers.

A. THE FREEDOM OF INFORMATION ACT

    1. Public Right of Access to Agency Records
    2. Exceptions to FOIA's Disclosure Requirements

B. DISCOVERY FROM THE GOVERNMENT IN LITIGATION

    1. Evidentiary Privileges
    2. Executive Immunity or Executive Privilege

C. OPEN MEETINGS REQUIREMENTS

    1. The Sunshine Act
    2. The Federal Advisory Committee Act (FACA)

A. The Freedom of Information Act

The Freedom of Information Act (FOIA), adopted by Congress in 1966, opens vast numbers of "agency records" to public inspection and creates a procedure (which was strengthened by amendments passed in 1974) for enforcement of agencies' obligations to make their records public. FOIA, codified as part of the Administrative Procedures Act (APA) at 5 U.S.C. §552, also contains several exceptions to the disclosure requirement. The two main issues arising under FOIA are whether the material sought constitutes an "agency record" within the meaning of FOIA and whether one of FOIA's exemptions authorizes the agency to withhold the material sought.

(1) Public Right of Access to Agency Records

FOIA requires that agencies publish certain matters and allow public inspection, upon request, of all other "records" unless the records sought fall within one of FOIA's exemptions. FOIA creates a federal cause of action against an agency that "improperly withhold[s]" requested agency records. 5 U.S.C. §552(a)(4)(B).

Agency records are those records that are created or obtained by the agency in the course of doing the agency's work and are in the control of the agency at the time of the FOIA request. See *Department of Justice v. Tax Analysts*, 492 U.S. 136 (1989). The fact that the records are physically located at the agency is not dispositive. Rather, the records must be the product of work on behalf of the agency. Private papers (or papers that were created in a different agency that an official keeps in an agency office) are not agency records merely because they are located on agency premises.

To understand how physical location of records on the premises of an agency does not necessarily mean that the records are those of the agency, consider *Kissinger v. Reporters Committee for Freedom of the Press*, 445 U.S. 136 (1980). In that case, a reporter directed a FOIA request to the Department of State for notes of Secretary of State and longtime presidential advisor Henry Kissinger's telephone conversations in which either the reporter's name was mentioned or the issue of information leaks was discussed with certain other government officials. The conversations occurred while Kissinger worked in the office of the President, but they were not sought until Kissinger became Secretary of State. Because the notes were stored in Kissinger's State Department office, the reporter sought them under FOIA as agency records of the State Department. The Court held that based on the following four factors, these notes were not records of the State Department: (1) the notes were never in the control of the State Department; (2) the notes were not generated in the State Department; (3) the notes were never placed in any State Department files; and (4) the notes were not used in any way by the State Department. This confirms the general rule that agency records must be the product of the agency's work, not merely papers of an agency official that happen to be stored at the agency.

> ## Sidebar
>
> ### OPENNESS IN GOVERNMENT
>
> The statutes examined in this chapter, FOIA, the Government in the Sunshine Act, and the Federal Advisory Committee Act, are all evidence of a strong movement in the late twentieth century toward openness in government. The presumption is that unless there are good reasons, all government activities should be conducted out in the open. From the executive branch's perspective, however, this series of reforms may be viewed as an attack by Congress on executive power.

F A Q

Q: What happens if an agency has lost possession of records sought in a FOIA request?

A: As noted, FOIA creates a legal claim, enforceable in federal court, when an agency **"wrongfully withholds"** agency records. An agency does not "wrongfully withhold" records that were not in its possession at the time the FOIA request was made, even if the records had once been agency records and were improperly removed from agency possession. FOIA does not create an obligation to retrieve records wrongfully removed. See *Kissinger, supra.*

The "agency records" and "wrongfully withheld" provisions of FOIA were both in dispute in *Department of Justice v. Tax Analysts*, 492 U.S. 136 (1989). Tax Analysts (a nonprofit organization that publishes Tax Notes, a weekly magazine on federal taxation) sought copies from the Department of Justice of the past month's district court decisions in tax cases litigated by the Department. The Department refused to provide the copies on two FOIA bases, first that they were not agency records and second that they had not been "wrongfully withheld" since they were publicly available from the district courts that had issued them. The Supreme Court ruled against the agency on both scores. First, the Court held that the decisions were agency records because the Department obtained them from the district courts and had them in Department files at the time the FOIA request was made. The Court also held that the Department, by not turning them over when requested, had "wrongfully withheld" the decisions regardless of whether they were available from another source. Justice Blackmun dissented, mainly on the ground that Congress did not intend, in enacting FOIA, to allow a publisher to impose its research costs on the government. In other words, since the decisions were already publicly available, no FOIA-related purpose was served by ordering the government to turn these decisions over to Tax Analysts who were merely trying to make it easier to produce their publication.

Only those records actually received and retained by the agency qualify as agency records. For example, data in the possession of a private party are not agency records, even if the data were created in an agency-funded study and even if the agency has, as a term of the grant, the right to receive copies of the documents created in the federally funded study. See *Forsham v. Harris*, 445 U.S. 169 (1980).

FOIA contains its own definition of "**agency**," which is somewhat broader than the APA definition. FOIA defines "agency" as "any executive department, military department, Government corporation, Government controlled corporation, or other establishment in the executive branch of government (including the Executive Office of the President), or any independent agency." 5 U.S.C. §552(f)(1). The narrower APA definition of "agency" has been held to apply only to agencies with authority to take actions with legal effect. The FOIA definition includes entities that may not be subject to other APA requirements, such as government corporations and executive branch entities that may collect information, but that have no power to take actions having legal effect.

FOIA COVERAGE CHECKLIST

1. Does the claimant seek records created or obtained in the course of the agency's work? If so, the records are covered by FOIA. If the records happen to be in possession of an agency, but were created or obtained by a different agency, they are not obtainable from the agency under FOIA.   ☑

2. Are the records in the possession of the agency? If so, the records are covered by FOIA. Agencies are not required, under FOIA, to retrieve records no longer in their possession. Note that the FOIA definition of agency is broader than the APA's definition and includes entities such as government corporations and military departments.   ☑

3. Is the agency wrongfully withholding agency records in its possession? If so, the claimant has a presumptive claim to the records under FOIA, and the remaining issue is whether they are covered by an exemption from disclosure.   ☑

Note: As detailed below, there are numerous exceptions to FOIA disclosure, many of them in the national security and law enforcement areas.

(2) Exceptions to FOIA's Disclosure Requirements

FOIA contains nine categories of exemptions from the requirement that agencies disclose their records. See 5 U.S.C. §552(b)(1)-(9). The exemptions protect several interests including privacy of the subjects of agency records, national security, law enforcement efforts, and internal agency management. The Supreme Court has stated repeatedly that FOIA exemptions should be narrowly construed so as not to interfere with FOIA's main purpose, which is to allow public access to government records. See, e.g., *Department of the Air Force v. Rose*, 425 U.S. 352 (1976). FOIA itself provides that if a record contains both exempt and non-exempt material, the non-exempt material must be provided with the exempt portions deleted.

Exemption (1) exempts records from disclosure that the executive branch determines should be kept secret in the interests of national defense or foreign policy. See 5 U.S.C. §552(b)(1). In order to be exempt, these records must be properly **classified** under the established procedure, set forth in Executive Orders, for classifying as secret records related to national defense or foreign policy interests. The secrecy determination cannot be made on an ad hoc basis in response to a FOIA disclosure request. See 5 U.S.C. §552(b)(1)(A).

Exemption (2) exempts records "related solely to the internal personnel rules and practices of an agency." This exemption is confined to those internal personnel rules that are unlikely to generate any substantial public interest, including matters cited in the legislative history, such as agency sick leave policies, regulation of lunch breaks, and employee use of parking facilities. This exception does not exempt matters from disclosure that are likely to be of concern to the general public. For example, in *Department of the Air Force v. Rose*, 425 U.S. 352 (1976), the Court rejected applying exemption (2) to case summaries, with names and other identifying facts deleted, of student honor code violations at the Air Force Academy. The Court reasoned that there was likely to be substantial public interest in disciplinary matters at the Academy. The Court did, however, agree with the lower courts that the district judge should carefully review the records before they are released to make sure that information that could lead to identifying particular students is redacted.

Exemption (4) exempts from disclosure "trade and commercial or financial information obtained from a person and privileged or confidential." 5 U.S.C. §552(b)(4). This is basically a **trade secrets** exception. A FOIA "trade secret" has been defined as "a secret, commercially valuable plan, formula, process, or device that is used for the making, preparing, compounding, or processing of trade commodities and that can be said to be the end product of either innovation or substantial effort." *Public Citizen Health Research Group v. FDA*, 704 F.2d 1280, 1288 (D.C. Cir. 1983). The *Public Citizen* court rejected applying the general tort law definition of "trade secrets" in favor of this definition, which it found was better suited to the purposes of FOIA.

"**Commercial information**" is information related to activity in commerce of the sort that would affect the submitter's commercial position if it were released. This exemption does not protect information from disclosure that is not related to commerce. For example, "a noncommercial scientist's research design is not literally a trade secret or item of commercial information, for it defies common sense to pretend that the scientist is engaged in trade or commerce." *Washington Research Project, Inc. v. Department of Health, Educ. & Welfare*, 504 F.2d 238 (D.C. Cir. 1974).

Exemption (4) applies only to "**privileged or confidential**" information. Information is confidential under FOIA if its disclosure would impair the government's ability to obtain information in the future or if disclosure would cause substantial harm to the competitive position of the person from whom the information was obtained. See *Worthington Compressors, Inc. v. Costle,* 662 F.2d 45 (D.C. Cir. 1981). In such circumstances, disclosure could harm the government's ability to obtain information in the future if the holder of the information would be reluctant to supply it without assurances that it will remain private.

When a private party is required by law to provide information to an agency, the government's ability to obtain information is not threatened by FOIA disclosure. Thus, in such cases, the primary interest weighing against disclosure is the provider's competitive interest in keeping important commercial information confidential. The government also has an interest in the quality of information provided. A party who knows that compulsory information may be disclosed may not provide complete or useful information as would be provided if confidentiality was ensured. See *Critical Mass Energy Project v. NRC,* 975 F.2d 871 (D.C. Cir. 1992) (en banc), *cert. denied,* 507 U.S. 984 (1993).

Because the government has an interest in encouraging people to provide commercial information voluntarily, the D.C. Circuit adopted a broader standard for keeping voluntarily provided information confidential under the fourth exemption. In such cases, "financial or commercial information provided to the Government on a voluntary basis is 'confidential' for the purpose of Exemption 4 if it is of a kind that would customarily not be released to the public by the person from whom it was obtained." *Critical Mass Energy Project,* 975 F.2d at 879.

For example, the Institute for Nuclear Power Operations (INPO) is an organization of the operators of nuclear power plants in the United States. It studies the construction and operation of nuclear power plants and provides its reports to the NRC on the understanding that the reports will remain confidential. Critical Mass Energy Project (CMEP) filed a FOIA request for the documents, and the NRC claimed that the reports were confidential commercial information within exemption (4). In *Critical Mass Energy Project,* the court held that the INPO reports were confidential and, under exemption (4), not subject to FOIA disclosure. The court reasoned that the reports were provided to the NRC voluntarily, and INPO would probably cease providing them if they were subject to FOIA disclosure. The court thus held that when a party voluntarily provides confidential information to an agency, that information should not be subject to FOIA disclosure if the provider would normally not release such information to the public.

Nothing in FOIA itself precludes an agency from voluntarily turning over records that FOIA exemptions would allow the agency to withhold. However, the **Trade Secrets Act**, 18 U.S.C. §1905, enacted in 1974, makes it a criminal offense for a government official to release information held to be within FOIA exemption (4). See *Bartholdi Cable Co. v. FCC,* 114 F.3d 274 (D.C. Cir. 1997). A person whose confidential information is threatened to be released by an agency has a "reverse-FOIA" cause of action under the APA's judicial review provisions (not the Trade Secrets Act itself) to prevent disclosure. See *Chrysler Corp. v. Brown,* 441 U.S. 281 (1979). There is no private right of action under the Trade Secrets Act, but an agency's decision to turn over information in violation of the Privacy Act would violate APA §706(2)(A) as "not in accordance with law." Id.

Exemption (6) exempts from disclosure "personnel and medical files and similar files the disclosure of which would constitute a clearly unwarranted invasion of personal privacy." 5 U.S.C. §552(b)(6). Additionally, a further exemption is found in exemption 7(C) for disclosure of "records or information compiled for law enforcement purposes, but only to the extent that the production of such law enforcement records or information . . . (C) could reasonably be expected to constitute an unwarranted invasion of personal privacy." 5 U.S.C. §552(b)(7)(C). These are the primary FOIA exemptions for which issues of personal privacy are important.

Determining whether exemption (6) exempts a particular personnel, medical, or similar file from disclosure "require[s] a balancing of the individual's right of privacy against the preservation of the basic purpose of the Freedom of Information Act 'to open agency action to the light of public scrutiny.' " *Department of the Air Force v. Rose*, 425 U.S. 352, 372 (1976). In *Rose*, the Court rejected the Air Force's argument that exemption (6) applied to summaries of cases of honor code violations by Air Force Academy cadets. The Court held that FOIA policies (including the public's ability to monitor the disciplinary practices of the Air Force Academy) favored disclosure, and that cadets' privacy concerns could be addressed by the elimination of identifying information from the summaries.

Determining whether exemption (7)(C) exempts law enforcement records from disclosure based on personal privacy concerns involves a balancing test similar to that involving personnel records. The subject of law enforcement records (such as a person charged with or convicted of a crime), has a substantial privacy interest against disclosure of the records.

This privacy interest exists even though the information was made public at the time of arrest, prosecution, or conviction. The public, on the other hand, has a substantial interest in monitoring the conduct of the activities of law enforcement agencies.

A good illustration of the application of the balancing test in the law enforcement context is *National Archives v. Favish*, 541 U.S. 157 (2004), in which the Court held that the government may withhold death scene photographs of Vincent Foster, Jr., a presidential aide who was found dead in a park, apparently by suicide. Although five separate investigations concluded that Foster's death was a suicide, a citizen requested the photographs as part of his own investigation, founded upon a belief that the government's investigations were "incompetent and untrustworthy." Favish argued that the personal privacy exception did not apply because Foster lost any interest in his privacy when he died. The Court held that Foster's family had a continuing privacy interest in keeping photographs of Foster's body out of the public eye and that this interest outweighed any public interest in disclosure without specific evidence to suggest that the investigations were not reliable.

Because the theory underlying FOIA is that disclosure facilitates government accountability, the public's interest in disclosure of information that would invade privacy is strongest when the information would reveal important matters concerning the agency's behavior and is weakest when the information would reveal nothing about the agency's conduct. For example, the Federal Bureau of Investigation (FBI) maintains a database of the records of criminal charges and convictions (rap sheets) of all law enforcement agencies in the United States, including state and local law enforcement agencies. In *Department of Justice v. Reporters Committee for Freedom of the Press*, 489 U.S. 749 (1989), the Department of Justice (DOJ) refused to turn over, to CBS news reporters and the Reporters Committee, the rap sheet of a member of a family whose company allegedly procured military contracts "as a result of an improper relationship with a Congressman." A rap sheet shows the subject's criminal record. Because the rap sheets are in files obtained and maintained by the FBI, they are clearly agency records. However, the Court held that the privacy interest of the subjects of the rap sheets outweighed the public's interest in obtaining them from the FBI.

The *Reporters Committee* decision is also interesting because of the sensitivity it shows to the realities of government record keeping. It could be argued that the subjects of rap sheets have little privacy at stake because all convictions are public when they occur. However, the Court recognized that the massive computerized database maintained by the FBI presents a great potential for spreading information regarding the criminal histories of the subjects of the rap sheets that may have been long out of the public eye. Further, most states place severe restrictions on the public's right to obtain criminal records. Finally, the public's interest in disclosing the FBI's records was slight, according to the Court, because they would reveal nothing about the operation of the FBI since the FBI was merely the custodian of records of arrests and convictions in other jurisdictions. Thus, the Court held that the rap sheets maintained by the FBI were exempt from FOIA disclosure under exemption (7).

The Privacy Act of 1974, codified at 5 U.S.C. §552a, is another federal statute that protects individuals' privacy interests in records maintained by the federal government. The Privacy Act prohibits agencies from disclosing records "except pursuant to a written request by, or with the prior consent of, the individual to whom the record pertains." The Privacy Act also restricts the information agencies are allowed to collect on individuals (only that information necessary to accomplish agency purposes), allows individuals to inspect records pertaining to them, and sets up a procedure for correcting erroneous records.

A large number of **law enforcement records** are not subject to FOIA disclosure. Exemptions (7)(A), (B), (D), (E), and (F) exempt law enforcement records from disclosure when disclosure would cause one of several enumerated harms to law enforcement interests. These interests include: (A) protecting against interference with law enforcement proceedings; (B) protecting the right of the accused to a fair trial; (D) protecting the identity of a confidential source of information; (E) protecting the secrecy of law enforcement techniques and enforcement guidelines; and (F) protecting the physical safety of individuals. Records are law enforcement records under FOIA even if they were originally compiled for other purposes as long as they are eventually used for law enforcement purposes. See *John Doe Agency v. John Doe Corp.*, 493 U.S. 146 (1980). Further, records do not lose their law enforcement status even if they are provided by a law enforcement agency to a non-law enforcement agency. See *FBI v. Abramson*, 456 U.S. 615 (1982) (FBI records did not lose their law enforcement status when summaries of the documents were provided to the White House for non-law enforcement purposes).

Exemption (5) exempts from FOIA disclosure "inter-agency or intra-agency memorandums or letters which would not be available by law to a party other than an agency in litigation with the agency." 5 U.S.C. §552(b)(5). This exemption protects the agency deliberative processes and other matters that executive privilege and privileges related to the attorney-client relationship would protect. The statutory reference to material that "would not be available by law to a party . . . in litigation with the agency" means material protected by the attorney-client and attorney work product privileges.

Exemption (5) does not apply to agency memoranda that, in effect, constitute final agency decisions on agency matters. For example, exemption (5) does not protect from disclosure a memorandum that explains why an agency decided not to go forward with an enforcement action. Exemption (5) does apply to agency memoranda that result in an agency taking further action in a matter, such as memoranda explaining why an enforcement action should go forward. Such memoranda are considered part of the process of intra-agency deliberation and are kept confidential to protect the deliberative process.

NLRB v. Sears Roebuck & Co., 421 U.S. 132 (1975), illustrates the issues surrounding disclosure of memoranda that might reflect deliberative processes. That case involved memoranda produced after a party files an unfair labor practice charge with the NLRB. The NLRB's General Counsel has final authority to decide whether to pursue the charge by issuing a complaint. The General Counsel operates through Regional Directors throughout the country. Regional Directors often consult with the General Counsel regarding whether to pursue a charge. If the Regional Director decides not to file a charge, the complainant can appeal to the General Counsel, and if the General Counsel agrees with the Regional Director, the General Counsel will prepare an "Appeals Memorandum" explaining the decision not to pursue charges. In some cases, as part of the consultation process, the General Counsel will prepare an "Advice Memorandum" to the Regional Director (which includes legal and factual reasoning) ordering the Regional Director either to issue a complaint or to dismiss a charge.

Sears made FOIA requests for disclosure of both types of memoranda, and the General Counsel denied the requests on the ground that the records were internal agency memoranda under exemption (5). The Supreme Court held that those memoranda ordering the General Counsel not to file an unfair labor practice charge were "final agency decisions" that must be made public under §552(a)(2). However, with regard to the memoranda ordering the Regional Director to file a complaint of an unfair labor practice, the Court held that these are not subject to disclosure because

Sidebar

AGENCY DELIBERATION

In general, the exemption for inter- and intra-agency memoranda is designed to protect the process of deliberation inside and among agencies. Early drafts of decision memos and other memoranda that are preliminary to actual decisionmaking should not be subject to disclosure. Otherwise, the agency decisionmaking process would be hampered by the fear that tentative views might be subject to public disclosure. However, memoranda containing final decisions are subject to disclosure.

they are part of an ongoing process of the General Counsel's involvement in the case, since the General Counsel may ultimately litigate the case before the NLRB and in court. As to exemption (5), the Court noted that these memoranda include the General Counsel's views on the facts and the law of the case, and thus are squarely within the exemption for attorney work product. See *NLRB v. Sears, Roebuck & Co.*, 421 U.S. 132 (1975).

Exemption (3) exempts from disclosure records that are "specifically exempted from disclosure by statute . . . provided that such statute (A) requires that the matters be withheld from the public in such a manner as to leave no discretion on the issue, or (B) establishes particular criteria for withholding or refers to particular types of matters to be withheld." 5 U.S.C. §552(b)(3). Exemption (3) identifies three distinct types of statutes that operate to exempt records from FOIA disclosure. The first type includes statutes that identify exempt records and leave no discretion regarding nondisclosure. In such cases, the agency would determine (subject to judicial review under FOIA) whether the agency lacked discretion to make the records public. If the agency had discretion, it might still attempt to withhold the records, and then the question would become whether withholding was statutorily authorized, even though it was not statutorily required.

The second type of statute that might affect FOIA disclosure under exemption (3) consists of statutes that establish criteria for withholding and do not contain a hard and fast rule of nondisclosure for certain types of records. In such cases, the agency (subject to judicial review under FOIA) would determine whether the criteria for withholding are met and would disclose the records only if the other statute's criteria for nondisclosure are not satisfied. The third type of statute that might affect FOIA disclosure includes statutes that refer to records containing particular types of matters that should be withheld. In such cases, the agency would decide (subject to judicial review under FOIA) whether the records contain matters within the types of information referred to in the relevant statute.

CIA v. Sims, 471 U.S. 159 (1985), is an example of how FOIA and other statutes interact to determine whether records are subject to disclosure. In *Sims*, the Court upheld the CIA's broad interpretation of its authority to withhold intelligence-related documents from FOIA disclosure. The Court found that former §102(d)(3) (since repealed) of the National Security Act of 1947 was a statute that "specifically exempted [matters] from disclosure" under 5 U.S.C. §552(b)(3). This is the third type of nondisclosure statute, focusing on a type of material contained in the records sought to be disclosed. Former §102(d)(3) stated that "the Director of Central Intelligence shall be responsible for protecting intelligence sources and methods from unauthorized disclosure." Sims sought the names of institutions and individuals that had performed research as part of a CIA project to study behavior-control techniques. Sims argued, and the Court of Appeals agreed, that §102(d)(3) protected only the identity of intelligence sources who would turn over intelligence information only on a guarantee of confidentiality. The Supreme Court disagreed, holding first that §102(d)(3) satisfied exemption (3)'s requirement that the statute refer to "particular types of matters" when it refers to "intelligence sources and methods" and second that §102(d)(3) gave the CIA broad discretion to withhold all information within the statutory categories. Thus, the CIA was allowed to withhold the identities of all providers of intelligence information, not merely those who require confidentiality before providing information. Therefore, the identities of the researchers are not subject to FOIA disclosure.

F   A   Q

Q: Given all of the exemptions and limiting doctrine, how effective is FOIA?

A: FOIA has undoubtedly opened up much of the working of government to public scrutiny. However, although FOIA creates a presumption that agency records are open to the public and must be provided if a proper request for them is made, there are numerous exemptions that give agencies discretion not to disclose certain records. The courts are supposed to operate with a presumption of openness, but in some areas, especially regarding national security and law enforcement, the courts have allowed relatively broad withholding of agency records. Thus, the record on FOIA's success is mixed.

B. Discovery from the Government in Litigation

Another way to obtain information from the government is through the litigation **discovery** process. The government can resist discovery on the same terms as a private litigant. In addition, the government has two additional privileges — **evidentiary privilege** and **executive immunity** (also known as **executive privilege**) that are not enjoyed by private parties.

(1) Evidentiary Privileges

Evidentiary privileges are privileges that protect categories of government matters from discovery or other use in litigation when release would be contrary to the public interest. These include things like state secrets, military secrets, and sensitive foreign affairs matters. Claims of evidentiary privilege must be made formally by the head of the department having control over the material, and that department head must have personally considered the matter. See *United States v. Reynolds*, 345 U.S. 1 (1953). It should

Sidebar

CRITICISMS OF DISCOVERY

Discovery in the United States is extremely broad and has been criticized as adding needlessly to the expense of litigation and as facilitating harassment by opposing parties. Periodically, proposals are made to limit discovery. The material in this section must be understood against the background of broad discovery.

be noted that the use of the state secrets privilege has been controversial in recent years due to claims that the Administration of George W. Bush overused it to the detriment of openness in government.

Whether the material sought in discovery is protected by a privilege is determined by balancing the litigant's need for the information against the government's interest in secrecy. A court should uphold a privilege claim without even looking at the actual material when there is a reasonable possibility that the material is privileged. Only if the balance appears to favor the litigant should a court examine the documents in camera to help determine whether the material is privileged.

(2) Executive Immunity or Executive Privilege

Executive immunity from discovery, also known as **executive privilege**, is a separation of powers-based claim for confidentiality of executive branch information. The executive branch rarely claims complete immunity from the discovery process. When such a claim is made, a court must balance the executive branch's need for confidentiality against the litigant's need for the material. The litigant's interest is held to be strongest in the criminal context, where the fairness of a trial may depend on the litigant's ability to discover material relevant to the case.

Sidebar

EXECUTIVE PRIVILEGE IN CRIMINAL CASES

In *United States v. Nixon*, the Supreme Court expressed grave concerns over the due process implications of allowing the President to withhold information that was necessary to allow a criminal defendant to present a complete defense to the charges.

Executive immunity is not absolute. In *United States v. Nixon*, 418 U.S. 683 (1974), President Nixon argued that once the President claims the privilege, separation of powers requires that courts defer to the claim of privilege without further inquiry. The Court rejected this argument and held that the court must determine for itself whether the claim of immunity is well founded and whether a litigant's need for information outweighs the executive branch's need for confidentiality. The Court held that the President's generalized interest in confidential communication within the executive branch, while weighty and entitled to respect, is not sufficient to defeat, as a blanket matter, all requests for discovery regarding such communication in a criminal case.

When the President invokes executive privilege, the presumption is that the material sought to be discovered is privileged, and the burden is on the party seeking discovery to demonstrate that the material is essential to justice. This burden is much more likely to be met in the criminal context because of the potential effects on the fairness of the trial.

C. Open Meetings Requirements

Requiring agencies to meet in public is obviously important to maintaining agency accountability. Various provisions of federal law require that agency meetings normally be open to the public. States have similar provisions. We look at two such federal provisions, the **Government in the Sunshine Act** and the **Federal Advisory Committee Act (FACA)**.

(1) The Sunshine Act

The Government in the Sunshine Act, passed in 1976 and codified at 5 U.S.C. §552b, was designed to open agency meetings to the public. Three issues are vital to a proper understanding of the Sunshine Act:

1. To what agencies does the open meetings requirement apply?
2. What is a "meeting of an agency" for the purposes of the Sunshine Act? and
3. Under what circumstances may a covered agency hold a meeting in private?

The Sunshine Act requires all agencies (using FOIA's definition of "agency") that are headed by a "collegial body composed of two or more individual members" to announce their meetings at least one week in advance and to open the meeting to the public unless a Sunshine Act exception applies.

A "meeting of an agency" within the Sunshine Act occurs if the members "jointly conduct or dispose of agency business." 5 U.S.C. §552b(b). The Sunshine Act does not apply to meetings that are purely consultative in character, at which the agency does not purport to conduct business beyond discussing matters of interest to the agency. See *FCC v. ITT World Communications, Inc.*, 466 U.S. 463 (1984). The Sunshine Act may be violated if the result of agency decisionmaking was predetermined at a closed meeting characterized by the agency as purely consultative. See id. Such a violation is more likely to be found if it is shown that the agency's attention at the closed meeting was focused on discrete proposals rather than an overview of matters of concern. See id.

The Sunshine Act contains ten categories of exceptions to its open meetings requirement, most of which track the exemptions from FOIA's disclosure requirements. See 5 U.S.C. §552b(c)(l)-(8). In addition to the exceptions that track FOIA exemptions, an agency may meet in private when an open meeting would have certain effects on financial markets or institutions, when the agency's purposes would be significantly frustrated if a closed meeting could not be held, or when the meeting concerns certain investigatory or adjudicatory matters. See 5 U.S.C. §552b(c)(9)-(10).

The Sunshine Act contains procedures that must be followed to hold a closed meeting, even if the agency has statutorily sufficient reasons for keeping the meeting closed. A meeting may be closed pursuant to the Sunshine Act exceptions only by a public vote of a majority of the members of the agency. Further, for each closed meeting, the chief legal officer of the agency must certify that the meeting qualifies for one of the Sunshine Act exceptions and must designate the applicable exception. Agency decisions to close meetings are subject to judicial review, and a verbatim transcript or recording must be kept of all closed meetings so that if the closure is ruled improper, the contents of the meeting can be disclosed.

> ### Sidebar
>
> **SINGLE-MEMBER AGENCIES**
>
> Agencies headed by a single individual (such as the EPA and the FDA) are not subject to the Sunshine Act, even when the head of the agency meets with subordinates to discuss agency business. This is because when an agency has a single administrator in charge of the entire agency, the agency is basically meeting anytime that person is working on agency business. There are no real deliberations that should be held in public.

(2) The Federal Advisory Committee Act (FACA)

FACA, enacted in 1972 and amended in 1976, regulates **advisory committees** "established or utilized" by the President or an agency to give advice to the executive branch. (FACA is not codified in the U.S. Code but is reproduced as appendix 2 to 5 U.S.C.) Advisory committees are not agencies but rather are groups with at least one private citizen (usually they are composed largely of private citizens) that advise the President or an agency. FACA essentially requires advisory committees to comply with the Sunshine Act with regard to their meetings, and to FOIA with regard to their records. The President or agency head may utilize the Sunshine Act's exceptions to close a meeting of an advisory committee.

Because it interferes with the President's ability to seek advice from private citizens, it has been argued that FACA violates the separation of powers. For example, in *Public Citizen v. DOJ*, 491 U.S. 440 (1989), Public Citizen argued that FACA applied to meetings of the ABA committee that assessed the qualifications of appointees to federal judgeships because the President utilized those recommendations. The majority of the Supreme Court held that FACA did not apply, but three concurring Justices found that FACA did apply but that FACA, as they understood it, unconstitutionally infringed on the President's appointment power. Even the majority may have been influenced by constitutional concerns, since it admitted that the ABA's advice may have fallen within the literal terms of FACA. However, the Court concluded that Congress did not intend FACA to have such broad application.

Because FACA applies only to groups that include private citizens, one way to avoid its requirements is to exclude private citizens from membership. Early in his presidency, President Clinton created a task force to develop a proposal for national health care legislation, chaired by the First Lady Hillary Clinton. Mrs. Clinton was the only private citizen on the task force, and when an association of medical professionals sued to force the task force to comply with FACA, the D.C. Circuit found that to avoid separation of powers concerns, Mrs. Clinton should be considered a government employee for FACA purposes. See *Association of American Physicians & Surgeons v. Clinton*, 997 F.2d 989 (D.C. Cir. 1993). However, the task force also had a working group that included numerous private citizens as "consultants." The court was concerned that this was merely a device to avoid FACA requirements, so it remanded the case to the district court to determine whether these "consultants" were de facto members of the task force. Id.

The de facto membership issue arose again in *Cheney v. U.S. Dist. Court for Dist. of Columbia*, 542 U.S. 367 (2004). In this case, the Supreme Court decided that the Vice President could resist complying with FACA's procedural and disclosure requirements based on separation of powers concerns without asserting executive privilege. That case involved a group known as President Bush's National Energy Policy Development Group. It was chaired by the Vice President and officially included only government officials, not private citizens. The group's secrecy, and reported widespread participation by private energy industry officials, led to suspicion that it had formulated energy policy in a manner that favored the interests of energy producers over environmental concerns.

Sidebar

CONSTITUTIONAL PROBLEMS WITH FACA

FACA raises serious separation of powers issues insofar as it restricts the President's ability to consult with private individuals. Congress, it should be noted, is under no similar set of restraints — Members of Congress are legally free to meet with private citizens in private as they see fit.

Because many private energy industry officials reportedly participated in the group's meetings without being made formal members, public interest plaintiffs seeking information about the group claimed that these private citizens were de facto members of the group, which would then subject it to FACA. The Court held that this group was not subject to FACA because all of its members were government officials. The Court was concerned about the separation of powers implications of FACA, and thus held that only those people with a vote or de facto veto over group decisions could be characterized as members for FACA purposes. Even if private citizens participated in the discussions, as long as all of the official members were government officials, FACA did not apply.

SUMMARY

■ The Freedom of Information Act (FOIA) grants the public a right of access to most agency records. In order for the presumption of public access to apply, the material sought must fit FOIA's definition of "agency records." Agency records are those records created or obtained by the agency in the course of doing the agency's work and in the control of the agency at the time of the FOIA request.

■ There are several exemptions from FOIA's disclosure requirement. The exemptions fall roughly into three categories: protection of proprietary business information, protection of personal privacy, and protection of internal government functions.

■ FOIA exemptions do not prevent the government from releasing information voluntarily. However, the Trade Secrets Act and the Privacy Act protect suppliers of covered information from government disclosure.

■ Government documents also are subject to disclosure through discovery in litigation. In addition to the usual doctrines governing discovery, the federal government has two sets of defenses to discovery, the evidentiary privileges, which protect sensitive information such as military secrets and foreign affairs information, and executive immunity, also known as executive privilege, which allows the executive branch, in limited circumstances, to claim immunity to disclosure of information.

■ The Government in the Sunshine Act requires that most agency meetings be open to the public. The Sunshine Act does not apply to agencies with only one person at the top. An agency may meet in private if one of the exceptions to the Sunshine Act is met. These exceptions are similar to the FOIA exemptions.

■ The Federal Advisory Committee Act (FACA) requires that nongovernmental bodies established to provide advice to the President or a federal agency follow the open meetings requirements of the Sunshine Act and the open information requirements of FOIA.

■ Serious constitutional questions exist regarding whether FACA unduly interferes with the President's ability to seek advice from private citizens or groups regarding matters within the President's constitutional powers.

CONNECTIONS

Separation of Powers and Open Government

All of the legislation that opens executive branch activities to public scrutiny may raise separation of powers concerns although they are unlikely to actually violate the separation of powers. See Chapter 2.

Presidential Secrecy and Separation of Powers

In particular, presidential assertions of executive privilege and resistance to opening advisory committee proceedings to public scrutiny under FACA should be considered in light of the separation of powers principles explored in Chapter 2.

Non-final Actions and FOIA

Internal agency memoranda regarding enforcement activities may not be subject to FOIA disclosure if they do not constitute final decisions. For issues surrounding reviewability of enforcement discretion, see Chapter 3.

TABLE OF CASES

TABLE OF STATUTES

INDEX